Gavin Douglas

The Palyce of Honour

T0154134

MIDDLE ENGLISH TEXTS SERIES

The Middle English Texts Series are scholarly texts designed for research and classroom use. Its goal is to make available to teachers, scholars, and students texts that occupy an important place in the literary and cultural canon but have not been readily available in print and online editions. The series does not include those authors, such as Chaucer, Langland, or Malory, whose English works are normally in print. The focus is, instead, upon Middle English literature adjacent to those authors that is needed for doing research or teaching. The editions maintain the linguistic integrity of the original work but within the parameters of modern reading conventions. The texts are printed in the modern alphabet and follow the practices of modern capitalization, word formation, and punctuation. Manuscript abbreviations are silently expanded, and *u/v* and *j/i* spellings are regularized according to modern orthography. Yogh (3) is transcribed as *g*, *gh*, *y*, or *s*, according to the sound in Modern English spelling to which the medieval pronunciation corresponds; thorn (þ) and eth (ð) are transcribed as *th*. Distinction between the second person pronoun and the definite article is made by spelling the one *thee* and the other *the*, and final *-e* that receives full syllabic value is accented (e.g., *charité*). Hard words, difficult phrases, and unusual idioms are glossed either in the right margin or at the foot of the page. Explanatory and textual notes appear at the end of the text, often along with a glossary. The editions include short introductions on the history of the work, its merits and points of topical interest, and brief working bibliographies.

Gavin Douglas

The Palyce of Honour

Edited by
David Parkinson

SECOND EDITION

Published for TEAMS
(Teaching Association for Medieval Studies)
in Association with the University of Rochester

by

MEDIEVAL INSTITUTE PUBLICATIONS
Kalamazoo, Michigan
2018

**Library of Congress Cataloging-in-Publication Data
are available from the Library of Congress**

ISBN: 9781580443722 (paperback)
ISBN: 9781580443739 (hardback)

Printed and bound by CPI Group (UK) Ltd, Croydon, CR0 4YY

CONTENTS

PREFACE AND ACKNOWLEDGMENTS

Since the first Middle English Texts Series edition of *The Palis of Honoure* (1992), research into the literary culture and history of late fifteenth-century Scotland has produced much new knowledge relevant to Gavin Douglas and his poem. As discussed below, recent work on the text of the poem has strengthened the case for basing a new edition on the London print (William Copland, c.1553). The case has also been gaining momentum for rebuilding the 1992 edition into a more strongly-established *Palyce* with wider prospects. As will be apparent at various points throughout what follows, the distinctiveness of this new edition is based on some contentions that have gained clarity and substance. With its largely superficial flaws, Copland's text of *The Palis* reflects linguistic and stylistic expectations and practices in late fifteenth-century Scotland. Through the lens of this text, the reader glimpses Douglas at work: his abiding interest in thoroughgoing, meaningful syncretism; his parallel refinement of form through the interweaving of disparate sources; a constant interplay of entertainment, prophecy, admonition, encomium, and downright foolery. Thus perceived through Copland's *Palis*, *The Palyce of Honour* emerges afresh as both rootedly Scottish and largely accessible to readers south of the border. Part of its Scottishness is the ambition with which it is pitched to celebrate wider international developments in scholarship, even while its extraordinary range of implication assures its continued relevance at home. In these ways, it is very much a Douglas poem.

Revisiting *The Palis of Honoure* in this spirit and rediscovering *The Palyce* has made possible a fresh look at fundamental aspects of text and interpretation. Throughout, the goal has been to consider what can be known of that "Palyce of Honour" ("Direction," line 122) to which Douglas alluded at the end of his *magnum opus*, his translation of Virgil's *Aeneid*. To an unusual degree in *The Palyce*, Douglas produced an introduction to late-medieval learning, statecraft, poetics, and manners, as they prevailed in Scotland. Written at the very end of the fifteenth century, the poem looks back into established practices of education, literature, pastime, and good counsel, but also announces the beginnings of new models of textual analysis as a means of ethical development. Thus *The Palyce* is extraordinarily well placed to afford its readers a number of perspectives at a crystallizing moment that is also a moment of profound change. Turning as it does from Chaucerian (and Gowerian) to directly Ovidian and Virgilian models, for example, *The Palyce* shows Scottish literature gaining new freedom of scope and movement. Douglas prepares for this new age by looking to humanist learning for models that engage with Classical and Biblical traditions. He does so with an urgency that deserves closer attention than it has received. In this poem, he is taking seriously the challenge to the poet to draw upon the conduit of ancient learning in order to improve the present world — to teach princes and not merely please them and to reawaken and reinvigorate religious knowledge. At the same time, and most remarkably, Douglas is creating a richly textured work in which farce, vision, encyclopedic learning, debate, encomium, and polemic come rapidly to the fore. It offers a remarkable realm of discourse that promotes a continuing appeal for many readers.

It has been what Douglas would call a "joyous discipline" to re-enter that realm, one that has involved help at every stage. Two initial steps prepared the way for work on this new edition: participation in a workshop at the Free University of Berlin, organized by Regina Scheibe and Andrew James Johnston, along with a research fellowship at Edinburgh University's Institute for Advanced Studies, under the direction of Jo Shaw. In Edinburgh, Philip Bennett, Sarah Carpenter, Sarah Dunnigan, Lucy Hinnie, Margaret Mackay, and Greg Walker showed me various ways to reconsider Douglas' achievement in *The Palyce of Honour*. In Durham, Elizabeth Archibald, who previously had encouraged me to develop my thinking about Douglas, suggested that I might yet have something to contribute. Had it not been for the opportunity to participate in a conference in May 2016 at the University of Rochester on *Older Scots Literature and Culture*, organized by Rhiannon Purdie and Thomas Hahn, the present edition would not have been imagined, let alone attempted. On that conference's closing day, Russell Peck, general editor of the Middle English Texts Series, encouraged me to revisit work done long ago on Douglas and make it new. More recently, Elizabeth Ewan gave me the opportunity to discuss *The Palyce* in a panel at the fifteenth International Conference on Medieval and Renaissance Scottish Language and Literature, and the comments from many at and after that session helped me to refine and develop various aspects of what follows; here I want especially to thank Margaret Connolly, Priscilla Bawcutt, and Kate McClune. What follows is a result of these various forms of encouragement. It is again a special pleasure to acknowledge Russell Peck's enlivening influence and guiding hand from start to finish of this project, and hope that the outcome, at least in some measure, repays his confidence.

I am glad to have the opportunity to thank the librarians and archivists who helped me locate and study the materials fundamental to this edition, and especially the copies of the sixteenth-century prints of the poem. This edition could not have proceeded without the gracious co-operation of the staff of the following libraries: the Bodleian Library, Oxford; the British Library; Cambridge University Library; Edinburgh University Library; the Folger Shakespeare Library, Washington, D. C.; the Henry E. Huntington Library, San Marino, California; the John Newberry Library, Chicago; the John Rylands Library, Manchester; the National Library of Scotland; the National Records of Scotland; and Queen's College Library, Oxford. Those librarians and archivists who have gone out of their way to assist me are numerous, but it is a special pleasure to thank Anne Anderton (Heritage Imaging Assistant, the John Rylands Library), Paul Fleming (Centre for Research Collections, Edinburgh University Library), Emily Goetsch (Special Collections Assistant, National Library of Scotland), Melanie Leung (Image Request Coordinator, Folger Shakespeare Library), Jennifer Ozers (Search Room Archivist, National Records of Scotland), Domniki Papadimitriou (Picture Library Co-ordinator, Cambridge University Library), and Lisa Schoblasky (Special Collections Services Librarian, Newberry Library).

Other help gave me the confidence to embark on and persist in this edition. As so often, Alasdair MacDonald gave my flagging efforts a gentle buoying-up at a key moment. Anne Kelly provided valuable and timely assistance, not least with study of copies at Oxford of the London print of the poem. Rhiannon Purdie gave considerable support and encouragement toward the completion of this project; she also advised me to invite Caitlin Flynn to review and comment on the edition in draft form. Caitlin's attention to the literary and other contexts for the points raised therein resulted in a great many corrections and improvements. Beth Richert also commented incisively on the introduction and explanatory notes, and especially on the classical allusions. Krupa Shah identified ways to strengthen the argument of the Introduction. Heather Giles caught persistent errors of style and argument throughout, and urged me to overcome my reluctance to improve my style and develop my conclusions. The METS staff have my enduring gratitude for the care and learning they have bestowed on the preparation of this volume. While drawing particular attention to Russell Peck's key role in this regard, I also want to recognize here the Associate Editor of the Series, Alan Lupack, and its indefatigable Assistant Editor, Pamela Yee. I am very grateful to staff editors Alison Harper, Kyle Huskin, and Ashley Conklin for the care and skill with which they carried out their work. On virtually every page, Peck, Lupack, Yee, and their colleagues showed me ways to fashion a more illuminating window into *The Palyce of Honour*. May this book merit a better fate than the one meted out in the poem itself, to dastardly intruders at such windows. Without these people's care, vigilance, and learning, this edition would have been much the poorer. Last but not least, I thank the College of Arts and Science at the University of Saskatchewan; without the backing of my academic home, this *Palyce* would have remained only a dream.

INTRODUCTION

1. GENERAL

The Palyce of Honour (*PH*) occupies a pivotal moment in Scottish literary history. Daringly combinative in style and subject, the poem exerts lasting influence into and beyond the Reformation. Its moment and maker are clearly identified. Completing his translation of Virgil's *Aeneid* in the summer of 1513, Gavin (or, as the name continues to be spelled in library catalogues, "Gawin") Douglas describes himself as having written "my Palyce of Honour" twelve years earlier. Douglas was a priest and a scion of a dominant noble family. In the 1490s he had maintained connections with the court of James IV, and the king had supported his efforts to gain ecclesiastical preferment. What is known about Douglas, and especially about his later political and ecclesiastical career, adds significance to the fact that, at the inception of that career, he writes about "Honour" as both a moral and a martial value. The poem embodies a vision of literature as the prime means to strengthen connections to the classical past and instill spiritual knowledge and moral renovation, but also to inculcate these values as intrinsic to kingly and noble power. With such high aspirations, *The Palyce of Honour* reflects its context in its striking combinations: medieval and humanist; comic, visionary, and epic; regional and international; Christian and pagan.

This blend seems distinctively, pervasively Scottish, grounded in national aspirations and anxieties. Scotland had a national myth of origin with its own eponymous founders, Scota and Gaythelos (as in "Scots" and "Gaels").[1] Asserting direct access to and legitimate descent from the ancient world, Scottish chroniclers had long asserted the antiquity of their kingship. This myth guaranteed an unmediated right of participation in European culture at large. Such myth-making also countered English claims of hegemony, in a war of words that sharpened recurrently into conflict. The neighboring kingdoms were not tidily fenced off from each other, the Borders between them remaining very much debatable land. In part for that reason, an awareness of the linguistic distinctiveness of Scots as the variety of English dominant in Scotland was only gradually emerging; and the linguistic landscape was further complicated by the continuing, if retreating, presence of Gaelic, identified as the link to national origins. It was still possible, if in a humorous context, for the poet Walter Kennedie to announce at court that "Irische" ought to be "all trew Scottis mennis lede" ("all loyal Scots' tongue").[2] It is in this setting of rising cultural distinctiveness, sustained political

---

[1] On the origins and distribution of this myth, see Bower, *Scotichronicon*, ed. Watt, 1:xx–xxi, xxiii–xxvii; further, see Broun, *Irish Identity*, pp. 5n29, 11–15, 119–21.

[2] *The Flyting of Dumbar and Kennedie*, lines 345–46 (*Poems*, ed. Bawcutt, 1:211).

rivalries, but also a certain volatility of affiliation, especially along the Borders, that *The Palyce of Honour* can be located.

PH is a dream vision that responds strongly to Chaucer's poems in this genre. It is not the earliest Scottish dream vision; that is the early fifteenth-century *Kingis Quair*, ascribed to King James I of Scotland. As he would later with Virgilian epic, Douglas advances beyond his literary models toward a distinctively Scottish rendering of the dream form. No mere imitator of Chaucer, Douglas devises a plot for *PH* that is designed to exhibit his inventiveness, not least in the foregrounding and combination of motifs. A would-be poet of love falls asleep and dreams of a wilderness through which divine cavalcades pass. Denouncing Venus, he faces her wrath and retaliation; but Calliope argues for leniency. The poet-dreamer joins the Muses en route to the mountain location of the palace of the god Honour. Aided by Calliope's nymph, the dreamer ascends and tours the palace within which he catches a glimpse of Honour and falls unconscious. The nymph teaches him that Honour judges traitors and usurpers; then she summons him across a moat into the garden of the Muses. He stumbles, awakens, and sings praises to Honour and James IV. Despite this freshness of design, critical commentary on *PH* has generally focused on its affinities with Chaucer's *House of Fame* in particular; but for much of the allusive fabric of his invention, Douglas is looking beyond Chaucer and especially to Ovid. It is as if he is legitimating his own literary lineage, much as Scottish historical writers had done in their cultivation of a Scottish myth of national origin.

Though only a shred of manuscript evidence exists for the text of the poem, and the earliest printed evidence dates to at least a decade after the poet's death in 1522, the textual situation of this poem is perhaps better grounded than has previously been assumed. With advances in research into the text, language, and interpretation of *The Palyce of Honour*, it has become possible to re-evaluate the status of the earliest extant complete witness of the poem, the London print of *The Palis of Honoure*, c. 1553 by William Copland. Several copies of Copland's print survive, and eight of them have been studied closely for the present edition. As a result of this attention, it has been possible to restore several readings to the text of the poem, and to reinstate an appreciation of the language of the poem as represented in that print. It is thus Copland's print that serves as the copy-text for the present edition, with emendations admitted sparingly from the other witnesses. Accepting Copland thus has involved a detailed reconsideration of the text at every point, especially with reference to the particulars of the 1579 Edinburgh print by John Ross for Henry Charteris; an important instance where the Edinburgh print is superior is its inclusion of lines 1711–19, a stanza omitted by Copland that itemizes a notably wide assortment of tales.

One might already go a little further in contrasting the London print to the Edinburgh: where the former relies on an assumed linguistic and cultural commonality between its Scottish and English readers, the latter contributes to a new national literary canon. Neither goal lies beyond Douglas' scope, however; with characteristic assertiveness, the poet espoused both nationalism and cosmopolitanism. In 1513, he declared that his Scottish version of Virgil's *Aeneid* would be "with every gentill Scot . . . kend, / And to onletterit folk be red on hight" ("known by every gentle Scot and read aloud to illiterate people").[3] He also envisioned its being read "[t]hrow owt the ile yclepit Albyon"; akin even in terms to the

---

[3] *Eneados*, "Exclamatioun," lines 43–44 (ed. Coldwell, 4:193). All *Eneados* quotations are from Coldwell's edition.

circulation of Chaucer's verse, "throu Albion iland braid."[4] Already in *PH* can be detected an eclecticism of language, style, and cultural affiliations that foreshadows this competitive spirit.

It has proven important, therefore, to situate this edition afresh in relation to the main print witnesses. This task has even affected the form of the title. Given these considerations and especially the affiliation this edition has with Copland's print (L), there is a sense in which the title should be *The Palis of Honoure*, as it appears on Copland's title page, and in the 1992 METS edition. The change to *Palyce* has been made to reflect what can be glimpsed of the poet's own general usage in the poem itself and subsequently.[5] In the present edition, *Palis* refers to William Copland's London print of the poem (L); *Palice* designates the later Edinburgh print by Ross and Charteris (E). The title has been changed to reflect the ways in which L has emerged more clearly than before as a sturdy platform from which to see an array of evidence about the making, transmission, and reception of the poem. It has proven to be valuable to see the poem as more than L. On this basis, it has been possible to revisit the literary affiliations of *PH*, for instance to re-evaluate its relations to Ovid and Chaucer in particular in the light of its purposive, thematically cohesive scriptural references and allusions. Reconsideration of the textual and literary evidence makes it possible to gain a new appreciation of *PH* as a vehicle of cultural continuity through the sixteenth century in Scotland, a period of extreme change.

2. AUTHOR

The dramatic political and religious alterations coming to Scotland (the defeat and death of James IV in 1513; the Reformation Parliament in 1560; the deposition of Mary, Queen of Scots in 1567; the coronation of James VI as James I of England, 1603) had roots in the fifteenth century. During this earlier period, however, dynastic struggles may have seemed to be part of the continuing fabric of public life. The changing fortunes of the Douglases, not least of the Angus branch of that family, exemplify this familiar pattern. At the age of fourteen, Archibald Douglas succeeded his father in 1463 as the fifth earl of Angus. Five years later, he married Elizabeth Boyd, eldest daughter of the Chamberlain of Scotland. Robert Lord Boyd was at the summit of his power, having taken control of the adolescent James III in 1466 as his official guardian. Boyd soon fell and went into exile; Archibald Douglas served on the parliamentary assize that condemned his father-in-law. In 1474 or 1475, but possibly as late as 1476, Elizabeth Boyd and Archibald Douglas had a son, Gavin, their third among four sons and three daughters.[6]

The prominent philosopher and academic John Mair ("Major") alluded to Gavin Douglas' having been born "not more than a Sabbath-day's journey" from his own home town of Gleghornie, near the burgh of Haddington; elsewhere he refers to their being

---

[4] *Eneados*, "Conclusio," line 11 (ed. Coldwell 4:186); *Eneados*, Prologue to Book 1, line 343 (ed. Coldwell, 2:12).

[5] *Palyce of Honour*, lines 1403, 1429, 1443, 1452, 1790, etc. (while *Palice* appears twice in the London print, L, lines 264 and 293), and in referring to it subsequently (*Eneados*, "Direction," line 122 [ed. Coldwell, 4:191]; "Mensioun," line 6 [ed. Coldwell, 4:139]). *Palice* predominates in E, the Edinburgh print.

[6] Paul, *Scots Peerage*, 1:183–85; Bawcutt, "New Light on Gavin Douglas," p. 96.

linked by "the stretch of land between Tantallon and Gleghornie."[7] Mair's comments point to Tantallon Castle as the birthplace of Gavin Douglas. Tantallon still forms an impressive landmark on the Lothian coast along the Firth of Forth. The natural advantages of the site made it possible to be defended with a single enclosing wall, an imposing curtain of red sandstone, blocking access from the mainland. Bracketing the wall stood two towers, the north-western one connected to a hall and probably containing the residence of the noble family.[8] Within that wall, one looks north toward the prominent Bass Rock. The promontory the castle encloses makes an excellent natural fortification. Apart from a fortified sea-gate, it would have been difficult or impossible to land at the foot of the steep basalt cliffs of that promontory. The buttresses of those cliffs do not invite convenient ascent from the sea.

The earlship of Angus was strongly but not solely based in the Borders, from Tantallon on the east coast to Kircudbright in the southwest. From this base, Archibald Douglas played a leading role in James III's attack on England in 1479. By 1482, with their discontent rising against James, the nobles met to decide how to nullify the coterie of royal advisors. At this meeting, as the seventeenth-century historian Hume of Godscroft depicted it, the fable of the mice and the cat was recounted. When the question was asked, "Who will bell the cat," Archibald volunteered. In later times, he was remembered as "Bell-the-Cat."[9]

In 1488, another aristocratic rebellion led to James' defeat and death at Sauchieburn, and the adolescent James IV took the throne. Among the power brokers, Patrick Hepburn, newly created earl of Bothwell, was Archibald Douglas' great rival in the Marches, the three militarized districts forming a buffer along the English frontier. The Hepburns and their allies the Homes amassed many honors, rewards, and offices from the overthrow of James III. The Hepburns' threat to Douglas' fortunes was mitigated by James IV's evident pleasure in Archibald's company. They played dice and cards, but such pastimes were not sufficient to counterbalance the progress of Bothwell's strategies.[10] Archibald sought recourse elsewhere and by other means. He visited Henry VII of England in 1489, and in 1491 promised to act on Henry's behalf by advocating peace between the two nations.[11] James besieged Tantallon because of the bond Angus had made with Henry VII.[12] Still, Douglas' fortunes were advanced by other means. The earl's niece Marion Boyd became the king's mistress, and Archibald became the king's Chancellor soon after.[13]

By 1489, when he was thirteen years old, Gavin Douglas' education had progressed to the point that he was matriculated at the University of St. Andrews. His studies would begin in Logic, then Physics and Natural Philosophy, then Metaphysics; all along, Aristotle would be the foundational authority.[14] In 1492, Douglas was named among those confirmed as

---

[7] Mair, *History of Greater Britain*, ed. Constable, pp. xxxi–xxxii; Broadie, "John Mair's *Dialogus*," pp. 421, 425, 430.

[8] Historic Environment Scotland, "Tantallon Castle." Online at http://canmore. org.uk/site/56630.

[9] *ODNB*, "Douglas, Archibald [nicknamed Bell-the-Cat], fifth earl of Angus (c. 1449–1513), magnate and rebel."

[10] Macdougall, *James IV*, p. 87.

[11] Macdougall, *James IV*, p. 88.

[12] *Accounts of the Lord High Treasurer of Scotland*, ed. Dickson, p. cvi.

[13] Macdougall, *James IV*, p. 152.

[14] *Acta Facultatis Artium Universitatis Sanctiandree*, ed. Dunlop, 1:lxxxiv.

Bachelors, and in 1494 he was listed among the *Licentiati*, or Masters of Arts, those who were qualified to teach the seven Liberal Arts.[15] The direction of his studies indicates the career for which he was intended, in the Church; a more specific indication of that purpose came in the form of a papal supplication in February 1489 for various ecclesiastical benefices, a canonry among them.[16] This request was based on the assumption that Douglas would do well in his studies at St. Andrews: an advanced academic degree was a legal requirement for becoming a Canon.[17] It was a time of increasing interest in education: an Act of Parliament (June 1496) required sons of noble and freeholding families to attend grammar school, acquire familiarity with Latin, and then receive basic legal training.[18]

Gavin Douglas was aspiring to positions that would demonstrate his family's prominence in ecclesiastical affairs. During the mid-1490s, he was spending at least part of his time at court: in the king's chamber in April 1495 he witnessed a legal deed and was described on that occasion simply as the Chancellor's son.[19] The papal chancery registers for 1494/96 contain a reference to "Gowinus de Wglas" as dean of Dunkeld; similarly identified as "dene of Dunkeldene," Douglas witnessed an indenture in Edinburgh in 1497 between his father and Lord Kennedy.[20] Signaling his direct interest, James IV attended a hearing of his Lords of Council in October 1497 to assert Douglas' right to this deanship.[21] By the end of the decade, however, the earl of Angus was entering a politically rocky time with gloomy implications for his family's future prospects. His cachet was no longer enhanced by the king's romantic attachments. Margaret Drummond had replaced Marion Boyd as the king's mistress; in 1496, Drummond was installed in Stirling Castle and Linlithgow Palace.[22] Archibald Douglas lost the Chancellorship in 1497, and his enemies the Hepburns made further inroads into his power.[23] About twenty-one at the time of his father's fall from office, Gavin Douglas would have to find his own way to advancement. The previous year, Douglas had been awarded an income from the proceeds of the parish of Monymusk (in Aberdeenshire); in 1498, the king granted him the parsonage of Glenholm (in Peeblesshire; now Tweeddale) when it should next become vacant; possibly at about the same time, Douglas became parson of Lynton and Rector of Hauch near Dunbar.[24] In passing, it is worth noting how much contentiousness was involved in the award of these positions; for instance, Douglas' royally supported appointment as dean of Dunkeld was successfully

---

[15] *Poetical Works*, ed. Small, 1:iv–v.

[16] Bawcutt, "New Light on Gavin Douglas," p. 95.

[17] *Poetical Works*, ed. Small, 1:v.

[18] *Records of the Parliaments of Scotland*, eds. Brown et al., A1496/6/4; Macdougall, *James IV*, p. 174.

[19] *Protocol Book of James Young*, eds. Donaldson and Paton, no. 790, p. 173; Macdougall, *James IV*, p. 284.

[20] Fraser, *Douglas Book*, 3:161–64; Bawcutt, *Gavin Douglas: A Critical Study*, p. 6.

[21] *Acts of the Lords of Council in Civil Causes*, eds. Neilson and Paton, 2:81–82.

[22] *Accounts of the Lord High Treasurer of Scotland*, ed. Dickson, p. cxxxiii; *ODNB*, "Drummond, Margaret (d. 1502), royal mistress."

[23] On the Hepburn rivalry, see Paul, *Scots Peerage*, 1:180; *ODNB*, "Douglas, Archibald [nicknamed Bell-the-Cat], fifth earl of Angus (c. 1449–1513), magnate and rebel."

[24] *Poetical Works*, ed. Small, 1:vi.

resisted by master George Hepburn — the family rivalry operating even at this level.[25] With the king's support, Douglas was nevertheless making some progress, despite his father's political eclipse.

In tracing the historical factors leading to *PH*, special significance can be attached to the development of the Scottish king's interests, pursuits, and concerns. Born in 1473, James IV was only a few years older than Douglas; the king was to exert particularly strong influence on the poet. Reaching the age of majority in 1495, James IV assumed direct control of his own government. The following year he was studied closely by the Spanish ambassador Pedro de Ayala, who wrote a detailed report to Ferdinand and Isabella about the young king, his realm, and his people. It was a flattering but also judicious portrait de Ayala provided of the multilingual, handsome, devout, courageous prince who "loves war" too much, not least for its being "profitable to him and to the country."[26] At the same time, the king made regular donations to religious houses and foundations.[27] James' religious devotion had a strongly penitential strain that led him to show particular favor toward the Observant Franciscans, a strict order gaining prevalence in many Scottish burghs. James' interest in this order led to his endowing the Observant house in Stirling, afterwards his annual retreat each Easter week.[28] James later commented to Pope Julius II that among the Observants "he found cleansing for his conscience."[29] Real or perceived complicity in the rebellion against his father James III helped motivate such acts of expiation.

During the first decade of his majority, James took up his father's interest in improving the royal palaces at Stirling Castle and Linlithgow.[30] Construction of the so-called Palace at Stirling Castle commenced in 1496. James also found time to cultivate an interest in gardens at both sites: payments for repairs and new planting may suggest a growing awareness that a garden is an integral appurtenance of a royal palace.[31] Building at Stirling was accompanied by the establishment of new kitchen gardens and orchards but also by more decoratively landscaped garden spaces. Hundreds of trees were purchased and planted. Much effort went into the digging of irrigation canals ("stankis"), and ponds stocked with fish and fowl.[32] Especially in the description of Honour's palace and its precincts, *PH* may reflect these royal projects.

Despite all his interest in building and landscaping, James was a monarch on the move. In March 1498, having completed "his perfyte aige of twenty-five yeiris," James IV made a formal revocation of all grants made in his name during his minority. He spent the next few

---

[25] *Acts of the Lords of Council in Civil Causes*, eds. Neilson and Paton, 2:241, 284; Bawcutt, "New Light on Gavin Douglas," p. 97.

[26] *Calendar of Negotiations between England and Spain*, ed. Bergenroth, 1:170.

[27] *Accounts of the Lord High Treasurer of Scotland*, ed. Dickson, pp. ccxxxi–ccxxxii.

[28] *Accounts of the Lord High Treasurer of Scotland*, ed. Dickson, pp. cclxxi, 391.

[29] *Letters of James the Fourth*, eds. Hannay and Mackie, p. 55; quotation from Macdougall, *James IV*, p. 217.

[30] Fawcett, *Scottish Architecture*, pp. 304–20; Dunbar, *Scottish Royal Palaces*, pp. 10–18, 40–49; MacDonald, "Princely Culture in Scotland," pp. 165–66.

[31] *Accounts of the Lord High Treasurer of Scotland*, ed. Dickson, pp. cclxv–cclxvi, 286; Cooper, "Ornamental Structures," p. 821.

[32] *Accounts of the Lord High Treasurer of Scotland*, ed. Dickson, pp. cclxv–cclxviii, 386, 389, 390.

months on a typically fast-paced round of visits to strategically, politically, and spiritually important places in his realm. His movements in early April display a criss-crossing of the realm: Dumbarton, Ayr, and the ancient religious center Whithorn in the southwest; then retracing his route and arriving at Stirling; then to Edinburgh, but returning to Stirling to celebrate Easter week there; soon to Dunbar, and thence to Linlithgow via Restalrig and its royal chapel housing the relics of St. Triduana. "[W]ith his characteristic restlessness and rapidity of movement,"[33] he returned to Dunbar in early May; then it was back to Dumbarton and thence by boat at Newark to Kintyre. It may be worthwhile to compare this strenuous royal itinerary with the cavalcades that dominate much of the first and second parts of *PH*.

It is possible to see *PH*'s genesis in the poet's intermittent attendance at court in the mid to late 1490s. Work on the poem would thus coincide with his embattled quest for ecclesiastical preferment. Years later, in the summer of 1513, with his translation of Virgil's *Aeneid* nearing completion, Douglas looked back at his making of the earlier poem:

. . . now am I fully quyt,	*discharged*
As twichand Venus, of myn ald promyt	*concerning; promise*
Quhilk I hir maid weil twelf yheris tofor,	*Which; fully twelve years ago*
As wytnessith my Palyce of Honour,	
In the quhilk wark, yhe reid, on hand I tuke	*you may read, I undertook*
Forto translait at hir instance a buke.	*request*
Sa have I doyn abufe, as ye may se,	*Thus; done*
Virgillis volum of hir son Enee,	
Reducit, as I cowth, intill our tong.	*was able, into*
(*Eneados*, "Direction," lines 119–26)	

In this passage, the writing of the *Palyce* appears to be synchronous with the experience of the dream that is recounted therein. It is difficult to treat this statement as the factual basis for a chronology of composition.[34] Douglas mentions the earlier poem again in the final addenda to his *Eneados*, but if anything complicates its compositional history even further:

Lo thus, followand the flowr of poetry,	*following the flower of poetry (Virgil)*
The batellys and the man translait have I,	*I have translated*
Quhilk yoir ago in myne ondantit youth,	*Which long; unrestrained*
Onfructuus idylnes fleand as I couth,	*Unprofitable; evading; was able*
Of Lundeys Lufe the Remeid dyd translait,	*Fleshly Love; Remedy*
And syne *Off hie Honour the Palyce* wrait —	*wrote*
"Quhen paill Aurora with face lamentabill,	
Hir russet mantill bordowrit all with sabill, etc."	
(*Eneados*, "Mensioun")	

From this comment, it would appear that the *Palyce* was the second literary project Douglas completed, preceded by a mysterious work of which no trace survives beyond this reference. Attempts have been to identify Ovid's *Remedy of Love* as the first translation Douglas made; and *Lundeys* can be derived from *loun(d)*, "ruffian, rascal" (in later

---

[33] *Accounts of the Lord High Treasurer of Scotland*, ed. Dickson, p. clxvi.

[34] For a counter-argument, see Lyall, "Stylistic Relationship," p. 70.

sixteenth-century instances, explicitly "lecher" or "strumpet").[35] Possibly Douglas is depicting his literary development in Virgilian terms: three works; twelve years between the second and the third.[36] It may be prudent, if less tidy, to consider *PH* as a product of the years 1497–1503.

Early in the new century, Douglas was awarded a significant ecclesiastical position with royal patronage, as Provost or Dean of the Collegiate Church of St. Giles in Edinburgh.[37] St. Giles' Church had very high status among collegiate (self-governing) churches in Scotland, next in importance and wealth only to the Chapel Royal at Stirling. As its Provost, Douglas presided over a community including sixteen endowed priests (prebendaries), a curate, and seven other clerics, and a well-funded array of altars and chaplainries. It is tempting to consider the Provostship as James IV's reward to Douglas for writing *The Palyce of Honour*, dedicated to the king, "Throw quhais mycht may humyll thyng avance" (line 2160) — through whose power a humble thing (like *PH*) can succeed.[38] Given Calliope's advocacy for the dreamer when he is under sentence in Venus' court, one might speculate that Douglas would be aware of the way his poetic vocation could also carry him through the controversies and competitions of his waking life.

After this inception on the literary stage and having achieved a leading position in an important ecclesiastical institution, it is all the more striking that Douglas vanishes from the extant Scottish records from 1505 to 1509.[39] At least some of this time, he appears to have been in Paris.[40] With the theologian David Cranston, he compiled the Index for the internationally famous Sorbonne scholar John Mair's commentary on the Fourth Book of Peter Lombard's *Sentences* (1509). Prefatory to the next volume of Mair's commentaries (on the First Book; 1510) appears a Dialogue in the persons of Douglas and Cranston. In this Dialogue, Cranston is depicted defending Mair's own scholastic commitments in theology. Douglas is given the role of the forward-looking humanist (*virum non minus eruditum quam nobilem*; "a man no less learned than noble") who cites the controversial Italian humanist Lorenzo Valla's critique of dialectic and Aristotelian philosophy, and who encourages Mair himself to "abandon school exercises and to return to his native soil, and there cultivate the Lord's vineyard."[41] In such an intellectually rigorous environment, and at a stimulating distance from the duties of the provostship of St. Giles, Douglas' own humanist interests take a momentous step toward his translation into Scots of Virgil's *Aeneid*.

In 1513, Douglas took care to record the occasion of his completion of the *Eneados* on the feast of St. Mary Magdalene, 22 July: eighteen months had elapsed, he declared, since

---

[35] *DOST, loun, lown* (n.). This interpretation follows Bawcutt, *Gavin Douglas: A Critical Study*, p. 215n10. For earlier attempts to connect *Of Lundeys Lufe the Remeid* to Ovid's *Remedia*, see, for example, *Poetical Works*, ed. Small, 1:cxxviii.

[36] Morse, "Gavin Douglas: 'Off Eloquence,'" p. 110; Suetonius, "The Life of Virgil," 2:454–57.

[37] *Poetical Works*, ed. Small, 1:vii; Macdougall, *James IV*, p. 284.

[38] *Poetical Works*, ed. Small, 1:viii; Bawcutt, *Gavin Douglas: A Critical Study*, p. 49; Fradenburg, *City, Marriage, Tournament*, p. 185; Bawcutt, *Dunbar the Makar*, p. 80.

[39] Bawcutt, *Gavin Douglas: A Critical Study*, p. 28.

[40] Rutledge, "Development of Humanism," p. 259.

[41] Broadie, "John Mair's *Dialogus*," p. 426.

he "fyrst set pen to wryte" this project.[42] Less than fifty days later, James IV and many of his earls, lords, knights, and soldiers had been killed at the Battle of Flodden. The King left a widow, Margaret Tudor, sister of Henry VIII, and their two sons (along with six illegitimate children from his liaisons with a series of four mistresses). For Douglas, Flodden effectively ended his literary career.

Politics claimed him. Douglas was appointed by the Lords of Council to attend Margaret Tudor; eleven months after Flodden, in August 1514, she wedded the sixth earl of Angus, another Archibald. A scant month later, the Lords of Council sent for John Stewart, duke of Albany and a descendant from James II, to assume the Governorship of Scotland. For a short period, September–November 1514, Gavin Douglas was Chancellor and being appealed to by Henry VIII's agents to assist the Queen and her two sons to depart Scotland for England. At this time Margaret and her brother recommended Douglas to Pope Leo X as the next Archbishop of St. Andrews. Once again, a family foe stood in opposition: John Hepburn, Prior of the Regular Canons at St. Andrews, claimed the right of election to the archbishopric and ousted the supporters of Douglas.[43] It was yet another candidate, Andrew Forman, bishop of Moray, who was ultimately successful in the competition. Undaunted, Queen Margaret nominated Douglas to be Bishop of Dunkeld, and in this she was again supported by her brother Henry VIII.

In May of 1515, the Duke of Albany arrived from France. As Governor, he acquired proof that Douglas had attained the bishopric of Dunkeld through the support of Henry VIII and hence sought to depose Douglas for treason. Called before the Lords of Council, Douglas argued that they were a secular court and had no jurisdiction over "ane spirituale man"; unsurprisingly, the Lords rejected this plea.[44] Found guilty, Douglas was imprisoned. Albany also warded Margaret in Edinburgh Castle, apart from her sons, but she escaped and fled to London. Frustrated in his aim to control potential rivals and adversaries, Albany released Douglas and allowed him to assume office as Bishop of Dunkeld. Even at this point of vindication, Douglas faced violent opposition. A rival's supporters barricaded the steeple and episcopal palace at Dunkeld and fired on the celebrants in the cathedral.[45]

The embattled beginning was an omen of things to come but hardly represented the best traditions of the bishopric. Housing relics of St. Columba, Dunkeld was an ancient center of Christianity and a gateway to the Gaelic-speaking Highlands. The Cathedral had a reputation for being tended by previous bishops, and for musical excellence.[46] Douglas did not long have the opportunity to contribute to these traditions. By 1517 he was in France as one of the negotiators of the Treaty of Rouen. His opponent the Duke of Albany also went to France, leaving his domestic duties to a cluster of earls, including Angus. Margaret Tudor, meanwhile, returned to Scotland, her marriage to Angus rapidly descending into estrangement. Angus continued to rely on his uncle the Bishop of Dunkeld. In 1520, the

---

[42] *Eneados*, "Tyme, Space and Dait," lines 1–4, 8, 12 (ed. Coldwell, 4:194); with skepticism on this count, Morse, "Gavin Douglas: 'Off Eloquence,'" pp. 118–19n2.

[43] *History of Scotland . . . by John Lesley, Bishop of Ross*, ed. Thomson, p. 101. For a photo-facsimile of this volume, see the Internet Archive: https://archive.org/stream/historyscotland00thomgoog#page /n6/mode/2up

[44] *Poetical Works*, ed. Small, 1:lxii–lxiii.

[45] *Poetical Works*, ed. Small, 1:lxxxii.

[46] Harrison, *Music in Medieval Britain*, p. 15.

Earl of Arran plotted to capture Angus in Edinburgh. Arran and his associates gathered in the residence of James Beaton, Archbishop of Glasgow. Angus sent Gavin Douglas there to negotiate the retreat of Douglas forces from Edinburgh. According to an apocryphal story, Beaton assured Douglas that he could not prevent Arran's hostilities; in a gesture of sincerity he struck his chest, and the armor he was wearing under his robes clanged. Douglas commented, "I persaue, me lord, your conscience be not 'goode for I heir thame clatter.'"[47] During the ensuing fracas, later known as "Cleinye Calsay" (cleanse the causeway), Douglas is supposed to have rescued Beaton.[48]

In the last year or so of his life, Douglas experienced both the collapse of his political ambitions and a resurgence of his cultural commitments. Angus' re-ascendancy ended late 1521 when Albany returned to Scotland. Angus responded by sending his uncle to England to request Henry VIII's help, to convey tales of intimacy between Margaret and Albany, and to paint a pathetic picture of the young James V, neglected and threadbare at court.[49] Learning about this mission, Margaret sought to deprive Douglas of the bishopric and to have him prosecuted in England. In his own defense, Douglas admitted to Cardinal Wolsey that he was "so full of sorowe and displesour that I am wery of my avne lyfe."[50] In London, Douglas had the good fortune to meet the historian Polydore Vergil. Douglas insisted that Vergil pay no heed to a recent history — almost certainly John Mair's *History of Greater Britain* (1521) — which treated skeptically the old stories about the royal descent of Scotland from an Athenian prince and a Pharaoh's daughter.[51] Priscilla Bawcutt observes that Mair, "the schoolman, is here aligned with Vergil, often regarded as the type of the new, rational historian"; Douglas, who had years earlier proclaimed his support for Lorenzo Valla and the new learning, now seems old-fashioned in his advocacy for the medieval narrative of Scottish origins.[52] One might reflect further, however, on Douglas' remarkable assertion of the potency of the national myth; finally, that myth, and the legitimacy it guaranteed, have outweighed all the allure of cosmopolitanism and progress.

The next year, 1522, Douglas died and was buried in the Hospital Church of the Savoy, in London. Polydore Vergil remembered him as a good as well as noble man, fired with commitment to scholarly debate and a vision of national identity. Within a few years of his death, Douglas was being praised by Scots poets as pre-eminent among literary figures of his nation. In his *Testament of the Papyngo* (1530), a poem rich in echoes of *Palyce of Honour*, Sir David Lyndsay praises Douglas more than he does any other poet, English or Scots:

Allace for one, quhilk lampe wes of this land!	*who was the shining light*
Of eloquence the flowand balmy strand	*flowing, fragrant stream*
And, in our Inglis rethorick, the rose.	*English rhetoric; finest bloom*
As, of rubeis, the charbunckle bene chose,	*rubies; carbuncle is choicest*

---

[47] Lindesay, *Historie and Cronicles of Scotland*, 1:281–82; compare *History of Scotland*, trans. Aikman, 2:278–79.

[48] Lindesay, *Historie and Cronicles of Scotland*, 1:283.

[49] *Poetical Works*, ed. Small, 1:xciii–xciv.

[50] *Poetical Works*, ed. Small, 1:civ.

[51] *Polydore Vergil's English History*, ed. Ellis, pp. 105–08.

[52] Bawcutt, *Gavin Douglas: A Critical Study*, p. 31.

And, as Phebus dois Synthia presell,   *the Sun surpasses the Moon*
So Gawane Dowglas, byschope of Dunkell

Had, quhen he wes in to this land on lyve,   *when he was living in this country*
Abufe vulgare poetis prerogatyve,   *precedence over vernacular poets*
Boith in pratick and speculatioun.   *craft and theory*
I saye no more. Gude redaris may discryve   *Good readers can describe*
His worthy workis, in nowmer mo than fyve,   *more than five in number*
And speciallye the trew translatioun   *accurate*
Of Virgill, quhilk bene consolatioun
To cunnyng men, to knaw his gret ingyne   *skilled; great ingenuity*
Als weill in naturall science as devyne.
              (lines 22–36)[53]

In giving Douglas a higher status than "vulgare poetis," Lyndsay may well be ascribing to him cultural leadership in forging the link between Scottish poetry and classical tradition.

In his *History of Scotland* (1571), John Lesley, Bishop of Ross, called Douglas "ane learned man, and ane guid poet."[54] Less disposed to praise bishops, George Buchanan concurred:

> [B]esides the splendour of his birth, and the dignity of his personal appearance, [Douglas] was distinguished for learning, exemplary conduct, and peculiar moderation of spirit, and for his unshaken probity and authority among adverse factions in turbulent times. He left some admirable monuments of his learning and genius in his native language.[55]

The leading poet in early seventeenth-century Scotland was William Drummond of Hawthornden, who alluded to Douglas in similar terms, as "a man noble, valiant, learned, and an excellent Poet, as his works, yet extant testifie."[56] Drummond likely knew *PH*; he owned the copy of E now in Edinburgh University Library. The combination of personal and literary excellence may be merely a eulogistic convention, but its consistency across sectarian and political divisions suggests that the poet's character and works were widely regarded as estimable and deserving of continued attention. In the storms and stresses of reformed Scotland, it was necessary that the writer of a good and important poem be seen as a good man, even if he was a bishop. In this way, Douglas and his poems retain standing in the national literary canon emerging in Drummond's lifetime, long enough to have influenced late sixteenth-century works such as Alexander Montgomerie's *The Cherrie and the Slae* and Elizabeth Melville's *Ane Godlie Dreame*, poems that would continue to attract audiences into the next century and beyond.

The Palyce of Honour is important for the course and direction of its maker's life, and the reverse is true also. Aspects of the poet's upbringing, education, and early career shed light on things in the poem: the understatedly wry handling of Aristotelianism; the allusions to

---

[53] *Sir David Lyndsay: Selected Poems*, ed. Hadley Williams, pp. 58–59.

[54] *History of Scotland . . . by John Lesley, Bishop of Ross*, ed. Thomson, p. 117.

[55] *History of Scotland*, trans. Aikman, 2:280.

[56] Quoted in Geddie, *Bibliography of Middle Scots Poets*, p. 239.

noble families shoved aside by importunate interlopers and schemers; the bad examples of
rebellious and lecherous princes; possibly the sense of cultural openness to England, but
more importantly to France, Italy, and the ancient world; behind it all, indeed, maybe even
the noble family and its household in the castle at the top of a cliff with a stormy sea roiling
below. As well, elements in the poem have a curious way of cropping up later for Douglas,
at moments of controversy: the legal plea that one's judges are not competent to hear one's
case; the insistence on retribution against those who seek advancement at others' expense
and for their own particular benefit. The biographical connections suggest a further
rootedness in the continuing public life of the nation; and the poet's own reputation in
public memory served to keep knowledge of *The Palyce* timely and fresh.

3. TEXT

A. WITNESSES

The following discussion provides a description and comparison of the textual witnesses of
PH. In this section appears a list of the key points at which these witnesses vary; this list
leads into a discussion of the ways these variations offer evidence of relations between the
witnesses themselves. Comparison of variants includes reference to possible causes of
variation: for instance, textual descent based on more than one authorial draft or version
in circulation; or editorial intervention by a scribe or a printer. A goal of this discussion is
to establish principles for the selection of one witness as the basis for this edition, and to
identify particular circumstances in which the text of that witness should be emended. These
activities and the decisions stemming from them underpin virtually every aspect of this
volume, from its title to the form and spelling of each word in the poem as presented, to the
emphases and conclusions in the introduction and explanatory notes.

The overall textual history of *PH* deserves some initial reflection. If one accepts
Douglas' statement that he completed the poem in 1501, at least thirty years pass before the
production of surviving material evidence for the circulation of its text. The textual history
of *PH* depends almost entirely on evidence in printed editions. This state of affairs contrasts
with the textual history of Douglas' major literary work, *Eneados*, his translation of Virgil's
Aeneid, which has a robust transmission in manuscript, with an early copy produced under
Douglas' supervision.[57] During this pre-history, the only signs of that circulation are
admiring allusions to *PH*, in poems by John Bellenden and David Lyndsay. Given their
close associations with the court of James V and their own literary activities, Bellenden and
Lyndsay were sufficiently well-placed, committed, and expert to play a role in the
transmission of *PH*. The earliest extant text is the printed edition by Thomas Davidson,
conjecturally dated c. 1530 to c. 1540. This edition exists in only one highly fragmentary
copy, as follows:

- D [Gavin Douglas.] *The Palyce of Honour*. [Edinburgh: Thomas Davidson (?), c.
  1530–40.] STC 7072.8. Edinburgh University Library De.6.123. [4+] leaves, 4°.

---

[57] Bawcutt, *Gavin Douglas: A Critical Study*, pp. 16, 108.

This edition is represented by four uniquely surviving fragments from the first sheet of four leaves of the printing. William Beattie identified one of the typefaces as identical with the black-letter type in Thomas Davidson's three other extant publications, and the other as identical with the smaller roman type in the chapter-headings of Davidson's edition of John Bellenden's translation of Hector Boece, *The Hystory and Croniklis of Scotland* (1541–42).[58] Ascribing D to Davidson is attractive on various counts, not least his "favored" status as printer of "government documents and 'croniklis.'"[59] A royal connection might suggest continued interest at court in Douglas and his poem.

William Beattie identified the watermark (in the design of a hand below a star) as identical with one used in two books in which Davidson is named as printer: Bellenden's *Boece* and *Ad serenissimum Jacobum Quintum Strena*. F. S. Ferguson identified a partially surviving woodcut with one in Jan van Doesborch's 1521 edition of *Die historie vanden stercken Hercules*, depicting Hercules prevented by Laomedon from entering Troy.[60] Also from van Doesborch is the fragment of a woodcut illustration on sig. 3v.[61]

D is a quarto in which the poem is presented twenty-nine lines to a page, as it is in both L and E (described below). The paginal distribution of the text matches that in L, with which it is also very similar orthographically.[62] The marginal note in L at lines 39–41 likely did not appear in D. At the bottom of the first recto of text (missing the top of the leaf, beginning at line 39 and ending at line 58) appears a signature, "A ii." but no catchword. The catchword at the bottom right of sig. B1v (the last page in D) reads "Certis"; given that the last line on this page appears to be 184, the following line (in L, "Quhilk is allace sa freuch and variant") appears to have been omitted in this copy. Beattie proposes that Copland, printer of L, may have been working from "a cognate edition now lost."[63] The comparable page in L is unusual in that it contains thirty lines instead of the usual twenty-nine, with some consequent compression and slight tipping of the text evident, especially at the top of the page. It remains possible that L derives from D but that at least at this point it was corrected with reference to another witness.

Manuscript evidence exists for the Scottish readership of D or perhaps another print roughly contemporary with and closely related to it. The Protocol Book of David Bowsie

---

[58] Dickson and Edmond, *Annals of Scottish Printing*, pp. 105–35. The identification of Davidson as the printer of D has more recently been only tentatively supported; Bawcutt, *Gavin Douglas: A Critical Study*, p. 193; Mapstone, "Editing Older Scots Texts," p. 322.

[59] Fradenburg, *City, Marriage, Tournament*, pp. 47–48.

[60] Beattie, "Fragments of 'The Palyce of Honour,'" p. 34.

[61] It is "used repeatedly" in his *Den oorspronck onser salicheyt*, 1517, and also appears in his *Thuys der Fortunen Ende dat Huys der Doot*, 1518 (quoted in Beattie, "Fragments of 'The Palyce of Honour,'" p. 34).

[62] The following differences are noted, with readings in D followed by their uncorrected counterparts in L: *silvir/silver*; *nold/nolde*; *stone/stunr*; *tyll/tyl*; *Cau[s]ys/Causis*; *twystis/twystes*; *amourous/amorous*; *fresch/fresche*; *neuyr/neuir*; *[ter]mys rud/termes rude*; *bene/byn*; *monsturis/monstruis*; *onblomy[t]/vnblomyt*; *[l]auchys/lauhcys*. For a fuller listing of all variants, including punctuation and capitalization, see Beattie, "Fragments of 'The Palyce of Honour,'" pp. 40, 43–46; it is still a very small list.

[63] Beattie, "Fragments of 'The Palyce of Honour,'" p. 33.

(alias David Alexander; Edinburgh, National Records of Scotland, MS B 21/1/1, fol. 1r) commences with the following inscription:

> My febill mynd seand this gret supprys
> was thane of wit and euery blys full baire
> Heir end the first part of this tret[. . .]
> And followis the secund part & c.

The lines correspond to 770–71, the end of the First Part of the poem; the inclusion of the rubric may suggest that the leaf was originally part of a longer transcription of the poem, and had been pressed into duty for a different purpose, and perhaps by a different scribe. Mapstone notes the similarities between the phrasing of this rubric and the one ending the "preambyll" in D; she observes that the entries in the protocol book proper commence in the early 1540s.[64]

- L ☙*The* | *Palis of* | *Honoure Compyled by* | *Gawyne dowglas Bys-*|*shope of Dunkyll.* | ¶*Imprinted at London in* | *fletstret, at the sygne of* | *the Rose garland by* | *wyllyam* | *Copland.* |*God saue Quene* | *Marye.* [1553?] [39] leaves, 4°; signatures A3, B–K4. Running title: The Palys | of Honour.

Printed in black-letter type, this is a quarto edition in ten gatherings, each of which is indicated in turn by the alphabetical signatures ABCDEFGHIK. For the present edition, the following copies of this item (*STC* 7073) have been consulted: Bodleian Library, Oxford (Mal.965, in which the fourth gathering has each pair of leaves in reverse order); British Library (G.11231); Cambridge University Library (Syn.6.55.9; missing the last leaf of the first gathering); Edinburgh University Library (De.6.37); Folger Shakespeare Library, Washington, D. C. (HH71/21); Henry E. Huntington Library, San Marino, California (60151); John Newberry Library, Chicago (Case 4A 906); John Rylands Library, Manchester (2039.2); National Library of Scotland (RB.m.517; incomplete, missing the last two gatherings); and Queen's College Library, Oxford (Sel.e.244[2]).

While Copland's edition was in press, a few changes were made in it, not all of which are obvious improvements. Most apparent are the alterations on the title page, which in some copies (Newberry's, for instance) reads as *Compeyled*, in others (such as Huntington's) as *Compeled*, and in still others (for instance, Folger's) correctly as *Compyled*. The edition does not move uniformly toward improvement, however: line 118 is complete in the *Compyeled* and *Compeled* copies, but in the copies with the apparently correct title page, that line lacks its last two words, "a space." Finally, two of the *Compyled* copies examined, Queen's and Rylands', add a marginal gloss at line 630: "He curseth the worlds felycité, fortune and all his pleasure." It is thus possible to glimpse four stages in the production of this edition: three evident in the changes on the title page, and one in the late inclusion of a new gloss.

Though no date of publication appears, it has been surmised to coincide with Copland's publication in 1553 of Douglas' *Eneados*, which has the following text on the title page:

> *THE* | *.xiii. Bukes of Eneados of* | *the famose Poete Virgill* | *Translatet out of Latyne* | *verses into Scottish me-* | *tir, bi the Reuerend fa-* | *ther in God, May-* | *ster Gawin Douglas*

---

[64] Mapstone, "Editing Older Scots Texts," p. 323n59.

| *Bishop of Dunkel &* | *vnkil to the Erle* | *of Angus. Euery* | *buke hauing hys* | *perticular* | *Prologe.* | *Imprinted at Londo*n | *1553.*

The typeface of Copland's *Palis* is identical with that used in his *Eneados*. It is conceivable that the *Palis* was designed by Copland to be a tailpiece to that much longer book, to comprise a Works of Douglas; the two are bound thus in the copy at Queen's College, Oxford (Sel.e.244).[65] As in Copland's *Eneados*, the text of Copland's *Palis* is accompanied by printed marginal notes that may show indications of being written by a Scot or for a Scottish readership.[66] As described below, these notes offer important evidence of early readership of the poem. At two points, the commentary has attracted critical attention. First and less controversially, when Venus hands the dreamer a "buke" (line 1749) a note appears saying, "By thys boke he menis Virgil," a point that is necessarily implicit in the text — Douglas has not yet written the translation, and to predict it might create expectations impossible to fulfill, not least if the poet does not receive the wherewithal to enjoy "mare lasere" (line 1757). A more tendentious note accompanies the Nymph's comment that the mirror of Venus "[s]ignifyis" nothing other than "the greit bewtie" (lines 1761–63) lovers find in their ladies' faces: alongside appears the note "The Auctors conclution of Venus merour."[67] Here the commentator has assigned authorial intention to a character's judgment. Evidently, the paratext of L repays close attention.

With some justice, L has been described as crudely edited and printed.[68] Given its persistence, this characterization calls for further attention. Evidence of a lack of sophistication is not far to seek: the text of the prologue begins on the verso of the title page. The first gathering is anomalous, as it contains three leaves, and the title page is the unsigned recto of what would have been the second; the signature "Aiii" appears on the recto of the second leaf of the first gathering as it stands. On the face of it, the book does have a certain roughness of design: section headings are inconsistently applied, with the Preamble headed only with the running title, and The First Part (sig. B1r) headed with the poem's title entire (and no running title), as *The Palys of Honour*. The later headings are better provided: ¶*The seconde parte.* (signature [D4]r); ¶*The thyrd parte* (signature G1r). The large capital letters at the beginning of sections are rather inconsistent: at the start of the Preamble, the "Q" in "Quhen" is framed and historiated six lines deep; at the start of the First Part, the calligraphic "T" in "Thow" stands without historiation, and is only three lines deep; the L of "Lo" at the start of "The seconde parte" is, again historiated, and five lines deep; and at the start of "The thyrd parte," the anthropomorphic Y of "Ye," has no frame and is again five lines deep.

Still, as edited and printed, the volume shows indications of care in its design. The text block is consistent, page for page. The imprint is clean and regular. Spellings and word distributions are consistent. Catchwords are generally correct; but see, for example signature E2v, where the catchword is written correctly as *Bydand*, and the corresponding

---

[65] Small (*Poetical Works*, 1:clxviii) comments that "copies of the two are sometimes bound in one volume."

[66] Mapstone, "Editing Older Scots Texts," pp. 315–16; Bawcutt (*Shorter Poems*, p. xvi) considered "Copland himself" to be the author of these notes.

[67] Morse, "Gavin Douglas: 'Off Eloquence,'" pp. 111–12.

[68] *Shorter Poems*, ed. Bawcutt, pp. xxi–xxii.

word commencing the text on E3r is *Byddand*. After the initial errors noted above, the running titles are consistent; signatures are regularly provided for the first and second leaf of each quire, though one is missing for C2. The first lines of most of the stanzas begin with a pilcrow, or, less frequently, a fleuron or a manicule. Aligning Douglas and his poem with English interests, Copland places a woodcut of the Tudor arms at the end of the Prologue. The ornamental frame of the title page displays triumphally classical elements. At each bottom corner is a cupid bearing a mace, the left one inscribed *VEL* and the right one *VT* (*velut*, "just as"); these inscriptions correspond to those in the pendants in the upper corners (the left one *SIC*, the right *VT*; *sicut*, "even so"). Around the box in which the title, author, and printer appear is a wreath Copland also used for *The History of Herodian* (1556; STC 13221), and for his edition of Douglas' *Eneados*. The impression evidently aimed for is one of prestige and authenticity.

Perhaps L has received more than its fair share of criticism. Copland evidently took care to correct errors in his text of *PH*. Faulty imposition of type evident in some copies are generally corrected in others, though occasionally new errors intrude. Where Copland's text of *Eneados* has been castigated for its numerous errors, his *Palis* appears comparatively tidy and correct. This difference can be ascribed to Copland's working here from printed copy rather than manuscript; and the admittedly fragmentary evidence suggests he followed D (or a related edition) with care. The eighteenth-century editor of the poem, John Pinkerton, exerted lasting influence on the reputation of L when he generalized that its "spelling . . . is more English," while that of the later Edinburgh print was "more Scottish; but minutiae are not attended."[69] R. J. Lyall has asserted that the later print E "is much closer to Douglas' OSc. orthography" than L, a relationship "confirmed by the readings of the surviving fragment" of D.[70] In fact, a comparison of L to D shows considerable similarity between the two texts, although Copland does not follow the rubrics in D.[71] As well, study of the language of L (see below, section 4) reveals a fairly consistent representation of late fifteenth-century word forms and Northern spellings. For its stalwart advocate John Norton-Smith, L "may well represent transcription direct from an authoritative manuscript or a previous printing which reflects such a manuscript."[72]

The Palis of Honoure occupies a distinctive place in William Copland's considerable output. During the reign of Edward VI (1547–53), Copland was heavily involved in the production of Protestant tracts: for instance, Lancelot Ridley, *Exposition upon the Epistle of Jude* (1549?); William Tyndale's *Parable of the Wicked Mammon* (1549); Thomas Paynell, *The Piththy and Moost Notable Sayinges of al Scripture* (1552). During the reign of the Catholic Mary Tudor (1553–58), the scope and focus of his booklist changed: John Skelton, *Colyn Clout* (1554); Thomas Malory, *The Story of the Moste Noble and Worthy Kynge Arthur* (1557); *The Godly Advertisement or Good Counsell of the Famous Orator Isocrates, Intitled Paraenesis to Demonicus wherto is annexed Cato in olde Englysh meter* (1577–78). Into Elizabeth's reign, Copland printed several medieval romances: *Bevis of Hampton* (c. 1560, c. 1565), *Sir Degaré* (c. 1565), *Sir Isumbras* (c. 1565), *Sir Tryamour* (c. 1561, c. 1565) *Sir Eglamour* (c. 1555; c. 1565), *The Squire of Low Degree* (c. 1560), and *A Mery Geste of Robyn Hoode and of his Lyfe, with*

---

[69] *Scotish Poems*, ed. Pinkerton, 1.51.

[70] Lyall, "Stylistic Relationship," p. 73n9.

[71] Mapstone, "Editing Older Scots Texts," p. 323.

[72] *The Kingis Quair*, ed. Norton-Smith, p. xxx.

a New Playe for to be played in Maye Games (c. 1560). In this context, and together with his *Eneados*, Copland's *Palis* stands out as a distinctively Scottish work. As such, the pair might represent an attempt to capitalize on Douglas' continued reputation in England as a proponent of rapprochement between the two kingdoms. It is more likely, however, that, given the evidence of Scottish circulation and ownership in some of the extant copies, the publication of the *Palis* and *Eneados* provides some indication of Copland's attempt at marketing north of the border. To judge from the limited evidence of a very few surviving copies, Scottish printing was not thriving in the 1550s: copies of a scant eight titles survive for the entire decade, including John Scot's two printings of Sir David Lyndsay's *Dialog Betwix Experience and an Courteour* (1554, 1559).[73]

It may make sense to consider L as in many ways a rather utilitarian, mercenary attempt by a London printer to take advantage of what appears to have been a lull in the Scottish book trade. The small evidence of L's reception suggests that it may have had some success: of the extant copies, several contain marginal annotations. Up the edge of one verso in the copy in the National Library of Scotland, a reader has inscribed with some ornate flourishes (and uncertain formation of some letters) the following lines:

1   I vm[beth]ocht quhow Jhoves and all Satorne
2   In tell a wolfe they did lycaon turne etc.
3   All haille dreid I tho forgett in hye
4   And all my woe Bot ȝit I wist not quarwhy

The last word is repeated, with less flourish, to the right of the line. Here a reader may be taking initial, perhaps wobbly, steps into retracing the poet's steps, or the dreamer's.

Owing the quality of its text to its likely derivation from D or a closely related Scottish print no longer extant, L preserves a great deal of linguistic and textual evidence that would otherwise have been lost or obscured. As will become clear in a discussion of the language of *PH*, L occupies an important place in the developing relations between two geographically and politically distinct varieties of English, one increasingly identified as Scots and another increasingly recognizable as the standard for vernacular texts printed in London. In seeking a mutually comprehensible linguistic ground with identifiably Scots features, L may indeed have remained in some sense true to the values of the poem: it cuts a path by which Scottish power and culture may achieve distinction, while at the same time it maintains active discourse with the southern interlocutor. In this sense, Copland's publication of *The Palis* alongside *Eneados* preserves some opportunity to glimpse the poet's balance between the national and the cosmopolitan. With minimal effacement of the poem's embodiment of a Scottish manner and ambition, the English printer would effectively be foregrounding its role in sustaining cultural dialogue — now, in 1553, between two precariously Catholic realms of Britain, Scotland effectively under the redoubtable Marie de Guise, and England under Mary Tudor.

- E ¶*Heir beginnis | ane Treatise callit the Palice | of Honour, Compylit | be M. Gawine | Dowglas |Bischop of | Dunkeld. [Printer's emblem, McKerrow no. 187] Imprentit at Edin-| burgh: Be Iohne Ros, | for Henrie Charteris. Anno. 1579. | Cum priuilegio Regali.* 40 leaves 4°: signatures A–K4. Running titles: *The Prologue.* [signatures A2–4]; *The Palice | of Honour.* [signatures B1v–K4r, paginated 2–71].

---

[73] National Library of Scotland, *Scottish Books 1505–1700*. Online at https://www.nls.uk.

Like L, this edition is a quarto in ten signed gatherings. The distribution of text per page in E differs from that in L: for example, the first page of The First Part contains 21 lines (in L, 29).

To judge from its surface indications, the 1579 Edinburgh *Palice of Honour* (STC 7074) is designed to outshine its predecessor. The reference to royal privilege is easy to overvalue: Ross and Charteris were never the King's printers but claimed royal patronage under the institution of copyright in Scotland.[74] On the final verso appears the larger of John Ross' two devices, featuring the emblem "of a woman with book labeled *Verbum Dei*" ("the Word of God") and a lit candle. The motto is *Vincet tandem Veritas* ("Truth will conquer at last"). These devices also appear in John Rolland, *The Court of Venus* (1575).[75]

The Edinburgh *Palice* deserves to be seen as part of a sequence of older literary works brought back in printed copy for educated, patriotic readers in recently reformed Scotland. Through the initiative of John Scot, John Ross, Robert Lekprevick, and with the increasingly active support of Henry Charteris, items such as Hary's *Wallace* (1570; *STC* 13149), Barbour's *Bruce* (c. 1571; *STC* 1377.5), Henryson's *Fables* (1571; *STC* 185.5), the anonymous *Rauf Coilyear* (1572; *STC* 15062), John Rolland's *Court of Venus* (1575; *STC* 21258), and *The Palice of Honour* came into print in Scotland in the 1570s. Most prominent in this group of literary titles is Sir David Lyndsay's *Works*, printed no less than four times in Edinburgh between 1568 and 1580 (*STC* 15658, 15660, 15661, 15662). It may make sense to see this modest flurry of literary interest owing more to association with the status of Lyndsay as a forerunner of Reformation than it does to any uprush of antiquarian spirit.

In his preface to the 1568 edition of Lyndsay's *Works*, Charteris points to the working of God's grace in preserving the poet in his criticism of contemporary abuses of religion. Charteris gives less credit to the protective function of comedy in Lyndsay's writings, but still acknowledges that Lyndsay's "writing was commounlie mixit with mowis, and collourit with craftie consaitis (as Chaucer and utheris had done befoir)" (signature +3r). In a poem appended to his preface, Charteris associates Douglas with the divinely inspired, excellently forthright Lyndsay:

> Thocht Gawine Dowglas, Bischop of Dunkell,
> In ornate meter surmount did euerilk man;
> Thocht Kennedie, and Dunbar bure the bell   *took the prize*
> For the large race of Rethorik thay ran:
> 3it neuer Poeit of our Scottische clan,
> Sa cleirlie schew that Monstour with his markis,   *showed; characteristics*
> The Romane God, in quhome all gyle began: *whom; deception*
> As dois gude Dauid Lyndesay in his warkis.[76]

Good poetry is a good thing, but poetry that confirms and strengthens the nation as a godly community is altogether better. In this context and spirit, the editing of Douglas by Ross and Charteris may reasonably be expected to highlight any flickerings of reforming spirit; indeed, such illuminations may even be enhanced where the opportunity exists.

---

[74] Mann, *Scottish Book Trade*, pp. 140–41.

[75] McKerrow, *Printers' and Publishers' Devices*, no. 189, p. 71.

[76] Charteris, "Ane Adhortatioun of All Estatis," lines 17–24 (*Works of Sir David Lindsay*, ed. Hamer, 1:404); sig. A2r.

For their edition of *The Palice*, Ross and Charteris provide a much shorter preface than they did for Lyndsay's *Works*. The verso of the title page presents a single paragraph, as follows (in slightly modernized spelling):

> To the Reidar. Qvhen we had sene and considderit the diuers Impressiones befoir Imprentit of this Notabill werk, to haue bene altogidder faultie and corrupt: not onlie that quhilk hes bene Imprentit at London, bot also the Copyis set furth of auld amangis our selfis: We haue thocht gude to tak sum panes and trawellis to haue the samin mair commodiously and correctly set furth: to the Intent, that the benevolent Reidar may haue the mair delyte and plesure in reiding, and the mair frute in perusing, this plesand and delectabill werk.

While the preceding editions may indeed have all been faulty and corrupt, saying so could be a good way to enhance the status of one's own product. Interestingly, reference is made to "copyis" made in Scotland but only *that* one coming from London. From this, one might justifiably posit that the fragmentary D is thus all that remains of two or more Scottish editions of *PH*; it has been suggested that there may have been more such, though the grounds for believing so are unclear.[77] The implication exists that a manuscript, now lost, may have been among the sources consulted for E; and that implication would of course heighten the status Charteris and Ross are claiming for their edition. They also appear to regard L as a unique incursion in Scotland of an English printing of this title. Although it came out about 24 years previously, it would be the principal competition for a new edition, and hence it particularly is to be regarded as "altogidder faultie and corrupt." What Ross and Charteris promise in its place is a commodious and correct edition, one that will doubtless enhance their contemporaries' experience of the poem. Resisting any uncritical acceptance of the Edinburgh editors' assertions, Priscilla Bawcutt detects a possible "element of 'knocking copy' in Charteris' method of advertising" that might recall his previous animadversions on the editions of David Lyndsay's works preceding his own.[78]

Ross and Charteris banked on a sustained healthy interest in their edition of *The Palice of Honour*. Their hopes seem to have been modestly rewarded. Ross died in 1580, and among the assets included in his will were 280 unbound copies of the book ("price of the dosane, xv s"); in his will of 1585, the bookbinder Robert Gourlaw mentioned "Palice of Honour, iij, at xij d. the peice."[79] Among the owners of their book was the poet William Drummond of Hawthornden, whose copy is now in Edinburgh University Library.[80]

Reading the poem in this edition, one immediately notices obvious differences from L. The typeface of the preface and Prologue is roman, while the poem proper is set in black letter. The running title remains in roman: verso "The Palice"; recto, "of Honour." Other headings are also in roman: for instance, "The Author directis his buik | to the richt Nobill and Illuster Prince Iames | the Feird [Fourth] King of Scottis" (p. 70). As well, in the third part of the poem, Latin terms and phrases are set in roman: "Se[s]que altra and decupla"; "Sancta Sanctorum"; "in periculo mortis"; "primum mobile"; "Trivmphous" (lines 495,

---

[77] Mapstone, "Editing Older Scots Texts," p. 323.

[78] *Shorter Poems*, ed. Bawcutt, pp. xxi–xxii.

[79] "Wills of Thomas Bassandyne, and Other Printers," eds. Laing, Scott, and Thomson, pp. 189, 205, 212, 214.

[80] Bawcutt, *Gavin Douglas: A Critical Study*, p. 193.

1454, 1705, 1840, 2143). Though each page contains twenty-nine lines of verse, as was usually the case in L, large title headings at the beginnings of the prologue and the first part produce a different spread of lines per page in E: "The Prologue" (sig. A2r); "The Palice of | Honour, Compylit be M. | Gawine Dowglas | Bischop of Dunkeld" (sig. B1r). Page numbers are printed on the outer top corners verso and recto throughout E. Signatures are provided on each leaf until the last, [K4]. In several respects, this looks a more correct, professional job than L. The right-hand margin is more regular, with extra-long lines hyphenated and remaining syllables and/or words placed immediately below on the right. With its frequent capitalization of main nouns, it also appears to present its text as having status and importance. This dignified impression is somewhat lessened by the ink from the impression on the other side of each leaf showing through the thin paper.

- E1[Handwritten emendations in the NLS copy of E]

The National Library of Scotland's copy of E contains handwritten marginalia that call for attention in a consideration of the text of *PH*.[81] Unlike the annotations in the Newberry Library's copy of L, which indicate a reader's efforts to comprehend a difficult text, those in the NLS copy of E seem more assured, as if they arise from additional knowledge about the poem and its language. The script is skillful and legible; the editorial marks are handled with precision and assurance, conveying the impression that the annotator is well-versed in commenting thus on such texts. The handwriting exhibits Scottish secretary features (for instance, "the form of *c* made by two short strokes . . . and the tendency for *e* to fall apart")[82] and may date from the late sixteenth or early seventeenth century. Unfortunately, cropping of the leaves for rebinding has resulted in the loss of the edges of the original pages, with consequent loss of the text of some annotations. Overall, the annotations are numerous; 53 pages of text in E contain one or more such markings.

The first of these annotations provides a meaningful example. As witnessed in both L and E, the first stanza of the Prologue contains at the end of the fifth and the eighth lines a prominent repeated word, given in E as "amiabill." The annotator of NLS E has drawn a box around the second appearance of this word, and in the right-hand margin has written "delectabil[l]," each letter distinctly and separately formed. To the same line, the annotator has also provided a caret between the *o* and *l* of the ambiguous form "Sol," with an *i* provided in the right hand margin. Such interventions sometimes seem, as here, designed to address potential semantic or stylistic difficulties. Similarly at line 167, the annotator provides "compaissit" in place of E's "compassit"; and here, the interest seems to have been to ensure the consistency in appearance and sound of the stanza's a-rhyme (in E, "abaisit," "arraisit," "betraisit," "compassit"; compare "violate/violait" in line 220). In various cases, the annotations sometimes revert to spellings and forms in L: in place of E's "swappis" (line 144), the annotator provides "skappis," returning to the reading in L and indeed in D; similarly, the annotator reinstates "four" as the number of milk-white horses pulling the chariot of Venus (line 213). Numerous such examples are to be found in the Textual Notes of this edition.

---

[81] Bawcutt (*Shorter Poems*, p. xix) cites William Beattie's groundbreaking discussion of these annotations, in a letter to *The Times Literary Supplement* (23 February 1946).

[82] Simpson, *Scottish Handwriting 1150–1650*, p. 16.

These editorial interventions offer what appear to be carefully considered changes, ones that may either represent the stylistic sensibility of the commentator or access to another source, whether in print or manuscript. They have sufficient interest to constitute a witness in their own right. Although the source of these emendations cannot be identified, they are of such interest that they have been collated and will be referred to here and in the Textual Notes as E1. Speculating further about the identity of the annotator and the purpose of the emendations, one might conjecture that this is someone with marked literary interests and training who is engaging in concerted editorial work with the text, someone who deserves to be considered as the fourth early editor of the poem, whose critical acumen repays close attention.

The source of these readings, and especially of the unique items, has not been possible to determine with any certainty. Perhaps the annotator is working with L or a related witness and in addition is contributing readings based on her or his own stylistic knowledge. If so, the unique readings might be treated as purely editorial. That at any rate is the position taken here: E1's readings are all recorded as shedding particular light on the early reading of *PH*, but are treated with some caution as textual evidence.

B. COMPARING THE WITNESSES

The differences between E and L can largely be explained in terms of different editorial principles, errors of understanding, or misprints. Some forms and words in L had become obsolete by the 1570s and appear to have been replaced by newer alternatives, as can be seen in a comparative sample from the first six hundred lines of *PH*:

L	E
Replennessed	Replenischit
puncys	pulsis
veray	vary
Corruppis	Corruptis
avision	Visioun
ranys	rymis
skauppis	swappis
royk	rock
tothyr	uther
Inoth	Inwith
gekgo	greik
velvos	velvot
lusum	luifsum

Typically, where L uses "quhou," E provides "how"; L's "till" is often replaced by "to," "atwene" by "betwene," "tofore" by "befoir"; in the present participle, the suffix "-ing" occasionally replaces "-and." For variant readings witnessed in fragmentary D, that print consistently agrees with L against E.

On the other hand, E gives indications of greater precision — and, one might add, editorial interventiveness.[83] Errors of typesetting are significantly less frequent than in L.[84] Apparent errors of terminology, grammar, or prosody are corrected. A sample follows:

L	E
eccon	Echo
monstruis	monstures
or brounvert	ovirbrouderit (E1 emends to "ovirbroudart")
Fare	France
Demoophan	Demophoon
involvit in dispyte	involupit in syte
in greif disdenyeit	and greit disdenyeit
as of a dedly cryme	of a deidlie crime
Twelf plagis in Egypt	Ten Plaiges in Egypt
pronounce a fals sentence	pronounce fals sentence

One or two such variants call for closer attention. For example, E preserves the older idiom "involupit in syte" (line 613), for which L provides "involvit in dispyte"; one way of explaining this difference would be to posit that some editorial intervention has taken place in L to make an obscure phrase accessible to southern readers; admittedly, L does not contain many such instances. Another case is E's apparent preservation of the word "Newand" (line 1705), obsolete by 1550; L provides the less semantically accurate but more familiar and current term "Mewand." Of special interest is E1's agreement with L. If "Mewand" were to have been used in D or a comparable Scottish print from the 1530s, then the case might strengthen for E's having been based here on an independent witness. A simpler explanation may be that, at this point, E1 has not recognized the validity of E's "Newand."

Bawcutt considered the relationship between E and L to be "complicated" and posited three ways in which the text might have been altered in transmission: authorial revision, especially in the Second Part; scribal/compositorial error; and "conscious 'editing' by Charteris, and perhaps by Copland also."[85] While much but not all of the variation can be explained as error, a reconsideration of the variants in the Second Part seems rather to indicate a pattern of editorial correction of apparent mistakes and updating of obscure old terms, especially in E.[86] While some of the lacunae can be explained straightforwardly as the result of mechanical error (for instance, the omission in E of lines 805 and 1043), the deletion in L of the stanza on popular tales (lines 1711–19) deserves further attention. The exclusion of this stanza from the text of L is likely editorial; and here, the challenge to the English printer-editor would have been one of sheer comprehension: Piers Plowman and Robin Hood might have been sufficiently familiar, but "Raf Coilyear," "auld Cowkewyis

---

[83] *Shorter Poems*, ed. Bawcutt, p. xxv.

[84] L has a comparatively high proportion of accidental errors: mistakes with similar letter forms (for instance, *f*/long *s*; *t*/*c*, *r*/*x*), reversed pairs of letters (for instance, *monstruis* for *monsturis*), and punctuation, especially opening and closing parentheses: about 130, or roughly one every sixteen lines overall. For E, the incidence of accidental error is about 35, or roughly one every 62 lines — almost four times more accurate.

[85] *Shorter Poems*, ed. Bawcutt, pp. xxvi–xxvii.

[86] For evidence and discussion, see the Textual Notes for lines 772–1287.

sow," and the wren that "come out of Ailssay" surely would not. By the late eighteenth century, the stanza was still eliciting strongly varied responses. On the one hand, James Scott, the first modern editor of the poem, expressed "pleasure" to "find here, two of Ossians celebrated heros, *viz.* Gow or Gaul the son of Morni and Fyn Macoul or Fyngal — The last verse alludes to their heroic, or god-like exploits in Ireland."[87] On the other hand, the poem's second editor, John Pinkerton, "could make nothing of the strange names" and called the stanza "ludicrous."[88] Perhaps Copland responded in a similar vein.

On balance, the evidence is surprisingly slender that Charteris and Ross had access to a superior exemplar apart from D and/or a printed edition closely related to it. As well, specific evidence is lacking for the kinds of purposive reworking that could be associated with authorial revision. What thus emerges is an adequate, economical explanation of textual relations through the occurrence of individual printers' errors and editorial decisions. These bits of evidence accumulate to support the hypothesis of a fairly unified textual descent, with D representing the previous generation, L an older (and expatriate) sibling offspring, and E a younger sibling attaining a distinctiveness by asserting loyalty to native values and practices.

Seeking in L and E for a preferable repertoire of editorial practices has no better results. Attempting to assign superiority to one or the other of the two prints for greater authenticity of its Scots spellings and word-forms is inconclusive at best. Southern forms occur in each, and especially in the rhetorically high-colored sections such as the Prologue, at least some of these can be identified as probably authorial: appearing in both L and E, "bonkis" (line 54) is an interesting example, with its southern -*o*- and northern -*is*; the b-rhymes in the next stanza also show what is probably the poet's own preference for southern -*o*- forms ("stone," "alone" rather than "stane," "alane"; for similar forms in rhyme position, see lines 422 and — in L but not E — 1920, 1923, and 1924). As a feature of style, Douglas occasionally, and especially in the Prologue, employs a characteristically southern form of negation, typical of Chaucer: for example, "nolde" for "ne wolde" (line 52), "not" for "ne wot" (line 60). By such indications, episodes and passages are set alongside if not within an English tradition of eloquence.

There is a modest handful of divergent readings where each witness offers what appears to be an equally good option (such as "rebell/rebald" in line 954).[89] Some of these competing options pertain to the thematic core of the poem, notably in the discrepancy between L's "a god armypotent" (line 1921) and E's "ane God Omnipotent" to denote the god Honour enthroned in his presence chamber.[90] Less observed has been a similar variation slightly later in the poem, when the Nymph refers to the "vailyeand folk" dwelling "[v]ictoriusly" — or as E has it, "[v]erteouslie" — in Honour's court (line 1966). One explanation for these differences would be that Charteris and Ross are restoring the spiritual sense at a point when Copland veered away from it; another would be that they have intervened at this

---

[87] *Select Works*, ed. Scott, p. 149.

[88] *Scotish Poems*, ed. Pinkerton, 1.122.

[89] In the Introduction to *Shorter Poems* (pp. xxiv–xxv), Bawcutt provides a list of these; in several of the cases cited, it is possible to perceive a historical priority in the options in L. See the Textual Notes, below, for discussion of individual cases.

[90] In *Anglo-Scottish Literary Relations*, pp. 117–18, Kratzmann resolves the difference firmly in E's favor. No less firmly does Hasler emphasize "armypotent" (*Court Poetry*, p. 99 and n37).

crucial juncture to heighten appreciation of Douglas as a forerunner for the forthrightly reformist spirit of Sir David Lyndsay. If Charteris and Ross are responsible for the change, they have discreetly engaged in the sort of reforming revision that has been noted, for example, in prints of Henryson's *Fables*.[91] Charteris and Ross would not thus be expurgating vestiges of the old religion, but coloring the moral import of *PH* more vividly, to bring to the fore a figural reading of their *Palice* as the new Jerusalem, and their *Honour* as Christ.

It is not necessary to assert the superiority of L over E in order to make the case that its text deserves attention and study in its own right. What is more valuable to demonstrate is that the surviving witnesses of *PH* provide evidence of a reasonably coherent line of descent and may even adequately represent the text as the author left it. In this descent, L holds a worthy place and offers opportunities for insight into the workings and import of *The Palyce of Honour* that are not possible elsewhere. It is possible to see in both L and E the indications of standardization: Copland, through his mediation of Scottish distinctiveness; Charteris and Ross, through a linguistic updating that accommodates the poem to the norms of late sixteenth-century Scots.

C. EDITORIAL PRACTICE

This edition presents a text based on the forms of L. Editing has involved a new comparison of the witnesses, with a fuller consideration of the states of the text as represented by the various extant copies of L. Accordingly, its textual commentary, though still selective rather than exhaustive, is founded upon a more inclusive concept of significant variation than was the case in its METS predecessor, with some attention paid to accidentals. In the interest of providing an edition of use to readers at various stages of training, the actual presentation of the text throughout this edition involves some modifications to spelling and punctuation that have been made as consistently as possible:

a.   The letter *i* represents a vowel, with *j* substituted where *i* stands for the consonant in L.

b.   The letter *u* represents a vowel, and *v* a consonant. This normalization is not extended to *w*, which is maintained in the distribution found in L.

c.   The yogh (ȝ) is replaced by *y*.

d.   With attention given in the notes to the punctuation of L, and especially the recurrence of *punctus flexus* as an indication of a brief medial or final pause, the punctuation of the text is largely editorial.

e.   Capitalization is editorially adjusted, so that proper nouns are capitalized (e.g., "Musis" for "musis"); as a result the serendipitous charm of such instances as "Maryguld," "Eliphant," "Dragonys," and "Dalyans" (lines 37, 330, 349, 600) has been rejected with some regret.

f.   Where a final -*e* has phonemic value as /i/, it is provided with an acute accent, *é*. In the form of the second person pronoun "the," the spelling is modified to "thee" in the interest of readability.

---

[91] *Poems of Robert Henryson*, ed. Fox, p. lx.

D. EDITIONS

The following list of modern editions is presented in chronological order.

- [James Scott, ed.] *Select Works of Gawin Douglass, Bishop of Dunkeld*. Vol. 2 of *The Scotish Poets*. 3 vols. Perth: Robert Morison Jr., 1787.

The copy-text is E, moderately accurately represented, with *quh* generally represented by *wh* and ʒ (yogh) by *z*; E's distribution of *u* and *v* is generally maintained. The introduction dwells much upon the poet's historical stature, and touches on the possibility that Douglas might have written "some of the pastoral and heroic ballads, or celebrated songs of his time" (p. xxx). Some effort is made to find an autobiographical reflection on the poet's own entry into holy orders in the concluding episode of *PH*: "The habitation of the honourable Ladies was surrounded by a deep ditch. When he attempted to pass over by the narrow Bridge by which, no doubt, he meant the ceremony of marriage, he fell into the water, and awakened from his dream" (p. xxxi). For the editor, "[t]he allegory is of that mixed kind which introduces ideal persons with such as are real, and the Greek and Roman mythology with sacred History" (pp. xxxi–xxxii). The poet earns praise for his "great powers of invention" in a poem that "abounds not only with moral lessons, but with lively and picturesque descriptions: and the language, tho' it may now appear barbarous to many, because of its obsolete words and seeming deficiencies in construction, is artfully compiled and wonderfully expressive" (p. xxxii). James Scott has been identified as the editor, though he is not named in the volume.[92] He displays a fondness for the Gothic as it can be detected in *PH*, the nightmare description of what he calls the "horrid desart" earning his accolade of being "very poetical" (p. 141).

- John Pinkerton, ed. *The Palice of Honour, Compylit be Mr. Gawine Douglas, Bishop of Dunkeld*. In *Scotish Poems: Reprinted from Scarce Editions*. 3 vols. London: John Nichols, 1792. Vol. 1, pp. xiv–xv, 51–142.

The copy-text is E, with some variants recorded from L. Pinkerton's introductory note is brief, with mention of a presumed source, "the *Sejour d'Honneur* by St. Gelais," and the critical comment that "[t]his poem of Douglas, amid many defects, has great merit for the age in which it was written" (p. xiv).[93] Pinkerton provides somewhat antique-looking Arguments for each part, for example at the outset: "The poet gangs into a gardyne — Falls in a swoun — Is transportit to a desert," etc.

- John Kinnear, ed. *The Palice of Honour by Gawyn Douglas*. Bannatyne Club. Edinburgh: James Ballantyne, 1827.

---

[92] *Poetical Works*, ed. Small, 1:clxx; Geddie, *Bibliography of Middle Scots Poets*, pp. lxxxviii, 244.

[93] In *The Lily and the Thistle* (pp. 48–51), Calin compares *PH* to the *Séjour d'Honneur*. For opposing views, see *Poetical Works*, ed. Small, 1:cxxxvii; Kratzmann, *Anglo-Scottish Literary Relations*, p. 108; Gray, "Gavin Douglas," p. 152. Saint-Gelais completed his long allegorical poem in 1494, rather late for sustained influence on *PH*.

This is an accurate facsimile of E, with a list of variants from L. The Bannatyne Club was a leading antiquarian society that had been led by Sir Walter Scott and that continued to thrive on the energies and acumen of the bibliophile and editor David Laing. This facsimile upholds the Club's interests in specifically Scottish literary and historical remains. Following on the two previous editions, the choice of E confirms the priority of that witness. That priority would be maintained in most discussions of the poem through the nineteenth and twentieth centuries.

• John Small, ed. *The Poetical Works of Gavin Douglas*. 4 vols. Edinburgh: Paterson, 1874.

Along with a groundbreaking biography of the poet, the first volume of this edition contains a text of *PH* that is founded on E, with a list of variants from L and facsimile pages from D. Small brought a new scholarly rigor to study of the poem: his influential account of the author's biography and the sources of his poem, and especially his recognition of the influence of Chaucer's *House of Fame*, determined the shape and emphases of research into and criticism of the poem for over a century.

• Priscilla Bawcutt, ed. *The Shorter Poems of Gavin Douglas*. Edinburgh: Scottish Text Society, 4th series, no. 3, 1967. 2nd edition STS 5th series, no. 2, 2003.

The bulk of this new edition is a paginary reprint of the excellent first edition with its authoritative discussion of text, language, and literary affiliations. Also including texts of *King Hart* (no longer attributed to Douglas) and the short poem "Conscience," this includes a parallel edition of L and E, with E being given some priority by virtue of its fuller editorial treatment and principal attention in the notes and glossary. In each part of the volume, effort is taken to distinguish between the various texts presented; the combination is such that the distinctive features of L, though often cited, sometimes recede from focus. The second edition includes some valuable new notes on, for instance, aspects of the sources, reception and influence of the poem. Some of this new material presents additional evidence for the strength of variant readings in L. Given this evidence, this second edition opens the door for fuller attention to Copland's text in the further study of the poem.[94]

• David J. Parkinson, ed. *Gavin Douglas: The Palis of Honoure*. Kalamazoo, MI: Medieval Institute Publications, 1992.

Sally Mapstone commented that this was "in fact the first full modern edition to prefer the London edition to the Edinburgh one."[95]

---

[94] In revising *Shorter Poems*, Bawcutt commented further on the importance of L, for the "medieval forms" of several of the names, but even more for the increased recognition of possibly superior readings therein (p. 300).

[95] Mapstone, "Editing Older Scots Texts," pp. 323–24; Mapstone notes a prior edition of lines 1828–90 from L, in *Late Medieval Verse and Prose*, ed. Gray, pp. 320–23, 477–78.

4. LANGUAGE

The following comments provide a basis for the contention that, as represented by L, the language of *PH* balances authoritatively between readability and distinctiveness. Thus represented, this is a recognizably northern, Scottish poem with international connections. In its spellings and vocabulary, it intermittently signals an affiliation with southern English. It is both conservative in its forms and innovative in its coinages. At various levels, from sound and spelling to style and versification, these principles work cohesively in *PH*.

A. SOUNDS

To a great extent the vowels in the L text of *PH* can be determined from its rhymes. As discussed below, the dominant stanza form consists of nine lines with only two rhymes, with a secondary form in three rhymes and two inset passages of ten-line stanzas. Despite the formal demands across the 240 stanzas of the poem, the rhymes tend to be full and consistent. Understandably, rhymes are commonest where lexical resources are richest, so that the vowel /i/ (as in "see"), for instance, recurs frequently, while the diphthong /ɔɪ/ (as in "joy") rhymes rarely. Given the poem's ample length, study of its rhyming vowels produces sufficient evidence to show consistency with currently accepted accounts of phonology as represented in late-medieval Scottish texts. The effects of the major sound-change known as the Great Vowel Shift are evident here in ways consistent with Jeremy Smith's description of the consequences: "Whereas in the South all Middle English long vowels were affected, in the North . . . only front vowels underwent raising or diphthongisation."[96] One aim of the following discussion is to muster the evidence to consider whether L might represent this process accurately and coherently. For this reason, considerable attention is paid to the phonological evidence provided by rhymes, and to specific features of grammar. International Phonetic Alphabet (IPA) symbols and descriptions are meant to offer some standard orientation for the sounds involved. Following is a survey of the vowels and diphthongs detectable in the rhymes of *PH* as witnessed by L:

i   *see* (close unrounded front vowel), e.g., *seis, tapestreis, greis, gleis, treis; heid, reid* (OE *read*), *deid* (OE *dead*); *yeir, cleir* (ME *cler*), *speir* (OFr *espere*), *heir; complete, hete* (OE *hæto*), *swete* (OE *swéte*), *sprete* (AN *spirit*), *replete; nystee, thee; remede, dede, rede, plede* (AN *plaid*); *virginité, fre* (OE *freoh*), *feminyté; slep* (OE *slapan*), *pepe, depe* (OE *díop, déop*);[97]

e   *say* (mid-close unrounded front vowel), e.g., *curage, age, rage, vissage; May, affray, day* (OE *dæg*), *away* (OE *aweg*); *naturale, availe, ale, assaile; space, face, cace, place, grace; twane, frane* (OE *fregnan*), *slane;*

ɪ   *pin* (mid-close unrounded centralized vowel), e.g., *mycht, sycht, wycht, lycht* (OE *leoht*; ME *ligt, liht*), *richt; blys* (OE *blisse*), *this, yys, i-wys; lippis, eclippis; king, livyng; salusyng, bening, sudjournyng;*

---

[96] Smith, *Older Scots: A Linguistic Reader*, p. 30.

[97] This vowel represents the confluence of close and open -*e*, which are distinct in earlier Scots; *Poems of Robert Henryson*, ed. Fox, p. 492.

ɜ	p*e*n (mid-open unrounded front vowel), e.g., *fret, set, wet, yet; cruell, sell, tell, Hell; effek, blek, nek;*
æ–a	f*a*ther (open unrounded front vowel), e.g., *wary, vary, sary, tary, fary; infernall, naturall, fall, boryall; agast, wast, upcast, blast, fast; part, art, eftirwart, depart; vigillant, skant; immutabill, stabyll, abil, innumerabill;*
u	p*oo*l (close rounded back vowel), e.g., *respirature, nature, cure, creature; blume, tume, dume, grume; proportioun, doun, broun, fassioun; bowr, lowr, dour, clour; blud, flud, rude; quuke, tuke, luke;*
ʊ	p*u*ll (near-close rounded near-back vowel), e.g., *fundyr, undyr, thundyr; joyous, tedius, thus; Peneus, Tmolus, Emus, Heliseus;*
o	b*oa*t (mid-close rounded back vowel), e.g., *stone, fanton, allone, schone; one, alone, mone, apone; Plato, Cicero, go; chariote, velvote, wote, hote, note; ost, bost;*
ʌ	b*u*n (mid-open unrounded back vowel), presumed in unstressed syllables in polysyllabic words: e.g., *i* in *aggreabill, e* in *battell, y* in *fowlys, u* in *monsture* or *quhilum;*
ɔ	c*o*t (mid-open rounded back vowel), e.g., *spokkyn, brokkyn, lokkyn, tokkyn, wrokkyn; nocht, wrocht, mocht, thocht; astond, grond, confond, wond; sok, knok;*
ɒ	c*ou*rt (open rounded back vowel), e.g., *report, overwhort, schort, sort, port; accord, discord, record, lord, remord; implore, forlore, more; raw, schaw, saw, knaw, aw; blaucht, kaucht;*
ø	p*u*rr (mid-close rounded mid-front vowel), e.g., *Saturn, turn, sudjourn, murn, spurn;*
ʌɪ	wh*y*, e.g., *pryce, ryce; pungitive, vivificative, restorative, hyve; extasy, by, cry, I, espy; quhyt, parfyte, polyte, delyte; fyne, divine, nyne;*
ʌu	*ou*t, e.g., *routyt, schoutyt, doutyt, sproutyt, moutyt; about, out; brow, sow, fow;*
ɪʊ	n*ew*, e.g., *hewyt, renewyt, eschewyt, thewyt, unpersewyt; new, hew, trew, schew, Grew, schrew; slewch, eneuch; persew, drew;*
ɔɪ	c*oy*, e.g., *tranoynt, anoynt, disjoynt, poynt; convoy, joy.*

B. SPELLINGS AND FORMS

Some variation is to be expected in any text by a late fifteenth-century writer in any variety of English; in one written in Edinburgh that is printed half a century later in London, variant spellings and forms will arise from the interplay of at least two distinct dialects; and the distribution of these spellings and forms may intermittently be influenced by stylistic considerations. Given predictable variation, therefore, it is striking how often L represents an apparent preference for northern spellings over southern ones, a preference that could be due to its exemplar being a text printed in Scotland such as D. It is also striking how rhymes show the choice of a southern English option at key moments to have been authorial, as for instance in the b-rhymes of the seventh stanza, *stone, fanton, alone, schone*: in each of these instances except the second, a northern speaker could be expected to have opted for a spelling with *-a*, *stane*, *alane*, *schane*; southern options broaden the stylistic and prosodic palette of *PH*. In its "extensive admixture" of southern and northern forms, the language of *PH* has been described as a development from that of *The Kingis Quair*.[98] Remaining alert to spelling variation may thus enable the reader to perceive patterns: thus *a* varies in some frequent instances with *e* (*war/wer*, *wes/wa*); *i*, *y* with *e* (*nyxt/next*; more idiosyncratically, *vigitant*, *rillik* where one would expect *vegetant*, *relic*); more superficially, *y* varies with *i*, *ie* (*-is/-ys*; *-yng/-ing*; *lyk*, *py*; *rays/rais*; *dais/dayis*). Following is a brief, informal selection of recurrent patterns, largely consistent with spelling practices in fifteenth-century Scottish texts, with occasional variations:

a, *ai* for *o*: *maist*, *na*, *behald*, *laith*, *blaw*, *knaw*, *mare*, *bald*, *ane*, *rais*, *hald*, *raid*, *schaw*, *baith* (consistent with regular practice in northern Middle English texts; but see the intermittent reversals of this trend, toward southern norms: *no*, *bonkis*, *mony*, *bore*, *tone*, *one*, some of which may be authorial, especially in rhyme positions);

-is, *-ys* for *-s*, *-es*, *-se*: *dois*, *goddis*, *ellis/else*, *lois/loss* (compare *signifyes*, line 1762, where *-es* is a more explicit form of the suffix following *y*) — and it is worth noting that the vowel in the final *-is* usually lacks syllabic value;

-it, *yt* for *-ed*: *ratlit/rattled*; *deliverit*, *answerit*, *walkyt* (compare *fulfyllet* for *fulfilled*, line 251);

quh for *wh*, *h*: *quhilk*, *quhair*, *quhow* (but note the contrasts, such as the unusual word *overwhort*, line 284; and *what*, line 941 — the unique appearances of this spelling in L);

i, *y* following another vowel as an indicator of length: *beistis/bestis*, *thoill/tholyt*, *luif/luf*, *fluid/flude*; *clos/clois*, *maid/made*;

s alternating with *sh* (*sall/shall*);

-ny- appearing where *-gn-* would be expected in modern English (*fenyeit* for *feigned*).[99]

Some spelling variations appear to have little or vestigial phonological significance: *w*, *u*, and *v* are interchangeable, so that *w* often serves in place of *u* (*owt* for *out*). Sometimes *w* and *v* are exchanged (*wariance* for *variance*; *varyit* for *waryit*, and, as in the title pages to L and E, *Gawine* for *Gavin*).

In all these cases, the dominant option in L turns out to be the usual spelling and form in northern and especially Scots usage.

A survey of the forty most frequent words in *PH* reveals broad similarities in spelling with modern English forms. Amongst these words occur the following: *the*, *and*, *of*, *I*, *in*, *with*, *that*, *a*, *my*, *all*, *to*, *for*, *on*, *be*, *me*, *as*, *his*, *not*, *is*, *saw*, *this*, *now*, *he*, *so*, *at*, *we*. This survey also begins to reveal some patterns of difference from modern English: *wes* in place of *was*; *thair*,

---

[98] *The Kingis Quair*, ed. Norton-Smith, p. xxx.

[99] For a more systematic introduction to these features, see Smith, *Older Scots: A Linguistic Reader*, pp. 25–34.

thare for *their* but also *there* (e.g., lines 527, 529, 544, 570, 576; compare lines 248, 368, 542, 562). Some potential traps can be found in the list of common spellings: thus the spelling *be* sometimes but not consistently represents a preposition equivalent to modern English *by* (e.g., lines 3, 42, 95, 280 etc.; compare the spelling *by* in lines 168, 170, 198, 266 etc.); *til*, *till* often appears where *to* would in modern English (e.g., lines 5, 51, 55, 329, 337, 361, 383, 396 etc.), but it is not consistent, so that *to* is one of the most frequent words in *PH* (e.g., lines 6, 39, 79, 142, 209, 248, 283, 309; but compare the even greater frequency of *to* in E).

Among the frequent words, those with the initial *quh-* spelling give prominence to *PH* as a Scots text. The most commonly occurring item among these is *quhilk*, the relative pronoun (for the modern English relative and interrogative pronoun *which*, but also *who*; e.g., lines 21, 31, 33, 139, 157, 321, 380), sometimes in the construction *the quhilk* (e.g., lines 280, 361, 365). This common occurrence is related to the form *ilk* (compare modern English *each*, *very*, *same*; e.g., lines 215, 221, 296, 1647). The plural form takes the *-is* suffix (e.g., lines 430, "sternys . . . quhilkis schone"; 436–37, "bellys . . . in sound quhilkis excellis"; 1381, "folk, quhilkis quhyle thay ar here"). Also quite common is *quhat* (for the modern English relative and interrogative *what*; e.g., lines 173, 235, 238, 382, 385, 387). The adverbs *quhen* and *quhil(l)* are similarly prominent (e.g., lines 1, 14, 28, 110, 116); see also *quhare*, *quhair* (*where*; lines 143, 153, 200, 208) and *quhairin* (lines 151, 204), as well as *quhy* (*why*; e.g., lines 167, 782, 956). Also highly recurrent are the pronouns *quho*, *quha* (e.g., line 86, 183–84; see also the possessive form *quhois*, e.g., lines 24, 70, 106) and the pronoun/adjective *quhat* (*what*, e.g., lines 173, 235, 238). In L but not E, this spelling convention is extended to the adverb *how* (*quhow*, *quhou*, e.g., lines 92, 118, 197). The inflected personal pronoun *quham*, *quhom* has a rather wider range of uses than the rather more exclusive reference to persons performed by its modern English equivalent *whom* (e.g., lines 101, 146, 211).

One encounters various ways in which common words apparently familiar from modern English are "false friends" that turn out to have quite distinct meanings and/or functions.[100] For instance, *be* is a recognized form of the preposition *by*, as mentioned above; *gyf* can represent the verb *give* but often appears as a form of *if* (e.g., lines 471, 529). The spelling *not* is frequent; occasionally *nocht* appears in its place (e.g., lines 49, 307, 368, 459; compare E, where *nocht* is more frequent) — and as generally in Middle English, the spelling *not* can also be a contracted form of *ne wot*, "did not know" (e.g., line 60, 118), or "do not know" (e.g., line 382). Used as a preposition (*except*) or conjunction, *but* is often spelled *bot* (e.g., lines 149, 162, 304, 336, 368); spelled as in modern English, the word tends to be used more often as a preposition (*without*; e.g. "but caus," line 163; "but dout," line 241; lines 254, 380, 381, etc.; compare, e.g., lines 387, 738, 1166).

PH also displays variation in the use of compound forms: *in til*, *in to/into*; *to fore/before*; *every thing*, *na thing/nothyng*, *over fret/Ovyrfret*, *ilk ane*, *erd quake*, *thairfra*, *thairfore*; *throw out*, *Quhare so*, *quhair of/Quhairof*, *with all*. L also contains some unique, apparently idiosyncratic spellings — *eccon*, *vigitant*, *rillik*, *problewm*, *optene*, *rowme*, *feminité* — that may nevertheless reflect prior and even authorial choices.

---

[100] Such false friends are a prime focus of the Glossary to this edition.

C. Grammar

The following points indicate some prominent ways in which the morphology of *PH* as represented by L differs from that of standard modern English. An account of the historical descent of the forms and structures mentioned has not been attempted here.[101]

Nouns: The usual plural ending is *-s*, with variants *-is/ys/es*; depending on metrical constraints, this suffix may or may not have syllabic value (compare *droppis*, line 27, with *leves*, line 20). Other plural forms: zero change (*hors, fysche*; compare *horsys, fyschis*), mutation of medial vowel (*feit* from *fut*; *teith* from *tuth*), and *-ir* suffix (*chyldir*); occasionally, the southern plural form *-n* appears (*eyn*, line 480). As with the plural, the usual possessive ending is *-s*, with variants *-is/ys/es* (e.g., *mannys voce*, line 441; *lustis art*, line 532).

Pronouns: The 1st person singular nominative is *I*, oblique *me*, possessive *my*, *myn(e)*; the plural forms are *we*, *us*, and *our/owr*. The 2nd person singular nominative is *thou*, *thow*, oblique *tha* or much more commonly *the(e)*, possessive *thy*; *thine/thyn(e)*. The plural forms are *you/yow*; and *your*, *youris*. The 3rd person singular masculine nominative is *he*; oblique form *him*, *hym*; possessive *his*, *hys*. The 3rd person singular feminine nominative is *scho*, *sche*; oblique form *her*, *hir*; possessive *her*, *hir*; [*hers*, *hirs*]. The 3rd person plural nominative is spelled *thay*, *they*; oblique form *thaim*, *thaym*, *them*; possessive *thair*, *thayr*, *thare*, *their*. The demonstratives are *this*; *thair/their/thir* (modern English *these*); *that*; *tha* (line 148), *thay* (modern English *those*, as in line 2109).

Articles: The definite article is *the*. The indefinite article is *a*, *ane*. Of interest is the recurrent demonstrative form *thir* (*these*).

Adjectives: Strong/weak and singular/plural inflection are not evident. The comparative ending is normally *-er* (lines 523, 676, 958, etc.), but also *-ar* (line 532). The superlative normally ends *-est* (e.g., lines 360, 451, 1904, 2017, 2117).

Adverbs: As in standard modern English, the adverbial ending is spelled and rhymed *-ly* (as in lines 1765, 1772, 1835, 1841), but occasionally *-lyk* (e.g., *tratourlyk*, line 284), with the suffix rarely provided as a separate word (for instance, *poete lyk*, line 820; also line 1571).

Verbs: Rather than attempting a full description of this large category, the following observations focus on points where forms differ significantly from those in standard modern English. The infinitive usually appears without a suffix (as in lines 188, 200); but sometimes with *-ing*, *-yng* (lines 666, 729, 1067, 1399, 1814).[102] In the present indicative, the 1st person singular commonly lacks a suffix, as does the 1st person plural. The 2nd person singular commonly has *-is*, *-ys* (e.g., *thow denyis*, *knawis thou not*, *quhy standis thou*; compare *thow hes*) but occasionally *-yst* (*thow seyst*); cumulative internal rhyme can affect this form (as in line 2139). The 3rd person singular commonly has *-is*, *-s*, *-ys* (for instance, lines 331, 561, 965, 1633, 1973, 1989), with syllabic significance as the metre requires (for instance, lines 31, 33) and sometimes with the southern ending *-ith/yth* (lines 621, 860, 1030, 1061, 1115, etc.), *-oth* (*doth*, line 1265). The 2nd person plural commonly lacks a suffix (as in lines 725, 1389,

---

[101] Further discussion of these features can be found in Smith, *Older Scots: A Linguistic Reader*, pp. 45–50; see also Macafee and Aitken, "A History of Scots to 1700," section 7.

[102] "Inflected infinitives in *-in* occur as an anglicism (also spelled *-ing*)" (Macafee and Aitken, "History of Scots to 1700," section 7.8.9). See also the discussion of this hallmark of Douglas' style in Bawcutt, *Gavin Douglas: A Critical Study*, pp. 144–45.

1391), but see also -*is* (line 1388). The 3rd person plural sometimes lacks a suffix (as in lines 264, 632, 1716, 1965), but see also -*is*, -*ys* (for instance, lines 1382, 1816), -*en* (line 1778), and often -*yng* (as in lines 210, 227, 600, 643, 824, 1076, 1253).

The past indicative calls for particular attention. Strong verbs (where vowel mutation signals the past tense) include, e.g., *crap* (from *creip*), *fand* (from *fynd*), *flaw*/*flew* ("fly"), *gat* (from *get*), *gaif*/*gave* (from *gyf*), *hard* (from *here*, "hear"), *raid* (from *ryd*), *ran* (from *ryn*), *schane* (from *schyne*), *schew* (from *schaw*), *schuke* (from "shake"), *straid* ("stride"), *sang* (from *syng*), *tuke* (from *tak*). Weak verbs (those that in modern English add the ending -*ed* or -*t* to signal the past tense) have the endings -*it*, -*t*, -*yt*. If the meter demands, the weak past tense ending can be syllabic (e.g., *alychtit*, *commandit*, *convoyt*, *dynnyt*, *onheldit*), or not (*playt*, *passit*, *knelyt* [line 675]; *lerit* [line 1104], *opprest*, *remanyt*); the -*ed* ending occurs rarely, as in *blasphemed* (line 670). Some irregular verbs show the past tense by a suffix and a vowel change: for instance, *brocht* (from *bryng*), *kaucht* ("catch"), *betaucht* (compare *teche*); comparable formations of the past tense occur in the modal verbs *can* (*culd*), *may* (*mocht*), *sall* (*suld*), and *will* (*wald*).

In the present participle, the distinctive ending is -*and* (for instance, *blomand*, *makand*, *syngand*, *confessand*, *addressand*, *traistand*, *fordynnand*, etc.); but alongside it the southern -*ing* form also recurs (e.g., *rynnyng*, *rowmyng*, *quakyng*, *quhislyng*, *approchyng*, *stampyng*, *bathyng*, *corruppyng*, etc.): of interest is the combination in line 1709, "With questyng hundis, syrchand to and fra," where the purely adjectival item preceding the noun takes -*yng*, in contrast to the -*and* item following. For the past participle: with alteration of the medial vowel, strong verbs take the ending -*in*, -*en*, occasionally also the initial *y*- (for instance, *yschappit*, line 41, *ydronken*, line 357; compare *songin*, *wryttyn*, *blawin*, *wordyn*, *biddin*). In weak verbs, the past participle takes the same ending as the past tense, -*it*, -*yt* (e.g., *devoryt*, *offeryt*, *dullit*, *trappit*, *festnyt*, *bylappit*, *caryit*, etc.). Verbal nouns take the -*ing* ending, which can be followed by a plural suffix (for instance, *werking*, *hering*, *stychlyng*, *knawlegyng*, *harnasyngis*, *tarying*, *havinges*).

The copular verb *to be* follows a fairly consistent pattern: present singular *am*, *art*, *is*; plural *ar*, *are* (but sometimes *bene*); past *was*/*wes*, *war*/*wer*. Some intermittent forms (e.g., *bene* for the usual plural *are*, lines 527, 716–26, 1735; once, *werren* for the plural past tense, line 528) reflect southern English usage. Of interest is the 3rd person singular form *beis* (lines 708, 2028), which appears to function predictively; in both instances, the form appears with negation, *beis no(ch)t*.

The special handling of phrases and sentences is core to literary style. Before delving into that large topic as it pertains to *PH*, some mention should be made of underlying aspects of syntax. The usual order of syntactic elements follows the general pattern in English of Subject–Verb–Object/Complement: "beis wrocht material"; "His luke was grym." For stylistic variation, a frequent inversion places the Object at the start: "Every invasybill wapyn on him he bare." In questions, the Verb typically precedes or phrasally envelops the Subject: "hes my self bene gylty?"; "Quhow plesys thee our pastance and effere?" In negation, *not*/*nocht* occasionally serves as the sole marker (e.g., "we not presume"; "not tell can I"). As do other aspects of language, these elements suggest both a determination to assert a distinctive identity and an effort to communicate to a wide diversity of readers, in Scotland but also south of the border. The signs of that effort and determination are deeply enough seated in the text to be regarded as authorial.

D. Terms, *Colouris*, and Style

Douglas evidently took pains to make even the finer details of his poem striking, new, and yet rooted in classical tradition. At this level, newness of language may catch the reader's attention. A prominent feature of *PH*, especially in the Prologue, is the inclusion of unusual, rare, or unprecedented words. With reference to the etymological information in the relevant entries in *The Dictionary of the Older Scots Tongue* (*DOST*), a few of these apparently new words can be informative:

> *reparcust* (Latin *repercuss-*, past participial form of *repercutere*)
> *umbrate* (Latin, *umbrat-*, past participial form of *umbrare*)
> *vivificative* (Old French *vivificatif*; Latin *vivificat-*, past participial form of *vivificare*)
> *respirature* (Latin *respirat-*, past participial form of *respirare*)
> *assucurit* (Latin *assecurare*)
> *virgultis* (Latin *virgulta*, plural of *virgultum*)
> *effere* (noun from Middle English verb *aferen*)
> *muskane* (uncertain: Gaelic *mosgain* or Norwegian *mausken*, Shetland *moskin*)
> *bubbys* (perhaps imitative)
> *apyrsmart* (Old French *aspre* + *smart*)

This sample of words for which *PH* provides the earliest evidence reveals some of the qualities of the poem: its classicism, but also its recourse to regional vernaculars and vividly imitative formations. Sometimes Douglas extends the meaning of a word already in use in restricted contexts: for example, his description of May as the "maternall moneth" (line 65), his reference to the "brownys" of the olive branches (line 81) or to the branches of the trees in the nightmare, all "moutyt" (moulted) of their leaves (line 152). Occasionally his innovation seems fanciful, as in "sulfuryus" (line 354; almost a portmanteau word in the manner of Lewis Carroll). It begins to appear that this poet has identified such newness as a hallmark of literary excellence.

In *PH*, Douglas works purposefully with various levels and areas of diction. It is conventional to see fairly straightforward alternation between *ugsome* (horrifying, loathsome) and *amene* (agreeable, pleasant) language according to mood and topic: C. S. Lewis wrote influentially about the "weird energy of the description" of the nightmare forest, "rattling with broad Scots words of the *boisteous* style" in "careful contrast" to the polished terms of the earlier *locus amoenus*.[103] Bawcutt has suggested instead that "familiarity with Latin as a second tongue may have led" Douglas to transfer "learned, polysyllabic words, often of Latin origin" in a thoroughgoing way into his text, "almost unconsciously."[104] It is worth noting that considerations of the especially ornate style of the Prologue have preponderated in discussions of the language of *PH*. Considering the markers of subordination Douglas employs in the opening stanzas (e.g., *Quhen, So, Quhil, Quhilk, Quhois*), John Norton-Smith commented acerbically on "lengthening the poetic period to achieve the effect of Latinate continuousness" as having become "almost a vice of style."[105] The demands of fluency and

---

[103] Lewis, *Allegory of Love*, p. 291.

[104] Bawcutt, *Gavin Douglas: A Critical Study*, pp. 64–65.

[105] *The Kingis Quair*, ed. Norton-Smith, p. xxix.

compendiousness can produce a flattening of emphasis, in which topics and terms are presented as if in "a kind of catalogue."[106] R. J. Lyall focused more appreciatively on the fifth stanza of the Prologue (with its a-rhymes on *onlappit*, *happit*, *wappit*, *yschappit*, and *gnappit* and its b-rhymes *pungitive*, *vivificative*, *restorative*, and *hyve*), particularly on the fact that "Douglas here weaves his latinate rhyme-sequence in with one which is unmistakably Scots."[107] The integration of latinate and native elements can be seamless.

Douglas employs the abundant jargon associated with a host of specializations: acoustics, music, clothing and fashion, the law, geography, preaching, gardening, architecture and the decorative arts, jewels, astronomy and cosmology, landscaping. One might add the local display of rhetorical *colouris* (devices, figures), with which Douglas again produces striking effects of amplitude: *repetitio* (e.g., lines 128–34, 174–81, 403–10; that figure with "much charm and also impressiveness and vigor,"[108] *apostrophe* (e.g., lines 1282–87, 1288–96, 1588–94), *ratiocinatio* (e.g., lines 183–90). All these various, richly elaborated passages assert the range and depth of the poet's specialized knowledge and eloquence, but more importantly, like turns in a maze, they present a series of obstacles and opportunities to the reader, who is thereby challenged to determine a cognitively satisfying line of signification and progression. The risk is that, like the dreamer himself caught gazing at the ornamentation on the threshold to Honour's palace, the reader may lose momentum and fall prey to "dotyng" (line 1868). As becomes blatantly obvious, for example, in the poet's characterization of his profuse recounting of musical terms, seeing the signs and knowing the words does not necessarily betoken knowing the art. Here Douglas resituates and sharpens the impression of pedantry that attends the Eagle's discourses in Chaucer's *House of Fame*: he conveys an awareness that prolonged terminological indulgence only deepens the impression of folly.

Douglas turns to a different set of *colouris* to spur the reader to greater alertness. Not all *colouris* work expansively: Douglas finely musters effects of forceful brevity, and especially in narration and direct discourse: *asyndeton* (e.g., lines 944, 1695–99, 1710), *sententiae* (e.g., lines 272–73, 762, 985–87, 1410, 1879, 1989), the Nymph's tidy *paronomasia*: "Thow art prolixt" (line 1462), *articulus* (e.g., line 1372); and as a recurrent ironic gesture of closure, *occultatio* (e.g., lines 410, 517–20, 1165, 1408–10, 1427). By such figures as these, just as the Nymph urges the protagonist to recognize and understand what he is experiencing, the poet calls for the reader's attention and reflection.

John Small wrote influentially that the stylistic faults of *PH* "are those of superabundance, rather than deficiency."[109] Charles Blyth argued that in *PH* Douglas resorts to "a rhetorical mode which consists of excessive piling up of descriptive phrases, aureate diction, and ornate imagery"; while noting that this is "only one of the modes of the poem," he concludes that it provides a stylistic model that is too static for use with extended

---

[106] Lydgate, *Poems*, p. 169n218–23, quoted in *Chaucerian Dream Visions and Complaints*, ed. Symons, p. 122n218–24; on the prevalence of catalogues as the "basic structural device" of *PH*, see Fox, "Scottish Chaucerians," p. 198.

[107] Lyall, "Stylistic Relationship," p. 75.

[108] Quoted in Murphy, *Rhetoric in the Middle Ages*, p. 365. See also Bawcutt, *Gavin Douglas: A Critical Study*, p. 57 for the poet's "fondness" for this rhetorical color.

[109] *Poetical Works*, ed. Small, 1:cxxviii.

narrative.[110] So prominent are the local displays of specialized terms that, distracted by them, readers may fall into the trap of considering the poem as a loosely coordinated sequence of areas of rich allusion and topical jargon. It would be unfortunate to leave the matter thus, as the poem has more to offer. The usual mode of narration is decisive; an increasingly deft, understated handling of terms reflects the changing balance between emphasis and fluency. To see this technique in operation, it is necessary to proceed beyond the stark contrasts and set-pieces of the First Part and into the more concerted progression of the Second. The plot advances in passages such as these:

> All haill my dreid I tho foryet in hy   *wholly; then; at once*
> And all my wo, bot yit I wyst not quhy,   *I did not know why*
> Save that I had sum hope till be relevyt.   *rescued*
> I rasyt than my vissage hastely   *raised*
> And with a blenk anone I did espy   *look*
> A lusty sycht quhilk nocht my hart engrevit.   *did not grieve my heart*
> (lines 781–86)

In a poem given to powerful, transformative sights and sounds, this foreshadowing is structurally significant, and yet the language employed in this passage is efficient rather than gaudy; the distance between the dreamer's lack of self-awareness and the poet's more knowing recollection is given point by the litotes of the last line quoted.[111] It can be a surprisingly concise style, with values of directness and fluency akin to those Quintilian found in Sallust and Livy, two writers Douglas evidently admired (see note to line 252).

As if in a Livian vein, Douglas enlivens his narrative with direct discourse. Here his management of tonal effects can be spiritedly evocative:

> Styl at the hillys fute we twa abaid,   *Still; base; two lingered*
> Than suddandly my keper to me said,
> "Ascend, galand!" Tho for fere I quuke.   *fine gentleman! Then; fear; trembled*
> "Be not effrayit," scho said. "Be not mismaid,"   *upset*
> And with that word up the strait rod abraid.   *rushed up the narrow path*
> I followit fast; scho be the hand me tuke
> Yit durst I nevir for dreid behynde me luke.
> (lines 1306–12)

The abruptly jocular reference to the quailing dreamer as "galand" complicates the tone even as it accelerates the pace (and note the prominence of active verbs in the following lines); the resulting hesitation produces a more solicitous tone, and a repetition of a key term in the poem, "mismaid."[112] Previously, the dreadful court proceedings "mysmaid" the dreamer (line 683); as if in unconscious irony, Calliope asks Venus who had "mismaid" her (line 941). Later, gradually regaining consciousness after having been smitten by a sight of

---

[110] Blyth, *"The Knychtlyke Stile,"* p. 164.

[111] Amsler, "Quest for the Present Tense," p. 195.

[112] As consideration of the Glossary to this edition will reveal, Douglas can rely on a repetitiveness of phrasing; for instance, the high frequency of the phrase *I saw* can be detected through the profusion of citations of *saw* in the review of the forms of the verb *se*. Very often, however, he handles repetition with grace and skill.

the god Honour, the dreamer is mocked for being "so mysmaid" (line 1938). Through the whole stanza, an unobtrusive but evocative selection of terms contributes to the meaningful counterpoise of movement and hesitation.

E. VERSIFICATION

The stanzas of *PH* have attracted some attention, mostly for their presumed Chaucerian antecedents: notably in the complaints proper in Chaucer's *Anelida and Arcite* (lines 211–55, 273–316, 333–57) and *The Complaint of Mars* (lines 155–298). In Scottish verse before *PH*, the nine-line stanza had appeared in *The Quare of Jelusy* and *The Lufaris Complaynt* (included in the *Kingis Quair* manuscript, Bodleian Arch. Selden. B. 24; *Quare*, lines 191–316; *Complaynt*, lines 72–107, 124–77) but also in a lyric complaint in Hary's *Wallace* (2:171–332). Gregory Kratzmann has written appreciatively about "the sonorous finality of Douglas's ingeniously contrived stanzas, with their . . . self-consciously ornate and 'poleit' eloquence."[113] Denton Fox described Douglas, drawing upon Chaucer's fifteenth-century reputation, "as a metrical innovator and as a technical virtuoso."[114] What has been insufficiently noticed is that Douglas puts this stanza to various different uses: rapid narrative, vigorous debate, and vivid, concrete description as well as the rhetorical mode of complaint to which it is largely confined in his predecessors' work. The flexibility and responsiveness of the nine-line stanza in *PH* calls for further discussion, especially given the variation of rhyme schemes as the poem progresses. What becomes apparent is that, at least in his pushing increasingly heavy metrical constraints to extremes, Douglas is something of a metrical innovator, seeking to outdo his prosodic models.

This technical variation deserves closer attention in its own right but also for what it may imply about the composition of *PH*. For the Prologue, First Part, and Second Part of the poem, the dominant form is a stanza of nine pentameter lines with two rhymes (*aabaabbab*). An inset complaint of three ten-line stanzas of three rhymes with a refrain (*aabaabbcbC*, with the last line as a refrain; lines 163–92) interrupts this pattern. Later, another complaint is interposed, again in three ten-line stanzas, each in two rhymes (*aabaabbabb*; lines 607–36). Marking an end to this sequence of lyric insets, a third ten-line lyric of expiatory praise appears, this one in two rhyme-schemes, its first two stanzas being in two rhymes (*aabaabbaba*; lines 1015–34), and the last stanza in three rhymes (*aabaabbcbC*; lines 1035–44). These variant stanzas make sense as markers of special rhetorical functions interrupting the narrative. Other variations are harder to explain. In the description of the Muses is a single stanza in three rhymes (*aabaabbcc*; lines 862–70); here an attempt is made in E to assert consistency, with the first *c*-rhyme (L's "and sistir schene") being converted to the *a*-rhyme ("sister with Croun"). Three other instances of this scheme occur in the Second Part (lines 916–24, 943–51, and 1189–97), in only the second of these instances is an attempt made in E to assert the two-rhyme norm, where "velanie" replaces L's "wallaway" in the eighth line (line 950). A significant change takes place at the start of the Third Part, where the previously intermittent scheme in three rhymes (*aabaabbcc*) becomes the norm. Finally, closure demands special measures: two stanzas in the two-rhyme form serve to conclude the work. The first of these also displays cumulative internal rhyme: two rhyming words per line

---

[113] Kratzmann, *Anglo-Scottish Literary Relations*, p. 105.

[114] Fox, "Scottish Chaucerians," p. 197; see also Spearing, *Medieval Poet as Voyeur*, p. 241.

in the first stanza, three in the second, and — clangorously — four in the third. Given the pains Douglas has taken to establish and maintain highly demanding verse forms, the variations deserve further attention. They may be artifacts of revision, markers of rhetorical emphasis, or simply evidence of the technical leeway the poet has permitted himself.

Turning from the stanza to the decasyllabic line, what is most impressive is the metrical regularity Douglas maintains. He allows a degree of license in his handling of the third and even the fourth feet of the pentameter, where inversion of stress is an infrequent option, as the following examples show:

> Amyddys quham, borne in ane goldyn chare (line 211)
> Thair saw I, weil in poetry ygroundyt (line 895)
> No woman is, rather a serpent fell (line 984)
> In ane instant scho and hir court wes hence (line 1052)
> Now out of France tursyt in Tuskane (line 1086)
> Ovir Carmelus, quhare twa prophetis devyne (line 1105)
> Maid sobir noys, the schaw dynnyt agane (line 1151)
> My Nymphe in grif schot me in at the yet (line 1865)

Elision of unstressed syllables ending or beginning with a vowel is also optional: "Furth past my Nymphe; I followyt subsequent" (line 1441); "That men in story may se, or cornakyll reid" (line 1694). As well, the final foot sometimes ends with an additional unstressed syllable: "Amyd my brest the joyus heit redoundyt" (line 891). Hyper- and hypometrical lines are rare, and may be due in part to scribal handling of suffixes. For instance, line 25, "Of reparcust ayr the eccon cryis," appears to contain a maximum of nine syllables; but the problem may have arisen in the transcription of the second word, the suffix of which could be fully articulated as *reparcussit*. Hypermetrical lines are slightly more common in E than L, for instance, line 1040, "Till Venus, and under hir guerdoun all houris"; for *guerdoun*, L provides the metrically regular *gard*. A notable instance in E is the replacement of *Quincyus* with the correct but metrically excessive name *Marcus Curtius* (line 1676; see Textual Note to line 1676). While allowing that Douglas does not metrically "break down so often or so badly" as his English contemporary Stephen Hawes, George Saintsbury disliked "the name-catalogues, which [Douglas] rather affects," and cited the following line as an illustration: "Galien, Averroes, and Plato" (line 258) — and indeed, many lines in the poem display greater or lesser ingenuity in stitching together names.[115] More serious, perhaps, is Saintsbury's disapproval (in the same note) of the following lines: "I understude be signes persavabill / That was Cupyd, the god maist dessavabill" (lines 481–82). The first of these lines can be resolved if one reads the suffix of *signis* as so reduced that it is not registered as a separate syllable; such reduction is a regular option throughout the poem. The second line is more problematic. The only way to reduce its eleven syllables to metrical regularity is to speculate on the intrusion of *maist* at some point in the transmission of the text. An even more serious challenge arises shortly after this passage, in the line "Accumpanyit lusty yonkers with all" (line 490); here the second foot manifests an inversion of stress, a rare departure from the metrical norm. Attention to metrical variation evidently increases the scope for textual analysis but, more importantly, it can

---

[115] Saintsbury, *History of English Prosody*, 1:276 and footnote.

assist the reader to appreciate the stakes and hazards of Douglas' poetic practice, and to recognize the extreme measures he is prepared to take to meet the demands of his rhyme scheme.

Overall, *PH* is an extraordinary achievement: an extended, rhetorically variegated narrative poem in an ornate, demanding stanza. As such it is a very Scottish poem, one that repays comparison with the earlier compositions in the alliterative thirteen-line stanza such as *The Knightly Tale of Golagros and Gawane* and Richard Holland's *The Buke of the Howlat*, as well as Alexander Montgomerie's later dream-vision in fourteen-line stanzas, *The Cherrie and the Slae*. Like those other assertions of cultural distinctiveness, *PH* deserves recognition as a place in which the whole resources and potential of language and verse are expanded in Scottish literature. What L reveals is how these achievements might have continued to be appreciated and learned from within and beyond Scotland's borders, through the sixteenth century.

5. THE POEM

A. OVERVIEW

Turning from the text and language of *PH* to a more sustained consideration of its literary qualities with their affiliations and reception, one may be impressed afresh by the scope and coherence of the poem as it stands. It is a dream vision, a form coming to Scotland apparently quite late, in the fifteenth century, but remaining current and vital up to the seventeenth. The earliest examples of the genre that are associated with Scotland are *The Kingis Quair* of James I (c. 1424) and Richard Holland's *The Buke of the Howlat* (c. 1450); among its later Scottish instances are *Ane Schersing of Trew Felicitie* by John Stewart of Baldynneis (completed in the 1580s or possibly a little earlier) and Elizabeth Melville's *Ane Godlie Dreame* (printed 1603). For Douglas as for James I decades earlier, Chaucer provided an enabling precedent, not least in making the dream vision the frame for vivid representation of a personal identity. The trick was to be more than merely Chaucerian in writing one's dream. While the plot and episodes of *PH* owe much to *The House of Fame*, the Prologue to *The Legend of Good Women*, and *The Knight's Tale*, Douglas is purposefully reshaping these elements. For instance, as discussed above, he employs for sustained narrative a stanza previously associated with set-pieces of complaint. Like Chaucer in drawing on Ovid and Virgil, Douglas nevertheless bestows a more heroic character than does his English predecessor to the material he draws from these and other classical sources. Of special prominence in the making of *PH* are its recurrent catalogues: diverse personages in cavalcades (in their interactions recalling perhaps the pilgrims in *The Canterbury Tales*); performers at a banquet and the stories they recite or perform (like the entertainers in *The House of Fame*); events from literature, history, and pastime as witnessed in a marvelous mirror; finally, the briefly glimpsed residents in the hall of Honour. In the closing moments of the poem, the relation of dreaming to waking is quite decisively made problematic; as recurrently in the vision just experienced, ascent and descent are only too easily mistaken for each other; and recurrently, troubling, threatening figures are included in the zones of celebration and reward.

Before proceeding to further discussion of the literary qualities of the poem, a synopsis of its action may be helpful. The Prologue places the poem in the usual context of late-medieval dream-poems. Before dawn one May morning, the narrator recalls, he visited a beautiful garden to pick flowers and sing, as one customarily does in the springtime. The sun rises, and the visitor hears a disembodied, anonymous voice singing praises to May. The excellent performance discourages him so that he laments his unworthiness to praise Nature, May, and Venus. Preparing to return home, he is overcome by a glare of light in the atmosphere and loses consciousness. He seems to awaken, but it is into a dream.

The First Part begins with the dreamer finding himself crawling in a filthy, noisy, dying landscape. He gives vent to a song against Fortune. A fine cavalcade approaches, attending a queen in a chariot. Two stragglers identify themselves as Ahithophel and Sinon, hopeless hangers-on to Minerva's court — whose followers they name — en route to the faraway palace of the god Honour. The unworthy pair tell the dreamer that two more deities are approaching, Diana and Venus. Expectant, the dreamer sees Actaeon, a hart chased by his hounds. With her small entourage, Diana arrives, mounted on a chaste elephant.[116] Their passing by leaves the dreamer miserable. A glow and a high-pitched sound catch his attention — and the poet digresses into the topic of acoustics. The joyful onset depresses him for the moment, but he remembers it with delight. The arrival of Venus and her entourage of lovers and musicians inspires him retrospectively to appreciative description. In the moment, however, he responds by singing a complaint in which he curses Cupid and Venus. His performance does not go over well. The more impish courtiers beat and bedaub him. A trial for blasphemy and treason commences. Venus rebukes the dreamer, who fearfully anticipates being metamorphosed.

The Second Part gradually releases the tension just created. The dreamer's upswing of unreasoning hope presages the arrival of the Muses and their songful followers. The Muse Calliope urges Venus to relent. At Calliope's command the dreamer writes a poem, which Venus accepts before departing. Calliope orders the dreamer to accompany her entourage, in the care of a Nymph. Mounted, they embark on a fantastic journey, arriving at the Hippocrene spring where everyone crowds for a drink so that the dreamer gets none. Accompanied with pastimes, a feast takes place. The cavalcade re-embarks and approaches their mountain destination.

The Third Part begins with the dreamer lingering at the bottom of the steep slope. The Nymph leads him up until he encounters a fiery chasm in which lie those who aspired to honor but gave way to pleasure. She lifts him by the hair and carries him to the summit. Instructed to look down, he sees the world below as a stormy sea in which a sailing vessel runs aground, its occupants drowning or struggling to the foot of the mountain. Those who drown are unfaithful, the Nymph declares; and the ship is Grace acquired through baptism; sin brings shipwreck, and then only Christ's help in performing good deeds can avail. Invited to look the other way, the dreamer sees an edenic garden, a richly ornamented palace in its midst. The Nymph guides him through the outer gate, and he sees tournaments. Vexed by his protracted staring, the Nymph urges him into a garden where Venus is enthroned. A mirror on a tripod sits before her, with the power to heal those hurt in the tournaments, and in which the dreamer sees all the deeds and fates of earthly history, along with various amusements. Venus notices the dreamer and hands him a book, commanding him to put its long-neglected contents into rhyme. As the dreamer departs, the Nymph remarks that the mirror shows lovers the beauty of the women they love.

Conveyed to the main citadel, the dreamer sees crowds of the unworthy seeking access

---

[116] See the Explanatory Note to line 330.

by any means, shoved or falling away while a guard denounces falsehood, envy, and greed. The Nymph identifies the officers of this court as virtues. The pair of visitors approach the door of the palace proper, its frame ornamented with a cosmography of images. The Nymph urges him forward and warns him against becoming dazed by what he sees. Through a peephole the dreamer glimpses the bejeweled place, its heroic denizens, and the mighty god, whose face is so bright it knocks the dreamer unconscious. Reviving him, the Nymph mocks his weakness. She dismisses his vexation but recognizes his limitations and offers to show him the Muses' garden. On the way there, she provides the information to which the dream appears to have been tending: the heroes in the hall, whom she lists, have attained true honor. If he had been endowed with enough fortitude, he would have seen that god execute justice on evil pretenders to honor. Instead, he can visit a garden where Muses are gathering the colors of rhetoric. The Nymph speeds over the separating moat across a log bridge, but the dreamer falls, and awakens. The garden where he first fell unconscious now seems hellish by comparison with his visions. He writes two lyrics, one in praise of Honour, and another humbly dedicating his poem to King James IV.

B. DESIGN

As is evident from this summary, *PH* is so eventful and decorated that one's attention may not gravitate towards elements and indications of larger design or purpose. Accusing its poet of a tendency to indulge stylistic excess, C. S. Lewis tartly observes that the poet himself has become "happily overwhelmed" by his poem's ornamental outerwork.[117] Even as his dreamer is rebuked for lingering over details, Douglas tempts the reader into such self-indulgence. That self-indulgence may be as inevitable as it is for the all-too-human dreamer to fall out of the vision and into frustrated wakefulness.

Engagement with the overall design of *PH* has rarely been attempted but was the aim of a 1978 essay by Alice Miskimin. She approached the poem numerologically; one need not be convinced by every element of the analysis for her approach to yield insights. Among the recurrent praise of craft and artistry in the poem are some leading indications that these values can be applied to the poem itself. In his stanza on musical proportion, Douglas provides a technical, densely terminological way to perceive a comparable proportion in his poem. With stanzas as the significant measure, one way of considering the three-part structure is as symmetrical constructions around three focal centerpoints. Thus each part "is centered on a crucial recognition at the mid-point, at each of the dreamer's three confrontations with Venus in his dream." Venus first appears at stanza 36 in the 71 stanzas of the First Part. In the 56 stanzas of the Second Part, the dreamer sings gratefully to Venus in the three stanzas beginning at number 28. The longest of the three parts is the Third, 99 stanzas including the two final lyrics; at stanza 50, "Venus turns her face at last in recognition." Thus focused, the poem enthrones Venus and gives priority to the resolution of the dreamer's problematic attitude to her.[118]

A less formal interchange operates through *PH*, with the impulse or ambition to rise, to learn, and to praise repeatedly met by a counter-impulse of failing and falling. In the Prologue, the protagonist rises to praise the month of May; proving unable to do so, he is

---

[117] Lewis, *English Literature in the Sixteenth Century*, p. 78.

[118] Miskimin, "The Design of Douglas's *Palice of Honour*," p. 400.

smitten by a blaze of light and "[a]s femynine so feblyt fell I doun" (line 108). In the nightmare of the First Part, he has three opportunities to declare his allegiance to a ruling deity; instead, he denounces Venus and is dragged before her for trial and punishment.[119] The Second Part proceeds more buoyantly, with the dreamer on the Muses' grand ride, first to Helicon and then to the foot of Honour's mountain. As Louise Aranye Fradenburg asserts, "In the 'Court Rethoricall' of Douglas's Muses is, then, to be found, not the shifting and uncertain ground of *The House of Fame*, but the 'constant ground of famous storeis sweit', 'the facound well Celestiall', 'the Fontane and Originall / Quhairfra the well of Helicon dois fleit' (ll. 835ff.)."[120] Indications of countering downward motion are implicit: the Muses' route retraces the places scorched in Phaethon's disastrous career in the chariot of the Sun.

Through the ascent and entry of the Third Part, overthrows and collapses emerge as dominant motifs. Sustained by the Nymph, the dreamer approaches the summit only to recoil in fear, first at the obstacle of the burning chasm of the indolent, and then, far below, at the inevitable shipwreck of earthly hopes. Entering the outer precincts of Honour, the dreamer proceeds to the "garth" of Venus (line 1466) rather than going directly to see the presiding god himself; and in the mirror of Venus, he sees at least as many defeats, rebellions, and acts of treason as he does triumphant deeds of honor: the fall of the angels, the Flood, the confusion at Babel, Sodom's destruction, Pharaoh drowning in the Red Sea, Gideon succeeded by the homicidal Abimelech, Rehoboam's misrule and the division of the kingdom, the destruction at Thebes, the first and second falls of Troy. Later history includes emphasis on episodes of portentous downfall: "every famus douchty deid" (line 1693) brings its gloomy consequence:

The miserie, the crewelté, the dreid,	
Pane, sorow, wo, baith wretchitnes and neid,	*both misery and indigence*
The gret envy, covatus, dowbilnes	*covetousness, treachery*
Twychand warldly onfaithful brukkylnes.	*Concerning worldly false instability*

(lines 1696–99)

For much of the episode of Venus' mirror, the sequence of allusions to the falls of princes can seem like an accelerated, expanded version of Chaucer's Monk's Tale. At the end of this sequence, the goddess herself gives the dreamer-poet a book and commissions him to work on it. It is a moment of exaltation and new purpose; but a certain uneasiness prevails. The failure of the unworthy to enter Honour's palace may only prefigure the dreamer's own much humbler failures, recent and yet to come. Viewing the poem as a succession of falls suggests a trend countervailing the vaunting display and the intent assemblage of an intricate, harmonious structure that are also very much part of the poem Douglas has made. Enthralled by the scenes he sees in Venus' mirror, the poet imbibes the inevitability of failure.

---

[119] A particular interest seems to adhere to forthright, incompletely motivated criticism of a powerful being, when the likely consequence would be harsh punishment. While this event is comparable to Cresseid's renunciation of Venus and Cupid in Henryson's *Testament of Cresseid*, it may be more productive to consider both as instances of a larger trend.

[120] Fradenburg, *City, Marriage, Tournament*, p. 187; as typical in critical comment on *PH*, the E text is quoted.

C. IMPORT

Even in synopsis it becomes apparent that *PH* offers a series of possible routes and apparent destinations. The traveler's capacities and limitations, but also his patrons and guides, determine his course and destination.[121] A visitor, a dreamer, a cleric, a traveler, a courtier, as well as a poet, the narrator experiences the anxieties of choice. In the process his poem gives readers the opportunity to choose their own course vicariously. Such choices are visceral: the dreamer's attempts at affiliation cannot but be insufficient, and his dismay is genuine in recoiling from the articulate manifestations of the sought-after ideal.[122] Thus he reacts with self-regarding discouragement to the competent performance of praise by the clear voice in the garden where the poem takes its beginning; it is as if the myth of Narcissus and Echo has been reversed, with the male role now one of incomplete, frustrated imitation. Later, though it may have something to do with being left behind in the horrible forest, he feels similar dismay once the potentially vengeful Diana has departed. Most blatantly, he cannot resist being "deeply engaged but strongly ambivalent" toward Venus, even though in both the dream and his evocation of it in his poem he experiences delight at her arrival.[123] Finally, he cannot endure the gaze of the mighty god Honour.

Implicitly, *PH* is built on the supposition that its ideal reader's inclinations and purposes are inaccessibly exalted. At least from the perspective of the concluding lyric, that reader is James IV. While the whole construction can be seen as a compliment or spur to that reader's royalty, at the same time its protagonist is a self who adores such beings from a distance, but quails — or is rebuffed — from too close association with them. Though the poet will end his poem meekly craving reward, in a lyric addressed to James IV, neither there nor in the vision itself does he envision kingliness as absolutely protective or benevolent.[124] What he can do is praise such lofty beings for being endowed with the full scope and determination to identify, pursue, and punish intruders, meting out retribution upon worse offenders than he, and displaying their victims' torments for the satisfaction and admonition of their loyal subjects. In this regard, and especially in his final paroxysms of humility, Douglas may well be articulating the consequences of his poetic labor to view and address the prince. In such expressions of inferiority Robert Meyer-Lee diagnoses "a

---

[121] Given the shaping of the narrator's poetic vocation, it is understandable that some readers of the poem have considered it a Portrait of the Artist; e.g., Kinneavy, "Poet in *The Palice of Honour*," p. 281; Amsler, "Quest for the Present Tense," pp. 186–87. For a countering emphasis on "the moral agency of the narrator," see Honeyman, "*The Palice of Honour*: Gavin Douglas' Renovation of Chaucer's *House of Fame*," p. 66.

[122] In contrast to the optimistic readings of, e.g., Kinneavy ("The Poet in *The Palice of Honour*," pp. 281, 283, 295–303) and Ebin (*Illuminator Makar Vates*, pp. 91–97; see also Honeyman, "*The Palice of Honour*"), Bawcutt has held that the dreamer "often reverts to the fearful, uneasy mood in which his dream began" (*Gavin Douglas: A Critical Study*, p. 60). As Leahy has noted, "That Douglas's dreamwork is not so easily dissolved into a moral interpretation is what distinguishes it from many of its antecedents: there are real trees in his allegorical forest" ("Dreamscape into Landscape, p. 157).

[123] Spearing, *Medieval Poet as Voyeur*, p. 238.

[124] Compare this interpretation with Fradenburg's comment on the vision of kingship as the "reward" of the dreamer's quest (*City, Marriage, Tournament*, pp. 190–91).

nervous tic" by which means the poet "relieves the pressure created by basic tensions" between his "intent to speak the truth," and his "economic and political dependence."[125]

The resulting adoration/repulsion is especially intense when the sovereign figure viewed and addressed is female. Fradenburg has described this threat as stemming from the dreamer's "unrationalized ambivalence" at the "sight of the erotic woman."[126] Some readers have been disquieted, others intrigued, by the inclusion of such women (Zenobia, Semiramis, even Medusa) among the inner circle of Honour.[127] Andrew Johnston and Margitta Rouse have gone so far as to posit that the defining myth of at least the Third Part of *PH* is that of Perseus and Medusa. They quote W. J. T. Mitchell's observation that "Medusa is the image that turns the tables on the spectator and turns the spectator into an image: she must be seen through the mediation of mirrors."[128] Seen along with the god Honour who detects the dreamer peeping through the keyhole and with a searching gaze shuts down his access and awareness, the dominant female figures of *PH* have a retaliative quality. After all, he may have been led through a visionary labyrinth by a knowledgeable female guide, but he is surely no Theseus.

There is in fact something labyrinthine about the progression of episodes in this poem. In the preamble, the visitor enters the garden in the approved way, to sing a song and gather flowers. The language of pleasure and delight becomes rather claustrophobic in its self-reflexive repetitiousness. For the time being, the garden of the preamble has been purged of the malign influences of Eolus, Saturn, and Neptune. The visitor hears a song discouraging in its excellence and in turn can express only inadequacy and frustration. There seems nowhere else to go but home, before the "impressioun" of light (line 105) sends him into a trance. The dreamscape in which he now finds himself appears to be the direct and emphatic opposite of the pleasant place; and yet both have something of a cul-de-sac about them. As well, both have elements of potentially or actually violent opposition or retaliation. Two clever malefactors skulk after Minerva. Diana's wrath is immediately apparent in the apparition of Actaeon metamorphosed. Not all who accompany Venus are happy; and when the dreamer utters his complaint, violence erupts and is channeled into a legal process. Even knowledge can entrap, if the digressions on acoustics or musical theory and performance are any indication. What had appeared in prospect a promise of fulfilment becomes self-consuming in experience.

With the coming of the Muses, the recurrent sense of entrapment gives way to rapid, free movement toward ideal but inaccessible destinations; the Hippocrene spring and then the mountain-top palace of Honour. Reaching for fulfilment involves besetting frustrations. At the Muses' fountain, the dreamer is crowded out; at the palace, he falters and fails. However, the persistent undertone of dissatisfaction evident in the First Part of the poem has been replaced by a more purposively exploratory mode. The dreamer has a Nymph to guide him. She has an angelic energy and decisiveness, not least when she lifts the dreamer over a hellish chasm, "As Abacuk wes brocht in Babilone" (line 1341); but if she is an angel, then the dreamer must be at least a little like a prophet, if a minor one. Her guidance of the

---

[125] Meyer-Lee, *Poets and Power*, pp. 82–83.

[126] Fradenburg, *City, Marriage, Tournament*, p. 188.

[127] Morse queries, "Can Honour's Palace encompass Dis-Honour?" ("Gavin Douglas: 'Off Eloquence,'" p. 112).

[128] Johnston and Rouse, "Facing the Mirror," p. 180; Mitchell, *Picture Theory*, p. 172.

dreamer through infernal difficulties may evoke memories of the Sibyl guiding Aeneas through Hades, in *Aeneid* VI. There is also something of a marketplace manner to the Nymph. Once at the palace, she can be relentless in her determination to keep the dreamer moving through a sequence of engrossing places, and her rebukes at his hesitations have an increasingly earthy swing to them. When the Nymph races across the moat, the lagging dreamer immediately loses stability and falls awake. For the reader, it may be the stiffest rebuff of the poem that waking existence at its most pleasant now seems joyless. Rather than containing the dream, earthly reality has been revealed to be circumscribed and contingent.

The Palyce of Honour is so thoroughly designed that small recurrences can assume significance. Patterns large and small are enlaced throughout the structure: for example, the May garden, the hellish wasteland, the environs of the Hippocrene; at Honour's palace, the "garth" of Venus (line 1466), the garden of the colors of rhetoric, and the now-threadbare return to the May garden "maist lyk to hel" (line 2094). Within that sequence, meaningful smaller motifs become apparent; for instance, the bees at work gathering sustenance from the flowers (line 45) are heard afresh at the Muses' spring (line 1152), where their activity leads as if logically to the rapturous dispersal of the women "playand, syngand, dansand ovir the bentis" (line 1154); and in the final moments of the dream, the Nymph directs attention to the Muses and their women again, "bissy as the beis," gathering the colors of rhetoric from their moated garden — "our gardyng, lo" (lines 2065, 2063). The poem ends where it began, in "russet weid" (lines 2162, 2). With such attention to detail, *PH* is evidently a work that repays attentive reading and especially alertness to recurrent parallels and reversals.

Gavin Douglas relies on literary allusion concisely to stir awareness of such alternating, contrastive patterns. Myths function especially evocatively thus. In the May garden, it is as if Echo precedes Narcissus when the disembodied voice sings the perfect praises of the season; followed by the self-concerned outpourings of the visitor. It is a self-regard that has profuse consequences when, late in the dream, the dreamer looks in Venus' mirror: "What he 'behalds,' however," Antony Hasler observes, "is a compilation that catches up an entire medieval library within the loose and permeable bounds of universal history, and which is then named, retroactively, as the face of the beloved."[129] The sunrise at the poem's outset awakens associations of the chariot of Phoebus and its well-managed horses — and much later, the well-managed horses of the Muses' cavalcade travel in an itinerary that retraces Phaethon's disastrous course in that same chariot. Sandra Cairns has noted how in the ride of the Muses, upward to Helicon and then toward the mountain of Honour, Douglas creates a counterpoint to Ovid's depiction of Phaethon's downward career in the chariot of the sun.[130] Douglas is not alone in drawing attention to this tale. In *The Meroure of Wysdome*, James III's confessor John Ireland summarized it thus:

> [O]uid þe poet sais in secundo methamorposeos that quhen the sone left his counsal and grauntit his sone phiton to reule his char a day for faut of knawlage his sone couth nocht gowerne þe hors na þe char and þan þe hors drew þe chayr out of þe rycht gait and brint

---

[129] Hasler, *Court Poetry in Late Medieval England and Scotland*, p. 105.

[130] Cairns, "*The Palice of Honour* of Gavin Douglas, Ovid, and Raffaello Regio's Commentary," p. 25.

a part of hevin . . . and eftir þe cart of fyr come sa neir þe Erd þat it consumyt þe humedite of þame of ethiop Ind et de gente maurorum and has maid þame all blak.[131]

In each of these cases, delighted purposefulness cannot fail to summon recollections and maybe predictions of the disastrous consequences of over-reaching. Or to see this the other way around, myths of failure and transgression — Narcissus, Phaethon, Actaeon — reverse into vision, progress, and creation.

One might regard Calliope's assumption of responsibility for the dreamer as an indication of his attaining a means of access to power that suits his talents and limitations. It is striking how often in her retinue and under the tutelage and guidance of the Nymph she assigns to his care he falls just short of attainment. He is crowded away from tasting the well of inspiration at Helicon; he cannot ascend Honour's peak without being hauled up, at one point by his hair; at the gate of the palace itself, his attention is diverted by the imagery and he loses momentum; he collapses at a glimpse of the hall of Honour and its denizens; he cannot even cross the rough bridge into the garden of the Muses. His sense of what the courtiers of Venus describe as Calliope's "kyngly stile . . . [c]lepyt in Latyne heroicus" (lines 877–78) is not articulated in Latin but in the vernacular: within the Scottish scene he is implicitly no Archibald Whitelaw or Walter Ogilvie, both of whom addressed English kings in Latin orations.[132] Instead, his concept of literary discourse is more allusive and shifting, with pastime but also moral admonition and apocalyptic vision frequently at hand.

Douglas extends this principle of variegation most economically in his lists: the courtiers of Minerva, Diana, and Venus; the Muses and their poets; the repertoire of entertainments at the Muses' banquet, from Ovid's heroic tales to Poggio spitting and growling at Lorenzo Valla; the conspectus of history and pastime in the mirror of Venus; the officers of Honour's household; the natural, astronomical and mythological images on the doorway of the palace; the great ones in Honour's presence chamber. These catalogues — and especially the extended mirror-of-Venus sequence — have attracted adverse criticism for their accumulation of detail and thus their impeding of narrative;[133] in them has been detected "a cultural memory that embodies authority" but also its Derridean nemesis, "an 'anarchivic' death drive that annihilates the archive even as it seeks to construct it."[134] Seen thus, Douglas is undoing the ostensible meaning and purpose of the dream, to celebrate virtuous honor, the chivalric *summum bonum* tinged with humanist values, as Douglas Gray has noted, of "nobility of soul."[135]

The catalogues in *PH* evidently merit attention. The potential for conflicting significations is already apparent in the sequence of female names at the head of Minerva's procession: twelve Sibyls (when the dreamer first sees them, he thinks they are Minerva's privy council; line 222), as well as (or possibly including) Cassandra, Deborah, Circe, Judith,

---

[131] *Meroure of Wysdome*, eds. Macpherson, Quinn, and Macdonald, 3:118.

[132] Whitelaw in 1484 and Ogilvie in 1502 (Rutledge, "Development of Humanism," pp. 239, 242–44).

[133] Norton-Smith, "Ekphrasis as a Stylistic Element," p. 240; Blyth, "*The Knychtlyke Stile*," p. 158.

[134] Hasler, *Court Poetry in Late Medieval England and Scotland*, p. 100.

[135] Gray, "Gavin Douglas," p. 156.

and Jael (lines 243–46).[136] As they have come by the late fifteenth century to be understood, the Sibyls epitomize the interplay of pagan and Christian prophecy;[137] and the rest of the list shows a readiness to conflate the two worlds of signification. It is a well-established practice; Ernst Robert Curtius commented on the medieval "theory of the parallelism of exemplary figures" by which "Antique and Christian exempla are systematically co-ordinated."[138] It may not be too far-fetched to think about syncretic combinations imparting cohesion and even purpose — one might say, a grammar — to the sometimes long lists of names in *PH*. They display learning, or at least the ambition to reach further into literature, history, and philosophy; they may also challenge the reader to seek subordination, contrast, and parallel in what often appears to be straightforward coordination. Recurrent motifs provide signposts for that quest.

Combining the pagan with the scriptural was very much to the fore of discourse in late fifteenth-century Scotland, as John Ireland shows. In the *Meroure of Wysdome*, he provides a list of rulers fallen into lustful intemperance through incautious hearing and sight: Ahab, Nabugodonsar, Holofernes, Herod, and so on into pagan record,

> for we knaw be noble storeis þat sic blind and daft luf that paris and elena had to giddir distroyit þe noble tovne of troye it expellit tarqwyn and all his blud riall out of rome for þe inordinat luf of his sone anens the noble lady lucres be it dalida causit þe distruccioun of sampsone þe luf of bersabe causit þe gret syn of dauid þe prophet; it causit þe fallin of wys salamon it causit þe flud of noye the distruccioun of þe [five] noble citeis and land þat was pentopolis & altera paradisus terrestris of þe quhilk was sodome and gomor and for þe oppressioun of a lady as sais þe scriptur it causit þe slauchtir of [60] thousand men it was þe caus of þe distruccioun of anthonius and cleopatra . . .[139]

It is not the mixture of sources that is most challenging about the lists Douglas presents, however, but their tendency, noted above, to include without comment extremely problematic figures. One such is Circe, a seer with transformative powers over the natural world and a revealer of men's inner natures, but also a vengeful, duplicitous sorceress.[140] Such fearsome pre-eminence recurs in later lists: among those walking up and down before Honour is Medusa (see note to line 2025). Given the way inconsistency acts throughout the poem as a stimulus to the reader to seek additional levels of signification, such moments of dissonance seem entirely fitting.

These intermittently disturbing presences relate to the misgivings about female power that the dreamer expresses in one way in his complaint against Venus and, in another, in his retorts to the masterful Nymph.[141] The making of the poem has been described as the

[136] Spearing, *Medieval Poet as Voyeur*, p. 236.

[137] See the discussion of lines 243–44 in the Explanatory Notes. Later in the poem, there is the marvelous moment when the Muses and their entourage offer prayers of gratitude to "gret God" for the success of their journey (line 1462).

[138] Curtius, *European Literature and the Latin Middle Ages*, p. 363.

[139] *Meroure of Wysdome*, eds. Macpherson, Quinn, and McDonald, 3:121–22.

[140] Wood, "Folkloric Patterns in Scottish Chronicles," p. 121.

[141] These misgivings have been ascribed to a "deeply engaged but strongly ambivalent" attitude to sexuality (Spearing, *Medieval Poet as Voyeur*, p. 238).

victory of "overflowing" eloquence over "(feminine) caprice."[142] That caprice may be too deeply dyed into the texture to be dissolved thus. As the Nymph reminds the dreamer, "kyrkmen wer ay jentill to ther wyvys" (line 1944). Similarly, the appearance of troubling figures amongst those awarded with the highest accolades suggests a counteractive unease in the workings of Honour as conceived in this vision. *PH* derives much of its continuing energy and appeal from the complex interactions of these disparate areas of meaning, that in combination resist simple categorization.[143] Each of the main character-sets in the poem is finally inscrutable: the god-king as bestower and tormentor; the beneficent, enlightening, rebuking, retaliative queen; the poet who serves and betrays Venus, who "has a superior and wider-reaching power of observation" and "sees the whole range of human experience preserved by written authority"[144] but who can also act like a blithering idiot.

Writing his *Dreme* a quarter-century or so after the completion of *PH* (c. 1526), Sir David Lyndsay recalled the sorts of stories he told the young James V; progressing from the "marciall" to the "amiabyll" to the "plesand,"[145] he was following the sequence of narrative types in Venus' mirror. In the mirror episode, but also throughout *PH*, Douglas provides an influentially variegated sequence of incidents, many of which reveal themselves as surprising, disparate variations on motifs: the sudden apprehension of more or less articulate sound (the echo in the garden; the yelling fish; the onset of music; the "garatour"'s warning cry, line 1779); marvelous flights and ascents (the Muses' ride; the miraculous ascent of Honour's mountain, but also Hay of Naughton's as-yet obscure flight to "madin" land [line 1719], or even the wren's no less mysterious foray from Ailsa Craig); plunges, sometimes wilful, sometimes inadvertent, into fearsome unknowability and imminent death (Empedocles, the fiery "sewch" [line 1316], the doomed carvel, *Curtius*, the terrified waterfowl, the ditch into which the dreamer falls). About unexpected voices, perceptive comment is not far to seek: on the echo, Hasler has written, "The voice intrudes from without as alien object; the dreamer errs . . . and is suddenly engulfed in a strange corporeal delirium."[146] Further connections would be valuable to make between that voice and other aural phenomena in the poem. As well, critical attention has been lavished upon the more obvious instances of ascent and enlightenment.[147] Calling for similar attention is the comparatively neglected counter-motif of plunging, falling, tumbling, and failure to recognize or understand. Indeed, the imminence of downfall may be part of the import of the poem for its sovereign reader, James IV. Johnston and Rouse comment that in the poet's evocations of "the grace and elegance of the courtly world," may be sensed that world's "darker side of ambition and power-struggles and the steep hierarchies that govern

---

[142] Fradenburg, *City, Marriage, Tournament*, p. 187.

[143] Gray goes so far as to ascribe to *PH* a "daring juxtaposition of a high seriousness that is almost mystical with pantomime knockabout" ("Gavin Douglas," p. 153).

[144] Kratzmann, *Anglo-Scottish Literary Relations*, p. 114.

[145] *The Dreme*, lines 31, 39, 44 (*Sir David Lyndsay: Selected Poems*, ed. Hadley Williams, p. 2).

[146] Hasler, *Court Poetry in Late Medieval England and Scotland*, p. 101.

[147] Kinneavy, "The Poet in *The Palice of Honour*"; Amsler, "The Quest for the Present Tense"; Ebin, *Illuminator Makar Vates*, pp. 92–96; Honeyman, "*The Palice of Honour*: Gavin Douglas's Renovation."

it."[148] The king who as a youth took part in rebellion against his father and who was present at the battle at (or after) which James III died may well have regarded the reiterative allusions to usurpation and rebellion as occasions for penitential reflection. That James IV was inclined to engage in such reflection as salutary for his spiritual health is apparent from Don Pedro de Ayala's depiction of him in the late 1490s but also from his continued support for the rigorous Observant order.[149]

D. SOURCES AND AFFILIATIONS

The whole arc of *PH* arises from a coherent group of literary sources: primarily the Bible (especially Genesis, Judges, 1 and 2 Samuel, 1 and 2 Kings, and Daniel with its apocryphal chapters), Ovid (mostly *Metamorphoses,* but more locally *Heroides* and the *Art of Love*), Chaucer (*House of Fame* [*HF*], but again more locally the *Knight's Tale, Troilus and Criseyde, Legend of Good Women,* and *Parliament of Fowls;* and the likely sources of the stanza forms, *Anelida and Arcite* and *The Complaint of Mars*), and, hardly less important, Gower (*Confessio Amantis*).[150] For specific passages and topics, Douglas also draws upon a secondary array of more diverse materials: for instance, Aristotle, Quintilian, humanist discourse, *The Flyting of Dunbar and Kennedie,* probably *The Kingis Quair,*[151] Holland's *Buke of the Howlat,* Livy, Virgil.[152] Some of these elements appear locally in the poem; others re-emerge repeatedly; a few impart shape and purpose to the narrative. Whether apparent in a few lines or recurrently, such elements are often even more important in combination than they are individually. Indeed the combination turns out to convey important things about the function and import of this powerfully syncretic poem. Some surprising omissions ought to be noted: little or no evidence exists that Douglas had read Henryson, beyond the possibility he had already seen *Orpheus and Eurydice,* and his reading of Lydgate may not have extended far beyond *The Siege of Thebes* and *The Complaynte of a Lovers Lyfe* (which he would have known as *The Maying and Disport of Chaucer*).[153] The array has tended to be studied

---

[148] Johnston and Rouse, "Facing the Mirror," p. 173.

[149] See above, footnote 29.

[150] Martin detects a deftness and evocativeness in the allusions Douglas makes to Gower's *Confessio Amanatis,* especially in "the subtle echo and reworking of narrative episodes, images, and diction" ("Responses to the Frame Narrative," p. 571).

[151] Generally skeptical about the influence of *The Kingis Quair* on late fifteenth-century Scottish poetry, Norton-Smith made something of an exception for Gavin Douglas, "who may have seen the manuscript in [Henry, third lord] Sinclair's library" (*The Kingis Quair,* p. xiiin2).

[152] R. D. S. Jack argued that Petrarch's *Trionfi,* especially the sequence of triumphs of Love, Chastity, and Fame, provided a precedent for the cavalcades of Minerva, Diana, and Venus. He went further by suggesting that Petrarch's *Trionfi* provided inspiration for "the whole scheme of Douglas's poem" (*Italian Influence on Scottish Literature,* pp. 23–27, quote on p. 24). This proposal has not been widely accepted.

[153] Boffey and Edwards comment that "we have only the evidence of some jotted extracts from the *Fables* in a student notebook (the 'Makculloch' manuscript) that [Henryson's] poems circulated at all during his lifetime ("Literary Texts," p. 564). Edwards has also noted the paucity of evidence for circulation of Lydgate's poems in Scotland prior to 1500 ("Lydgate in Scotland," pp. 191, 194).

piecemeal, so that specialist readers — usually literary scholars with particular interest in Chaucer — have tended to concentrate their attention in that direction. Further study reveals a more diverse and thriving complex of influences. Consequently Chaucer's *House of Fame* appears less pervasively influential than has been thought. To assert control over this influence, Douglas dis- and re-assembles his source materials. Douglas is seeking a way around and beyond a narrow Chaucerianism; he is drawing more widely on literary options than has generally been recognized, hence perhaps his extreme stylistic and linguistic range.

Since the connection between *HF* and *PH* has long been insisted upon, its grounding deserves to be considered. John Small's comments on this topic might be recalled:

> It may . . . be surmised, that Douglas had before him Chaucer's "Temple of Fame," when he drew the outline of his Palace of Honour. Chaucer's allegory takes the form of a dream, in which the poet finds himself in the Temple of Venus, whence he is carried, not by a nymph, but by an eagle, to a magnificent palace built upon a mountain of ice, and supported by rows of pillars, on which are inscribed the names of the most illustrious poets. Many of the names given by Chaucer are to be found in Douglas; yet, on the whole, the arrangement and versification of the two poems are so unlike, that to Douglas must be accorded the praise of having conceived and successfully completed an original design.[154]

After one has progressed from a surveying perspective to more detailed scrutiny, the differences between the two poems become more striking than the similarities. In *HF*, the dream begins instantly "Withyn a temple ymad of glas" (line 120), the temple of Venus; in *PH*, the dreamer will not reach any building until after 1,400 lines have passed, and indeed, the inner sanctum seems always inaccessible. In Chaucer's temple of Venus, the reigning poet is Virgil, a version of whose tale of Troy and Aeneas is engraved "on a table of bras" (line 142). Douglas pays heed to Chaucer's interposed list of faithless and unfortunate lovers: Demophon and Phyllis, Achilles and Breseyda, Paris and Oenone, Jason and Isiphile, Jason again and Medea, Hercules abandoning Deianeira for Iole, Theseus and Ariadne, leading back to Aeneas and Dido (lines 388–432). Only after studying the brazen tablets does Chaucer's dreamer go outside; and, as Conor Leahy has noted, the desert that greets him is a place of negation, "Withouten toun, or hous, or tree, / Or bush, or grass, or eryd lond" (lines 484–85).[155] In place of the alarmingly active scenes with which *PH* proper commences, full of cavalcades, self-exculpatory explanations, apparently spontaneous denunciations, all leading to a mobbing and a trial, Chaucer provides a bewildered pause and a rescue by Eagle.

Similarly, the long explanation and instruction the inimitable Eagle then imparts has no counterpart in *PH*, where Calliope and her Nymph instruct and inform the dreamer comparatively tersely. Douglas comes closest to Chaucer's example in a digression on acoustics; but in place of the Eagle's lecture, it is the poet himself who in retrospect attempts to explain the phenomenon of sound traveling over water (*PH*, lines 364–81). Arriving at the House of Fame, Chaucer's dreamer studies the rock on which it stands; and what appears hard and durable turns out to be a "roche of yse, and not of stel" (*HF*, line 1130).

The *Maying and Disport of Chaucer* is included with this title in the *Kingis Quair* manuscript, Bodleian Arch. Selden. B. 24, fols. 120v–129v (title given in colophon).

[154] *Poetical Works*, ed. Small, 1:cxxxviii.

[155] Leahy, "Dreamscape into Landscape," p. 156.

Here, at a point of close resemblance, Douglas stresses that his "roch" consists "of slyde, hard merbyll stone" (*PH*, line 1300), and thus distinguishes his chiseled poem from Chaucer's melting surfaces. In place of the crowds of arbitrary Fame's entertainers, memorialists, and disparate suitors, Honour's household is well-regulated, with the unworthy thrust away. Instead of a House of Rumor, Douglas provides a vision of just rule and abundant eloquence, neither of which his dreamer is worthy enough to attain.

Given these significant differences between *HF* and *PH*, it may be valuable to review at least a representative sample of the points at which Douglas appears to draw closest to Chaucer: the retelling of antique story (with Ovid as the epic master in place of Virgil; but compare the summary of the *Aeneid*, lines 1630–56, with *HF*, lines 143–396); the list of faithless and unfortunate lovers (*HF*, lines 397–404); the guide's rebuke (*HF*, lines 556–57; *PH*, lines 1460–62, 1936–44); the list of those carried into the heavens (*HF*, lines 588–92); the disquisition on sound; the sky-high glimpse of the earth far below (*HF*, lines 896–903); the description of the mountain atop which the destination place stands; ornamental features of palatial architecture (*HF*, lines 1184–94); musicians, magicians, and poets (*HF*, lines 1197–1281; 1456–1512). None of this is slavish copying. It is as if Douglas purposively takes apart Chaucer's motifs and reassembles them in a very different sequence and with strikingly different context, emphasis, tone, and import. What is experienced directly in *HF* is often alluded to comparatively in *PH*.

Parallel with these developments in vernacular literary style, the prevailing syncretism of fifteenth-century humanism provides another encouragement to seek and develop analogies within the whole body of ancient literature and scripture. It may be worthwhile to distinguish Douglas' handling of this array of materials in relation to the fifteenth-century practices of vernacular humanism, which Andrew Galloway, citing Warren Boutcher, has described "as an idiom forged by a deep involvement with ancient sources and their style and outlook but merged with contemporary vernacular traditions and speaking more directly to secular power."[156] Douglas can reveal more interest in striking combinations than extended investigation. As one example out of many, Byblis and Absalom appear in a single line (582). Such analogical thinking achieves highly compressed form when the dreamer recalls "quhow in a stone / The wyfe of Loth ichangit sore did wepe" (lines 752–53); in their mirrored fates, Niobe and Lot's wife are fused in the memory. In this regard, it may be valuable to consider the places in the Bible to which Douglas turns in his catalogues and allusions. Some of these correspond with the repertoire of the cycle plays: the fall of the angels, the creation of Adam and his expulsion with Eve from Eden, Noah's flood, the rise and fall of Babel, the destruction of Sodom, the patriarchs, Pharaoh's destruction in the Red Sea, and the wandering in the desert (lines 1499–1510). Douglas also alludes to righteous, heroic, and suffering women: Deborah, Judith, Jael, Jephthah's daughter, Esther, Susanna (lines 244, 246, 338, 579, 1563–64). Of particular interest are the allusions to rulers, successors, and champions: righteous Gideon (lines 1514–15); Samson victorious and deceived by Delilah (lines 580, 1516–20); Saul, whose evil spirit was allayed awhile by David's music (lines 509–10); and David the young hero and old king, his beloved Bathsheba and his rebellious son Absalom (lines 276–81, 570, 1525–32); the indomitable Maccabees (lines 1570–76). Some at least of these figures offer exaggerated reflections of

---

[156] Galloway, "John Lydgate and the Origins of Vernacular Humanism," p. 446; see Boutcher, "Vernacular Humanism in the Sixteenth Century, p. 196."

the ideal function of poetry: Samson the upholder and destroyer of noble edifices, himself subject to female sovereignty; David the driver-out of evil spirits at court. Political considerations came to the fore, when shameful successors receive special attention: with Absalom, the murderous Abimelech (line 1515), haughty Rehoboam (lines 1542–43), and usurping Tryphon (lines 1775–76). Alongside their often unworthy, even rebellious sons and heirs, Old Testament judges and kings provide inspiring and warning examples for James IV; they may even be timely subjects for his penitential contemplation. With the downfalls of deceitful protectors and advisors (Achitefell, Tryphon; lines 271–81, 1768–69, 1775–76) and the denunciation of ambitious intruders (lines 2033–52), a Douglas poet is also taking the opportunity to glance at Douglas rivals (notably the hostile Hepburns) at the Scottish court. Much that has been described as proto-Reformationist about Sir David Lyndsay's interweaving of Scripture and world history into contemporary political controversy is present already in *PH* and its handling of kingship and prophecy — and not least, its depictions of heroic women traduced, retaliating, and triumphant. Douglas seems drawn to the topic of female illustriousness but sometimes infuses it with irony (e.g., lines 332–36, 1588–93). Douglas' turn to the critical humanism epitomized for him by the writings of Lorenzo Valla may have enabled him to view the Bible alongside the classics, in an apparently direct, independent-minded way, unshackled from scholastic commentary, and readily aimed at targets near to home.

The ease of transition between classical and scriptural is not the only coalescence of note in *PH*. Native and continental literary practices also intersect. In each, invective is a prime means of literary representation; by demolishing the character of one's opponent, one articulates one's own values and virtues. Paul Kristeller observed the close connection in fifteenth-century humanist treatises between "concern for style and elegance" and excoriating invective; he notes how such invective "enabled the authors to give a more personal tone to their discourse and to exaggerate their points beyond the limits of plausibility, something they evidently enjoyed"; similarly, the "dialogue also gave a personal and almost dramatic vivacity to the problems discussed."[157] Both, Kristeller observes, "provided a literary excuse for avoiding the tight argument and precise terminology that had characterised the philosophical literature of the ancient Greeks and of the medieval scholastics."[158] Recreation, sportive elaboration, even grotesquery seem curiously linked to self-assertion in this observation, in ways that seem relevant to the characterization of authorship in *PH*. Thus Poggio and Valla are locked in scabrous dispute during the course of the Muses' entertainments, with Poggio memorably "spyttand and cryand fy" (line 1233). Included in the cavalcade of the Muses is a trio of Scottish poets, Dunbar, Kennedie, and Quintin; as Bawcutt has noted, the combination strongly evokes the way these three are brought together in *The Flyting of Dunbar and Kennedie*. It is tempting to see that most uncourtly of courtly entertainments as very much to the fore of recent memory at the time Douglas was making *PH*; and it has been argued that, at least at an early stage of its development *The Flyting* was a creation of the 1490s.[159] Through such evocations of

---

[157] Kristeller, "Humanism," p. 125.

[158] Kristeller, "Humanism," p. 125.

[159] McDiarmid, "Early William Dunbar and His Poems," pp. 130–32; noting references to events post 1500, Bawcutt expresses skepticism about so early a date, but suggests that the *Flyting* may have been revised before it was printed in 1508 (*Poems*, 2:429, 428).

invective, Douglas places his compatriots alongside some luminaries of Italian humanism, and implicitly asserts his own right of access to the great topics of the age.

One especially pressing question for a poet at the end of the fifteenth century had to do with the study of the classics and the identification of Latin writers most deserving of study and emulation. Douglas contributes decisively to this topic by bringing several of the ancients into his poem, along with their books and characters. For instance, Ovid figures in *PH*, and so do various characters from his books; in a sense, he and the other authors over whom he effectively presides "embody their works."[160] Given the prominence he enjoys at various points, Ovid is effectively the major literary presence in *PH*, and even more so is *Metamorphoses* its major source. His are the authoritative versions of the myths that underpin the import of the poem. Indeed, the epic dimension of *PH* is primarily Ovidian: Douglas turns to *Metamorphoses* for the Argonauts, for the siege and fall of Troy; only belatedly and locally does Virgil's *Aeneid* take primary attention instead (lines 1630–56). Douglas follows contemporary trends in commentary on *Metamorphoses* in drawing upon that book as "a dictionary of correct Latin usage, a repertory of examples of figurative diction, and a veritable encyclopedia of information on geography, astrology, music, physical science, and moral and natural philosophy."[161] Riding with the Muses, Nymph and dreamer traverse a largely Ovidian world, and Douglas draws especially upon "the prototypical humanist" Raffaelle Regio's oft-reprinted, much-read commentary on *Metamorphoses* to identify many of its mountains and rivers.[162] Ovid's dominance in *PH* comes with consequences for the way readers perceive the Scottish poem itself. Discussions of *PH* tend to divide on whether it is thematically coherent and structurally cohesive, and in this, the alignment with Ovid is significant. When Douglas was writing his dream vision, the debate was already long-established about the Roman poet's "unrestrained wit (*ingenium*), friskiness (*lasciuia*), and license (*licentia*)," not to mention the "rhetorical, erotic, and social freedoms Ovid conferred upon his Muse."[163] Ovid's characteristic latitude gives Douglas an enabling if risky precedent for the extraordinary variegation of his own work.

E. INFLUENCE

Later Scottish writers responded to *PH* as a durable model for eloquent allegory. They were also interested in its language and versification. If Rod Lyall is correct, then the very earliest instance may be William Dunbar's *The Goldyn Targe* (printed 1508), which he argues is a "refinement and concentration" of the profuseness and ornament of *PH*.[164] A more straightforward case of indebtedness can be found in the opening stanzas of *The Testament of the Papyngo* (1530), in which Sir David Lyndsay employs the nine-line stanza in three rhymes that Douglas had used in the Third Part; Lyndsay appears to follow Douglas (and Dunbar) in praising the English poetic triumvirate "Chawceir, Goweir, and Lidgate

---

[160] Hasler, *Court Poetry in Late Medieval England and Scotland*, pp. 106.

[161] Moss, *Renaissance Truth and the Latin Language Turn*, p. 243.

[162] Cairns, "*The Palice of Honour* of Gavin Douglas, Ovid, and Raffaello Regio's Commentary," pp. 20–25. Quotation from Knox, "Commenting on Ovid," p. 336.

[163] James, "Ovid and the Question of Politics," pp. 343–44.

[164] Lyall, "Stylistic Relationship," p. 77.

laureate" whose verses "throuch Albione bene soung" (ed. Hadley Williams, lines 12, 14). It may be relevant that Lyndsay ends this stanza praising Kennedie and Dunbar (the latter with reference to *The Goldyn Targe*). The "notis musycall," "balmy droppis," and "tender twystis" that are clustered in one stanza of *The Papyngo* (lines 136–40) recall the "notis," "balmy dewe," "silver droppis," and "twistis" in the Prologue to *PH* (lines 24, 13, 16 and 27, 22).[165] An even more ambitious engagement with *PH* can be found in the poems of John Bellenden, notably the *Proheme to the Cosmographe* at the outset of his translation of Hector Boece's *Chronicles of Scotland* (c. 1531). Bellenden used the nine-line stanza in two rhymes of the first two Parts of *PH* for his *Proheme*, at the start of which he also drew especially heavily on the diction of *PH*.[166] Thomas Rutledge summarizes the verbal echoes of *PH* in the Proheme ("balmy dew," "heit maist restorative," "diffundant grace," pp. vii, viii) but further he emphasizes that Bellenden's poem is pervasively indebted to the prologue to *PH*; in this way, he argues, Bellenden provides "a programmatic articulation of literary and political affiliation" and "signals his indebtedness to Douglas expressly to situate himself as Douglas's literary successor."[167]

In *The Court of Venus* (1560; printed by John Ross in 1575), John Rolland also draws heavily on *PH*.[168] With various inset passages in other stanza forms, the poem proper is largely cast in the nine-line stanza in two rhymes used by Douglas. Rolland bases the design of his plot in some part on *PH*: a character, Desperance, denounces love and is summoned to answer charges of treason against Venus. Desperance seeks an advocate far and wide; finally Vesta agrees to defend him. He is found guilty, but, relenting at last, Venus grants him clemency and makes him her liege. Rolland praises Douglas as the author of *PH* (*Court of Venus* 3:109–17). In his more satirical treatment of court life and manners, not to mention his interest in the benefits and fallacies of hope, Rolland seems closer in spirit to Octovien de Saint-Gelais' *Séjour d'Honneur* than to *PH*, however.[169] Even more fanciful in its remaking of *PH* is John Burel's *Passage of the Pilgremer* (1595/96), which commences with a lengthy conspectus of the kingdom of the animals and birds wracked by a storm, while the weak ones are preyed upon by the predators. The second part takes a different tack, with a survey of a mythological landscape that focuses on mountains, such as Mount Erix, on which stands the temple dedicated by the Trojans to Venus, and Haemus, "[q]uhair Orpheus leird his harmonie" (2.33; compare *PH*, lines 1102–04). The rocks "repercust and rang" with music (2.43). The dreamer turns to a royal-seeming woman standing nearby, who offers to escort him to Venus. Seeming to vanish, she suddenly reappears in monstrous form. These later

---

[165] For these elements of versification and diction, see also the opening *Epistill* and Prologue of Sir David Lyndsay's influential *Ane Dialog betwix Experience and ane Courteour*, for the latter especially lines 135–38 (*Sir David Lyndsay: Selected Poems*, ed. Hadley Williams, pp. 183–93).

[166] Bawcutt, *Gavin Douglas: A Critical Study*, pp. 194–95.

[167] Rutledge, "Gavin Douglas and John Bellenden," pp. 94–98, quote in pp. 95–96. Rutledge also identifies echoes of *PH* in Bellenden's Prologue to his translation from *Livy's History*, ed. Craigie, p. 96.

[168] *Ane Treatise Callit The Court of Venus*, ed. Gregor, pp. xx–xxiv; Bawcutt, *Gavin Douglas: A Critical Study*, pp. 195–96.

[169] For a discussion of the satirical depiction of court life in the *Séjour d'Honneur*, see Armstrong and Kay, *Knowing Poetry*, p. 150.

sixteenth-century Scottish dream-visions reject *PH*'s balance of chivalry and morality, and emphasize its theme of retaliative femininity.

A more carefully considered development of interest in the allegorical potential of *PH* can be traced in the Latin humanist dialogue *De tranquillitate animi* by Florence Wilson (1543).[170] Here a visionary garden leads a dreamer to a house of tranquility complete with allegorical columns, and finally to a culminating vision of Christ.[171] This more insistently spiritualized treatment of what might be called the *PH* tradition undergoes further development during the Reformation in Scotland. In the late 1570s or early 1580s, John Stewart of Baldynneis composed *An Schersing of Trew Felicitie*,[172] in which the dream-journey to a celestial vision (in the nine-line stanza with three rhymes) commences with the narrator setting out at dawn to seek felicity in a pleasant springtime setting ("The Mateir," stanzas 3–4). He comes to an encircling transparent wall of "christaline preclair" (stanza 5, line 1), the gate to which is kept by "the chast virgin Charitie" (6.7), who shows him two paths, one "dour and rycht difficill" that leads to failure for most who attempt it, so that they are "outthrust / from plesand plaice of perfyt repois" (19.1, 20.7–8). The other "plesand passage plaine" (64.3) leads through delights to damnation. More insistently than Rolland, Stewart is bestowing attention on the ways in which the appearance of worthiness tends more often than not to disgrace and perdition; like Rolland, though, he is intensifying the anti-courtly satire that is more intermittent in *PH*. Stewart comes closest to Douglas in his scriptural summary, as in the detail that "Duck Sangor" (Shamgar) "Sex hundreth slew with ane pleuch sok in teine" (179.1–2; compare *PH*, lines 1520–21: "I saw duke Sangor there with many a knok / Sax hundreth men slew with a plewchis sok"). Approaching the "plesand palice," the protagonist is advised by "Esperance, my ladie fair and frie" to enter a "glorious garding . . . / The[e] to refresche" (212.4, 214.1, 8–9). Reminiscences of Douglas abound: the comparison of "seimlie ceder" to "widdrit rammall," the call of the "garitour" (here, "Grace"), and the throng of singers and musicians accompanying "fair felicitie most brycht," too bright to be seen (217.5–6, 221.8, 235.2, 7). Yet another female guide leads the protagonist into the palace toward the throne "Quharon ane God omnipotent devyne / Was hichlie set" (256.1–2). In the closing stanzas, the narrator glimpses the name of James VI inscribed in the book of life, "Contining all Gods chosin childreine fair" (261.9, 260.7). Stewart has read *PH* thoroughly in order to produce a Calvinist allegory that he concludes with a royal compliment.

Stewart of Baldynneis is not the last to draw upon *PH*. Printed in Edinburgh by Robert Charteris in 1603, Elizabeth Melville's *Ane Godlie Dreame* shows the persistence of allegorical dream visions, and the influence of *PH*, to the end of the sixteenth century in Scotland.[173] Grieved by the prevalence of evil in this world, Melville's narrator falls asleep and in her dream appears an "Angell bricht with visage schyning cleir" that offers to guide her toward her "heauie hearts desyre" (lines 92, 118). She asks him his name, and he replies, "I am thy God for quhom thou sicht sa sair" (line 127). He warns her that the journey they will take will bring them "[t]hrow greit deserts, throw water and throw fyre" (line 150). So they proceed: "[t]hrow mos and myres, throw ditches deip wee past, / Throw pricking thornes,

---

[170] Sage, "Life of Gawin Douglas," p. 15.

[171] *De animi tranquillitate dialogus*, ed. Sutton, 2.95–3.258.

[172] *Poems of John Stewart of Baldynneis*, ed. Crockett, 2.193–268.

[173] Melville, *Ane Godlie Dreame*, pp. 4–7, 9, 11.

throw water and throw fyre" (lines 165–66). They traverse mountains, braes, deserts, and waters. The dreamer trembles on the brink of a pit in which the damned are tormented, and has to be lifted over by her guide. At last he shows her that "pleasant place, quhilk semit to be at hand"; she sees a "Castell fair, / Glistring lyke gold, and schyning siluer bricht," the towers of which "blindit mee, they cuist sa greit ane licht" (lines 207, 209–10, 212). Encouraged at last by her progress, the dreamer rushes ahead of her guide, and is pulled back from mounting the stairs on her own. She is warned, "[i]t is to hie thou cannot clim so stay" (line 254). Instead she is directed to look downwards into a black pit, which she is told is Hell, her next destination. Assured by Jesus that "thou art past the paine," she awakens in the realization that "To seik the Lord, we mon be purgde and fynde" (lines 320, 333).

Just over a century later, that intensity of response and recreation had cooled into scholarly explication and literary appreciation. Perhaps understandably, given his embattled and even fugitive career as a nonjuring Episcopalian bishop, John Sage wrote an appreciative life of Douglas for Thomas Ruddiman's 1710 publication of *Eneados*. For Sage, *PH* offers a premonition of the travails Douglas would later experience as Bishop of Dunkeld: "The Author's excellent design is, under the similitude of a Vision, to represent the Vanity and Inconstancy of all worldly Pomp and Glory; and to shew that a constant and inflexible Course of Vertue *and* Goodness, is the only way to true Honour and Felicity, which he allegorically describes as a magnificent Palace, situate on a very high Mountain, of a most difficult Access."[174] Sage supposed that Douglas had based his idea on a Hellenistic dialogue, the *Tablet* ascribed to Cebes, in which the narrator describes an enigmatic painting that is explained by an old man as a depiction of life and its choices; in his *History of English Poetry*, Thomas Warton echoed this supposition.[175] Despite all such searching after antecedents, what may impress the reader of *PH* instead is its originality of conception and boldness of execution. These are not the least of the qualities that this strikingly influential work imparted to Scottish literary tradition, and it is for these qualities that it continues to attract attention.

---

[174] Sage, "Life of Gawin Douglas," p. 15.

[175] Warton, *History of English Poetry*, 2:294.

THE PALYCE OF HONOUR

Prologue

	Quhen pale Aurora with face lamentable	*When; sorrowful face*
	Hir russat mantill borderit all with sable	*mantle bordered*
	Lappit about be hevinlye circumstance	*Wrapped around with; elaborateness*
	The tender bed and arres honorable	*tapestry*
5	Of Flora, quene till flouris amyable,	*kindly queen of [the] flowers*
	In May I rays to do my observance	*arose; perform my customary service*
	And entrit in a garding of plesance	*entered into an enclosed garden*
	With sole depaint, as paradys amyable,	*ground painted*
	And blisfull bewes with blomed wariance,	*boughs; floriated changeability*

10	So craftely dame Flora had over fret	*skilfully; had adorned*
	Hir hevinly bed, powderit with mony a set	*sprinkled*
	Of ruby, topas, perle, and emerant,	*emerald*
	With balmy dewe bathit and kyndly wet,	*Bathed with gentle dew; naturally*
	Quhil vapours hote, right fresche and wele ybet,	*While warm vapors; well-mixed*
15	Dulce of odour, of flewour most fragrant,	*Sweet; scent*
	The silver droppis on dayseis distillant,	*on daisies [were] distilling*
	Quhilk verdour branches over the alars yet,[1]	
	With smoky sence the mystis reflectant.	*incense; reflecting*

	The fragrant flouris, blomand in their seis,	*blooming; places*
20	Overspred the leves of Naturis tapestreis,	*tapestries*
	Above the quhilk with hevinly armoneis	*which; harmonies*
	The birdes sat on twistis and on greis,	*twigs; levels*
	Melodiously makand thair kyndly gleis,	*making; melodies*
	Quhois schill notis fordinned al the skyis.	*Whose high; filled with noise*
25	Of reparcust ayr the eccon cryis	*From impacted air; echo resounds*
	Amang the branchis of the blomed treis,	*blossomy*
	And on the laurers silver droppis lyis.	*laurels; lie*

	Quhyll that I rowmed in that paradice	*roamed*
	Replennessed and full of all delice,	*Imbued; delight*

---

[1] *Which green branches poured over the pathways*

30	Out of the sea Eous alift his heid —	*raised his head*
	I meyne the hors quhilk drawis at device	*mean; pulls according to plan*
	The assiltré and goldin chaire of pryce	*axle-tree; chariot; great worth*
	Of Tytan, quhilk at morowe semis reid.	*Apollo; in the morning appears red*
	The new colowr that all the night lay deid	*dead*
35	Is restored; baith fowlis, flowris and ryce	*both; thickets*
	Reconfort was throw Phebus gudlyheid.	*Revived; through Apollo's generosity*

	The dasy and the maryguld onlappit	*opened out*
	Quhilkis all the nicht lay with thair levis happit	*That; wrapped up*
	Thaim to preserve fra rewmes pungitive.	*from stinging damp*
40	The umbrate treis that Tytan about wappit	*shady; wrapped*
	War portrait and on the erth yschappit	*portrayed; fashioned*
	Be goldin bemes vivificative	*By; enlivening*
	Quhois amene hete is most restorative.	*pleasant*
	The gershoppers amangis the vergers gnappit,	*gardens munched*
45	And beis wrocht materiall for thair hyve.	*bees constructed*

	Richt halsom was the sessoun of the yeir.	*healthful; season*
	Phebus furth yet depured bemes cleir,	*poured forth purified*
	Maist nutrityve tyll all thynges vigitant.	*Most nutritious for all growing things*
	God Eolus of wynd list nocht appeir,	*Aeolus; chose not to be present*
50	Nor ald Saturne with his mortall speir	*deadly influence*
	And bad aspect contrar til every plant.	*malevolent look unfavorable to*
	Neptunus nolde within that palace hant.	*would not; walled garden stay*
	The beriall stremes rynnyng men micht heir	*sparkling streams flowing*
	By bonkis grene with glancis variant.	*banks; varying flashes (of light)*

55	For till beholde that hevinly place complete —	*to see that entire heavenly place*
	The purgit ayr with new engendrit hete,	*cleansed; newly generated*
	The soyl enbroude with colowr, ure and stone,	*embroidered; ore*
	The tender grene, the balmy droppes swete —	*sweet*
	So rejoysyt and confort wes my sprete	*comforted; mood*
60	I not wes it a vision or fanton.	*do not know [if] it was; delusion*
	Amyd the buskys rowmyng myn alone	*bushes; by myself*
	Within that garth of all plesans replete,	*garden full of all delight*
	A voce I hard, preclare as Phebus schone,	*heard, [as] clear; shone*

	Syngand, "O May, thow myrrour of soles,	*utmost example (acme) of happiness*
65	Maternall moneth, lady and maistres,	*month*
	Tyl every thing adoun respirature,	*To; on earth [the] reviver*
	Thyn hevinly werk and worthy craftines	*skilfulness*
	The small herbis constrenis tyl encres.	*compel to grow*
	O verray ground tyl werking of nature,	*truly the basis for the*
70	Quhois hie curage and assucuryt cure	*Whose noble spirit; constant care*
	Causis the erth his frutis tyll expres,	*to bring forth*
	Dyffundant grace on every creature,	*Diffusing*

"Thy godly lore, cunnyng incomparabyl,   *knowledge*
Dantis the savage bestis maist unstabyl   *Tames; unpredictable*
75   And expellis all that nature infestis.   *everything that assails nature*
The knoppit syonys with levys agreabyl   *budding shoots; pleasant leaves*
For tyl revert and burgione ar maid abyll.   *to sprout again and swell; able*
Thy myrth refreschis birdis in thair nestis,
Quhilkis thee to pryse and Nature never restis,   *Which; praise*
80   Confessand you maist potent and lovabyll   *Confessing*
Amang the brownys of the olyve twystes.   *brown hues; branches*

"In thee is rute and augment of curage,   *origin; increase of vitality*
In thee enforcis Martis vassalage.   *Mars' valor intensifies*
In thee is amorus luf and armony
85   With incrementis fresche in lusty age.   *new increases; vigorous time of life*
Quha that constrenit ar in luffis rage,   *Whoever; constrained; love's passion*
Addressand thaim with observans ayrly   *Preparing themselves; early*
Weil auchtys thee tyl glore and magnify."   *incumbent on you*
And with that word I rasyt my vissage   *raised*
90   Sore effrayit, half in a frenisye.   *Acutely alarmed; frenzy*

"O Nature quene and O ye lusty May,"
Quod I tho, "Quhow lang sall I thus forvay   *Said I then; shall go astray*
Quhilk yow and Venus in this garth deservis?   *That; serves*
Reconsell me out of this gret affray   *Restore; great fear*
95   That I maye synge yow laudis day be day.   *praises; by*
Ye that al mundane creaturis preservis,   *earthly created beings*
Confort your man that in this fanton stervis   *Comfort; delusion perishes*
With sprete arrasyt and every wit away,   *spirit downcast; all mental faculties*
Quakyng for fere, baith puncys, vane, and nervis."   *fear, both arteries, veins*

100   My fatal werd, my febyl wit I wary,   *fated destiny; curse*
My dasyt heid quham lake of brane gart vary   *dazed head which lack; made wander*
And not sustene so amyabyll a soun!   *endure; sound*
With ery curage, febyl strenthis sary,   *fearful spirit, feeble paltry faculties*
Bownand me hame — and list no langer tary —   *Betaking myself home; wanted; tarry*
105   Out of the ayr come ane impressioun   *came a flash*
Throw quhois lycht, in extasy or swoun,   *light; trance; swoon*
Amyd the virgultis, all in tyl a fary   *shrubbery, utterly into a stupor*
As femynine so feblyt fell I doun.   *As enfeebled as a feminine being*

And with that gleme so dasyt wes my mycht   *flash; dazed; strength*
110   Quhill thair remanit nothir voce nor sycht,   *Until; remained neither*
Breth, motione, nor hetis naturale;   *natural warmth*
Saw nevir man so faynt a levand wycht —   *Never did [any] man see; living being*
And na ferly, for over excelland lycht   *no wonder; overly intense light*
Corruppis the wit and garrys the blud availe   *Corrupts; mind; causes; descend*
115   On tyl the hart that it no danger ale.   *Into; so that no danger affects it*

Quhen it is smorit, membris wyrkes not richt;   *(the blood) is congested, parts of the body*
The dredfull terrour sua did me assaile.   *thus beset me*

Yyt at the last, I not quhou longe a space,   *But; know not how; time*
A lytell hete aperyt in my face   *warmth; appeared*
120   Quhilk had to fore beyn pale and voyde of blud.   *before been*
Tho in my sweven I met a ferly cace.   *dream I dreamed a weird occurrence*
I thought me set within a desert place   *imagined myself put; deserted*
Amyd a forest, by a hydous flud   *hideous river*
With grysly fysche; and, shortly tyl conclud,   *fish; to*
125   I shall descryve, as God wil geve me grace,
Myn avision in rurell termes rude.   *rough rustic words*

Finis.

The First Part

Thow barrant wyt overset with fantasyis,   *sterile; overwhelmed*
Schaw now the craft that in thy memor lyis,   *Show; skill; memory*
Schaw now thy shame, schaw now thy bad nystee,   *deplorable silliness*
130   Schaw thyn endyt, repruf of rethoryis,   *writing, scandal to rhetoric*
Schaw now thy beggit termis mare than thryis,   *scrounged; more; thrice*
Schaw now thy ranys and thyn harlottree,   *rigmaroles; thy ribaldry*
Schaw now thy dull, exhaust inanytee,   *empty inanity*
Schaw furth thy cure and wryte thir frenesyis   *diligence; these frenzies*
135   Quhilkis of thy sempyll cunnyng nakyt thee.   *Which; paltry skill exposed*

My ravyst sprete in that deserte terrybill   *abducted spirit*
Approchit nere that ugly flude horrybill   *river*
Lyk tyll Cochyte the ryver infernall   *Cocytus*
Wyth vyle wattyr quhilk maid a hydduus trubbyll,   *commotion*
140   Rynnand overhed, blud red, and impossybyll   *Rushing headlong*
That it had byn a ryver naturall.   *As if it*
With brayis bare, raif rochis, lyke to fall,   *bare banks, crags split, about*
Quhare on na gers nor herbys wer visibyll,   *Upon which no grass or plants*
Bot skauppis brynt with blastis boryall.   *Only knolls scorched by north winds*

145   Thys laythly flude, rumland as thondyr, routyt,   *loathsome; rumbling; roared*
In quham the fysche, yelland as elvys, schoutyt.   *which; yelling; elves shouted*
Thair yelpis wylde my hering all fordevyt.   *deafened my hearing*
Tha grym monsturis my spretis abhorryt and doutyt.   *shrank from and dreaded*
Not throu the soyl bot muskan treis sproutyt   *Nothing; decayed trees*
150   Combust, barrant, unblomyt, and unlevyt;   *Burnt, sterile, unblossomed; leafless*
Ald rottyn runtis quhairin no sap was levyt,   *stumps in which; left*
Moch, all wast, widdrit, with granis moutyt —   *Soggy; withered; branches broken*
A ganand den quhair morthurars men revyt.   *The sort of ravine; murderers; robbed*

155 Quhairfore my selvyn was richt sore agast.   *[I] myself; afraid*
    This wyldernes abhomynable and wast,   *waste*
    In quhom na thing wes Nature confortand,   *which in no way; comforting*
    Was dyrk as royk the quhilk the see upcast.   *dark; fog*
    The quhislyng wynd blew mony byttir blast.   *whistling; fierce gust*
    Runtis ratlit, and uneth myght I stand.   *Tree stumps creaked, and hardly could*
160 Out throu the wode I crap on fut and hand.   *crept*
    The ryvar stank. The treis clattryt fast.   *rattled continuously*
    The soil was not bot marres, slyik, and sand.   *nothing but marsh, mud*

    And not but caus my spretis were abaysit   *not without; dismayed*
    All solitare in that desert arrasyt.   *downcast*
165 "Allas," I said, "is non other remede?   *is [there] no other solution?*
    Cruel Fortoun, quhy hes thow me betrasyt,   *why; betrayed*
    Quhy hes thou thus my fatall end compasyt?   *planned*
    Allas allas, sall I thus sone be dede   *shall; so soon; dead*
    In this desert and wait non uther rede   *expect no other recourse*
170 Bot be devoryt wyth sum best ravanus?   *by some ravenous beast*
    I wepe, I wale, I plene, I cry, I plede,   *wail; lament; plead*
    Inconstant warld and quheil contrarius.   *contrary wheel*

    "Thy transitory plesans quhat avaylys?   *pleasure is of what advantage?*
    Now thare, now heir, now hie, and now devalys,   *sinks*
175 Now to, now fro, now law, now magnifyis,   *humble; gains status*
    Now hote, now cald, now lauchys, now bewalys,   *laughs; bewails*
    Now seik, now hail, now wery, now not alys,   *sick; healthy; weary; not troubled*
    Now gud, now evyll, now wetis and now dryis —
    Now thow promittis and rycht now thou denyis —   *you promise; you refuse*
180 Now wo, now weill, now ferm, now frevilus,   *woeful; fortunate; firm; flighty*
    Now gam, now gram, now lovys, now defyis —   *fun; distress; extols; renounces*
    Inconstant warld and quheil contrarius.

    "Ha, quha suld haif affyans in thy blys?   *who; trust*
    Ha, quha suld haif fyrm esperans in this   *hope*
185 Quhilk is allace sa freuch and variant!   *fragile*
    Certis none. Sum hes. No wicht. Suythly yys.   *Certainly; Nobody. Surely yes*
    Than hes my self bene gylty? Ya, iwys.   *Yes, indeed*
    Thairfore allace sall danger thus me dant?   *risk of harm intimidate me thus?*
    Quhyddyr is bycum sa sone this duyly hant   *From whence; come; fast; dismal spot*
190 And veyr translat in wyntyr furyus?   *spring turned into raging winter*
    Thus I bewale my faitis repugnant,   *unpleasant prospects*
    Inconstant warld and quheil contrarius."

    Bydand the deid thus in myn extasy,   *Awaiting*
    A dyn I hard approchyng fast me by   *loud noise; heard come close by me*
195 Quhilk movit fra the plage septentrionall   *northern quadrant*
    As heyrd of bestis stampyng with loud cry.   *As from a herd*

Bot than God wate quhow afferyt wes I, *then; knows how frightened I was*
Traistand tyl be stranglyt with bestiall. *Expecting to; trampled by livestock*
Amyd a stok richt prevaly I stall *hollow tree-stump; stealthily; crept*
200 Quhare, lukand out, anone I dyd espy *Where, looking; straightaway*
Ane lusty rout of bestis rationall — *fine herd; intelligent animals*

Of ladyis fair and gudly men arrayit
In constant weid — that weil my spretis payit. *matching clothing; contented*
Wyth degest mynd quhairin all wyt aboundyt, *serious manner; wisdom abounded*
205 Full sobyrly thair haknais thay assait *maneuvered their saddle-horses*
Eftyr the feitis auld and not forvayt. *traditional practices; did not err*
Thair hie prudence schew furth and nothyng roundit, *and cut no corners*
With gude effere quhare at the wod resoundyt. *fine ceremoniousness at which*
In stedfast ordour, to vysy onaffrayit, *unafraid to look about*
210 Thay rydyng furth, with stabylnes ygroundyt, *ride forth, seated with assurance*

Amyddys quham, borne in ane goldyn chare *Amongst whom, carried; chariot*
Ovyrfret with perle and stonys maist preclare *Adorned; lustrous*
That drawin wes by haiknays four, mylk quhyt,
Was set a quene, as lylly swete of sware, *lovely as a lily; neck*
215 In purpur robe hemmid with gold ilk gare *purple; edged; each gore (decorative pleat)*
Quhilk jemmyt claspes closyd all parfyte, *bejeweled clasps all fastened exactly*
A Diademe maist pleasandly polyte *attractively polished*
Set on the tressys of her gyltyn hare, *gilded hair*
And in her hand a sceptre of delyte.

220 Syne next her, rayed in granyt violate, *Then; arrayed in cloth thoroughly dyed violet*
Twelve Damysylles, ilk ane in theyr estate *each according to their rank*
Quhilkis semyt of hyr consell most secré, *seemed; her council; confidential*
And nixt thaym wes a lusty rout, God wate: *fine throng; knows*
Lordis, ladyis, and mony fair prelate, *ecclesiastical leader*
225 Baith borne of hie estate and law degré. *Both; high and low rank*
Furth with thair quene thay al by passit me. *passed by me*
Ane esy pase thay rydyng furth the gate, *gentle pace; ride along the path*
And I abaid alone within the tre. *remained*

And as the rout wes passyt one and one
230 And I remanand in the tre alone,
Out throw the wode come rydand cativis twane, *two wretches*
Ane on ane asse, a wedy about his mone, *donkey, a noose around his head*
The tothir raid ane hiddows hors apone. *on a hideous horse*
I passyt furth and fast at thaym did frane *came out; eagerly; ask*
235 Quhat men thay wer. Thay answeryt me agane, *What sort of men; in reply*
"Our namys ben Achitefel and Synone
That by our suttell menys feil hes slane. *sly tricks have killed many*

"Wait ye," quod I, "quhat signifyis yon rout?"   *Do you know*
Synon sayd "Ya," and gave ane hyddows schout,
240 "We wrechys bene abject thairfra, iwys.   *expelled from there, indeed*
Yone is the Quene of Sapience but dout,   *without doubt*
Lady Minerve, and yone twelve hir about   *around her*
Ar the prudent Sibillais full of blys,   *Sybils*
Cassandra, eik Delbora and Circis,   *Circe*
245 The Fatale Systeris twynand our weirdes out,   *spinning; destinies*
Judith, Jael and mony a prophetis,   *prophetess*

"Quhilkis groundyt ar in fyrm intelligens.   *Who are grounded; knowledge*
And thair is als in to yone court gone hens   *also within*
Clerkis divine, with problewmys curius,   *Scholars; skilled with hard questions*
250 As Salomon the well of sapiens   *source of wisdom*
And Arestotyl, fulfyllet of prudens,   *replete with knowledge*
Salust, Senek, and Titus Livius,   *Seneca*
Picthagoras, Porphure, Permenydus,   *Pythagoras, Porphyry, Parmenides*
Melysses with his sawis but defence,   *sayings without refutation*
255 Sidrag, Secundus, and Solenyus,   *Sidrak; Solinus*

"Ptholomeus, Ipocras, Socrates,   *Ptolemy, Hippocrates*
Empedocles, Neptennebus, Hermes,   *Nectanabus*
Galien, Averroes, and Plato,
Enoth, Lameth, Job, and Diogenes,   *Enoch, Lamech*
260 The eloquent and prudent Ulisses,
Wyse Josephus and facund Cicero,   *eloquent*
Melchisedech, with othyr mony mo.
Thair viage lyis throw out this wildernes;   *journey; across*
To the Palice of Honour all thay go.

265 "Is situat from hens liggis ten hundyr.   *[It] is located; leagues; hundred*
Our horsys oft, or we be thair, wyll fundyr.   *often, before; stumble*
Adew, we may no langer heir remane."   *Goodbye; stay here*
"Or that ye passe," quod I, "tell me this wondyr,   *Before*
How that ye wrechyt cativis thus at undyr   *in subjection*
270 Ar sociat with this court soverane?"   *associated*
Achitefell maid this answer agane,
"Knawis thou not? Haill, erd quake, and thundyr   *earthquake*
Ar oft in May, with mony schour of rane.   *shower of rain*

"Rycht so we bene in tyll this company.   *We are just like that among*
275 Our wyt aboundit, and usyt wes lewdly.   *intelligence; wickedly*
My wysdome ay fulfyllyt my desyre,   *always satisfied*
As thou may in the Bybyl weil aspy   *certainly discover*
How Davidis prayer put my counsell by.   *averted my advice*
I gart his sonne aganys hym conspyre,   *made; against*
280 The quhilk wes slane, quhairfore up be the swyre *killed, for which reason; neck*

My self I hangit, frustrat sa fowlily.   *foiled so shamefully*
This Synon wes a Greik that rasyt fyre   *started fire*

"First in to Troy, as Virgyll dois report —
Sa tratourlyk maid him be draw overwhort   *traitorously; to be taken across*
285   Quhill in he brocht the hors with men of armys   *So that he brought in; [Trojan] Horse*
Quhairthrow the towne distroit wes at schort."   *By which; was rapidly destroyed*
Quod I, "Is this your destany and sort?   *fate*
Cursit be he that sorowis for your harmys,   *grieves; misfortunes*
For ye bene schrewis baith, be Goddis armys.   *are both villains*
290   Ye will optene nane entres at yone port   *get no access to that entrance*
Bot gif it be throw sorcery or charmys."   *Unless; through; spells*

"Ingres tyll have," quod thay, "we not presume.   *Entry to*
It sufficis us tyl se the Palice blume   *suffices for us to see; flourish*
And stand on rowme quhare bettyr folk bene charrit.[1]
295   For tyll remane, adew, we have na tume.   *adieu; leisure*
This ilk way cummis the courtis, be our dume,   *very; opinion*
Of Diane and Venus that feil hes marryt."   *who has ruined many*
With that thay raid away as thay wer skarryt,   *as if; scared*
And I agayne, maist lyk ane elrych grume,   *elvish man*
300   Crap in the muskane akyn stok mysharrit.   *Crept; decayed ruined oak stump*

Thus wrechitly I maid my resydence
Imagynand feil syse for sum defence   *Taking thought often about*
In contrar savage bestis maist cruell,   *Against*
For na remeid bot deid be violence   *remedy but death by*
305   Sum tyme asswagis febill indegence.   *overcomes weak insufficiency*
Thus in a part I reconfort my sell   *heartened myself*
Bot that so lityll wes, I dar nocht tell.   *could not say [for sure]*
The stychlyng of a mows out of presence   *rustling; mouse; sight*
Had bene to me mare ugsum than the hell.   *horrifying*

310   Yit glaid I wes that I with thaym had spokkyn.
Had not bene that, certis my hart had brokkyn   *surely*
For megirnes and pusillamytee.   *inadequacy; timidity*
Remanand thus within the tre al lokkyn,   *tightly ensconced*
Dissyrand fast sum signys or sum tokkyn   *Desiring keenly; token*
315   Of Lady Venus and of hir companee,
A hart transformyt ran fast by the tree,   *transformed deer; close*
With houndis rent, on quham Dian wes wrokkyn;   *Lacerated by dogs; whom; avenged*
Tharby I understude that sche wes nee.   *nigh*

---

[1] *And stand far apart (from) where (even) better folk are rejected*

Thay had tofore declarit hir cummyng.	*previously announced her arrival*
320 Mare perfytly, forthy, I knew the syng;	*accurately, therefore; understood; sign*
Wes Action quhilk Diane nakyt watyt	*Actæon who; watched*
Bathyng in a well, and eik hir madynnys yyng.	*also; young*
The goddes wes commovyt at this thing	*enraged*
And hym in forme hes of a hart translatit.	*has turned into the form of a hart*
325 I saw, allace, his houndis at him slatit.	*incited against him*
Bakwert he blent to gyf thaym knawlegyng	*Backward he glanced; understanding*
Tha raif thair lord, mysknew hym at thaym batit.	*tore at; that baited them*
Syne ladyis come with lusty giltyn tressys	*Then; golden*
In habit wild maist lyke till fostaressys,	*And clothing; female forest-dwellers*
330 Amyddys quham, heich on ane eliphant	*high*
In syng that sche in chastité incressys,	*As a sign; grows in chastity*
Raid Diane, that ladyis hartis dressys	*Rode; who prepares women's hearts*
Tyl be stabil and na way inconstant.	*To be loyal*
God wait that nane of thaym is variant;	*knows; changeable*
335 All chast and trew virginité professys.	*[are] chaste and profess true virginity*
I not, bot few I saw with Diane hant.	*do not know; associate with Diana*
In til that court I saw anone present	*soon*
Jeptyis douchtir, a lusty lady gent	*Jephthah's daughter; fine noble lady*
Offeryt tyl God in hir virginité.	*Offered; virginity*
340 Pollixena I wys wes not absent.	*Polyxena indeed*
Panthessilé with mannys hardyment,	*Penthesilea; fortitude*
Effygyn and Virgenius douchter fre,	*Iphigenia; Virginius' noble daughter*
With uthyr flouris of feminyté	
Baith of the New and the Ald Testament,	
345 All on thay raid and left me in the tre.	*They all rode past; tree*
In that desert dispers, in sondyr skattryt,	*dispersed, scattered asunder*
Wer bewis bare quham rane and wynde on battryt.	*boughs; battered upon*
The water stank, the feild was odious	
Quhar dragonys, lessertis, askis, edders swattryt	*lizards, asps, adders wallowed*
350 With mouthis gapand, forkyt tayles tattryt,	*tattered*
With mony a stang and spoutis vennomous	*fang; venomous squirts*
Corruppyng ayr be rewme contagious.	*Polluting; by toxic vapor*
Maist gros and vyle enposonyt cloudis clatteryt,	*Very massive; poisonous; rumbled*
Rekand lyk hellys smoke sulfuryus.	*Reeking*
355 My dasyt hed, fordullit dissyly,	*dazed head, stupefied dizzily*
I rasyt up, half in a letergy,	*stupor*
As dois a catyve ydronken in slep	*wretch intoxicated*
And so opperyt tyl my fantasy	*appeared to my mind's eye*
A schynand lycht out of the northest sky.	*shining; north-east*
360 Proportion soundis dulcest hard I pepe	*I heard sweetest sounds pipe melody*
The quhilk with cure till heir I did tak kepe.	*attentiveness to hear; pay heed*

In musyk, nowmer full of harmony,   *intervals full*
Distant on far, wes caryit be the depe.   *afar, was carried by the deep water*

365 Farther by wattyr folk may soundis here   *can hear sounds*
     Than by the erth, the quhilk with poris sere   *various pores*
     Up drynkis ayr that movit is by sound,   *Soaks up air; is disturbed*
     Quhilk in compact wattir of ane rivere   *dense*
     May nocht entre bot rynnys thare and here   *Cannot enter; moves here and there*
     Quhil it at last be caryit on the ground —   *is conveyed over*
370 And thocht throw dyn, be experience is found,   *though because of noise [as] by*
     The fysch ar causyt within the rivere stere,   *to stir*
     Inoth the wattyr the nois dois not abound.   *Within*

     Violent dyn the ayr brekkis and deris,   *breaks and disturbs the air*
     Syne gret motion of ayr the watyr steris.   *Then; stirs*
375 The wattyr steryt, fischis for ferdnes fleis;   *fear escape*
     Bot, out of dout, no fysch in wattyr heris,   *beyond doubt; hears*
     For, as we se, rycht few of thaym has eris —   *ears*
     And eik forsuyth, bot gyf wyse clerkis leis,   *also indeed, unless; scholars tell lies*
     Thair is nane ayr inoth watters nor seis,   *no air within; seas*
380 But quhilk na thing may heir, as wyse men leiris,   *Without which; teach*
     Lyik as but lycht thair is na thyng that seis.   *Just as without light; sees*

     Anewch of this; I not quhat it may mene.   *Enough; do not know what*
     I wyll returne till declare all bedene   *to; completely*
     My dreidfull dreme with grysly fantasyis.   *frightening*
385 I schew tofore quhat I had hard and sene,   *showed before*
     Perticularly sum of my paynfull tene.   *sorrow*
     But now God wate quhat ferdnes on me lyis.
     Lang ere I said — and now this tyme is twyis —   *Long before; twice*
     A sound I hard, of angellys as it had bene,   *heard, as if from angels it had come*
390 With armony fordynnand all the skyis,   *making all the skies resound*

     So dulce, so swete, and so melodius
     That every wycht thair with mycht be joyous   *everyone might be delighted by it*
     Bot I and cativis dullit in dispare;   *Except; dulled by despair*
     For quhen a man is wreth or furius,   *angry; insane*
395 Malancolyk for wo or tedius,   *Depressed; weary*
     Than is al plesance till hym maist contrare;
     And semblably than, so did wyth me fare.   *apparently then, so happened with me*
     This melody intonyt hevinly thus
     For profund wo constrenyt me mak care;   *compelled me to express grief*

400 And murnand thus as ane maist wofull wicht,   *mourning*
     Of the maist plesand court I had a sycht
     In warld adoun sen Adam wes create.   *the world below since*
     Quhat sang? Quhat joy? Quhat armony? Quhat lycht?

Quhat myrthfull solace, plesance all at ryght?	*in due proportion*
405 Quhat fresch bewté? Quhat excelland estate?	*beauty; fine mode of existence*
Quhat swete vocis? Quhat wordis suggurate?	*honeyed words*
Quhat fair debatis? Quhat lufsum ladyis bricht?	*discussions*
Quhat lusty gallandis did on thair servyce wate?	*courtiers; wait*

Quhat gudly pastance, and quhat menstraly?	*pastime; [musical] performance*
410 Quhat game thay maid? In faith, not tell can I,	*pastime*
Thocht I had profund wit angelicall.	*Even if; intelligence*
The hevinly soundis of thair armony	
Has dymmyt so my drery fantasy,	*gloomy understanding*
Baith wit and reason, half is lost of all.	*perception*
415 Yit as I knaw, als lychtly say I sall:	*as readily shall I say*
That angellyk and godly company	*angelic and divine*
Tyll se me thocht a thyng celestiall.	*To see seemed to me; heavenly*

Procedand furth wes draw ane chariote	*Proceeding; was pulled*
Be cursuris twelf trappit in grein velvote.	*twelve stallions caparisoned; velvet*
420 Of fyne gold wer juncturis and harnasyngis.	*links; trappings*
The lymnuris wer of byrnyst gold, God wote.	*carriage-shafts; burnished; knew*
Baith extré and quhelis of gold, I hote.	*axle-tree; wheels; avow*
Of goldyn cord wer lyamys, and the stryngis	*thongs; reins*
Festnyt conjunct in massy goldyn ryngis;	*Fastened together*
425 Evyr hamys convenient for sic note;	*Ivory collar-frames; such [a] purpose*
And raw silk brechamys ovyr thair halsys hyngis.	*collars hang over their necks*

The body of the cart of evir bone	*chariot of ivory*
With crysolytis and mony pretious stone	*chrysolites*
Wes all ovirfret in dew proportioun	*encrusted; due*
430 Lyke sternys in the firmament quhilkis schone.	*stars; shone*
Reperalit wes that godlyk, plesand wone,	*Furnished; divine; abode*
Tyldyt abone and to the erth adoun	*Covered*
In rychest claith of gold of purpur broun;	*dark brown*
But fas or othyr frenyeis had it none	*tassel; fringes*
435 Save plate of gold anamallyt all fassioun,	*enameled [in] every pattern*

Quhairfra dependant hang thair megyr bellys,	*these tiny bells*
Sum round, sum thraw, in sound the quhilkis excellis.	*twisted*
All wer of gold of Araby maist fyne,	*finest gold from Arabia*
Quhilkis with the wynd concordandly so knellys	*rings so harmoniously*
440 That to be glad thair sound al wycht compellys.	*compels every person*
The armony wes so melodius fyne	
In mannys voce and instrument divine,	
Quhare so thay went, it semyt nothyng ellys	*Wherever; else*
Bot jerarchyes of angellys ordours nyne.	*hierarchies; nine orders of angels*

445 Amyd the chare, fulfillyt of plesance,	*abounding in delight*
A lady sat, at quhais obeysance	*whose bidding*
Wes all that rout; and wondyr is till here	*to hear*
Of hir excelland lusty countenance.	
Hir hie bewté, quhilk mayst is til avance,	*is most to be praised*
450 Precellys all — thair may be na compere —	*Surpasses; could be no equal*
For lyk Phebus in hiest of his spere	*at the zenith of his orbit*
Hir bewtye schane, castand so gret a glance	*shone, casting; intense a reflection*
All farehed it opprest, baith far and nere.	*prettiness; overwhelmed both*
Scho wes peirles of schap and portrature.	*peerless of figure; looks*
455 In hir had Nature fynesyt hir cure.	*used up her skill*
As for gud havyngis, thair wes nane bot sche.	*manners; no one like her*
And hir array wes so fyne and so pure	*spotless*
That quhair of wes hir rob, I am not sure,	*of what material was her robe*
For nocht bot perle and stonys mycht I se,	*nothing but; could I see*
460 Of quham, the brychtnes of hir hie bewté	*Because of which*
For till behald my sycht mycht not endure	*could not*
Mair than the brycht sonne may the bakkis e.	*[Any] more; sun can; bat's eye(sight)*
Hir hair as gold or topasis wes hewyt.	*topazes; hued*
Quha hir beheld, hir bewtie ay renewyt.	*Whoever saw her; always revived*
465 On heid sche had a creste of dyamantis.	*[her] head*
Thair wes na wycht that gat a sycht eschewyt,	*no one escaped who got a sight*
Wer he nevir sa constant nor weil thewyt,	*However loyal or virtuous he might be*
Na he was woundit and him hir servant grantis.	*But; avows himself [to be] her servant*
That hevinly wycht, hir cristall eyn so dantis,	*eyes so overcome*
470 For blenkis swete, nane passit unpersewyt,	*sweet glances; none; un-pursued*
Bot gyf he wer preservit as thir sanctis.	*Unless; like the saints*
I wondryt sore and in mynd did stare	*wondered greatly; obsess*
Quhat creature that mycht be wes so fare,	*[who] was so beautiful*
Of sa peirles, excelent womanheid.	*peerless*
475 And, farlyand thus, I saw within the chare	*wondering*
Quhare that a man wes set with lymmes square,	*seated; powerful limbs*
His body weil entalyeit every steid.	*well built all over*
He bare a bow with dartis haw as leid,	*carried; blue-grey as lead*
His clethyng wes als grene as ane hountare,	*hunter['s]*
480 Bot he forsuyth had none eyn in his hed.	*eyes*
I understude by signis persavabill	*evident signs*
That wes Cupyd, the god maist dissavabill;	*deceitful*
The lady, Venus his mother, a goddes.	
I knew that wes the court so variabill	*inconstant*
485 Of erdly luf, quhilk sendill standis stabill.	*which seldom remains constant*
Bot yit thayr myrth and solace, nevertheles —	*But even so their*
In musik, tone, and menstraly expres	*sound, and actual performance*

So craftely with corage aggreabill — *skilfully gratifying to the vital spirits*
Hard never wicht sik melody, I ges. *No one ever heard such, I suppose*

490 Accumpanyit lusty yonkers with all. *Fine young men played along besides*
Fresche ladyis sang in voce virgineall *pure voice*
Concordes swete, divers entoned reportis, *Sweet harmonies; melodic responses*
Proportionis fyne with sound celestiall: *Fine musical intervals*
Duplat, triplat, diatesseriall, *Seconds, thirds, fourths*
495 Sesque altra and decupla resortis; *Eleventh and tenth converge*
Diapason of mony syndry sortis *Melodic range[s]; different*
War songin and plait be seir cunnyng menstrall *played by many skilled musicians*
On luf ballattis with mony fair disportis. *In; pastimes*

In modulatioun hard I play and syng *music-making; heard*
500 Faburdoun, priksang, discant, conturyng, *Fauxbourdon; counter-melodies*
Cant organe, figuration, and gemmell, *Chant, ornament; gemel*
On crowd, lute, harp, with mony gudly spring, *bowed lyre; dance*
Schalmis, clarionis, portativis hard I ring, *Shawms; portatives I heard resound*
Monycord, orgain, tympane, and symbell, *Monochord; tympani; cymbal*
505 Sytholl, psaltery, and vocis swete as bell, *Citole, psaltery*
Soft releschyngis in dulce delyveryng; *ornamentations; performance*
Fractyonis divide, at rest, or clos compell. *Rhythms subdividing; converging*

Not Pan of Archaid so plesandly plays *Arcadia*
Nor King David, quhais playng, as men sayis, *whose playing*
510 Conjurit the spreit the quhilk Kyng Saul confoundit, *Exorcized; overcame King Saul*
Nor Amphion with mony subtile layis *well-made songs*
Quhilk Thebes wallit with harpyng in his dayis, *Who built the walls of Thebes*
Nor he that first the subtile craftis foundit, *invented the refined techniques*
Was not in musik half so weil igroundit *well schooled*
515 Nor knew thair mesure tent dele be no wayes. *system a tenth part as much at all*
At thair resort baith hevyn and erd resoundit. *their concord*

Na mare I understude thir noumeris fyne, *these musical proportions*
Be God, than dois a gekgo or a swyne, *cuckoo*
Save that me think swete soundis gude to heir. *Except; sweet sounds seem to me*
520 Na mair heiron my labour will I tyne. *waste*
Na mair I wyl thir verbillys swete diffyne, *describe their sweet warblings*
How that thair musik tones war mair cleir
And dulcer than the movyng of the speir *heavenly spheres*
Or Orpheus harp of Trace with sound divyne; *the harp of Orpheus of Thrace*
525 Glaskeryane maid na noyes compeir. *Glascurion; no sound equal [to them]*

Thay condescend sa weil in ane accord *agree; chord*
That by na juynt thair soundis bene discord, *at no juncture; discordant*
In every key thay werren sa expert. *were*
Of thair array gyf I suld mak record,

530 Lusty spryngaldis and mony gudly lord,   *young men*
    Tendyr yonglyngis with pietuous virgin hart,   *youths; merciful*
    Eldar ladyis knew mair of lustis art,   *ladies [who] knew more about lust's*
    Divers utheris quhilkis me not list remord,   *others; do not interest me to consider*
    Quhais lakkest weid was silkis, or brounvert. *poorest garment; gold and dark green*

535 In vesturis quent of mony syndry gyse,   *elegant clothes; different fashions*
    I saw all claith of gold men mycht devise,   *might imagine*
    Purpur coulour, punyk and skarlot hewis,   *Purple; red-purple; bright red hues*
    Velvot robbis maid with the grand assyse,   *made; ample cut*
    Dames, satyn, begaryit mony wyse,   *Damask; striped variously*
540 Cramessy satin, velvos enbroude in divers rewis, *Crimson; velvet embroidered; rows*
    Satyn figuris champit with flouris and bewis —   *overlaid; branches*
    Damesflure tere pyle, quhare on thair lyis   *Foundation damask of triple thickness*
    Perle orphany, quhilk every state renewis.   *Gilt embroidery with pearls*

    Thare ryche entire, maist peirles to behald,   *attire; peerless*
545 My wyt can not discrive, howbe it I wald.   *however much I wished*
    Mony entrappit stede with sylkis sere,   *caparisoned steed; profuse silks*
    Mony pattrell nervyt with gold I tald,   *breastplate ribbed; noticed*
    Full mony new gylt harnasyng not ald,
    On mony palfray, lusum ladyis clere;   *many [a] fine riding horse, lovely*
550 And nyxt the chare I saw formest appere   *foremost*
    Upon a bardyt cursere stout and bald,   *armored warhorse big and bold*
    Mars, god of stryf, enarmyt in byrnist gere.   *burnished equipment*

    Every invasybill wapyn on hym he bare.   *offensive weapon; carried*
    His luke was grym, his body large and square,   *muscular*
555 His lymmys weil entailyeit til be strang,   *limbs; built; strong*
    His nek wes gret, a span lenth weil, or mare, *width of an outstretched hand easily*
    His vissage braid, with crisp, broun, curland hare,   *broad, with wavy; curling hair*
    Of statur not ovyr gret nor yit ovyr lang.   *too burly; too tall*
    Behaldand Venus, "O ye my luif," he sang,
560 And scho agane with dalyans sa fare   *dalliance*
    Hir knycht hym clepis quare so he ryde or gang.   *calls wherever; or walk*

    Thair wes Arsyte and Palemon alswa   *Arcite*
    Accumpanyit with fare Emylya,   *by fair Emily*
    The quene Dido with hir fals luf Enee,   *Aeneas*
565 Trew Troylus, unfaythfull Cressida,
    The fair Paris and plesand Helena,   *attractive; pleasing*
    Constant Lucres and traist Penolype,   *Faithful; loyal*
    Kynd Pirramus and wobegone Thysbe,
    Dolorus Progne, triest Philomena,   *Procne, sorrowful Philomela*
570 King Davidis luif thare saw I, Barsabe.   *David's love; Bathsheba*

Thare wes Ceix with the kynd Alcyon,
And Achilles wroth with Agamemnon — *angry*
For Bryssida his lady fra hym tane; — *Briseida; taken*
Wofull Phillys with hir luf Demophon, — *Phyllis*
575 Subtel Medea and hir knycht Jasone; — *Artful*
Of France I saw thair Paris and Veane; — *Vienne*
Thare wes Phedra, Thesyus, and Adriane, — *Phaedra; Ariadne*
The secrete, wyse, hardy Ipomedon,
Asswere, Hester, irraprevabill Susane. — *Ahasuerus, Esther, unimpeachable*

580 Thare wes the fals unhappy Dalida, — *ill-omened Delilah*
Cruel, wikkyt and curst Dyonera, — *accursed Deianeira*
Wareit Bibles and the fair Absolon, — *Accursed Byblis*
Ysyphele, abhomynabil Sylla, — *Hypsipyle; Scylla*
Trastram, Yside, Helcana and Anna, — *Tristram, Iseult, Elkanah*
585 Cleopatra and worthy Mark Anthon,
Iole, Hercules, Alcest, Ixion, — *Hesione*
The onely pacient wyfe Gressillida, — *Griselda*
Nersissus that his hed brak on a ston. — *broke his head*

Thare wes Jacob with fair Rachel his make, — *spouse*
590 The quhilk become til Laban for hir sake — *Who became*
Fourteen yere boynd with fyrm hart immutabill. — *indentured; firm, unchanging heart*
Thair bene bot few sic now, I undertake. — *such nowadays; dare say*
Thir fair ladyis in silk and claith of lake — *fine linen cloth*
Thus lang sall not all foundyn be so stabyll. — *Up till now; found to be so dependable*
595 This Venus court quhilk wes in luif maist abil — *adept*
For till discrive my cunning is to wake. — *describe; too weak*
A multitude thay wer, innumerabill,

Of gudly folk in every kynd and age;
With blenkis swete, fresch lusty grene curage, — *sweet glances; young vitality*
600 And dalyans, thay rydyng furth in fere. — *dalliance; ride forth together*
Sum leivys in hope and sum in great thyrlage, — *Some live; servitude*
Sum in dispare, sum findis his panys swage. — *sufferings alleviated*
Garlandis of flouris and rois chaplettis sere — *many rose chaplets*
Thay bare on hede and samyn sang so clere, — *wore; together*
605 Quhil that thair myrth commovit my curage — *Until; stirred my energy*
Till syng this lay, quhilk folowand ye may here: — *To sing this song; hear*

"Constrenyt hart, bylappit in distres, — *Constrained; enwrapped*
Groundit in wo and full of hevynes, — *Rooted*
Complene thy paynfull caris infinyte, — *Lament; grievous woes*
610 Bewale this warldis frele unstedfastnes, — *frail*
Havand regrait, sen gone is thy glaidnes, — *Feeling regret, since*
And all thy solace returnyt in dispyte. — *repaid in hatred*
O cative thrall, involupit in syte, — *enveloped; sorrow*

Confesse thy fatale, wofull wrechitnes; — *destined*
615   Divide in twane and furth diffound all tyte — *two; pour forth all at once*
Aggrevance gret in miserabill endyte. — *Great grievance; writing*

"My crewell fait, subjectit to penance, — *made subject to*
Predestinat sa void of all plesance, — *Destined [to be] so empty*
Has every greif amyd myn hart ingrave. — *engraved into my heart*
620   The slyd, inconstant destany or chance — *slippery*
Unequaly doith hyng in thair ballance — *hang in their weighing scales*
My demeritis and gret dolour I have. — *misdeeds; [the] great sorrow*
This purgatory redowblys all the lave. — *rest*
Ilk wycht has sum weilfare at obeysance, — *well-being after submission*
625   Save me, bysnyng, that may na grace ressave. — *wretch; can; receive*
Dede, thee addresse and do me to my grave. — *Death, prepare thyself; send*

"Wo worth sik strang mysforton anoyus — *A curse upon such; grievous*
Quhilk has opprest my spretis maist joyus,
Wo worth this worldis freuch felicité, — *frail*
630   Wo worth my fervent diseis dolorus, — *severe, grievous distress*
Wo worth the wycht that is not pietuus
Quhare the trespassor penitent thay se,
Wo worth this dede that dayly dois me de, — *makes me die*
Wo worth Cupid and wo worth fals Venus,
635   Wo worth thaym bayth, ay waryit mot thay be, — *accursed may*
Wo worth thair court and cursyt destané."

Loude as I mocht, in dolour al distrenyeit, — *could, utterly constrained by misery*
This lay I sayng and not a lettir fenyeit. — *sang; did not make up a syllable*
Tho saw I Venus on hir lyp did byte, — *Then*
640   And all the court in hast thair horsys renyeit, — *reined*
Proclamand loude, "Quhare is yone poid that plenyeit — *toad*
Quhilk deth diservis committand sik dispite?" — *[for] committing such [an] offence*
Fra tre to tre, thay serchyng but respyte, — *they search ceaselessly*
Quhill ane me fand, quhilk said in greif, disdenyeit, — *one found me; anger, disgusted*
645   "Avant, velane, thou reclus imperfyte." — *Come out, churl*

All in ane fevyr out of my muskan bowr — *decayed bower*
On knees I crap and law for feare did lowr. — *crept and low; cower*
Than all the court on me thayr hedis schuke,
Sum glowmand grym, sum grinand with vissage sowr, — *frowning; snarling*
650   Sum in the nek gave me feil dyntis dowr, — *many heavy blows*
"Pluk at the craw," thay cryit, "deplome the ruke!" — *crow; de-plume the rook*
Pulland my hare, with blek my face they bruke. — *Pulling; boot-blacking; stain*
Skrymmory fery gaif me mony a clowr. — *[the] lively gave; hit; (see note)*
For Chyppynuty full oft my chaftis quuke. — *jaws trembled*

655   With payne torment, thus in thayr teynfull play,   *Tortured with injuries; spiteful*
        Till Venus bund they led me furth the way,   *fettered*
        Quhilk than wes set amyd a golden chare;   *Who; seated in; chariot*
        And so confoundit into that fell affray   *overcome in that terrible encounter*
        As that I micht consydyr thair array.   *could*
660   Me thocht the feild — ovirspred with carpetis fare,   *The field seemed to me overspread*
        Quhilk wes tofore brint, barrant, vile, and bare —   *previously scorched, barren*
        Wox maist plesand, bot all, the suyth to say,   *Grew; truth*
        Micht not amese my grewous pane full sare.   *soothe my grievous pain most sore*

        Entronit sat Mars, Cupyd, and Venus.   *Enthroned*
665   Tho rais a clerk wes clepit Varius   *Then arose an attorney named*
        Me tyl accusyng as of a dedly cryme;   *To accuse me; capital crime*
        And he begouth and red a dittay thus,   *began; read an indictment*
        "Thou wikkyt catyve, wod and furious,   *insane and raging*
        Presumptuusly now at this present tyme
670   My lady here blasphemed in thy ryme;
        Hir sonne, hir self, and hir court amorus
        For till betrais, awatit here sen prime."   *betray, lay in wait since sunrise*

        Now God Thow wate, me thocht my fortune fey.   *know, my fate seemed to me sealed*
        Wyth quakand voce and hart cald as a key   *quavering; cold*
675   On kneys I knelyt and mercy culd implore,   *did beg for mercy*
        Submyttand me, but ony langer pley,   *myself, without any further plea*
        Venus mandate and plesour till obey.   *To obey Venus' command and wish*
        Grace wes denyit and my travel forlore   *Mercy; withheld; effort wasted*
        For scho gaif chargis till procede as before.   *gave orders to proceed*
680   Than Varius spak rycht stoutly me till fley,   *fiercely to scare me*
        Injonand silence tyll ask grace ony more.   *Imposing silence [not] to*

        He demandit myn answere, quhat I sayd,
        Than as I mocht, with curage all mysmaid,   *spirit utterly downcast*
        Fra tyme I undirstude na mare supplé,   *Once; help*
685   Sore abasyt, belive I thus out braid,   *dismayed, at once I blurted out*
        "Set of thir pointis of cryme now on me laid   *Though; these; imputed to me*
        I may me quyte giltles in verité,   *exonerate myself*
        Yit fyrst, agane the juge quhilk here I se,   *against; whom I see here*
        This inordenat court, and proces quaid,   *improper; irregular proceedings*
690   I wyll object for causys twa or thre."

        Inclynand law, quod I with pietuus face,   *Bowing low; pitiful*
        "I me defend, Madame, plesyt your grace."   *legally represent myself; may it please*
        "Say on," quod sche. Than said I thus but mare,   *without more [delay]*
        "Madame, ye may not syt in till this cace,
695   For ladyis may be jugis in na place;   *are nowhere allowed to be judges*
        And mare attour, I am na seculare;   *furthermore; no lay-person*
        A spirituall man (thocht I be void of lare)   *lacking in learning*

Clepyt I am and aucht my lyvys space   *I am called; duration*
To be remyt till my juge ordinare.   *referred; ecclesiastical judge*

700 "I yow beseik, Madame, with byssy cure,   *beseech; relentless earnestness*
     Till gyf ane gracius interlocuture   *favorable judgment*
     On thir exceptionys now proponyt late."   *pleas; put forward just now*
     Than suddanly Venus, I yow assure,
     Deliverit sone and with a voce so sture   *Decided swiftly; harsh*
705 Answeryt thus: "Thow subtyle smy, God wait!   *rascal*
     Quhat wenys thou? Till degraid myne hie estate?   *What do you intend; debase*
     Me till declyne as juge, curst creature,   *to reject*
     It beis not so. The game gois othir gate.   *shall not be so; direction*

     "As we thee fynd, thou sall thoill jugement.   *adjudge you; undergo*
710 Not of a clerk we se thee represent   *Nothing about a clergyman; uphold*
     Save onely falsehed and dissaitfull talys.   *tales*
     Fyrst quhen thow come, with hart and hail entent   *firm intent*
     Thow thee submyttit till my commaundement.   *submitted thyself to*
     Now now, thairof me think to sone thow falys!   *it seems to me you fail too soon*
715 I weyn nathyng bot foly that thee alys.   *suppose; ails you*
     Ye clerkis bene in subtyle wordis quent   *skilled with cunning words*
     And in the deid als scharpe as ony snalys.   *deed; keen; snails*

     "Ye bene the men bewrays my commandis.   *You are; [who] disclose*
     Ye bene the men distrublys my servandis.   *harass*
720 Ye bene the men with wikkyt wordis fele   *many wicked words*
     Quhilk blasphemys fresch, lusty, yong gallandis   *abuse*
     That in my servyce and retenew standis.   *retinue*
     Ye bene the men that clepys yow so lele,   *call yourselves; loyal*
     With fals behest quhill ye your purpose stele,   *vow; get your way by fraud*
725 Syne ye forswere baith body, treuth and handis.   *Then; renounce; faith*
     Ye bene sa fals — ye can no word consele.   *conceal*

     "Have doyn," quod sche, "syr Varius. Alswyith   *"Stop," she said; Immediately*
     Do writ the sentence. Lat this cative kyith[1]
     Gyf our power may demyng his mysdeid."   *authority can deliver sentence on*
730 Than God Thow wait gyf that my spreit wes blyith.   *know whether; blithe*
     The feverus hew in till my face dyd myith   *feverish hue; show*
     All my male eys, for swa the horribill dreid   *distress; dread*
     Hail me ovyrset, I mycht not say my Creid.   *Completely overwhelmed me; Creed*
     For feir and wo, within my skyn I wryith.   *squirm*
735 I mycht not pray, forsuyth, thocht I had neid.   *could*

---

[1] *Have the sentence inscribed. Let this wretch exhibit*

Yit of my deth I set not half a fle —   *I didn't give half a fly*
For gret effere, me thocht na pane to de —   *fear; die*
But sore I dred me for sum othyr jape   *trick*
That Venus suld throw hir subtillyté   *guile*
740 In till sum bysnyng best transfigurit me,   *monstrous beast transform*
As in a bere, a bair, ane oule, ane ape.   *bear, a boar, an owl*
I traistit so for till have bene myschaip   *expected; deformed*
That oft I wald my hand behald to se
Gyf it alteryt, and oft my vissage grape.   *If it had changed; touch my face*

745 Tho I revolvit in my mynd anone   *reflected*
Quhow that Diane transformyt Acteone,
And Juno eik as for a kow gert kepe   *also; made to keep*
The fare Yo that lang wes wo begone —   *Io who was miserable for a long time*
Argos hir yymmyt that eyn had mony one,   *Argus guarded her; eyes*
750 Quhom at the last Mercurius gert slepe   *Mercury put to sleep*
And hir delyverit of that danger depe.   *And rescued her from*
I remembrit also quhow in a stone   *how into*
The wyfe of Loth ichangit sore did wepe.   *Lot transformed [note]*

I umbethocht quhow Jove and ald Saturn   *called to mind*
755 In tyll a wolf thay did Lycaon turn,
And quhow the mychty Nabugodonosore   *mighty Nebuchadnezzar*
In bestly forme did on the feild sudjourn   *form of a beast; dwell*
And for his gilt wes maid to wepe and murn.   *guilt*
Thir feirfull wondris gart me dreid ful sore,   *fearful wonders made*
760 For by exemplys oft I herd tofore
He suld bewar that seys his fallow spurn.   *sees his neighbor stumble*
Myschans of ane suld be ane otheris lore.   *One's mishap; another's lesson*

And rolland thus in divers fantasyis,   *reflecting; imaginings*
Terribil thochtis oft my hert did gryis,   *horrify my heart*
765 For all remeid wes alterit in dispare.   *changed into*
Thare wes na hope of mercy till devyis.   *to consider*
Thare wes na wycht my frend be na kyn wyis.   *no one; no way at all*
Alhalely the court wes me contrare.   *Unanimously; against me*
Than wes all maist wryttyn the sentence sare.   *almost; dire*
770 My febyll mynd, seand this gret suppris,   *seeing; mishap*
Wes than of wit and every blys full bare.

The Seconde Parte

Lo thus amyd this hard perplexité,
Awaytand ever quhat moment I suld de   *Awaiting constantly; die*
Or than sum new transfiguration,
775 He quhilk that is eternall verité,

The glorious Lord ryngand in personis thre,   *reigning*
Providit has for my salvation
Be sum gude spretis revelation,   *By; spirit's communication*
Quhilk intercessioun maid, I traist, for me;   *made, I believe*
780   I foryet all imagination.   *forgot; fanciful notion[s]*

All hail my dreid I tho foryet in hy   *wholly; then; at once*
And all my wo, bot yit I wyst not quhy,   *I did not know why*
Save that I had sum hope till be relevyt.   *rescued*
I rasyt than my vissage hastely   *raised*
785   And with a blenk anone I did espy   *look*
A lusty sycht quhilk nocht my hart engrevit.   *did not grieve my heart*
A hevinly rout out throw the wod eschevyt   *throng out from; emerged*
Of quhame the bonty, gyf I not deny,   *goodness, if I do not disagree*
Uneth may be in till ane scripture brevit.   *Hardly can be recorded in a text*

790   With lawrere crownyt in robbis syd all new,   *laurel; long gowns*
Of a fassoun, and all of stedfast hew,   *one design; hue*
Arrayit weil, a court I saw cum nere
Of wyse, degest, eloquent fathers trew   *dignified; honorable*
And plesand ladyis quhilkis fresch bewtie schew,   *whose youthful beauty was evident*
795   Syngand softly, full swete, on thair manere,   *in their way*
On poete wyse, all divers versis sere,[1]
Historyis gret in Latyne toung and Grew   *Greek*
With fresche endyt and soundis gude till here;   *style; to hear*

And sum of thaym ad lyram playit and sang   *accompanied by the lyre*
800   So plesand vers quhill all the rochys rang,   *Such; until; cliffs*
Metyr Saphik and also elygee.   *Sapphic meter; elegiac*
Thair instrumentis all maist wer fydlys lang   *mostly; long fiddles*
Bot with a string, quhilk nevyr ane wreist yeid wrang.   *With only one; peg went wrong*
Sum had ane harpe and sum a fair psaltree;   *psaltery*
805   On lutis sum thair accentis subtellé   *timbres skilfully*
Devydyt weil and held the mesure lang   *Articulated; sustained the full note value*
In soundis swete of plesand melodie.

The ladyis sang in vocis dulcorate   *sweet voices*
Facund epistillis quhilkis quhilum Ovid wrate   *Eloquent letters; previously; wrote*
810   As Phillys quene send till duke Demophon,   *sent*
And of Pennolepe the gret regrate   *lamentation*
Send till hir lord, sche dowtyng his estate,   *not knowing his state*
That he at Troy suld losyt be or tone.   *killed; captured*
Quhow Acontus till Cedippa anone   *Acontius to Cedippe promptly*

---

[1] *In poetical style, various different verses*

815	Wrate his complaint, thair hard I weil, God wate,
	With othir lusty myssyvis mony one.

heard
missives

	I had gret wondir of thair layis sere
	Quhilkis in that arte mycht have na way compere
	Of castis quent, rethorik colouris fyne,
820	So poete lyk in subtyle, fair manere
	And elaquent, fyrme cadens regulere.
	Thair vayage furth contenand rycht as lyne
	With sang and play, as sayd is, so dyvine,
	Thay fast approchyng to the place well nere
825	Quhare I wes torment in my gastly pyne;

their diverse lays
no peer at all
ingenious expressions
poetical
steady, regular meter
voyage; maintaining straight

rapidly approach
tormented; horrible suffering

	And as the hevynly sort now nomynate
	Removyt furth on gudly wyse the gate
	Towert the court quhilk wes tofore expremit,
	My curage grew — for quhat cause I not wate,
830	Save that I held me payit of thayr estate,
	And thay wer folk of knawlage, as it semit.
	Als in til Venus court full fast thay demit,
	Sayand, "Yone lusty rout wyll stop our mate
	Till justefy thys bisning quhilk blasphemit.

group just named
Traveled; the route
described
I knew not
felt myself [to be] gladdened by

But; criticized
That fine throng; companion
administer justice to this monster

835	"Yone is," quod they, "the court rethoricall
	Of polit termys, sang poeticall,
	And constand ground of famus historyis swete.
	Yone is the facund well celestiall.
	Yone is the fontayn and orygynall
840	Quharefra the well of Hylicon dois flete.
	Yone ar the folkis that comfortes every sprete
	Be fyne delyte and dyte angelicall,
	Causand gros lede all of maist gudnes glete.

There
polished words, lyric song
firm foundation
ample
source
From which Helicon flows
who comfort; mood
style
rough language; all gleam with

	"Yone is the court of plesand stedfastnes,
845	Yone is the court of constant merynes,
	Yone is the court of joyus disciplyne
	Quhilk causys folk thair purpos till expres
	In ornat wyse, provocand with gladnes
	All gentyll hartis to thare lare inclyne.
850	Every famus poet men may devyne
	Is in yone rout. Lo yondir, thair prynces,
	Thespis, the mothyr of the Musis Nyne;

elaborate style, enticing
adapt to their teaching
think of
princess

	"And nixt hir syne, hir douchter fyrst byget,
	Lady Cleo, quhilk craftely dois set
855	Historiis ald lyk as thay wer present.
	Euterpe eik, quhilk dayly dois hir det

after; first-born
Clio, who skilfully puts in writing
Ancient histories just as [if]
also; duty

In dulce blastis of pipis swete, but let. — *sounds; without cease*
The thyrd systir, Thalia diligent,
In wanton wryt and cronikillis doith imprent. — *fix in the mind*
860 The ferd endityth oft with chekis wet — *fourth composes; tear-stained cheeks*
Sare tragedyis, Melphomyne the gent. — *Distressing; noble*

"Tarpsychore the fyft with humyll soun — *fifth; gentle sound*
Makis on psaltreis modolatioun. — *Makes melody on psalteries*
The sext Erato, lyk thir luffirs wylde, — *these wild lovers*
865 Will syng, play, dans, and leip baith up and doune. — *dance, and leap*
Polimnya, the sevynt Muse of renoun, — *Polyhymnia*
Ditis thir swete rethorik cullouris mylde — *Composes these; colors of rhetoric*
Quhilkis ar so plesand baith to man and chylde.
Uranya, the aucht and sistir schene, — *eighth; fair*
870 Wrytis the hevyn and sternys all bedene. — *Chronicles; stars all fully*

"The nynt, quham till nane othir is compere, — *to whom; equal*
Caliopé, that lusty lady clere,
Of quham the bewtye and the worthynes,
The vertuys gret, schynis baith far and nere, — *great virtues shine*
875 For sche of nobillis fatis hes the stere — *nobles' fates; control*
Till wryt thair worschyp, victory, and prowes
In kyngly style, quhilk dois thair fame encres, — *makes*
Clepyt in Latyne heroicus but were, — *heroic (see note); without doubt*
Cheif of al wryt lyk as scho is maistres. — *Highest; writing just as she is mistress*

880 "Thir Musis nyne, lo yondir, may ye se
With fresch Nymphis of watir and of see — *river[s]; sea[s]*
And Phanee, ladyis of thir templis ald, — *Fanae; these ancient temples*
Pyerides, Dryades, Saturee, — *Pierides, Wood-nymphs, Satyrs*
Neriedes, Aones, Napee, — *Nereids, Aonians, Napaeae*
885 Of quham the bontyis nedis not be tald." — *good qualities need not be listed*
Thus dempt the court of Venus monyfald, — *judged; diversely*
Quhilk speche refreschyt my perplexité, — *soothed*
Rejosand weil my sprete afore wes cald. — *[that] previously was cold*

The suddand sycht of that fyrme court foresaid — *unexpected; stable; named previously*
890 Recomfort weil my hew tofore wes faid. — *[that] previously was pale*
Amyd my brest the joyus heit redoundyt, — *In; the welcome warmth returned*
Behaldand quhow the lusty Musys raid, — *rode*
And al thair court quhilk wes so blyith and glaid,
Quhois merynes all hevynes confoundyt. — *overcame all dejectedness*
895 Thair saw I, weil in poetry ygroundyt, — *well-versed in poetry*
The gret Homere, quhilk in Grew langage said — *Greek; spoke*
Maist eloquently, in quham all wyt aboundyt. — *knowledge*

	Thare wes the gret Latyn Virgillyus,	*Virgil*
	The famus fathir poet Ovidius,	
900	Ditis, Daris, and eik the trew Lucane,	*Dictys, Darius; truthful*
	Thare wes Plautus, Pogius, Parsius,	*Poggio, Persius*
	Thare wes Terens, Donat and Servius,	*Terence, Donatus*
	Francys Petrark, Flakcus Valeriane,	*Valerius Flaccus*
	Thare wes Ysop, Caton, and Alane,	*Aesop, Cato, and Alan*
905	Thare wes Galterus and Boetius,	*Boethius*
	Thare wes also the gret Quintilliane.	

	Thare wes the satyr poete Juvinale,	*satiric*
	Thare wes the mixt and subtell Marciale,	*versatile; Martial*
	Of Thebes bruyt thare wes the poete Stace.	*fame; Statius*
910	Thare wes Faustus and Laurence of the Vale,	*Lorenzo Valla*
	Pomponeus, quhais fame of late, sans fale,	*Pomponazzi; doubtless*
	Is blawin wyd throw every realme and place.	*trumpeted*
	Thare wes the morale, wyse poete Orace;	*Horace*
	With mony other clerkis of gret avayle,	*writers; great*
915	Thare wes Brunell, Claudyus and Bocace.	*Brunellus, Claudian; Boccaccio*

	So gret a pres of pepill drew us nere,	*crowd; came near us*
	The hunder part thare namys is not here.	*hundredth; [of] their names*
	Yit thare I saw, of Brutus Albion,	*of the English nation*
	Goffryd Chaucere as A per se, sance pere	*paragon, unequaled*
920	In his wulgare, and morell John Gowere.	*vernacular*
	Lydgat the monk raid musand him allone.	*pondering by himself*
	Of this natioun I knew also anone	*nation [of Scotland]; immediately*
	Gret Kennedy and Dunbar, yit undede,	*not yet dead*
	And Quyntyne with ane huttok on his hede.	*little hat*

925	Howbeit I couth declare and weil endyte,	*Even if I could put in words*
	The bonteis of that court dewlye to wryt	*virtues; sufficiently*
	Wer ovir prolyxt, transcendyng myne engyne	*abundant, exceeding my thinking*
	Twychand the proces of my panefull syte.	*Concerning; narrative; grief*
	Belive I saw thir lusty Musys quhyte	*At once*
930	With all thair route towart Venus declyne	*turn their course*
	Quhare Cupyd sat with hir in trone divyne,	
	I standand bundyn in a sory plyte	*tied up; plight*
	Bydand thair grace or than the dedly pyne.	*Awaiting; or else*

	Straucht til the quene sammyn thir Musis raid,	*Directly; together; rode*
935	Maist eloquently thare salutationys maid.	*made*
	Venus agane yald thaym thair salusyng	*in return gave; greeting*
	Rycht reverently and on hir fete upbraid,	*Very ceremoniously; arose*
	Besekand thaym to lycht. "Nay, nay," thay said,	*dismount*
	"We may as here make na lang tarying."	*while here*
940	Caliopé, maist facund and bening,	*eloquent; gracious*

Inquyryt Venus what wicht had hir mismaid	*Asked; person; upset*
Or wes the cause thair of hir sudjournyng.	*making a halt*
"Syster," sayd scho, "behald that bysnyng schrew.	*monstrous villain*
A subtyle smye — considyr weil his hew —	*rascal; take good notice of his hue*
945 Standis thair bond," and bykkynit hir to me.	*directed her attention*
"Yone cative hes blasphemyt me of new	*just now*
For tyl degraid and do my fame adew;	*make my reputation vanish*
A laithly ryme dispitefull subtellé	*hateful, spiteful rhyme craftily*
Compelit hes, rehersand loud on hie	*Has composed, reciting loud and clear*
950 Sclander, dispite, sorow and wallaway	*Slander, scorn; lamentation*
To me, my sonne, and eike my court for ay.	*also; forever*
"He hes deservit deth, he salbe dede,	*shall be*
And we remane forsuith in to this stede	*place*
Till justefy that rebell renygate."	*adjudge; renegade*
955 Quod Caliopé, "Sister, away all fede.	*retaliation*
Quhy suld he de? Quhy suld he leis his hede?	*lose*
To sla him for sa small a cryme, God wate,	*slay*
Greter degradyng wer to your estate	*debasement; noble rank*
All out than wes his sclander or sich plede.	*Utterly; before such controversy*
960 Quhow may a fule your hie renoun chakmate?	*fool; checkmate*
"Quhat of his lak! Your fame so wyd is blaw,	*So what for his slander; blown (spread)*
Your excellens maist peirles is so knaw,	*peerless; well-known*
Na wrichis word may depare your hie name.	*wretch's; impair*
Gyf me his lyfe and modefy the law,	*Give; tone down*
965 For, on my hed, he standis now sic aw	*by my judgment; is so afraid*
That he sall eft disserve nevir mare blame.	*never afterward merit further*
Not of his dede ye may report but schame.	*Nothing; death can you; except*
In recompence of this mysyttand saw	*offending speech*
He sall your hest in every part proclame."	*proclaim your bidding everywhere*
970 Than Lord quhow glad becam my febil gost!	*spirit*
My curage grew, the quhilk afore wes lost,	*spirits revived; before*
Seand I had so gret ane advocate	*Seeing*
That expertly, but prayer, pryce, or cost,	*without; bribe*
Opteynit had my frewel accion all most	*Won; frivolous lawsuit*
975 Quhilk wes afore perist and desolate.	*demolished; abandoned*
This quhyil Venus stude, in ane study strate,	*Meanwhile; in strict contemplation*
Bot fynally scho schew till all the ost	*signified; assemblage*
Scho wald do grace and be not obstinate.	*show mercy*
"I wyll," said sche, "have mercy and pyeté,	*pity*
980 Do slake my wreth and lat all rancour be.	*Reduce; set aside all rancor*
Quhare is mare vice than till be ovir cruel,	
And specially in wemen sic as me?	*such*

A lady, fy, that usis tirranné   *tyranny*
No woman is, rather a serpent fell.   *fierce*
985   A vennamus dragon or a devill of hell
Is na compare to the inequyté   *not equal; injustice*
Of bald wemen, as thir wyse clerkis tell.   *fierce; these*

"Gret God diffend I suld be ane of tho   *prohibit*
Quhilk of thare fede and malyce nevir ho!   *hostility; cease*
990   Out on sik gram, I wyll serve na repreif.   *trouble; deserve no reproof*
Caliope, sistir," said til Venus tho,   *Venus said then to [Calliope]*
"At your request this wreche sall frely go.
Heir I remyt his trespas, and all greif   *forgive; injury*
Salbe foryet, swa he wil say sum breif   *Shall be forgotten if; recite; letter*
995   Or schort ballat in contrare pane and wo,   *ballade; in opposition to*
Tuychand my laud and his plesand releif.   *Concerning; praise*

"And secundly the nixt resonabil command
Quhilk I him charge, se that he not ganestand.   *show resistance*
On thir conditions, sister, at your requeist,   *these*
1000 He sall go fre." Quod Caliope, inclynand,   *bowing*
"Grant mercy, sister. I oblys by my hand   *Great thanks; guarantee*
He sall observe in al poyntis your beheist."   *command*
Than Venus bad do slake sone my arreist.   *ordered my arrest to be dropped*
Belyve I wes releschit of every band,   *released from every restraint*
1005 Uprais the court and all the perlour ceist.   *discussion ceased*

Tho sat I doun lawly upon my kne   *Then; humbly*
At command of prudent Caliopé,
Yeildand Venus thankis a thousand sith   *Giving; times*
For sa hie frendschip and mercyfull pieté,   *great amity; pity*
1010 Excelland grace and gret humanyté,
The quhilk to me, trespassour, did scho kyth.   *show*
"I thee forgeve," quod sche. Than wes I blyth.   *happy*
Doun on a stok I set me suddanlye   *tree stump; seated myself*
At hir command and wrate this lay als swyth: *promptly wrote this song*

1015 "Unwemmyt wit, deliverit of dangear,   *Unblemished; rescued from*
Maist happely preservit fra the snare,   *fortunately*
Releschit fre of servyce and bondage,   *Released free from*
Expell dolour, expell diseyses sare,   *grievous distresses*
Avoyd displesour, womentyng, and care,   *Expel; lamenting*
1020 Ressave plesans and do thy sorowe swage,   *Accept; make; alleviate*
Behald thy glaid, fresche, lusty, grene curage,   *youthful spirit*
Rejois amyd thir lovers lait and air,   *late and early [always]*
Provyde a place till plant thy tendir age   *Prepare; youthful stage of life*
Quhair thou in joy and plesour may repair.   *visit*

1025   "Quha is in welth? quha is weill fortunat?   *Who; well-being*
       Quha is in peace, dissoverit from debbat?   *kept apart from strife*
       Quha levys in hop? quha levys in esperance?   *lives; hope [both times]*
       Quha standis in grace? quha standis in ferme estat?   *assured status*
       Quha is content, rejosyt air and lat,   *glad early and late*
1030   Or quha is he that fortune doith avance   *causes to advance*
       Bot thow, that is replenyst with plesance?   *well provided*
       Thow hes comfort, all weilfare dilligat;   *luxurious well-being*
       Thow hes gladnes, thow hes the happy chance,
       Thow hes thy wyll; now be not dissolat.   *cheerless*

1035   "Incres in myrthfull consolatioun,
       In joyus, swete ymaginatioun;
       Habond in luif of purifyit amouris   *Abound; love*
       With diligent trew deliberatioun;   *consideration*
       Rendir lovyngis for thy salvatioun   *praises*
1040   Till Venus; and, ondir hir gard all houris,   *protection*
       Rest at all ease, but sair or sytful schouris.   *without suffering or grievous pains*
       Abyde in quyet, maist constant weilfare.   *happiness*
       Be glaid and lycht now in thy lusty flouris,   *youth*
       Unwemmyt wyt, delyverit of dangare."   *rescued from (the lady's) disdain*

1045   This lay wes red in oppyn audience   *read in public hearing*
       Of the Musis and in Venus presence.   *Venus'*
       "I stand content thow art obedient,"   *remain satisfied*
       Quod Caliopé, my campion and defence.   *advocate and legal representative*
       Venus sayid eik it wes sum recompence   *said also; atonement*
1050   For my trespas I wes so penytent,
       And with that word all sodanly sche went.
       In ane instant scho and hir court wes hence,   *were gone*
       Yit still abayd thir Musis on the bent.   *remained; field*

       Inclynand than, I sayd, "Caliopé
1055   My protector, my help, and my supplé,   *rescue*
       My soverane lady, my redemptioun,
       My mediatour quhen I wes dampnyt to de,   *condemned to die*
       I sall beseik the Godly Majesté   *ask Lord God*
       Infynyt thankis, laud, and benysoun   *praise; blessing*
1060   Yow till acquyte, accordyng your renoun.   *to repay, befitting; renown*
       It langyth not my possibillité   *is not within my capacity*
       Till recompence ten part of this gwardoun.   *To repay a tenth part of this reward*

       "Glore, honour, laude, and reverence condyng   *praise, and suitable respect*
       Quha may foryeild yow of so hie a thyng?   *requite; for so high*
1065   And in that part your mercy I implore,
       Submyttand me my lyftyme induring
       Your plesour and mandate till obeysyng."   *to obey*

	"Silence," said scho, "I have eneuch heirfore.	*enough on this account*
	I will thow passe and vissy wondris more."	*decree; go to see more marvels*
1070	Than scho me hes betaucht in kepyng	*has entrusted me*
	Of a swete Nymphe, maist faythfull and decore.	*comely*

Ane hors I gat, maist rychely besene,   *got; richly decked out*
Was harnyst all with wodbynd levis grene.   *harnessed; woodbine leaves*
On the same sute the trappuris law doun hang.   *In; fashion; trappings; low*
1075 Ovir hym I straid at command of the quene.   *mounted*
Tho sammyn furth we rydyng all bedene   *together; rode; together*
Als swyft as thocht with mony a mery sang.   *thought*
My Nymphe alwayis convoyt me of thrang,   *guided me out of the crowd*
Amyd the Musys till se quhat thay wald mene,   *see what they intended*
1080 Quhilkis sang and playt bot nevir a wrest yeid wrang.   *tuning-peg went awry*

Throw cuntreis seir, holtis, and rochys hie,   *many countries, woods; cliffs*
Ovir valys, planys, woddis, wally se,   *valleys, plains; wave-tossed sea*
Ovir fludis fare and mony strate montane   *fine rivers; impassable*
We wer caryit in twynklyng of ane e.   *eye*
1085 Our horssis flaw and raid nocht, as thocht me.   *flew rather than ran; it seemed to me*
Now out of France tursyt in Tuskane,   *carried into Tuscany*
Now out of Flandris heich up in Almane,   *high; southern Germany*
Now in till Egypt, now in Ytalie,
Now in the realme of Trace, and now in Spane.   *Thrace*

1090 The montayns we passit of all Garmanie,
Ovir Appenynus devydand Ytalie,   *Apennines dividing*
Ovir Ryne, the Pow and Tirbir fludis fare,   *Rhine, the Po; Tiber*
Ovir Alpheus, by Pyes the ryche citie,   *Pisa*
Undir the erth that entres in the see;   *That flows underground into the sea*
1095 Ovir Ron, ovir Sane, ovir France and eik ovir Lare   *Rhône; Seine; Loire*
And ovir Tagus the goldin sandyt ryvare.
In Thessaly we passit the mont Oethé   *Oeta*
And Hercules in sepulture fand there.   *sepulchre*

Thare went we ovir the ryver Peneyus.   *Peneus*
1100 In Secil eik we passyt the mont Tmolus,   *Cilicia*
Plenyst with saphron, huny, and with wyne;   *Well stocked*
The twa toppyt famus Pernasus;   *twin-peaked*
In Trais we went out ovir the mont Emus   *Thrace; Haemus*
Quhare Orphius lerit his armony maist fyne,   *learned*
1105 Ovir Carmelus, quhare twa prophetis devyne
Remanyt, Helyas and Heliseus,   *Continued living, Elijah and Elisha*
Fra quhom the ordur of Carmelitis come syne;   *came afterwards*

And nixt untill the land of Amyson   *the Amazons*
In hast we past the flude Termodyon,   *Thermodon*

1110	And ovir the huge hill that hecht Mynas.	*Mimas*
	We raid the hill of Bachus Citheron	*crossed; Citheraon*
	And Olympus, the mont of Massidon,	*Macedonia*
	Quhilk semys heich up in the hevyn to pas.	
	In that countré we raid the flude Melas	
1115	Quhais watter makith quhite scheip blak anon;	*white sheep; immediately*
	In Europe eik we raid the flud Thanas;	*also; Don*

	We raid the swyft revere Sparthiades,	*Spercheios*
	The flud of Surry Achicorontes,	*river; Syria Orontes*
	The hill so full of wellis clepit Yda,	*named*
1120	Armany hillis and flude Eufrates,	*Armenian*
	The fluid of Nyle, the pretius flude Ganges,	*holy*
	The hyl of Secyle ay byrnand Ethna,	*Sicily; ever-burning*
	And ovir the mont of Frygy, Dindama,	*Phrygia, Dindyma*
	Hallowit in honour of the Modir Goddes;	*Consecrated*
1125	Cauld Cacasus we passit in Sythia;	*Cold Caucasus; Scythia*

	We passyt the fludis of Tygris and Phison,	
	Of Trace the riveris Hebrun and Strymon,	*Thrace; Hebrus*
	The mont of Modyn and the flud Jordane,	
	The facund well and hill of Elicon,	*ample*
1130	The mont Erix, the well of Acheron,	
	Baith didicat to Venus en certane.	*dedicated; doubtless*
	We past the hill and desert of Lybane,	*Libya*
	Ovir mont Cinthus quhare God Appollo schone,	*Cynthus; shone*
	Straucht to the Musis Caballyne fontane.	*Straight; Hippocrene*

1135	Besyde that cristall strand swete and degest,	*shining brook; calm*
	Them till repois, thayr hors refresch and rest,	*repose; horses*
	Alychtit doun thir Musis clere of hew.	*Alighted; complexion*
	The cumpany all halely, lest and best,	*together, of lowest status*
	Thrang to the well tyl drink, quhilk ran southwest	*Thronged*
1140	Throw out a meid quhare alkyn flouris grew.	*meadow; all sorts of flowers*
	Amang the layf, ful fast I did persew	*others; hasten*
	Tyll drynk, bot sa the gret pres me opprest	*throng crowded me*
	That of the watir I micht never tast a drew.	*drop*

	Our hors pasturyt in a plesand plane,	*pleasant open space*
1145	Law at the fute of a fare grene mountane,	
	Amyd a meid schadowed with cedir treys;	*shaded; cedar trees*
	Save fra al heit, thare micht we weil remane.	*Safe; heat*
	All kynd of herbis, flouris, frute, and grane	
	With every growand tre, thair men micht cheis.	*choose*
1150	The byrriall stremys rynnand ovyr sterny greis	*sparkling; flowing over glittering steps*
	Maid sobir noys; the schaw dynnyt agane	*Made (a) gentle sound; wood resounded back*
	For byrdys sang and soundyng of the beis.	*bees*

The ladyis fare on divers instrumentys   *fair*
Went playand, syngand, dansand ovir the bentis.   *dancing over the fields*
1155 Ful angelyk and hevynly wes thair soun.
Quhat creatour amid his hart imprentis   *Whatever being*
The fresche bewty, the gudly representis,   *appearances*
The mery spech, fare havinges, hie renounn —   *manners*
Of thaym wald set a wyse man halfe in swoun.   *Of these things [it]*
1160 Thair womanlynes writhyt the elementis,   *transformed*
Stonyst the hevyn and all the erth adoun.   *Astonished; below*

The warld may not consydyr nor discryve   *imagine; describe*
The hevynly joy, the blys I saw belyve,   *soon*
So ineffabill, abone my wyt so hie,   *above*
1165 I wyll na mare thairon my forhed ryve,   *rack my brains*
But breifly furth my febill proces dryve.   *forward; direct my feeble course*
Law in the meid a palyeon pycht I se,   *pavilion pitched*
Maist gudlyest and rychest that myght be.
My governour ofter than timys fyve   *more often*
1170 Untill that halde to pas commandit me,   *abode; go*

Swa fynally strycht to that rial steid   *straight; royal place*
In fallowschip with my leder I yeid.   *guide; went*
We entryt sone, the portar wes not thra,   *gate-keeper; stubborn*
Thare wes na stoppyng, lang demand nor pleid.   *dispute*
1175 I knelyt law and onheldit my heid,   *uncovered*
And tho I saw our Musis twa and twa
Sittand on deace, famylliaris to and fra   *Sitting; dais, familiar servants*
Servand thaym fast with Epocres and meid,   *spiced wine and mead*
Dilligate meatis, daynteis sere alswa.   *Tasty; many delicacies also*

1180 Grete wes the preis the feist ryall to sene.   *crowding*
At ease thay eit with interludyis betwene,   *ate; interludes between [courses]*
Gave problemys sere and mony fare demandis   *Posed various problems; questions*
Inquirand quha best in thair tymys had bene,   *Asking; had been best in their times*
Quha traist lovers in lusty yeris grene;   *Who [were] faithful; youthful years*
1185 Sum said this way and sum thairto ganstandis.   *disagree*
Than Caliope Ovid till appere commaundis: *commands to come forward*
"My clerk," quod scho, "of regestere, bedene   *official recorder, fully*
Declare quha wer maist worthy of their handis."   *deeds*

With lawrere crownyt at hir commaundment   *Crowned with laurel*
1190 Up stude this poet degest and eloquent   *poised*
And schew the fetis of Hercules the strang,   *feats*
Quhow he the grysly hellis houndis out rent,   *dragged out*
Slew lyonys, monstreis, and mony fell serpent,
And to the deth feil mychty giantis dang.   *many; struck*
1195 Of Thesyus eik he tald the weris lang   *narrated the long wars*

Agane the quene Ypollita the swete, *Against*
And quhow he slew the Mynotaure in Crete.

Of Persyus he tald the knychtly dedis
Quhilk vincussyt, as men in Ovid redis, *Who vanquished*
1200　Crewell tyrrantis and monsturis mony one;
Of Dianis bore in Callydon the dredis,[1]
Quhow throw a ladyis schot his sydis bledis,
The bretheris deith, and syne the systeris mone. *brothers' death; then; sister's lament*
He schew quhow Kyng Priamusis sonne Ysacon *son of King Priam, Aesacus*
1205　Efter his dede, body and all his wedis *clothes*
In till a skarth transformyt wes anon. *cormorant*

He schew at Troy quhat wyis the Grekis landis, *how the Greeks come ashore*
Quhow fers Achylles stranglyt wyth his handis *fierce*
The valyeant Cignus, Neptunus sonne maist dere, *Cycnus, Neptune's dearest son*
1210　Quhilk at Grekis aryvale on the strandis *Who during; arrival; beaches*
A thousand slew that day apon the sandis,
Faucht with Achill and blontit al his spere — *Fought; completely dulled his spear*
Na wapyn wes that micht him wond nor dere — *wound; injure*
Quhill Achylles bryst off his helm the bandis *Until; tore the straps off his helmet*
1215　And wyrryit hym be fors for all his fere. *strangled; by force despite; mightiness*

He schew full mony transmutationis *metamorphoses*
And wondirfull new figurationis *forms*
Be hondris mo than I have here expremyt. *hundreds more; identified*
He tald of lovys meditacionis, *expounded on discourses of love*
1220　The craft of love and the salvationis, *art; remedies*
Quhow that the furie lustis suld be flemyt. *frenzy [of] lusts; expelled*
Of divers other materis als he demyt, *topics; expressed opinions*
And, be his prudent scharpe relationys, *considering his; witty discourses*
He wes expart in all thyng, as it semyt. *appeared*

1225　Up rais the gret Virgilius anone *Virgil the great promptly stood up*
And playd the sportis of Daphnis and Coridon. *performed; pastimes*
Syne Therens come and playit the commedy *Terence*
Of Permeno, Thrason and wyse Gnaton. *Parmeno, Thraso; Gnatho*
Juvynale lik a mower hym allone *mocker by himself*
1230　Stud skornand every man as thay yeid by. *ridiculing; went*
Marcyall was cuyk till rost, seith, fars or fry, *cook to roast, boil, stuff*
And Pogyus stude with mony gyrn and grone, *snarl and groan*
On Laurence Valla spyttand and cryand fy. *spitting; fie*

---

[1] *The terrors in Calydon [caused] by Diana's boar*

With myrthys thus and meatis diligate, — *On entertainments; tasty dishes*

1235 Thir ladyis, festit accordyng thair estate, — *[having] feasted befitting their rank*
Uprais at last, commandand till tranoynt. — *giving the order to decamp*
Retret wes blawyn lowd, and than, God wate, — *Retreat; signaled*
Men micht have sene swyft horssys halden hate, — *kept at top speed*
Schynand for swete as thay had bene anoynt. — *Shining; sweat; anointed*

1240 Of all that rout wes never a pryk disjoynt — *jot out of place*
For all our tary, and I furth with my mate, — *sojourn; companion*
Montyt on hors, raid sammyn in gude poynt. — *together in fine style*

Ovir many gudly plane we raid bedene, — *at once*
The Vail of Ebron, the Campe Damascene, — *Vale of Hebron; Field*

1245 Throw Josaphat and throw the lusty vail, — *fine valley*
Ovir waters wan, thorow worthi woddis grene, — *dark, through fine*
And swa at last, in lyftyng up our eyne, — *eyes*
We se the fynall end of our travail, — *ultimate destination; travel*
Amyd ane plane a plesand roch till wail. — *flat expanse; crag; descry*

1250 And every wycht fra we that sycht had sene, — *once*
Thankand gret God, thare hedis law devail. — *bow their heads low*

With syngyng, lauchyng, merines, and play — *merriment*
On till that roch we rydyng furth the way. — *rock; ride*
Now mare till writ, for fere trymlys my pen. — *fear my pen trembles*

1255 The hart may not thynk nor manis toung say, — *heart; man's tongue*
The eyr not here nor yet the e se may, — *hear; can the eye see*
It may not be ymagyned with men, — *among*
The hevynly blys, the perfyte joy to ken — *to realize*
Quhilk now I saw; the hundreth part all day

1260 I micht not schaw, thocht I had tonges ten. — *could not show, even if*

Thocht al my membris tongis were on raw, — *Though; body parts were tongues in a row*
I wer not abill the thousand fald to schaw, — *the thousands of times; show*
Quhairfore I fere ocht forthirmare to wryte; — *anything more*
For quhiddir I this in saule or body saw, — *whether*

1265 That wait I not, bot he that all doth knaw, — *knew*
The gret God wait, in every thyng perfyt. — *perfect in every way*
Eik gyf I wald this avyssyon endyte, — *Also if; vision*
Janglaris suld it bakbyt and stand nane aw, — *Fault-finders; deride; feel no dread*
Cry "Out on dremes quhilkis ar not worth a myte." — *Away with; penny*

1270 Sen thys til me all verité be kend, — *Since; is known to me to be all truth*
I reput bettir thus till mak ane end — *consider; to end here*
Than ocht til say that suld herars engreve. — *to say anything; upset listeners*
On othir syd thocht thay me vilepend, — *On the opposing side; they mock me*
I considdir prudent folk will commend

1275 The vereté and sic janglyng rapreve. — *truth; censure such fault-finding*
With quhais correction, support, and releve — *help, and aid*

Furth till proceid this proces I pretend,   *continue this discourse; propose*
Traistand in God my purpose till escheve.   *Trusting; to achieve my purpose*

Quhowbeit I may not every circumstance   *Even though; detail*
1280   Reduce perfytly in rememorance,   *Capture; memory*
Myn ignorance yit sum part sal devyse   *shall describe*
Twychand this sycht of hevynly, swete plesance.   *Regarding*
Now empty pen, wryt furth thy lusty chance,   *onward; fine opportunity*
Schaw wondris fele, suppose thow be not wyse[1]
1285   Be dilligent and rypely thee avyse,   *maturely bethink thyself*
Be qwyke and scharpe, voydit of variance,   *lively and witty, purged of inconsistency*
Be swete, and cause not jentill hartis gryse.   *to shudder*

The Thyrd Parte

Ye Musis nyne, be in myne adjutory,   *at my aid*
That maid me se this blys and perfyte glory.
1290   Teche me your facund castis eloquent.   *ample, eloquent techniques*
Len me a recent, scharp, fresch memory   *Lend; undiminished, keen, vivid*
And caus me dewly til indyt this story.   *appropriately to compose*
Sum gratius swetnes in my brest imprent   *grace-endowed delightfulness; embed*
Till make the heraris bousum and attent,   *listeners compliant and attentive*
1295   Redand my wryt illumynyt with your lore;   *Reading; enlightened; teaching*
Infynyt thankis rendrand yow thairfore.

Now breifly to my purpose for til gone,   *to proceed concisely to my main point*
About the hyll lay ways mony one   *Around; hill; paths*
And to the hycht bot a passage ingrave,   *only one pathway carved out up to the summit*
1300   Hewyn in the roch of slyde, hard merbyll stone. *Hewn; slippery*
Aganne the sonne, lyk as the glas it schone.   *In the sunlight*
Ascens wes hie and strait for till consave,   *difficult to plan out*
Yit than thir Musis, gudly and suave,   *poised*
Alychtyt doun and clam the roch in hy   *climbed*
1305   With all the route, outtane my Nynphe and I.   *except*

Styl at the hillys fute we twa abaid,   *Still; base; two lingered*
Than suddandly my keper to me said,
"Ascend, galand!" Tho for fere I quuke.   *fine gentleman! Then; fear; trembled*
"Be not effrayit," scho said. "Be not mismaid,"   *upset*
1310   And with that word up the strait rod abraid.   *rushed up the narrow path*
I followit fast; scho be the hand me tuke;
Yit durst I nevir for dreid behynde me luke.

---

[1] *Reveal many marvels, even though you are unwise*

With mekill pane thus clam we nere the hycht, *great difficulty; climbed toward; peak*
Quhare suddandly I saw ane grysly sycht.

1315 As we approchit nere the hillis heid, *hilltop*
A terrible sewch — birnand in flawmys reid, *ditch; burning*
Abhominable and hol as heill to se, *deep as hell*
All full of bryntstane, pyk, and bulnyng leid, *brimstone, pitch, and boiling lead*
Quhair mony wrechit creatour lay deid
1320 And miserable catywis yeland loude one hie — *wretches; yelling in [a] high [voice]*
I saw, quhilk den mycht wele comparit be *a ravine that could well be compared*
Till Xantus the fluid of Troy so schill *Xanthus; cold*
Byrnand at Venus' hest contrar Achill. *Burning; command against*

Amyd our passage lay this wgly sicht, *ugly sight*
1325 Not brayd, but so horrible till eviry wicht *broad*
That all the warld to pas it suld have dreid.
Wele I considerit nene upparmar I mycht, *thought I could [go] no further up*
And to discend, sa hiddous wes the hicht,
I durst not aventur for this erth on breid. *attempt; for this wide world*
1330 Trymland I stud with teith chatterand gud speid. *Trembling; [at] high speed*
My Nymphe beheld my cheir and said "Lat be, *noticed my face; Enough*
Thou sall not aill, and lo the caus," quod sche. *suffer; here [is] the reason*

"To me thou art commyt. I sall thee keip. *entrusted; take care of you*
Thir pieteous pepill amyd theis laithly deip *pitiful; this hateful chasm*
1335 War wrechis quhilkis in lusty yeris fair *Were wretches who in vigorous years*
Pretendit thaym till hie honour to creip *Put themselves forward to; creep*
Bot suddandly thay fell on sleuthfull sleip *slothful*
Followand plesance, drynt in this loch of cair." *drowned; lake of sorrow*
And with that word, sche hynt me by the hair, *grabbed*
1340 Caryit me to the hillis hed anone *summit*
As Abacuk wes brocht in Babilone. *Habakkuk; brought into Babylon*

As we bene on the hie hill sittuate, *Once; positioned*
"Luke doun," quod scho, "Consave in quhat estat *Determine in what condition*
Thy wrechyt warld thou may considdir now." *estimate now [to be]*
1345 At hir command with mekill dreid, God wate, *great fear*
Out ovir the hill sa hiddous, hie, and strate *steep*
I blent adoun and feld my body grow. *looked down; felt; tremble*
This brukkill erth, sa littyl to allow, *crumbling; little to be commended*
Me thocht I saw byrn in a fyry rage *It seemed to me; burn*
1350 Of stormy see, quhilk mycht na maner swage. *which could in no way relent*

That terribbill tempest, hiddous wallys huge, *waves*
Wer maist grysly for till behald or juge, *estimate*
Quhare nothyr rest nor quyet mycht appere. *neither*
Thare wes a peralus palyce, folk to luge. *to house*

1355   Thare wes na help, support, nor yet refuge.
        Innowmerabill folk I saw flottrand in fere   *Innumerable; floundering together*
        Quhilk peryst on the weltrand wallys were;   *were sunk in the tossing waves*
        And secondly I saw a lusty barge   *fine boat*
        Ovirset with seyes and mony stormy charge.   *Beset by seas; surge*

1360   This gudly carvel — taiklyt traist on raw   *rigged secure in order*
        With blanschyt sail, mylk quhyte as ony snaw,   *bleached; snow*
        Rycht sover tycht, and wondir strangly beildyt —   *securely watertight; built*
        Wes on the boldyn wallys quyte ovirthraw.   *swollen waves utterly capsized*
        Contrariusly the bustuus wynd did blaw   *In opposition; rough; blow*
1365   In bubbys thik, that na schip sail mycht weld it.   *heavy squalls, so; could navigate*
        Now sank scho law, now hie tyl hevyn upheldyt.   *she; raised*
        At every part the see and wyndis drave,   *thrust*
        Quhill on a sand the schip tobryst and clave.   *sandbar; broke apart; split*

        It wes a pietuus thyng, allake allake,   *pitiful*
1370   Till here the duylfull cry quhen that scho strake, *hear; sorrowful; ran aground*
        Maist lamentabill the peryst folk till se   *shipwrecked*
        Sa famyst, drokyt, mait, forwrocht and wake,   *famished, wet, defeated, tired; weak*
        Sum on a plank of firre and sum of ake,   *oak*
        Sum hang apon takill, sum on a tre,   *rigging; mast*
1375   Sum fra thair gryp sone weschyne with the se.   *[dislodged] from; washed away*
        Part drynt, and part to the rolke flet or swam.   *Some drowned; crag floated*
        On rapis or burdis syne up the hill thay clam.   *ropes or planks then; climbed*

        Tho at my Nynphe breifly I did inquere
        Quhat sygnyfyit tha feirfull wondris sere.   *many fearsome portents*
1380   "Yone multitude," said scho, "of pepill drint   *drowned people*
        Ar faythles folk, quhilkis quhyle thay ar here
        Mysknawys God and followys thare plesere,   *Fail to acknowledge God*
        Quhairfore thay sall in endles fyre be brynt.
        Yone lusty schip thow seyst peryst and tynt,   *wrecked and lost*
1385   In quhame yone pepill maid ane parralus race,   *journey*
        Scho heycht the Carvell of the State of Grace.   *She is called*

        "Ye bene all borne the sonnys of ire, I ges,   *guess*
        Syne throw baptyme gettis grace and faythfulnes,   *baptism*
        Than in yone carvell suyrly ye remane,   *safely*
1390   Oft stormstad with this warldis brukkyllnes,   *beset by storms; uncertainty*
        Quhill that ye fall in synne and wrachitnes;   *Until; wretchedness*
        Than schipbrokyn sall ye droun in endles pane   *shipwrecked*
        Except bye fayth ye fynd the plank agane,
        Bye Chryst, vorkyng gud vorkys, I onderstand.   *working; works*
1395   Remane thair with, thir sall you bryng to land.   *Stay with that, these shall bring you*

	"This may suffice," said scho, "twychand this part.	*concerning this direction*
	Returne thy hed, behald this othir art,	*Turn back; district*
	Considdir wondris and be vigyllant	
	That thow may bettir endytyng eftirwart	*write afterwards*
1400	Thyngis quhilkis I sall thee schaw or we depart.	*before*
	Thow sall have fouth of sentence and not skant.	*abundance of language; scant*
	Thare is no welth nor welfare thow sall want.	*happiness; lack*
	The gret palyce of Honour salt thou se.	
	Lift up thy hed, behald that sicht," quod sche.	
1405	At hir commaund I rasit hie on hycht	*raised up high*
	My vissage till behald that hevenly sycht.	
	Bot tyl discryve this matter in effek	*in fact*
	Impossibill wer till ony erdly wicht;	*for any earthly being*
	It transcendes sa far abone my micht	*above*
1410	That I with ynk may do bot paper blek.	*can only make paper blackened*
	I man draw furth; the yok lyis in my nek,	*must pull onward; the yoke lies upon*
	As of the place to say my lewd avyse,	*offer my ignorant opinion*
	Plenyst with plesance, lyke to parradyce.	*Filled with delight*
	I saw a plane of peirles pulcritude	*plain; peerless beauty*
1415	Quhare in abondyt every thingis gude:	*In which abounded all*
	Spyce, wyne, corn, ule; tre, frute, flour, herbis grene,	*olive oil; timber*
	All foulys, bestis, byrdys and alkynde fude,	*fowls; every [sort of] foodstuff*
	All maner fyschis, bayth of see and flude,	*salt and fresh water*
	Wer kepit in pondis of polist silver schene	*polished, shiny silver*
1420	With purifyit wattir as of the cristall clene.	
	Till noy the small the grete bestis had na will,	*hurt the small animals*
	Nor ravanus fowlys the littil volatill.	*birds of prey; little birds*
	Styll in the season all thyng remanyt thare;	*Always in season everything*
	Perpetually, but othir noy or sare,	*without either hurt or harm*
1425	Ay rypyt were bayth herbys, frute, and flouris.	*Always ripened*
	Of every thyng the namys till declare	
	Until my febill wyt impossybill ware.	*To; would be impossible*
	Amyd the med replete of swete odouris,	*meadow abounding with*
	A palyce stude with mony riall touris	*stood; magnificent towers*
1430	Quhare kernellys quent, feil turretis, men mycht fynd	*ingenious crenels; many*
	And goldyn fanys wavand with the wynd.	*banners*
	Pynnakillis, fyellis, tournpikes mony one,	*Turrets, finials, spiral staircases*
	Gylt, byrnyst torris, quhilk lyk til Phebus schone,	*Gilded, polished knobs*
	Skarsement, repryse, corbell, and battelyngis,	*Ledges, recesses; battlements*
1435	Fulyery, borduris of mony pretius stone,	*Sculpted foliage; borders; precious*
	Suttyl muldry wrocht mony day agone	*moldings; ago*

On buttres, jalmys, pilleris, and plesand spryngis.[1]   *Lifelike motifs*
Quyke ymagry with mony lusty syngis
Thare mycht be sene, and mony worthy wychtis
1440   Tofore the yet arrayit all at rychtis.   *gate; in every way*

Furth past my Nymphe; I followyt subsequent.   *On went*
Straucht throw the plane to the first ward we went   *yard; precinct*
Of the palyce and entryt at that port.   *gate*
Thare saw we mony statelie tornament,
1445   Lancis brokyn, knychtis layd on the bent.   *knocked to the ground*
Plesand pastance and mony lusty sport   *entertainment*
Thair saw we als, and sum tyme battel mort.   *also; mortal combat*
"All thir," quod scho, "on Venus service vakis   *spend time in service of Venus*
In dedis of armys for thayr ladyis sakis.

1450   Vissyand I stude the principal place but pere,   *I stood inspecting; without peer*
That hevynly Palyce, all of crystall clere,
Wrocht, as me thocht, of polyst beriall stone.
Bosiliall nor Oliab, but were,   *Bezaleel; Aholiab, without doubt*
Quhilk Sancta Sanctorum maid, maist ryche and dere,   *the Ark of the Covenant*
1455   Nor he that wrocht the tempill of Salomon,
Nor he that beild the riall Ylyon,   *built; Ilion*
Nor he that forgete Darius sepulture   *constructed*
Couth not performe sa craftely a cure.   *carry out a project so skilfully*

Studiand here on, my Nimphe on to me spak,   *While [I was] gazing at this*
1460   "Thus in a stare quhy standis thou stupefak,   *in a state of wonderment; stupefied*
Govand all day and na thyng hes vissyte.   *Gaping; viewed*
Thow art prolixt. In haist retourn thy bak.   *tiresome; Quickly turn thy back*
Go efter me, and gud attendence tak.   *pay close attention*
Quhat thow seyst, luke eftirwartis thow write.   *take care*
1465   Thow sall behald all Venus blys perfyte."   *bliss*
Thair with sche till ane garth did me convoy   *garden; convey*
Quhare that I saw eneuche of perfyte joy.   *plenty*

Amyd a trone with stonys ryche ovirfret   *adorned with costly jewels*
And claith of gold, Lady Venus wes set.   *cloth; seated*
1470   By hir, hir sonne Cupyd quhilk nathing seys.   *who sees nothing*
Quhare Mars entrit, na knawlege mycht I get,   *entered; information could*
Bot straucht afore Venus vissage but let   *right in front of; directly*
Twelf amarant stagis stude, twelf grene precius greis,   *emerald tiers; steps*
Quhare on thare grew thre curius goldyn treis   *trees*
1475   Sustenttand weil the goddis face aforne   *Carrying; before the goddess' face*
A fair myrrour, be thaym quently upborn.   *ingeniously supported by them*

---

[1] *On buttresses, jambs, pillars, and pleasing arch supports*

Quhare of it makyt wes, I have na feil — *Of what substance it was made; sense*
Of beriall, cristall, glas, or byrnyst steil, *beryl; steel*
Of diamant or of the carbunkill jem — *carbuncle stone*
1480 Quhat thing it wes diffyne may I not weil, *I cannot adequately describe*
Bot all the bordure circulare, every deill, *circular frame; detail*
Wes plate of gold — cais, stok and uthir hem — *frame, base and edging*
With vertuus stanis picht that blud wald stem. *powerful jewels set; bleeding; stop*
For quha that wound wes in the tornament *whoever was wounded*
1485 Wox hale fra he apon the myrrour blent. *Became healed once; looked*

This riall rillik, so ryche and radius, *treasure; radiant*
Sa pollyst, plesand, purifyed, precius,
Quhoys bontyis half to wryt I not presume, *Half of whose powers; I cannot*
Thairon tyll se wes sa dellicius *delightful*
1490 And sa excelland schadois gratius, *[with] such very lovely reflections*
Surmontyng far in brichtnes, to my dome, *Exceeding; by my opinion*
The costly, subtil, quent spectacle of Rome *ingenious, elegant mirror*
Or yet the myrrour send to Canycé *Canace*
Quhairin men micht ful many wondrys se.

1495 In that myrrour I mycht se at a sycht
The dedes and fetes of every erdly wycht, *deeds and feats; earthly being*
All thinges gone lyk as they wer present,
All the creacion of the angellys brycht,
Of Lucifer the fall for all his mycht,
1500 Adam fyrst maid and in the erth ysent. *banished into the world*
And Noys flude thair saw I subsequent, *Noah's*
Babilon beild, that toure of sic renoun, *Babel built; such*
Of Sodomus the fele subversyoun. *massive overthrow*

Abram, Ysak, Jacob, Josoph I saw, *Isaac*
1505 Hornyt Moyses with his ald Ebrew law, *Horned*
Twelf plagis in Egypt sent for thair trespas, *plagues*
In the Reid See with al hys court on raw *Red Sea; one after another*
Kyng Pharo drynt that God wald nevir knaw — *drowned; would never acknowledge*
I saw quhat wyse the see devydyt was
1510 And all the Ebrewes dry fut ovir it pas — *walked dry-shod across it*
Syne in desert I saw thaym fourty yeris.
Of Josuy I saw the worthy weris. *Joshua; honorable wars*

In Judicum, the batellis strang anone *Judges; fierce battles straightaway*
I saw of Jepty and of Gedione, *Jepthah; Gideon*
1515 Of Ameleth the cruel homosyd, *Abimelech; homicide[s]*
The wonderful werkis of douchty duke Sampsone *brave*
Quhilk slew a thousand with ane assys bone, *a donkey's [jaw]-bone*
Rent templis doun and yettis in his pryde, *gates*
Of quhais strenth mervalys this warld so wyde.

1520	I saw duke Sangor there with many a knok	*Shamgar*
	Sax hundreth men slew with a plewchis sok.	*ploughshare*
	The praphet Samuell saw I in that glas	*mirror*
	Anoynt Kyng Saule, quhais sonne Jonathas	*whose*
	I saw wyncus ane gret ost hym allane;	*vanquish; army by himself*
1525	Yong David sla the grysly Golyas	*[I saw] Young David slay; Goliath*
	Quhais speirheid wecht thre hundreth uncis was,	*Whose spear-head['s] weight; ounces*
	Jesbedonab the giant mekill of mane	*of great might*
	Lay be the handis of douchty Davyd slane,	*Lay dead at the hands of brave David*
	With fyngris sax on athir hand, but weir.	*six fingers; each; without doubt*
1530	David I saw sla baith lyon and beir.	*bear*
	This David, eik, at ane onset astond,	*also; surprised at an ambush*
	Aucht hundreth men I saw hym bryng to grond.	
	With hym I saw Bananyas the strang	
	Quhilk twa lyonys of Moab did confond	*two; defeat*
1535	And gave the stalwart Ethiop dedis wond	*a fatal wound*
	With his awyn spere that of his hand he thrang.	*he forced out of his hand*
	Onabysytly this champion saw I gang	*Boldly; go*
	In a deip sistern and thare a lyon slewch	*cistern; slew*
	Quhilk in a storme of snaw did harm eneuch.	*snow did plenty of harm*
1540	Of Salomon the wysdom and estate	
	Thare saw I, and his ryche tempill, God wate;	
	His sonne Roboam, quhilk throw his hely pride	*Rehoboam; overweening*
	Tynt all his ligis hartis be his fate.	*Lost; lieges' loyalty; action*
	He wes to thaym sa outragius ingrate,	*grossly ungrateful*
1545	Of twelf tribis, ten did fra hym devyd.	*ten separated from him*
	I saw the angell sla be nychtis tyd	*at night*
	Four score thousandis of Synachorybis ost	*Sennacherib's army*
	Quhilkis come to weir on Jowry with gret bost.	*wage war; Judea; much threatening*
	I saw the lyfe of the Kyng Esachy	*Hezekiah*
1550	Prolongit fifteen yere, and the prophet Hely	*Elijah*
	Amyd a fyry chare to Paradyce went.	*In a blazing chariot*
	The stories of Esdras and of Neamy	*Ezra; Nehemiah*
	And Danyell in the lyonys cave saw I,	
	For he the dragon slew, Bell brak and schent;	*broke and destroyed Bel*
1555	The chyldir thre amyd the fornace sent;	*three youths into*
	I saw the transmygracion in Babillon	*exile into*
	And baith the bukis of Paralipomenon.	*Chronicles*
	I saw the haly archangell Raphell	*Raphael*
	Mary Sara the dochter of Raguell	*Marry; daughter of Raguel*
1560	On Thobyas for his just fatheris sake,	*To Tobias*
	And bynd the crewell devyll that wes sa fel	*cruel; fierce*

Quhilk slew hir sevin first husbandis, as tha tel;
And quhow Judyth Olyfarnus heid of strake   *cut off Holophernes' head*
Be nychtis tyd and fred hir town fra wrake;   *At night time; freed her; destruction*
1565   Jonas in the quhalys wame dais thre   *whale's belly three days*
And schot furth syne, I saw, at Ninive.   *vomited forth afterwards; Nineveh*

Of Job I saw the patyence maist degest;   *most calm*
Of Alexander I saw the gret conquest,
Quhilk in twelf yeris wan nere the warld on breid;   *conquered almost the whole world*
1570   And of Anthiacus the gret onrest,   *Antiochus; turmoil*
Quhow tyrrand lyk all Jowrye he opprest;   *tyrannically; Judea; oppressed*
Of Macabeus, full mony knychtly deid   *Judas Maccabeus; deed*
That gart all Grece and Egypt stand in dreid,   *made; hold back; fear*
In quyet brocht his realm throw his prowes;   *To peace brought*
1575   I saw his brethir Symon and Jonathas,

Quhilkis wer maist worthy quhil thair dayis rang.   *during their lifetimes*
Of Tebes eik I saw the weris lang,   *I saw the protracted wars of Thebes*
Quhare Thedeus allone slew fyfty knychtis;   *Tydeus*
Quhow fynaly of Grece the campyonys strang,   *mighty champions of Greece*
1580   All hail the floure of knychtheid, in that thrang[1]
Wes distroyit, quhill Thesyus with his mychtis   *until; forces*
The toun and Creon wan for all his slychtis.   *conquered despite; tricks*
Thare saw I quhow, as Stacius dois tell,   *Statius*
Amphiorax the bischop sank to Hel.

1585   The faithfull ladyis of Grece I mycht considdir   *could perceive*
In clathis blak all barfute pas togyddir   *black clothes; barefoot walk together*
Till Thebes sege, fra thair lordis wer slane.   *To the siege of Thebes, after*
Behald, ye men that callys ladyis liddir   *indecisive*
And lycht of latis, quhat kyndnes brocht thaym thidder,   *flighty of behavior; generosity*
1590   Quhat treuth and luif did in thair brestis remane.   *faithfulness*
I traist ye sall reid in na wryt agane   *expect [that]; in no text elsewhere*
In a realme sa mony of sic constance.   *loyalty*
Persave thairby wemen ar til avance.   *Recognize; to be praised*

Of duke Pyrrotheus the spousage in that tyd   *wedding; time*
1595   Quhare the Centauris reft away the bryd   *carried off the bride*
Thare saw I and thair battell huge till se,   *to see*
And Hercules, quhais renoun walkis wyd,   *is widespread*
For Exiona law by Troyis syd   *Hesione down; shore*
Fecht and ovircome a monsture of the se,
1600   For quhilk, quhen his reward denyit wes, he   *was disallowed*

---

[1] *All the best (soldiers) of knightly rank, in that melée*

Maid the first sege and the distructioun
Of mychty Troy, quhylum the rial town.   *once*

To wyn the fleys of gold, tho saw I sent   *fleece; then*
Of Grece the nobillis with Jason consequent,   *nobles along with Jason*
1605   Hail that conquest and all Medeas slychtis,   *Medea's wiles*
Quhow for Jason Ysiphile wes schent,   *Hypsipyle was ruined*
And quhow to Troy as thay to Colchos went,
Grekis tholyt of Kyng Lamedon gret onrychtis,   *suffered from; injustices*
Quhairfore Troy distroyt wes be thair mychtis,   *was destroyed by; forces*
1610   Exiona ravyst, and Lamedon slane,   *Hesione abducted*
Bot Priamus restoryt the town agane.

The jugement of Parys saw I syne   *then*
That gave the appil, as poetis can diffyne,   *apple; poets recount*
Till Venus as goddes maist gudlye,   *the most beautiful goddess*
1615   And quhow in Grece he revest quene Helyne,   *abducted*
Quharefore the Grekis with thair gret navyne,   *navy*
Full mony thosand knychtis, hastely   *thousand*
Thaym till revenge, salyt towart Troy in hye.   *sailed; with speed*
I saw quhow be Ulixes with gret joy   *by*
1620   Quhat wyse Achil wes fond and brocht to Troy.   *By what means; discovered; brought*

The crewel battellys and the dyntis strang,   *mighty blows*
The gret debate and eik the weris lang   *quarrel; lengthy hostilities*
At Troy sege, the myrrour to me schew,   *siege; showed me*
Sustenit ten yeris, Grekis Troianys amang,   *Protracted; amid [the] Trojans*
1625   And athir party set ful oft in thrang,   *placed; melée*
Quhare that Hector did douchty dedis enew   *courageous deeds aplenty*
Quhilk fears Achil — baith hym and Troylus — slew.   *Whom fierce*
The gret hors maid, I saw, and Troy syn tynt,   *horse built; then destroyed*
And fair Ylion al in flambys brynt.   *all burnt up in flames*

1630   Syne out of Troy I saw the fugityvys,
Quhow that Eneas, as Virgill weil discrivis,
In countries seir wes by the seis rage   *many lands was; sea's*
Bewavyt oft, and quhow that he arryvys   *Swept repeatedly*
With all his flote, but danger of theyr lyvys,   *fleet, without*
1635   And quhow thay wer reset, baith man and page,   *sheltered, both; child*
Be quene Dido, remanand in Cartage,   *By; abiding*
And quhow Eneas syne, as that they tell,   *afterwards*
Went for to seik his father doun in Hell.   *seek*

Ovir Stix the flude I saw Eneas fair,   *go*
1640   Quhare Carone wes the bustuus feryair.   *Charon; rough-mannered ferryman*
The fludis four of Hell thair mycht I se,   *four rivers; could I see*
The folk in pane, the wayis circulair,   *circular paths*

The weltrand stone wirk Sisipho mych cair,   *rolling; cause; much grief*
And all the plesance of the Camp Elysee,   *Elysian Fields*
1645   Quhare ald Anchyses did common with Enee   *converse; Aeneas*
And schew be lyne all his successyon.   *by descent; lineage*
This ilk Eneas, maist famus of renoun,   *same*

I saw to goddis make the sacrifice,
(Quhairof the ordour and maner to devyse   *Of which; sequence; itemize*
1650   Wer ovir prolext) and quhow Eneas syne   *Would be too lengthy*
Went to the schyp; and eik I saw quhat wyse   *also I saw in what manner*
All his navy gret hunger did suppryse;   *Great hunger afflicted his entire navy*
Quhow he in Italie fynalie with huge pyne   *great difficulty*
Arrivit at the strandis of Lavyne,   *shores*
1655   And quhow he faucht weil baith on land and seys
And Tarnus slew, the kyng of Rutuleis.   *slew Turnus; Rutulians*

Rome saw I beildit fyrst be Romulus,   *first built by*
And eik quhow lang, as wryttis Levius,   *Livy writes*
The Romane kyngis abone the pepill rang;   *ruled over the people*
1660   And how the wickit proud Terquinius,
With wyfe and barnis, be Brutus Junius   *children, by*
Wer exilit Rome for thair insufferabil wrang,   *exiled [from]; unendurable*
Bot al the proces for to schaw wer lang   *narrative; show would be*
Quhow chast Lucres, the gudliest and best,   *most beautiful and virtuous*
1665   Be Sextus Terquine wes cruelly opprest.   *overcome*

The Punik batalis in that mirrour cleir   *Punic Wars*
Atwene Cartage and Romanis mony yeir   *Between*
I saw, becaus Eneas pietuus   *for the reason that pious Aeneas*
Fled fra Dido be admonicionis seir.   *because of many warnings*
1670   Atwene thair pepil rais ane langsum weir.   *Between their nations; protracted war*
I saw quhow worthy Marcus Regulus,
Maist valiant, prudent, and victorius,
Howbeit he micht at liberty gone fre,   *Even though*
For common profyt chesyt for till de.   *public benefit chose to die*

1675   Tullus Servilius dowchty in his daw   *Servius Tullius valiant in his lifetime*
And Curtyus eik in the myrrour I saw,   *Curtius; also*
Quhilk throw his stowtenes in the fyry gap   *Who because of his courage: abyss*
For common profyt of Rome him self did thraw   *throw*
Richt onabasitly, havand na dreid nor aw,   *fearlessly; hesitation*
1680   Montit on hors, onarmyt, thairin lap;   *Mounted; without weapons; leapt*
And Hannyball I saw by fatell hap   *destined advantage*
Wyn contrare Romanys mony fair victory   *against*
Quhyll Scipio eclypsyt all hys glory.   *Until; eclipsed*

This worthy Scipio clepyt Affrycane | *named Africanus*
1685 I saw vincus thys Hannyball in plane | *defeat; on the battlefield*
And Cartage bryng untyll fynall rewyn, | *to ultimate destruction*
And to Rome conquerit all the realme of Spane. | *subjected*
Quhow Kyng Jugurtha hes his brethir slane | *has killed his brothers*
Thare saw I eik, and of his were the fyne. | *also, and the outcome of his war*
1690 Rycht weil I saw the batellis intestyne | *civil wars*
Of Catulyna and of Lentulus,
And atwine Pompey and Cesar Julyus; | *between*

And breifly, every famus douchty deid | *in short; mighty exploit*
That men in story may se, or cornakyll reid. | *read [in] chronicle[s]*
1695 I mycht behald in that myrrour expres | *definitely*
The miserie, the crewelté, the dreid,
Pane, sorow, wo, baith wretchitnes and neid, | *both misery and indigence*
The gret envy, covatus, dowbilnes | *covetousness, treachery*
Twychand warldly onfaithful brukkylnes. | *Concerning worldly false instability*
1700 I saw the Fend fast folk to vicis tist | *Devil ceaselessly; lure into vices*
And al the cumming of the Antecrist.

Plesand debaitmentis, quha sa rycht reportis, | *recreations, whoever; tells*
Thare mycht be sene, and al maner disportys: | *all kinds [of] entertainments*
The falkonnis for the revere at thair gate | *falcons on their way to the river*
1705 Newand the fowlys in periculo mortis, | *Chasing; danger of death*
Layand thaym in be companeis and sortis; | *Bringing them in by flocks; species*
And at the plunge, part saw I handlyt hate. | *during the dive, some; treated roughly*
The wery huntare, byssy ayr and late | *weary; busy early*
Wyth questyng hundis, syrchand to and fra | *searching*
1710 To hunt the hart, the bare, the da, the ra. | *boar; doe; roe-deer*

I saw Raf Coilyear with his thrawin brow, | *Ralph the Collier; frowning*
Craibit Johne the Reif and auld Cowkewyis sow | *Irritable; Reeve; Colkelbie's*
And how the wran come out of Ailssay, | *wren; Ailsa Craig*
And Peirs Plewman that maid his workmen fow, | *well-fed*
1715 Gret Gowmakmorne and Fyn Makcoull and how | *Goll mac Morna; Finn mac Cumhaill*
Thay suld be goddis in Ireland as thay say. | *used to be*
Thair saw I Maitland upon auld Beird Gray,
Robene Hude and Gilbert with the quhite hand,
How Hay of Nauchtoun flew in Madin land. | *Fairyland*

1720 The nigramansy thair saw I eik anone | *magic*
Of Bonitas, Bongo, and frere Bacon, | *Bonatti, Bungay; friar*
With mony subtell poynt of juglory: | *feat of conjuring*
Of Flandris peys, maid mony precius stone, | *peas*
A gret lade sadil of a sychyng bone, | *pack-saddle; sighing*
1725 Of a nutmog, thay mayid a monk in hy, | *nutmeg; made; in haste*
A parys kirk of a small penny py, | *parish church; pie*

And Bonytas of a mussil made ane ape,   *mussel*
With mony othir subtell mow and jape.   *clever jest; trick*

        And schortly til declare the veryté,   *briefly to state the truth*
1730   All plesand pastance and gemmys that micht be,   *pastime and games; could*
        In that myrrour wer present to my sycht.
        And as I wondryt on that grete ferlye,   *spectacle*
        Venus at last in turning of hir e   *her gaze*
        Knew weil my face and said, "Be Goddis micht,
1735   Ye bene welcum, my presoner, to this hycht.   *summit*
        Quhow passit thou," quod scho, "that hidduus depe?"   *chasm*
        "Madame," quod I, "I not more than a schepe."   *do not know any more; sheep*

        Na fors thairof," said scho, "Sen thow art here,   *No matter about that; Since*
        Quhow plesys thee our pastance and effere?"   *pleases; entertainment and ceremony*
1740   "Glaidly," quod I, "Madame, be God of hevyn."
        "Remembris thow," said scho, "withouten were   *without doubt*
        On thy promyt quhen of thy gret dangere   *promise; peril*
        I thee deliverit — as now is not to newyn?"   *liberated; which; need not be specified*
        Than answerit I agane with sober stevyn,   *in a serious tone of voice*
1745   "Madame, your precept, quhat so be your wyll,   *command, whatever*
        Here I remane ay reddy till fulfill."

        "Weil, weil," said scho, "thy wyll is suffycyent.
        Of thy bousoum answere I stand content."   *obedient*
        Than suddandly in hand a buke scho hynt   *she took a book*
1750   The quhilk to me betaucht scho or I went,   *she entrusted to me before*
        Commandand me to be obedient
        And put in ryme that proces, than quyt tynt.   *narrative, then utterly lost*
        I promised hir, forsuyth, or scho wald stynt,   *even before she was finished*
        The buke ressavand, thairon my cure to preve.   *Receiving the book; to try my skill*
1755   Inclynand syne lawly, I tuke my leve.   *made my exit*

        Twychand this buke, peraventur ye sall here   *Concerning; perhaps; hear*
        Sumtyme efter quhen I have mare lasere.   *leisure*
        My Nymphe in hast tho hynt me by the hand   *took*
        And as we sammyn walkyt furth in fere,   *walked onward together side by side*
1760   "I thee declare," sayd scho, "yone myrrour clere,
        The quhilk thow saw afore dame Venus stand
        Signifyes nothing ellis till understand   *else*
        Bot the gret bewty of thir ladyis facis,
        Quhairin lovers thinkis thay behald all gracis."   *see all special favors*

1765   Scho me convoyit, finally to tell,   *brought me*
        With gret plesance straucht to the ryche castell,   *much delight straight*
        Quhare mony saw I pres til get ingres.   *try to get entry*
        Thare saw I Synon and Achittefell

	Pressand til clym the wallis, and how thay fell.	*Pushing forward to climb the walls*
1770	Lucyus Catalyn saw I thare expres,	*Catiline; indeed*
	In at a wyndow pres til have entres,	*push to gain entry*
	Bot suddandly Tullius come with a buke	*Cicero came*
	And strake hym doun quhill all his chaftis quuke.	*struck; until; jaws trembled*
	Fast clymmand up thay lusty wallys of stone	*those fine stone walls*
1775	I saw Jugurtha and tressonabill Tryphon,	
	Bot thay na grippis thair mycht hald for slyddir.	*grip could hold there; slipperiness*
	Preissand to clym stude thousandis many one,	*Thronging; many thousands*
	And into the ground thay fallen, every one.	*they fall*
	Than on the wall a garatour I considdir,	*tower watchman*
1780	Proclamand lowd, that did thayr hartis swiddir,	*made their hearts quake*
	"Out on falshed, the mother of everye vyce,	*Away with falsehood*
	Away invy and brynnand covetyce."	*burning covetousness*
	The garatour, my Nymphe tho to me tald,	*then*
	Wes clepyt Lawté, kepar of the hald	*named Loyalty, guard; stronghold*
1785	Of hie Honour, and thay pepyll out schete,	*expelled*
	Swa presand thaym to clym, quilum wer bald,	*exerting themselves; once; bold*
	Rycht vertuus young, but fra tyme thay woux ald,	*grew old*
	Fra honour hail one vice thair mindis sete.	*entirely on; fixed*
	"Now sall thow go," quod sche, "straucht to the yete	*gate*
1790	Of this palyce and entre but offence,	*without*
	For the portar is clyped Pacience.	*gatekeeper; named*
	"The mychty prynce, the gretest Empriour	
	Of yone Palyce," quod scho, "hecht hie Honour,	*is called high*
	Quham to disservys mony traist officiare.	*Who is served by; loyal*
1795	For Charité, of gudlynes the flour,	*the paragon of virtue*
	Is Maister Houshald in yone cristall tour,	*that shining tower*
	Ferme Constance is the kyngis Secritare,	*Constancy; Secretary*
	And Liberalité heicht his Thesaurar.	*Treasurer*
	Innocens and Devocyon as efferis	*as is fitting*
1800	Bene clerkis of closet and cubeculeris.	*chapel clerks; grooms of the chamber*
	"His Comptrowere is clepyt Discretioun.	*Comptroller; named*
	Humanyté and Trew Relatioun	*Truthful Report*
	Bene yscherris of his chalmer morow and eve.	*ushers; chamber; morning*
	Peace, Quyet, Rest, oft wakis up and doun	*walk*
1805	In till his hall as marchellis of renoun.	*marshals*
	Temperance is cuke, his mete to tast and preve.	*cook; taste and test*
	Humylyté karvar, that na wycht lyst to greve.	*carver; who wishes to grieve no one*
	His maister sewer hecht Vertuus Discipline.	*butler*
	Mercy is copper and mixis weil his wyne.	*cupbearer*

1810 "His Chanceller is clepyt Conscyence
Quhilk for na meid will pronounce fals sentence. *bribe*
With him are assessouris four of one ascent, *assessors; one mind*
Science, Prudence, Justice, Sapience,
Quhilkis to na wycht lyst committing offence. *wish to commit*
1815 The chekker rollys and the kyngis rent *exchequer rolls*
As auditouris thay ovirseis quhat is spent. *auditors; oversee*
Labourus Diligens, Gud Werkis, Clene Livyng *Hard-working*
Bene out stewartis and catouris to yone kyng. *estate officers; purchasers*

"Gud Hope remanys ever amang yone sort, *resides always*
1820 A fyne menstral with mony mow and sport; *minstrel; jest*
And Pieté is the kyngis almoseir; *almoner*
Syne Fortitude, the rycht quha lyst report, *whoever wants to report accurately*
Is lieutenand al wrachys to comfort. *deputy; unfortunate people*
The kyngis mynyeon roundand in his eyr *familiar servant whispering*
1825 Heicht Verité, did nevir leyl man deir, *[who] never harmed a loyal man*
And schortly, every vertew and plesance *in brief*
Is subject to yone kyngis obbeysance. *authority*

"Come on," sayd sche, "this ordenance to vysyte." *survey this edifice*
Than past we to that cristall Palyce quhyte,
1830 Quhare I abayd the entré til behald. *paused to view the gateway*
I bad na mare of plesance nor delyte, *wanted nothing more*
Of lusty sycht, of joy and blys perfyte,
Nor mare weilfare til have abone the mold *well-being; in this life*
Than for til se that yet of byrnyst gold, *gate; burnished*
1835 Quhare on thair was maist curiusly ingrave *On which; intricately engraved*
All naturall thyng men may in erd consave. *phenomena; consider in the world*

Thare wes the erth enveronyt wyth the see *surrounded by the sea*
Quhare on the schyppes saland mycht I se, *On which I could see the ships sailing*
The ayr, the fyre — all the four elymentis —
1840 The Speris Sevyn and primum mobile, *Spheres*
The sygnis twelf perfytly every gre, *twelve [astrological] signs; degree*
The zodiak, hale as bukis represents, *just as books expound*
The Poil Antertik that ever himselfe absentis, *Pole; keeps himself out of sight*
The Poil Artik, and eik the Ursis twane, *two Bears*
1845 The Sevyn Sterris, Pheton, and the Charle wane. *Pleiades; Phaethon; Ursa Major*

Thare wes ingraf quhow that Ganamedis *engraved*
Wes reft till hevyn, as men in Ovyd redis, *abducted to*
And on till Jupiter made his cheif butlare. *made chief butler to Jupiter*
The douchters, fare in to thayr lusty wedis, *attractive in their fine clothes*
1850 Of Dorida, amyd the see, but dredis, *Doris; without doubt*
Swymmand, and part wer figurit thare *depicted there*
Apon a crag, dryand thair yalow hare, *drying their blonde hair*

With facis not onlyk, for quha thaym seyng   *unlike; whoever sees them*
Mycht weil consyddir that thay al sisteris beyng.   *understand; are all sisters*

1855   Of the planetis all the conjunctionys,   *conjunctions*
        Thare episciclis and oppositionis   *epicycles*
        Wer porturyt thair, and quhow thair coursis swagis;   *subside*
        Thare naturale and dayly motionis,   *courses*
        Eclipse, aspectis, and degressyonys.   *positions; deviations*
1860   Thare saw I mony gudly personagis
        Quhilkis semyt all lusty quyk ymagis,   *fine lifelike depictions*
        The werkmanschip excedyng mony fold   *many times*
        The precyus mater, thocht it wes fynest gold.

        Wondrand here on, agane my wyll, but lete,   *Puzzling over this; without pause*
1865   My Nymphe in grif schot me in at the yet.   *annoyance shoved; gate*
        "Quhat Devyl!" said scho, "Hes thou not ellis ado   *What the devil; else to do*
        Bot all thy wyt and fantasy to set   *to lavish*
        On sic dotyng?" and tho for fere I swet   *foolishness; sweat*
        Of her langage; bot than anone said scho,   *Because of*
1870   "List thou se farlyes, behald thaym yondir, lo,   *[If it] please you to see marvels*
        Yit study not ovir mekil, a dreid thow vary   *overmuch, out of fear you will rave*
        For I persave thee halflyngis in a fary."   *halfway; daze*

        Within that Palyce sone I gat a sycht   *had a view*
        Quhare walkand went ful mony worthy wicht
1875   Amyd the close with all myrthys to wale;   *courtyard; delights to enjoy*
        For lyk Phebus with fyry bemys brycht
        The wallys schane, castand sa gret a lycht   *shone*
        It semyt lyk the hevyn imperiall,   *empyrean sphere*
        And as the cedir surmontyth the rammale   *cedar surpasses the shrub*
1880   In perfyt hycht, sa of that court a glance
        Excedis far all erdly vane plesance.   *earthly vain delight*

        For lois of sycht, considir micht I nocht   *loss*
        Quhow perfytly the ryche wallys wer wrocht.   *were constructed*
        Swa the reflex of cristall stanys schone,   *reflection from; shone*
1885   For brychtnes skarsly blenk thairon I mocht.   *scarcely look upon; could*
        The purifyit silver soithlie as me thocht,   *truly as it seemed to me*
        In steid of syment wes ovir all that wone,   *Instead; cement; habitation*
        Yet round about ful mony a beriall stone   *Poured; beryl*
        And thaym conjunctly jonyt fast and quemyt.   *joined together and fitted*
1890   The close wes paithit with silver, as it semyt.   *courtyard was paved*

        The durris and the wyndois all wer breddyt   *doors; paneled*
        With massy gold, quhare of the fynes scheddit.   *fineness glowed*
        With byrnyst evyr baith palyce and touris   *polished ivory*
        Wer thekyt weil, maist craftely that cled it: *shingled well; skilfully; covered*

1895	For so the quhitly blanchit bone ovirspred it,	*palely bleached*
	Mydlyt with gold, anamalyt all colouris,	*Intermixed; enameled*
	Inporturat of byrdis and swete flouris,	*Depicted with*
	Curius knottis, and mony sle devyse,	*Ornamental knots; intricate pattern*
	Quhilkis to behald wes perfyt paradice.	
1900	And to proceid, my Nymphe and I furth went	
	Straucht to the hall, throw out the Palyce jent,	*fine palace*
	And ten stagis of thopas did ascend.	*steps of topaz*
	Schit wes the dure. In at a boir I blent,	*Shut; peephole I looked*
	Quhare I beheld the gladdest represent	*appearance*
1905	That evir in erth a wrachit catyve kend.	*miserable wretch beheld*
	Breifly theis proces til conclude and end,	*narrative*
	Me thocht the flure wes al of amatist	*floor; amethyst*
	Bot quhare of war the wallis I ne wist.	*what substance; walls were; not know*
	The multitud of prectius stonis sere	*abundant precious stones*
1910	Thair on swa schane, my febill sycht, but were,	*without doubt*
	Mycht not behald thair vertuus gudlynes.	*Could; powerful beauty*
	For all the ruf, as did to me appere,	*ceiling*
	Hang full of plesand lowpyt saphyrs clere.	*wreathed sapphires*
	Of dyamantis and rubys, as I ges,	
1915	Wer all the burdis, maid of mast riches.	*tables; greatest costliness*
	Of sardanus, of jaspe, and smaragdane,	*sardonyx; jasper; smaragd (emerald)*
	Trestis, formys and benkis wer, pollist plane.	*Trestles, seats; benches; smooth*
	Baith to and fro amyd the hall they went,	
	Rial Princis in plate and armouris quent,	*plated and well-wrought armor*
1920	Of byrnist gold, cuchit with precyus stonys.	*furnished*
	Intronyt sat a god armypotent,	*Enthroned; warlike god*
	On quhais gloryus vissage as I blent,	*looked*
	In extasy, be his brychtnes, atonys,	*suddenly*
	He smate me doun and byrsyt all my bonys.	*knocked; bruised*
1925	Thare lay I still in swoun with cullour blaucht,	*ashen complexion*
	Quhil at the last my Nymphe up hes me kaucht.	*Until; has picked me up*
	Syne wyth gret pane, with womentyng and care,	*lamenting; sorrow*
	In hir armys scho bare me doun the stare	*carried; stairs*
	And in the clois full softly laid me doun,	*courtyard*
1930	Held up my hede to tak the hailsum ayre,	*health-giving air*
	For of my lyfe scho stude in gret dispare.	*she was in grave doubt*
	Me till awalk ay wes that lady boun,	*to awake; busy*
	Quhill finally out of my dedly swoun	*death-like swoon*
	I swyth ovircome and up my eyne did cast.	*suddenly awoke; eyes; open*
1935	"Be myrry, man," quod scho, "the werst is past.	

      "Get up," scho said, "for schame, be na cowart.

      My hede in wed, thow hes a wyfis hart   *I'd bet my head*

      That for a plesand sycht is so mysmaid!"   *undone*

      Than all in anger, apon my fete I start,   *Then; leapt*

1940 And for hir wordis wer so apyrsmart,   *because; biting*

      On to the Nymphe I maid a bustuus braid.   *threatening gesture*

      "Carlyng," quod I, "quhat wes yone at thow said?"   *Old woman; was it that thou*

      "Soft, yow," said sche, "thay ar not wyse that stryvys,   *Easy, you; quarrel*

      For kyrkmen wer ay jentill to ther wyvys.   *always courteous with their wives*

1945 "I am rycht glaid thou art wordyn so wycht.   *you have become so strong*

      Lang ere, me thocht thow had nothir fors ne mycht,[1]

      Curage nor wyll, for till have grevyt a fla.   *annoyed a flea*

      Quhat alyt thee to fall?" Quod I, "The sycht   *What troubled you (that made you) fall*

      Of yone goddes grym, fyry vissage brycht   *that god's*

1950 Ovirset my wyt and all my spretis swa,

      I mycht not stand." "Bot wes that suyth?" "Ya, ya."   *could not remain standing; true; Yes*

      Than said the Nymphe rycht merylie and leuch,   *laughed*

      "Now I considir thy malt hart weil eneuch.   *understand; tender heart*

      "I wyl," quod scho, "na mare thee thus assay   *test*

1955 With sic plesance quhilk may thy sprete effray.   *terrify*

      Yit sall thow se suythly, sen thou art here,   *since*

      My lydyis court in thair gudly array.   *ladies'*

      For till behald thair myrth, cum on thy way."

      Than hand in hand swyth went we furth in fere   *indeed; together*

1960 At a postrum towart the fair herbere.   *side door; flower-garden*

      In that passage full fast at hir I franyt,   *eagerly; asked*

      Quhat folk thay wer, within the hall remanyt?   *[who] stayed*

      "Yone wer," said scho, "quha sa the richt discrivys,   *whoever describes the truth*

      Maist vailyeand folk and vertuus in thair lyvys.   *courageous (valiant)*

1965 Now in the court of Honour thay remane

      Victoriusly, and in all plesance thryvys,

      For thay with spere, with swerdys, and wyth knyvys

      In just battell wer fundyn maist of mane.   *greatest of strength*

      In thair promyttis thay stude evir fyrm and plane.   *promises*

1970 In thaym aboundit worschyp and lawté,   *honor and loyalty*

      Illumynyt with liberalité.   *Illumined with generosity*

      "Honour," quod scho "to this hevinly ryng   *realm*

      Differris richt far from warldly honoring,

      Quhilk is but pompe of erdly dignyté   *only display of earthly*

1975 Gyvyn for estate or blude, micht, or sic thyng;   *rank or lineage, power, or such things*

---

[1] *A while back, it seemed to me you had neither strength nor ability*

And, in this countré, prynce, prelate, or kyng
Alanerly sall for vertu honoryt be;   *Shall be honored for virtue only*
For erdly glore is not bot vanyté   *nothing but*
That, as we se, sa suddandly will wend;   *will depart*
1980 Bot vertuus honour nevir mare sall end.

"Behald," said scho "and se this warldly glore
Maist inconstant, maist slyd and transitore.   *slippery and transitory*
Prosperitie in erd is bot a dreme   *on earth*
Or lyk as man wer steppand ovir a score.   *boundary-line*
1985 Now is he law that wes so hie to fore,   *low; before*
And he quhilum wes borne pure of his deme,   *formerly; poor; mother*
Now his estate schynys lyke the sonne beme.   *sunbeam*
Baith up and doun, baith to and fro, we se,
This warld weltrys as dois the wally see.   *tosses; stormy sea*

1990 "To papis, bischoppis, prelatis, and primatis,[1]
Empriouris, kinges, princes, potestatis,   *rulers*
Deth settis the terme and end of all thair hycht.   *height*
Fra thay be gan, late se quha on thaym watys.   *Once; let [us] see who waits on them*
Na thyng remanis bot fame of thair estatis,   *except the glory of their positions*
1995 And not ellis bot vertuus werkis richt   *nothing else except; rightly*
Sall with thaym wend — nother thair pompe nor mycht.   *go, neither*
Ay vertu ryngis in lestand honour clere;   *Forever; reigns; enduring; bright*
Remembir than that vertu hes no pere.   *peer*

"For vertu is a thing sa precyous
2000 Quhare of the end is sa delycious   *delightful*
The warld ma not consyddir quhat it is.
It makis folk perfyte and glorious,
It makis sanctis of pepill vicious,   *saints [out] of wicked people*
It causis folk ay leve in lestand blys,   *live; lasting*
2005 It is the way til hie honour, iwys,   *indeed*
It dantis deth and every vice thorow mycht.   *defeats; through*
Without vertu, fy on all erdly wycht.   *fie*

"Vertu is eik the perfyte sikkyr way,   *dependable*
And not ellis, til honour lestand ay.   *nothing else, to everlasting honor*
2010 For mony hes sene vitious pepil upheit,   *wicked people exalted*
And eftir sone, thair glory vanys away,   *soon after; vanishes*
Quhar of exemplis we se this every day.   *Examples of which; see*
His erdly pompe is gone quhen that he deyt;   *has died*
Than is he with no erdly frend suppleit,   *supplied with no earthly friend*

---

[1] *To popes, bishops, prelates, and leading bishops*

2015   Savand Vertu. Weill is him hes sic a fere.   *Except; It goes well for; comrade*
       Now wil I schaw," quod sche, "quhat folk bene here.

       "The strangest Sampson is in to yone hald,   *Samson the strongest; inside; dwelling*
       The forsy, pyssand Hercules so bald,   *strong, mighty; bold*
       The feirs Achill and all the Nobillis Nyne,   *fierce; Nine Worthies*
2020   Scipio Affricane, Pompeyus the ald,   *elder*
       Uthir mony quhais namys afore are tald,   *are already mentioned*
       With thousandis ma than I may here diffine,   *more; describe*
       And lusty ladyis amyd thay lordis syne,   *among those; too*
       Semiramis, Thamar, Ypolytha,   *Tamar, Hippolyta*
2025   Pantyssalé, Medus, Cenobia.   *Penthesilea, Medusa, Zenobia*

       "Of thy regyon yondir bene honorit part,
       The kyngis Gregor, Kened, and Kyng Robert,
       With otheris mo that beis not here rehersyt.   *shall not be listed here*
       Varyit," quod scho, "ay be thy megyr hart!   *Cursed; forever; puny*
2030   Thow suld have sene, had thou biddin in yon art,   *remained; that place*
       Quhat wyse yone hevynly company conversyt.   *way; conversed*
       Wa worth thy febyll brane, sa sone wes persit!   *Sorrow fall upon; impaired*
       Thow mycht have sene, remanand quhare thow was,   *remaining where*
       A huge pepyl punyst for thair trespas,   *numerous; punished; crime*

2035   "Quhilkis be wilfull, manyfest arrogance,
       Invyus pryd, pretendit ignorance,
       Fowle dowbilnes, and dissate unamendit   *treachery; uncorrected deceit*
       Enforcis thaym thair selvyn til avance   *Exert; to advance themselves*
       Be sle falsheid, but lawté or constance,   *sly; without loyalty or dependability*
2040   Wyth subtelnes and slychtys now commendit,   *deceit and tricks now praised*
       Betraisand folk that nevir to them offendit,   *Betraying*
       And upheis thaim self throw frawdful lippis,   *promote themselves; lying mouths*
       Thocht God cause oft thare erdly glore eclippis.   *their earthly glory to dim*

       "And nobillis cumyn of honorabill ancestry   *descended*
2045   Thair vertuus nobilité settis nocht by   *give no respect to*
       For dishonest, unlefull, warldly ways   *unlawful*
       And throw corruppit, covatus invy.
       Bot he that can be dowbill, nane is set by,   *Except; false, no one is esteemed*
       Dissate is wisdum, lawté, honour away is.   *Wisdom is banished*
2050   Rycht few or nane takis tent thairto thir days,   *pays heed; these*
       And thair gret wrangis till reforme but let   *without delay*
       In judgement yone god wes yondir set.

       "Remanand yondir, thow mycht have herd belyve   *heard promptly*
       Pronouncit the gret sentence diffinytive   *great, definitive judgment*
2055   Twichand this actioun, and the dreidful pane   *Concerning; legal case; punishment*
       Execute on trespassouris yit on lyve,   *Carried out; alive*

Swa that thair malyce sall na mare prescryve." *no longer prevail*
"Madame," quod I, "for Goddis saik, turn agane,
My spreit desyris to se thair torment fane." *eagerly*
2060 Quod scho, "Richt now thare sall thow be rejosyt *pleased*
Quhen thow hes tane the ayr and bettir apposyt. *recovered*

"Bot first thow sal considdir commoditeis *benefits*
Of our gardyng, lo, full of lusty trees,
All hie cypres, of flewer maist fragrant. *tall cypress; scent most*
2065 Our ladyis yonder, bissy as the beis, *busy; bees*
The swete florist colouris of rethoreis *flowery; rhetoric*
Gaddris full fast, mony grene tendir plant, *Gather*
For with all plesance plenist is yone hant *filled; that abode*
Quhare precious stanys on treis doyth abound — *stones do abound on trees*
2070 In sted of frute, chargyt with peirlis round." *laden; pearls*

On till that gudly garth thus we proceid,
Quhilk with a large fowsy fare on breid *ditch far around*
Inveronyt wes, quhare fysches wer enew. *Was set about; aplenty*
All wattir foulis wer swomand thair gud speid. *swimming there briskly*
2075 Als out of growand treis thair saw I breid *Also; sprouting; breed*
Foulys that hyngand by thair nebbis grew. *hanging; beaks*
Out ovir the stank of mony divers hew *water; assorted colors*
Wes laid a tre ovir quhilk behovyt we pas, *over which we had to go*
Bot I can not declare quhare of it wes. *of what kind it was*

2080 My Nymphe went ovir, chargeand me folow fast. *commanding; follow*
Hir till obbey my spretis woux agast, *grew afraid*
Swa peralus wes the passagis till aspy. *the route to identify*
Away sche went, and fra tyme sche wes past *once*
Apon the bryg I entrit at the last; *bridge*
2085 Bot swa my harnys trymlyt bissyly *brains trembled ceaselessly*
Quhyl I fell ovir, and baith my fete slaid by, *slipped away*
Out ovir the hede, into the stank adoun, *head; down*
Quhare, as me thocht, I wes in point to droun. *about to drown*

Quhat throw the byrdis sang and this affray, *What with; shock*
2090 Out of my swoun I walkynnyt quhare I lay *awakened*
In the gardyn quhare I fyrst doun fell.
About I blent, for richt clere was the day, *I looked about*
Bot all thys lusty plesance wes away. *pleasant place had disappeared*
Me thocht that fare herbere maist lyk to hel *flower-garden; hell*
2095 In till compare of this ye herd me tell. *In comparison with; heard*
Allace, allace, I thocht me than in pane *considered myself*
And langyt sare for till have swounyt agane. *wished very much*

The byrdis sang nor yit the mery flouris
Mycht not ameys my grevows gret dolouris.   *soothe my grievous; woes*
2100   All erdly thyng me thocht barrant and vyle.   *seemed to me barren*
Thus I remanyt in to the garth twa houris,
Cursand the feildis with all the fare coullouris,   *Cursing; lovely*
That I awolk, oft wariand the quhyle.   *awoke; reviling meanwhile*
Always my mynd wes on the lusty yle   *isle*
2105   In purpose evir till have dwelt in that art   *place*
Of rethorik cullouris til have fund sum parte.   *colors of rhetoric*

And maist of all my curage wes aggrevit   *mood was distressed*
Becaus sa sone I of my dreme eschevyt,   *departed from my dream*
Nocht seand quhow thay wrechis wer torment   *Not seeing how those*
2110   That honour mankyt and honesté myschevyt.   *Who; impaired; damaged*
Glaidly I wald amyd thys wryt have brevyt,   *into this text; recorded*
Had I it sene, quhow thay were slane or schent.   *If I had seen it; destroyed*
Bot fra I saw all thys weilfare wes went,   *after; good fortune had vanished away*
Till mak ane end, sittand under a tre,   *sitting*
2115   In laude of Honour I wrait thir versis thre: *wrote*

"O hie Honour, swete hevynly flour degest,   *sweet, dignified, heavenly flower*
Gem vertuus, maist precius, gudlyest   *Powerful gem; worthiest*
For hie renoun, thow art guerdoun condyng,   *you are [the] fitting reward*
Of worschyp kend the glorius end and rest,   *renown known [to be]; goal*
2120   But quham, in rycht, na worthy wicht may lest.   *Without which, indeed; last*
Thy gret puissance may maist avance all thyng   *power; benefit*
And poverale to myche avale sone bryng.   *poor people; much good soon*
I thee requere, sen thow, but pere, art best,   *request, since; without peer*
That eftir this in thy hie blys we ryng.   *continue*

2125   "Of grace thy face in every place so schynys,
That swete all spreit baith heid and feit inclynis   *courteously every being; lowers*
Thy glore afore, for til implore remeid.   *before; remedy*
He docht rycht nocht quhilk out of thocht thee tynis.[1]
Thy name but blame, and riall fame, dyvine is,   *without; is divine*
2130   Thow port, at schort, of our comfort and reid   *gateway, in brief; guidance*
Tyll bryng all thyng tyll gladyng eftir deid.   *happiness; death*
All wycht but sycht of thy gret mycht ay crinis.   *without; always dwindles*
O Schene, I mene, nane may sustene thy feid.   *Beautiful (one); endure; hostility*

"Hail rois maist chois til clois thy foys gret mycht.   *choicest rose; stop; foes'*
2135   Hail stone quhilk schone apon the trone of lycht,   *gem that shone; throne*
Vertew, quhais trew swet dew overthrew all vyce,   *sweet dew*
Was ay ilk day, gar say, the way of lycht,   *each; cause to say*

---

[1] *He achieves absolutely nothing who fails to keep you in mind*

Amend offend and send our end ay richt, — *misdeed; always justly*
Thow stant ordant as sant of grant maist wyse — *remain dedicated; saint; favor*
2140 Til be supplé and the hie gre of pryce. — *[a] support; platform; worthiness*
Delyte thee tite me quyte of syte to dycht, — *Please; quickly; free of misery; make*
For I apply schortly to thy devyse." — *commit [myself]; plan*

Dedication

The auctor direkit his buke to the rycht — *dedicated*
nobill Prynce James the Ferd, Kyng — *Fourth*
of Scottis.

Tryumphus laud with palm of victory, — *praise*
The laurere crown of infynyte glory, — *laurel*
2145 Maist gracius prince, our soverane James the Ferd,
Thy majesty mot have eternally, — *May your kingship*
Supreme honour, renoun of chevalry,
Felycité perdurand in this erd, — *Happiness enduring*
With etern blys in the hevyn by fatal werd. — *destined decree*
2150 Resave this rusty, rurall rebaldry — *crude, rustic discourse*
Lakand cunnyng, fra thye puyr lege onlerd, — *Lacking; poor untaught subject (liege man)*

Quhilk in the sycht of thy magnificence,
Confydand in so gret benevolence, — *Depending on such*
Proponis thus my wulgare ignorance, — *Proffers; vulgar*
2155 Maist humely wyth dew obedyence, — *humbly; due*
Besekand oft thy mychty excellence — *Beseeching*
Be grace til pardon all sic variance — *By; to; such imperfection*
With sum benyng respect of ferme constance, — *kindly consideration; firm stability*
Remyttand my pretendit negligence, — *Presenting; acknowledged*
2160 Throw quhais mycht may humyll thyng avance. — *Through whose; humble; find favor*

Breif, burall quair, of eloquence all quyte, — *rustic book; divested*
With russet weid and sentence imperfyte, — *coarse clothing*
Til cum in plane se thow not pretend tha. — *into the open; assert thyself*
Thy barrant termis and thy vyle endyte — *fruitless words; writing*
2165 Sall not be min, I wyll not have the wyte, — *mine; blame*
For, as for me, I quytcleme that I kend tha. — *renounce; knew you*
Thow art bot stouth — thyft lovys lycht but lyte.[1]
Not worth a myte, pray ilk man till amend tha. — *penny; correct thee*
Fare on with syte, and on this wyse I end tha. — *Journey on with sorrow*

Finis.

---

[1] *You are only theft; theft does not much love the light*

🌿 Explanatory Notes

ABBREVIATIONS: *ALHTS*: *Accounts of the Lord High Treasurer of Scotland*, ed. Dickson, vol. 1; *Aeneid*: Virgil. *Aeneid*, ed. Fairclough; **Bawcutt**: Priscilla Bawcutt, *Gavin Douglas: A Critical Study*; *BD*: Chaucer, *Book of the Duchess*, ed. Benson; *BH*: Richard Holland, *The Buke of the Howlat*, ed. Hanna; *Brill*: *Brill's New Pauly: Encyclopaedia of the Ancient World*, ed. Canok; *Bruce*: John Barbour, *Bruce*, ed. McDiarmid and Stevenson; **Burrow**: John Burrow, *Gestures and Looks in Medieval Narrative*; *CA*: John Gower, *Confessio Amantis*, ed. Peck; **Cairns**: Sandra Cairns, "*The Palice of Honour* of Gavin Douglas, Ovid and Raffaelo Regio's Commentary on Ovid's *Metamorphoses*"; *CLL*: John Lydgate, *A Complaynt of a Loveres Lyfe*, ed. Norton-Smith; *CT*: Geoffrey Chaucer, *The Canterbury Tales*, ed. Benson (with the titles of individual tales abbreviated as in the Riverside edition); **Curtius**: Ernst Robert Curtius, *European Literature and the Latin Middle Ages*; *D*: The print of *PH* ascribed to Davidson; *DOST*: *Dictionary of the Older Scottish Tongue*; *E*: The Edinburgh print of *PH*; *E1*: The handwritten emendations in the NLS copy of E; *Eneados*: *Virgil's Aeneid Translated by Gavin Douglas*, ed. Coldwell; *Heroides*: Ovid, *Heroides and Amores*, trans. Showerman; *HF*: Chaucer, *The House of Fame*, ed. Benson; *History*: Livy, *History of Rome*, ed. Foster; *KQ*: James I, *The Kingis Quair*, eds. Mooney and Arn; *L*: The London print of *PH*; *LGW*: Chaucer, *The Legend of Good Women*, ed. Benson; **Lyndsay**: *Sir David Lyndsay: Selected Poems*, ed. Hadley Williams,; *MED*: *The Middle English Dictionary*; *Meroure*: John Ireland, *The Meroure of Wysdome*, eds. MacPherson, Quinn, and McDonald; *Met*: Ovid, *Metamorphoses*, trans. Miller; *NLS*: National Library of Scotland; **Norton-Smith**: John Norton-Smith, "Ekphrasis"; *OED*: *The Oxford English Dictionary*; *OT*: Old Testament; *PF*: Chaucer, *The Parliament of Fowls*, ed. Benson; *PH*: *The Palyce of Honour*, ed. Parkinson; **Plin. *HN***: Pliny, *Natural History*, ed. Rackham; **Quint. *Inst.***: Quintilian, *Orator's Education*, ed. Russell; **Scott**: *Select Works of Gawin Douglass*, ed. Scott; *SP*: *The Palice of Honour*, ed. Bawcutt (in *The Shorter Poems of Gavin Douglas*); *ST*: John Lydgate, *The Siege of Thebes*, ed. Edwards; **Statius**: Statius, *Thebaid*, ed. Bailey; **STC**: *Short-Title Catalogue*; **STS**: The Scottish Text Society; *TC*: Chaucer, *Troilus and Criseyde*, ed. Benson; **Trev. *Prop.***: On the Properties of Things: John Trevisa's translation of *Bartholomaeus Anglicus De proprietatibus rerum*, eds. Seymour and Liegey; **Utley**: Francis Lee Utley, *The Crooked Rib*; **Whiting**: Bartlett Jere Whiting and Helen Prescott Whiting, *Proverbs, Sentences, and Proverbial Phrases from English Writings Mainly before 1500*; **Wyntoun**: Andrew Wyntoun, *The Original Chronicle of Andrew Wyntoun*, ed. Amours.

The following notes selectively elucidate difficult passages, identify likely sources, and comment on points of style. For transcriptions of the marginal glosses printed in L, see the Textual Notes. Unless otherwise indicated, classical texts are cited from Loeb editions. For Biblical references, *The Holy Bible: Douay Rheims Version* (ed. Challoner, 1889) is used, unless otherwise noted. Abbreviations are as provided above, with the authors and titles of classical works shortened following the *Oxford Classical Dictionary*, fourth edition. Unless otherwise indicated, citations of Chaucer's works refer to *The Riverside Chaucer*, third edition.

Title   *palyce*. This is a royal residence (*DOST palice* (n.1), senses 1a and b); later in the sixteenth century, the expression "palice of honour" could refer as if officially to a building in which the Scottish sovereign "was currently in residence" (sense 1b). A second significance pertains to a garden or habitation surrounded by a palisade (*DOST palice* (n.2)). In *The Dreme* (line 591), Sir David Lyndsay refers to heaven as "that palice preclare" (Lyndsay, p. 22). With varying emphasis and signification, the term recurs throughout *PH*. See the Glossary of the present edition for citations.

1   *Quhen pale Aurora with face lamentable*. Douglas begins with the same word as does Chaucer in the General Prologue to *CT*; but rather than surveying relations between natural and human existence in time, Douglas directs the reader's attention to a mythologically sorrowful dawn and only thereafter to a paradisal garden. At the very outset, grief seems uppermost. In Ovidian terms, a pale, sorrowful Aurora portends overthrow, uncertainty, disappointment, and loss: her advent sets Phaethon on his disastrous course; Medea's poisons appall her; she stands between light and darkness; she laments her husband's decrepitude (*Met* 2.144, 1:70–71; 7.209, 703, 1:356–57, 390–91). In Ovid's account of Memnon's funeral at Troy (*Met* 13.576–622, 2:268–73), Aurora, the hero's mother, had lost her wonted brightness (*ille color, quo matutina rubescunt tempora*) and had grown pale (*palluerat*) with grief, so that the skies became overcast (13.581–82, 2:268–70).

2   *russat*. The primary significance here is "reddish-brown colour" (*DOST russat* (adj.), sense 2), suiting the previous reference to Aurora, who is frequently called rosy-fingered in the classical sources; a secondary association is with the coarse cloth typically of this hue, used "by country people and the poor" (*DOST russat* (adj.), sense 1; *ALHTS*, pp. 14, 17, 234); the ambiguity may be meaningful in a poem that balances exalted discourse and aspirations against more lowly tendencies. The term recurs at the end of the poem, in the "envoy," where the poet mocks his work for being clad in "russat weid" (line 2162); there, the ambiguity is scornfully resolved.

         sable. The heraldic term for black (*DOST sabill* (n.2), sense 1), also the color of mourning (sense 2). In a secondary sense the term also refers, like modern English *sable*, to the costly fur, used to trim fine garments (*DOST sabill* (n.1)), thus contrasting with humble "russat."

3   *circumstance*. In KnT, Palamon sacrifices to Venus "Ful pitously, with alle circumstaunces" (*CT* I[A] 2263; rhymes with "observances," as here, line 6); the term has associations elsewhere with the commencement of a text, e.g., Wyntoun, prol., line 11.

6   *observance*. Chaucer's Arcite goes into the woods alone at dawn "to doon his observaunce to May," and there he makes "a gerland of the greves, / Were it of wodebynde or hawethorn leves," and sings a song to May (*CT* I[A] 1500–12). In

The Quare of Jelusy, the sun makes "every lusty hert" rise early in May "to done thair observance" (*Chaucerian Dream Visions*, ed. Symons, lines 11–13; see also p. 183n13).

7 *garding of plesance.* This may simply be a pleasant place, *locus amoenus*; a "plesance," however, is more precisely a walled garden like the ones in *Le Roman de la Rose* or *PF*, into which one enters at one's peril.

8 *amyable.* Though E1's emendation of "dilectabill" is tempting (see Textual Note for this line), the repetition of this term from line 5 may be significant in a set-piece prologue in the high style, featuring a "special stock" of latinate expressions, many of which are used "copiously and repetitively" (Macafee and Aitken, "History of Scots to 1700," §9.3.4; see also §9.2.9).

10–18 *So craftely dame . . . . the mystis reflectant.* The passage is intricate, allusive, and redundant. Flora has adorned her bejeweled bed with dew, while plentiful, fresh, sweet, fragrant vapors are distilling silver droplets on the daisies, which the green branches hanging over the garden paths let fall, reflecting the mists with smoky incense; *DOST verd(o)ur(e*, (n.), sense 2, signifies a "Tapestry sewn or woven with representations of trees, vegetation, etc.," sometimes used attributively (*verdoure bed*; *verdeour clathis*); the garden and its representation are spoken of in terms of each other.

11 *Hir hevinly bed, powderit with mony a set.* Douglas puns on "bed" (also line 4) and "set," the latter denoting a cluster of buds or jewels. Lyall comments that "powderit" "is a term in [heraldic] blason; we may therefore be invited to see in Douglas' scene not only a painting of some kind, but more specifically the stylised imagery of a heraldic device" ("Stylistic Relationship," p. 74).

16 *The silver droppis on dayseis distillant.* Silver drops are "hangynge on the leves" in KnT (*CT* I[A] 1496); Douglas repeats the term in line 27.

17 *Quhilk verdour branches over the alars yet.* Compare "So thik the bewis and the leves grene / Beschadit all the aleyes" (*KQ*, lines 218–19).

18 *reflectant.* The use of this word is unusual, with *DOST* citing this line as a nonce occurrence (*reflectant* (adj.)). Here and elsewhere, Douglas is pushing the linguistic bounds of the high style.

19 *The fragrant flouris, blomand in their seis.* DOST cites this line as a unique application of *se* ("throne") to refer to a flower-bed (*se* (n.2), sense 1c).

20 *Naturis tapestreis.* Lydgate speaks of a flourishing garden as Nature's tapestry (*CLL*, lines 50–52).

21–24 *Above the quhilk . . . . al the skyis.* Birdsong is integral to the pleasant place (Curtius, pp. 195, 197). The birds' "greis" (Scott glosses this as "on degrees, steps, one above another," p. 139; *DOST gre* (n.1), sense 1) imply precedence or even an artificial structure, as if the garden becomes an aviary (Cooper, "Ornamental Structures," pp. 818, 819). See further the note to line 2140. Birdsong is heard again at the end of *PH* (see line 2098 and note).

22   *twistis.* Compare "[O]n the small grene twistis sat / The lytill suete nyghtingale" (*KQ*, lines 225–26).

25   *reparcust.* To "repercuss" is to cause to rebound or recoil. Lyall cites *aere repercusso* in *Met* 4.783, 1:232–33, where "it refers to the reflection of light rather than echoing sound" ("Stylistic Relationship," p. 78n15); Ovid is referring to the bronze of Perseus' shield having reflected the image of Medusa. The line is hypometrical as it stands. If the suffix of "reparcust" were fully articulated ("reparcussit"), the anomaly would be resolved. Douglas contributes the term to later Scottish depictions of the pleasant place: e.g., *Dialog*, line 201 (Lyndsay, p. 190).

30–33   *Eous . . . semis reid.* The name *Eous* derives ultimately from Ovid's list of the four horses of the Sun (*Met* 2.153–54, 1:70–71). Discussing Henryson's reference to red Eous in *The Testament of Cresseid* (line 211), Denton Fox notes that "[t]he four horses of the sun . . . were often treated by medieval authors, who, with a considerable amount of variation, assign to each horse a part of the day"; Eous "was usually described as red, because of the colour of the rising sun" (*Poems of Robert Henryson*, ed. Fox, p. 357).

32   *assiltré.* On the chariot of the Sun, see *Met* 2.107–08, 1:66–67. The axle-tree can be read allegorically as the axis of the sun or its course across the sky (*OED axle-tree* (n.), sense 4a). Mythographically, the detail is a metonymy for the wheels of Apollo's chariot.

40   *wappit.* The verb "wap" means to "throw," "utter," or "strike" (*DOST, wap* (v.), senses 1, 2, 3); its occurrence in both L and E may be a mistake for "wrap."

41   *yschappit.* Douglas uses an archaic form of the past participle of "shape," where "shapin" would be the usual form.

42   *vivificative.* This is the earliest instance of the learned adjective "vivificative" (from Latin *vivifico*) in *DOST*.

43   *amene.* "Amene" (Latin *amoenus*) is a prominent element of courtly diction in late-medieval Scottish poetry. See note to line 8 above.

45   *beis.* The industrious bees reappear in the pleasant place where the Muses rest; they are also the subject of a simile near the end of the poem (see lines 1152, 2065 and note). Maggie Kilgour comments that "Classical and Renaissance writers commonly used contrasting kinds of insects as models to describe different forms of creativity. The bee's gathering and transformation of nectar from a variety of flowers is a common image for *imitatio*" (*Milton and the Metamorphosis of Ovid*, p. 278).

49–51   *God Eolus of wynd . . . . til every plant.* Echoed by Lyndsay in *The Testament of the Papyngo*: "That day Saturne, nor Mars, durst not appeir, / Nor Eole, of his cove, he durst nocht steir" (lines 113–14; Lyndsay, p. 62). Aeolus' sack of unfavorable winds (Homer, *Odyssey* 10.1–79; pp. 358–65) has a long heritage.

50   *speir.* A planet's "sphere" is its zone of movement and dominance in the heavens and thus contributes to its particular effect upon the earth (*DOST sper(e* (n.2), sense 2b).

53   *The beriall stremes rynnyng*. Beryl is proverbially associated with brightness (Whiting B263).

54–55   *By bonkis grene . . . . beholde that hevinly place*. "Bonkis" and "beholde" are the preferred forms in southern English; as befits the courtly style in Scottish verse, such forms are prominent in this Prologue. The latter term is key for the poem as a whole. See the Glossary for occurrences.

57–63   *The soyl enbroude . . . . as Phebus schone*. The *b*-rhymes ("stone," "fanton") use the medial vowel *-o-* characteristic of southern English in place of the northern *-a-*.

61   *rowmyng myn alone*. As Lydgate or Juvenal will be depicted (see lines 921, 1229–30 and notes), so the poet depicts himself musing, "alone"; the form of the word is southern (compare northern "alane").

63   *A voce I hard*. Hearing an authoritative voice (sometimes taken to be a bird's) is a convention in poems about a visit to the *locus amoenus* (e.g., the hymn to May in *KQ*, lines 232–38).

65   *Maternall moneth*. Calling May the maternal month is a Chaucerism; *TC* 2.50.

70   *curage*. For Fradenburg, "the martial aspect of 'curage' is being invoked alongside the maternal plenitude of May" (*City, Marriage, Tournament*, p. 188); Spearing glosses the word as "sexual desire" (*Medieval Poet*, p. 234). See further lines 83–85 and note.

81   *olyve twystes*. The olive branches betoken the poet's classicism, as well as the Mediterranean associations of his scene. Douglas includes them again in the no less literary scene depicted in the prologue to Book 12 of his *Eneados* (line 165, 4:71; Curtius, pp. 195–202); it is noteworthy that the disembodied voice, not the visitor to the garden, mentions the olive branches.

83–84   *In thee enforcis . . . . luf and armony*. Here is the first of several instances in *PH* of the rhetorical "colour" *repetitio*; see further lines 128–34, 174–81. Of note is the linkage of martial and amorous "curage," the first of many instances in *PH* where keenness to fight is given centrality in the array of virtues. See note to line 70 above.

89   *I rasyt my vissage*. The dreamer looks up to see something new four more times (lines 784, 1247–48, 1405–06, 1934).

94   *Reconsell*. Though the term is perhaps most straightforwardly glossed here as "To bring back, restore" (as in *DOST reconsell* (v.), sense 2; see also sense 3), it also reflects, Caitlin Flynn argues, other aspects of the term's meaning, notably "To bring (a person) back into right or friendly relations" (sense 2; see also sense 4; "Grotesque," p. 188). Along with the term "forvay" earlier in this stanza (line 92), "reconsell" indicates an awareness of being misaligned or imbalanced.

105   *impressioun*. The term has subjective associations, as in *TC* 5.372–04, "thorugh impressiouns, / As if a wight hath faste a thyng in mynde / That therof cometh swiche avysiouns" (and see *Troilus and Criseyde*, ed. Windeatt, notes to lines 372–07 and 374; *MED impressioun* (n.), sense 3c); the phenomenon is also

considered a natural occurrence, as when Bartholomaeus Anglicus describes atmospheric "impressiouns" ignited at various altitudes (Trev. *Prop.* 11.2, p. 569). Such flashes may be considered as apocalyptic portents: "For as lightning cometh out of the east and appeareth even into the west, so shall also the coming of the Son of man be" (Matthew 24:27).

100–08   *my feblyt wit . . . . so feblyt fell.* In this stanza, the narrator refers three times to his enfeebled state: "febyl wyt," "febyl strenthis," and "[a]s femynine so feblyt." Intensifying a fifteenth-century topic of poetic self-representation, Douglas appears to be returning to Chaucer's practice in his professions of authorial modesty, which David Lawton sees as "claim[ing] a space for fiction that is apart from the public world of truth" ("Dullness and the Fifteenth Century," p. 762). However, in the last line of this stanza Douglas is also setting up the complex, problematic attitude to femininity that resurfaces at various points in the poem. (See Introduction to this edition, pp. 43, 45–57.)

113–17   *And na ferly . . . . did me assaile.* For Bartholomaeus, the "sensible soul" receives sense impressions, has its source of vital power in the heart, and generates sleep; Bartholomaeus also discusses those stimuli that cause the blood to rush to the heart to preserve the heat of the body: fear, infection, injury, pollution, cold, "whanne the spirit *vitales* fleth his contray and closith himself in the innere parties of the herte" (Trev. *Prop.* 3.15; p. 106, lines 12–13).

121–24   *Tho in my sweven . . . . shortly tyl conclud.* In the visionary onset of foul weather, Douglas may have drawn from alliterative tradition as represented by the influential *Awntyrs off Arthure,* in which dalliance "vndur a lefesale [bower]" gives way suddenly to dark "[a]s hit were mydni3t myrke" and cold, "[f]or the sneterand snawe [swirling snow] that snaypped hem snell [hurt them keenly]" (lines 70, 76, 82).

127–35   *Thow barrant wyt . . . . cunnyng nakyt thee.* Stemming from Classical antiquity and prized by orators such as Cicero, the *captatio benevolentiae* had become a dependable topic of inception and conclusion by the fifteenth century (*Brill,* "Captatio benevolentiae"). Gregory Kratzmann compares this passage with *HF,* lines 523–27: "Neither is a simple *captatio benevolentiae*: both reflect a concern for clear and accurate expression" (*Anglo-Scottish Literary Relations,* p. 120); see further line 1268.

129   *nystee.* Andrew of Wyntoun accuses himself of "foly or nysetee" in a comparable admission of incapacity in the prologue to his *Original Chronicle* (Wemyss text, 1.prol.45).

131   *beggit termis.* The poet depicts himself as a scrounger of more eloquent poets' words; the terms he has acquired are not his by right. In this context, "begging" is a euphemism for "pilfering." In his prologue to *The Court of Venus* (line 320), John Rolland borrows the expression "beggit termes" from Douglas.

136–53   *My ravyst sprete . . . . morthurars men revyt.* Chaucer describes a dream-desert in *HF,* lines 482–91, but a closer parallel to Douglas' wasteland is the noisy, barren forest encircling the temple of Mars in KnT (*CT* I[A] 1975–80). Douglas may also be drawing on the sudden transformation of the setting from luxuriant lushness to purgatorial dreariness that is part of the tradition of visionary encounters between the living and the dead in Middle English poetry (Chism, *Alliterative Revivals*, p. 246).

136   *ravyst sprete*. Given the narrator's earlier reference to himself as "femynine" in falling unconscious in the garden (line 108), it is possible that mention of his "ravyst sprete" could evoke memories of Heurodis, Orfeo's queen, abducted by the fairies. In the fifteenth century, a Scottish Orpheus romance was in circulation, and fragments of it are preserved in a sixteenth-century manuscript and a nineteenth-century transcript; see Purdie's edition of these fragments in *Shorter Scottish Medieval Romances* (pp. 23–33, 113–23).

138   *Cochyte the ryver infernall*. The comparison with "Cochyte" may arise from a recollection of *Aeneid* 6.131–32, 1:542–43, where the entrance to Hades is in a wood, around which Cocytus meanders. Another Virgilian source may be *Georgics* 4.478–79 (ed. Fairclough, pp. 252–53), where Orpheus approaches Cocytus with its "black ooze" (*limus niger*) and "unsightly reeds" (*deformis harundo*).

139   *trubbyll*. In place of "trubbyll" in the printed witnesses, the reading in E1, "trybbill" ("treble"), improves the rhyme and sharpens the reference to sound; nevertheless, "trouble" has contemporary associations with loud noise as an element of tribulation, as when John Ireland writes about Paradise as a place where "na trubile nore commocioune js of wynd, rayne, snaw or vthire trubile" (*Meroure* 2:4, 1:77).

144   *skauppis brynt*. The burnt hills may be an apocalyptic touch, as in the Biblical prophecy against the "destroying mountain," Babylon, doomed to be made into "a burnt mountain" (Jeremiah 51:25).

146–47   *In quham the fysche . . . . hering all fordevyt*. Fishes' clamor pertains to the tradition of apocalyptic omens. For a list of versions, see Heist, *Fifteen Signs*, pp. 204–14. Underpinning the tradition are scriptural passages such as Luke 21:25, on the "confusion of the roaring of the sea and of the waves." In *The Prik of Conscience*, Jerome is cited as the authority for the signs following the coming of the Antichrist, including that for the fourth day, when "The wondursteful fysshes of the see / Shul come togedur and make roryng / Wondur hydous to monnes heryng" (ed. Morey, 5.760–62; also see *Northern Homily Cycle*, ed. Thompson, Homily 2, lines 117–20). The fish are described as "yelland as elvis" in that the noise they are making is otherwordly, or inhumanly strange; see the note to line 299, below.

149–53   *Not throu the soyl . . . . morthurars men revyt*. According to Bartholomaeus, "deserte is untiliede and ful of thornes and pricchinge busshes, place of crepyng wormes and venymouse bestes and of wylde bestes, and it is the home of flemyd [banished] men and of theves, londe of firste and of drynesse, londe of brennynge and disease, londe of wastynge and of grysenesse, londe of mysgoynge and of errynge" (Trev. *Prop.* 14.51, p. 721, lines 17–22). As well as preparing for the apocalyptic description at lines 346–54, Douglas is reversing the topic of creativity (sap, bees, flowers, herbs, cultivation) that predominates elsewhere in the poem.

160   *I crap on fut and hand.* A. C. Spearing perceives that the frightened, disgusted dreamer has already undergone a metamorphosis "into a cowering animal," on all fours (*Medieval Poet*, p. 236). See further the note to lines 756–58 below.

163–92   *And not but . . . . and quheil contrarius.* The stanza in ten pentameter lines with the rhyme scheme *aabaabbcbC* is perhaps understandably quite rare. The translation of a complaint in French on the death in 1445 of the Dauphine Margaret Stewart, daughter of James I (*Book of Pluscarden*, trans. Skene, pp. 382–88) is in a ten-line stanza with the same rhyme scheme but without the extra refinement Douglas employs, of a final refrain. In the lament in *Orpheus and Eurydice* (ed. Fox, lines 134–83), Henryson employs this stanza with refrain. A single ten-line stanza in this rhyme-scheme also appears near the end of *The Quare of Jelusy* (*Chaucerian Dream Visions*, ed. Symons, p. 152). See notes to lines 607–36 and 1015–44 below.

165–92   *"Allas," I said . . . . and quheil contrarius.* For the convention of the complaint against Fortune, see H. R. Patch's classic account (*Goddess Fortuna*, pp. 55–80).

174–81   *Now thare . . . . now defyis.* Utley commented about a similar medieval literary complaint that its speaker "imprisons the conflict between the walls of antithesis, but his rhetoric accentuates rather than resolves the difficulty" (Utley, p. 33). Antithesis is a rhetorical figure commonly used to express the variability of Fortune (and of Venus; see lines 601–02 and note); another figure employed here (and frequently elsewhere in *PH*) is anaphora, the repetition of a word or phrase at the beginning of consecutive clauses.

186–87   *Certis none . . . . Ya, iwys.* In the prologue to Book 1 of his *Eneados*, Bawcutt observes, Douglas "shows his mastery of *talking* in verse," and his "repeated use of *correctio* [as here in line 186] suggests a man in the act of thinking aloud" (pp. 166–67).

199   *Amyd a stok richt prevaly I stall.* Palamon in KnT similarly hides "in a bussh" because "soore afered of his deeth was he" (*CT* I[A] 1517–18).

199–300   *Amyd a stok . . . . akyn stok mysharrit.* Gower's Rosiphilee hides among trees to watch the procession of the courtly retinue of Venus; she also accosts a straggler who has failed to obey the laws of that court (*CA* 4.1292–434).

201   *Ane lusty rout of bestis rationall.* A faint reminiscence may be detectable here of a famous exploit of the poet's ancestor Sir James Douglas, who maneuvered his troops up to Roxburgh Castle by disguising them as a herd of oxen (*Barbour's Bruce*, ed. McDiarmid and Stevenson, 10.380–99, 2:254–55).

202–03   *Of ladyis fair . . . in constant weid.* Uniformity of dress prevails here and at the court of the Muses (line 791), but not at the court of Venus (lines 535–43), or among the courtiers of Chaucer's Fame (*HF*, lines 1323–28).

205–06   *Full sobyrly thair haknais . . . . eftyr the feitis auld.* Among riding horses, hackneys were "[l]ighter in frame and known for their high action in movement"

(Simmons, "Rejection of the Manege Tradition," p. 6); referring to the old style of riding, Douglas may be alluding to the humanist recovery of knowledge of ancient equestrianship, including Xenophon's *De re equestri*, which Leon Battista Alberti followed in his *De equo animante* (1444–47; Bergstein, "Donatello's *Gattamelata*," pp. 852, 863–64).

214   *swete of sware*. This is a traditional phrase: *DOST swire* (n.), sense 1.2; *MED swire* (n.), senses 1a, b), especially the citations from *Arthur and Merlin* (line 715, Lincoln's Inn text), *The Siege of Milan* (line 36), and *Le Bone Florence* (lines 90, 441).

215   *In purpur robe hemmid with gold ilk gare*. Pliny noted that a military victor honored in a Roman triumph wore a toga dyed purple with a golden trim (Plin. *HN* 9.127, 3:248–49). Here a "gare" is any "wedge-shaped or triangular piece of cloth forming part of a garment and serving to produce the difference in width required at different points" (*OED gore* (n.2), sense 3). The classicism of the image stops short enough that the actual clothing envisioned mirrors the mode of late fifteenth-century Scotland — amply cut gowns and not togas.

220   *granyt violate*. Cloth with ingrained dye was especially expensive and prized (*ALHTS*, p. clxxxiii); Pliny described the toilsome derivation of purple from sea mollusks (Plin. *HN* 9.125–27, 3:246–49).

224   *mony fair prelate*. The reference to "mony fair prelate" in the cavalcade of Venus is likely ironic; Chaucer's Monk is called "certeinly" a "fair prelaat" (*CT* I[A] 204).

232   *mone*. The form "mone" for "mane" (the hair to refer to the head) is an extreme example of substitution of the southern -*o*- form to fit the rhyme scheme, where it would not appear in southern usage; see *DOST mone*.

236   *Achitefel and Synone*. The Biblical and Greek names suggest treachery (see line 282). Compare Gower, *CA* 2.3090 for Ahithophel, and *CA* 1.1172 for Sinon, the Greek spy and trickster, who conspired against Troy with the wooden horse. See also lines 278–81, 282–86, and notes.

243–44   *the prudent Sibillais . . . . Cassandra, eik Delbora and Circis*. The term "sibyl" could be used loosely to refer to prophetic women; the ensuing sequence of notable women and "mony a prophetis" (line 246) could be referred to thus. Possibly Douglas is referring to a specific tradition of twelve Sibyls who foretold Christian truths: the Persian, Libyan, Erythrean, Cumaean, Samian, Cimmerian, European, Tiburtine, Agrippan, Delphic, Hellespontine, and Phrygian. Exemplifying the contemporary interest in crossovers from pagan to Christian, the Dominican inquisitor Philippus de Barberis (Filippo Barbieri) compiled the prophecies about Christ ascribed to the classical Sibyls, *Duodecim Sibyllarum vaticinia* (the second treatise in his *Opuscula*, as reprinted c. 1482). For a contemporary depiction of the twelve, see the Isabella Breviary, British Library, Additional MS 18851, fol. 8v.

244   *Cassandra, eik Delbora and Circis*. A diverse trio of prophetic women: Cassandra, also named "Sibille" in Chaucer, the unheeded prophet of Troy's destruction

and expounder of Troilus' dream (*TC* 5.1450–533); Deborah, judge of Israel and prophet of victory over the Canaanites (Judges 4:4–10); Circe, the deceiver and debasing enchanter of men, who directs Ulysses homeward (*Met* 14.223–319, 2:316–23; paired with Calypso in *CA* 6.1426–71; alongside Medea and Calypso in *HF*, lines 1271–72).

246   *Judith, Jael*. Potentially controversial Biblical women who overcame men: Judith beheaded Holofernes (Judith 13:4–9; Chaucer, *CT* VII[B²] 3741–64; *Heroic Women*, ed. Peck, pp. 109–53); Jael impaled Sisera's head with a tent-peg (Judges 4:21–22).

252   *Salust, Senek, and Titus Livius*. Sallust, Seneca, and Livy assume prominence in the fifteenth century as disparate models of Latin style: Douglas alludes later to Sallustian characters (Jugurtha, *PH*, lines 1688–89; Catiline, *PH*, lines 1690–91) and episodes from Livy (*PH*, lines 1657–80; *Eneados* 1.5.28n, 2:35); he may have been influenced by Quintilian's pairing of the "famous brevity of Sallust" with the "milky fullness of Livy" (Quint. *Inst.* 10.1.32, 4:268–69). Apparently spontaneous, often abrupt and antithetical, and commonly contrasted to Cicero's, Seneca's prose style exerted a lasting influence on the writing of philosophy and theology in the Middle Ages.

253   *Picthagoras, Porphure, Permenydus*. Here and elsewhere in this catalogue, the selection of names in the line can be more euphonious than cogent. In the Middle Ages, the ancient Greek philosopher Pythagoras was famous for his beliefs in monotheism and the transmigration of souls, but also being at or near the origins of the liberal arts of mathematics and music; his reputation for learning expanded to include unrelated specializations such as surgery (*CA* 6.1410–11) and chess (*BD*, lines 666–67). Principally known in fifteenth-century Europe through Boethius' translations, Porphyry would have been recognized as a commentator on Aristotle's logic; a copy of his *Isagoge super Organon*, "a set book in logic for first-year Arts students in the medieval universities," was donated by Bishop Elphinstone to King's College Library; now MS 223 (Macfarlane, "Elphinstone's Library Revisited," pp. 68, 70; quoted on p. 70). Parmenides, pre-Socratic Greek philosopher, founded the Eleatic school of philosophy.

254   *Melysses*. This has been supposed to refer to Melissus of Samos, follower of Parmenides, whose words were hardly irrefutable, being criticized by Aristotle (*Physics*, trans. Wicksteed and Cornford, 1.184b, 185b, 186a; 1:14–15, 20–21, 28–29). A less likely candidate is Melisseus, reputed discoverer of honey (and hence such sweet things as eloquence) and inventor of the art of beekeeping; Lactantius calls him the originator of sacrifices to the gods (*Divine Institutes*, trans. Fletcher, 1.22; Bühler, "'Kynge Melyzyus'").

255   *Sidrag, Secundus, and Solenyus*. Sidrak (derived from the Biblical Shadrach: Daniel 3:22, 23; alluded to later in the poem, line 1555) is the sage who answers the wide-ranging questions of the Babylonian king Bokkus in the widely distributed *Livre de la fontaine de toutes sciences*, translated into English as *Sidrak and Bokkus*; in *The Quare of Jelusy*, "the gret philosophoure / Sydrake" is cited as

a moral authority (*Chaucerian Dream Visions*, ed. Symons, p. 191n317–18). Though the cognomen recurs frequently, "Secundus" may refer to Julius Secundus, whom Quintilian commemorates as an important orator and friend (Quint. *Inst.* 10.1.120–21, 4:316–17; 10.3.12, 4:340–43). The *Polyhistor* (*Collectanea rerum memorabilium*) of the Roman geographer Caius Julius Solinus was published frequently in the late fifteenth century; John Ireland cites Solinus on kingship by election rather than lineal succession on the strictly regulated island of Caprobane (*Meroure* 7; 3:146–54).

257   *Empedocles, Neptennebus, Hermes.* Empedocles is the pre-Socratic Greek philosopher who reputedly leapt into the Sicilian volcano Etna (Horace, *Ars Poetica*, ed. Henderson, lines 465–66, pp. 488–89). There were two Egyptian kings of the thirtieth Dynasty named Nectanebus, the second of whom enters the medieval tradition of romances about Alexander the Great as a magician and the father of Alexander the Great (*CA* 6.1789–2366; *Brill*, "Alexander Romance"; "Nectanebus"). Hermes Trismegistus was the Greek counterpart of the Egyptian god Thoth (god of wisdom), pseudonymous author of the Hermetic writings on astrology, alchemy, magic, medicine, religion, and philosophy, and the legendary founder of Hermeticism (*CA* 4.2606–07 and 7.1476–92; *Brill*, "Corpus Hermeticum").

258   *Galien, Averroes, and Plato.* In addition to Plato, these are two authoritative, influential commentators: the Greek physician and philosopher Galen (on Hippocrates) and the Arabic philosopher Averroes (on Aristotle).

259   *Enoth, Lameth, Job, and Diogenes.* Enoch "walked with God" (Genesis 5:24) and was therefore thought to have explored the heavens (e.g., *HF*, line 588); Lamech the notorious bigamist (e.g., *CT* III[D] 54, V[F] 550–51; *Anelida and Arcite*, line 150); Job, whose Old Testament book recounts his sufferings, patience, and restoration. In this biblical group, the Cynic philosopher Diogenes may fit because of his praise of virtuous poverty, his rebuke of Alexander, but also, according to Gower, his use of a tub as an observatory from whence to view "the hevene / And deme of the planetes sevene" (*CA* 3.1201–311, quoted at lines 1215–16).

261   *Wyse Josephus.* Flavius Josephus, historian of the Jews and especially the Jewish war against Rome; calling him "Ebrayk Josephus the olde," Chaucer depicts him lifting "The fame up of the Jewerye" (*HF*, lines 1433, 1436).

262   *Melchisedech.* Melchizedek (Genesis 14:18–20), priest and king, merits a line to himself.

272–73   *Knawis thou not . . . . schour of rane.* The topic of youthful aspirations ignobly diverted reappears late in the poem, in the Nymph's reflections on those who fail to reach the summit of the mountain and who fall from the walls of the palace (lines 1334–38; 1785–88).

278–81   *How Davidis prayer . . . . frustrat sa fowlily.* David prays to God to "turn Ahithophel's advice to folly"; Ahithophel commits suicide upon learning that Absalom has rejected his advice; in battle against his father, Absalom was killed while caught in a tree by his hair (2 Kings 15:31; 17:23; 18:9–15, ed. Wansbrough).

283–86   *First in to Troy . . . . wes at schort.* Aeneas recounts the stratagems by which Sinon convinced the Trojans to bring the Wooden Horse into their city (*Aeneid* 2.57–198; 1:320–31). Gower draws attention to Sinon's lighting a fire in Troy to signal the Greek attack (*CA* 1.1172–77).

291   *sorcery or charmys.* While already advocating for the prerogatives of Honour, the dreamer raises the possibility that sorcery may penetrate the Palace.

294   *on rowme.* Douglas employs a well-established idiom; *DOST roum* (n.), sense 1d.

299   *elrych.* This is the earliest datable appearance of "elrych" (*DOST elrich(e* (adj.); compare *OED eldritch* (adj.)). The word may recall the jesting description of the pilgrim Chaucer as "elvyssh by his contenaunce" (*CT* VII[B²] 703). Alaric Hall argues that "elrych" derives etymologically from Old English **æl-rīce*, meaning "foreign" or "otherworldly" ("Etymology and Meanings of *Eldritch*," pp. 21–22).

316–27   *A hart transformyt . . . . at thaym batit.* Diana's transformation of Actaeon into a hart (*Met* 3.131–252, 1:132–43; retold in *CA* 1.333–82; see also the briefer allusion in *CLL*, lines 94–98). "[A]s in Lydgate's *Complaynt*, an apparently gratuitous treatment of Actaeon functions as a figure or symptom of the poet's sense of the shame and peril of his own voyeuristic position in his poem" (Spearing, *Medieval Poet*, p. 237). For the dreamer-protagonist of *PH* at least, the scene provides the context for his later fear of Venus (lines 738–44); it may also relate to his recurrent sense of being "mismaid" (see Glossary).

327   *Tha raif thair lord, mysknew hym at thaym batit.* This line exemplifies Douglas' recourse to the concise style: note the asyndeton (omission of a grammatically integral word, here the conjunction between "lord" and "mysknew") and the grim pun on "batit" (Actaeon used to feed his dogs as their master; now he feeds them as their prey); for another example of this style, see line 1680.

328–29   *Syne ladyis come . . . . lyke till fostaressys.* This rhyme recalls *HF*, lines 229–30, describing Venus at Carthage, "As she had ben an hunteresse, / With wynd blowynge upon hir tresse"; Douglas, however, is thus describing true votaries of Diana, the virgin deity of women and hunting.

330   *eliphant.* The elephant is an emblem of chastity: "Elephantes hateth the werk of leccherye but oonliche to gendre ofsprynge" (Trev. *Prop.* 18.45, p. 1196, lines 21–22).

334–36   *God wait that . . . . with Diane hant.* The insistency and overstatement of this praise of women's steadfastness and chastity hang on the word "professys"; in the late fifteenth century, the word is not proven to include the implication that the affirmation (of virginity in this case) is false (*DOST profes* (v.), sense 6; *OED profess* (v.), sense 3a). However, the absoluteness of "nane of thaym is variant" and "All chast" leads to an absolute reversal in the "few" of the stanza's last line. Behind the insistence of this passage may lie encomia of women's steadfastness such as Chaucer's in *LGW* (G prol.273–310; see Hansen, "Irony and the Antifeminist Narrator," pp. 14–15.)

338–39   *Jeptyis douchtir . . . . in hir virginité.* Jephthah's daughter, doomed by her loyalty; Jephthah the Israelite vowed to sacrifice to God "whosoever shall first come forth out of the doors of my house, and shall meet me when I return in peace"; his daughter was first to meet him, and "he did to her as he had vowed" (Judges 11:30–40, quoted at verses 31, 39; see also *CA* 4.1505–95, and the Middle English version of the story in *Heroic Women*, ed. Peck, pp. 121–24).

340   *Pollixena.* Polyxena, princess of Troy, carried off by Agamemnon and sacrificed to appease the ghost of Achilles (*Met* 13.439–80, 2:258–63; compare *Historia Destructionis Troiae*, trans. Meek, 30.297–337). A virgin when sacrificed, Polyxena suitably appears among Diana's attendants.

341   *Panthessilé.* Penthesilea, Amazon queen who, for love of Hector, fights at Troy and is killed by Pyrrhus (*Historia Destructionis Troiae*, trans. Meek, 28; *CA* 4.2139–72).

342   *Effygyn and Virgenius douchter fre.* Sacrificial daughters: Iphigenia, daughter of Agamemnon, offered at Aulis to Diana, who substitutes a doe for the human victim (*Met* 12.28–38, 2:182–83); Virginia, whose tale is told by Livy as a decisive instance of lustful oppression in ancient Rome (as in Bellenden's Scots translation, *History*, ed. Craigie, 3.44–48, 2:142–61), and retold by Gower (*CA* 7.5131–306) to point the need for kings to eschew lust, and also the subject of Chaucer's Physician's Tale.

359   *A schynand lycht out of the northest sky.* This northeastern glow occurs in a dream that is couched in a fiction; it may yet be valuable to note at Edinburgh at 6:00 UTC, Venus would have been visible in the northeast sky on 1 May in 1495, 1501 and 1502 (Walker, *Your Sky*). The northerly advent of Venus may recall the opening of *KQ*, in which the planet "North northward approchit the mydnyght" (line 7).

362   *nowmer.* "Number" refers to ratios and proportions as well as quantity in music, and thus to relationships between components in melody, rhythm and harmony (*DOST noumer* (n.), sense 9).

364–81   *Farther by wattyr . . . . thyng that seis.* Not least for its comic handling of learned discourse, this excursus on the transmission of sound over water bears comparison to *HF*, lines 765–80; Bawcutt notes more substantially philosophical similarities and differences in Vincent of Beauvais' *Speculum Naturale* 5.10, 5.14, 5.20, and 5.21, 18.2 and 18.7 (*SP*, p. 179n364–81). This is not the first indication in *PH* of a wide-ranging interest in the relation between sound and motion, and specifically between sound and water; see notes to lines 25, 146–47 above. In Douglas' university education, the topic would have had curricular status through the primary authority of Aristotle, for whom the production of sound involves percussion and the transmission involves vibration: "Echo occurs when air rebounds, like a bouncing ball, from another body of air unified by the vessel which confines it" (*De Anima*, trans. Hett, 2.419b.26–27, pp. 110–11).

418–35   *Procedand furth wes . . . . anamallyt all fassioun.* In this ekphrasis, Douglas exhibits particular interest in the depiction of the chariot of the sun in Ovid's story of Phaethon (*Met* 2.106–10, 1:66–69).

422 *hote*. The rhyme-word "hote" is the southern counterpart to the northern form *hecht*.

425 *hamys*. These are the ornamental frames on draught horses' collars; the traces are attached by means of the "hamys" (*AHLTS*, pp. 284, 291).

428 *crysolytis*. Chrysolite is the name "formerly given to several different gems of a green colour, such as zircon, tourmaline, topaz, and apatite" (*OED chrysolite* (n.), sense 1a). The reference seems Ovidian, with chrysolites being singled out as decorative elements on the yoke of the chariot of the sun (*Met* 2.109–10, 1:68–69).

429–32 *Wes all ovirfret . . . . the erth adoun*. More explicitly than in the brief description of the chariot of the sun earlier in *PH* (line 32), this chariot is endowed with cosmological significance, its jewels and cloths conveying "proportioun" and influence, "to the erth adoun."

434 *fas . . . frenyeis*. Tassels ("fassis") decorated the trappings of the Scottish kings' horses (*ALHTS*, pp. 22, 228).

444 *Jerarchyes of angellys ordours nyne*. In ascending order, the angelic hierarchies are (1) Angels, Archangels, and Virtues; (2) Powers, Principalities, and Dominations; (3) Thrones, Cherubim, and Seraphim (Trev. *Prop*. 2.7–18, pp. 68–84). Alluding to the creation of the angels, an earlier Scottish poet, Andrew of Wyntoun, cites "Sanct Gregour in ane omely [homily]" on the subject of "angellis orderis thrise thre" (Wyntoun, Wemyss text, 1.3, lines 33, 41); Wyntoun's editor F. J. Amours identifies the source, Gregory the Great, Homily 34.6–8 (Wyntoun, 1:4–5). The comparison with angels' song is proverbial (Whiting A128).

458 *hir rob*. The bejeweled gown Venus is wearing outdoes the best of women's fashion in Scotland c. 1498, when noblewomen's gowns were often of satin, velvet, or camlet, "adorned with the most expensive trimmings and embroidery," lined with broadcloth, silk, buckram, or fur, often with cloth or fur trimming at the hem (*ALHTS*, p. clxxxi).

462 *Mair than the brycht sonne may the bakkis e*. On the wide circulation of this Aristotelian commonplace (*Metaphysics*, trans. Tredennik, 2.1.3, 933b, pp. 84–85), see *Poems of Robert Henryson*, ed. Fox, p. 277n1636–42). Douglas could have encountered the passage during his studies at St. Andrews, where *Metaphysics* was a set text in Arts.

465 *creste of dyamantis*. Crests are often associated with helmets and heraldic designs (*OED crest* (n.1), sense 3a); they are designed more to awe than to allure. It is thus appropriate that mention of this crest introduces the topic of Venus' power.

478 *He bare a bow with dartis haw as leid*. Here, Cupid's arrows are all leaden; it is with a lead-tipped arrow that Cupid wounds Daphne so that she flees Apollo (*Met* 1.452–72, 1:34–35). Conventionally, lead-tipped arrows inspire hate in the victims they strike while gold-tipped ones inspire love.

480 *he forsuyth had none eyn in his hed*. Cupid without eyes; see also line 1470. Douglas intensifies the well-attested topic of Cupid's being blindfolded or blind; Cupid

is blind in *HF* (lines 137–38, 617), *CT* (I[A] 1965), *CA* (1.47), *CLL* (line 461), and *KQ* (line 654). Contrast Chaucer's more idealized description of the God of Love, who "al be that men seyn that blynd ys he, / Algate me thoghte that he myghte se" *LGW*, F prol.237–38); by emphasizing Cupid's blindness, Douglas depicts him as the "personification of illicit Sensuality" (Panofsky, *Studies in Iconology*, p. 121).

494–96   *Duplat, triplat, diatesseriall . . . . mony syndry sortis*. Douglas surveys tonal proportions in late-medieval music theory, with "sesquialtera" the eleventh (octave plus fourth) and "decupla" the tenth (octave plus third). While his discussion somewhat resembles a comparable passage in Robert Henryson's *Orpheus and Eurydice* (lines 226–39), it is likely that both poets are working from a curricular source such as Boethius' *De Institutione Musica*, or else Book 2 of Macrobius' commentary on Cicero, *De Somnium Scipionis* 3.15–16 (trans. Stahl, pp. 196–97).

500   *Faburdoun, priksang, discant, conturyng*. Douglas pulls out the stops: "faburdoun" refers to improvised three-part singing, with a plainchant treble and two parallel lower parts, in parallel fourths and sixths below the melody in treble (*Grove Music Online*, "Faburden"); "priksang" is notated music (*DOST prik* (adj.2), sense a); "discant" is polyphonic singing with a plainchant tenor line and the other voices providing the "countering."

501   *Cant organe, figuration, and gemmell*. These are practices of sung polyphony: "cant organe," the singing of a second voice parallel to a plainchant (*cantus*); "gemel" or "gymel," the splitting of a single voice part into two, as a solo duet, as attested in English songbooks contemporary with *PH* (*Grove Music Online*, "Gymel"); compare Henryson, *Orpheus and Eurydice*, ed. Fox, line 370.

502–05   *On crowd, lute . . . . swete as bell*. According to Gower, the retinue of Venus is announced by "a soon / Of bombard and of clarion / With cornemuse and schallemele" (*CA* 8.2481–83); see also *BH*, which includes a catalogue of musical instruments played in praise of the Virgin Mary, including "psaltery," "sytholis," "crovde," "monycordis," and "portatiuis" (lines 757–67; see especially pp. 134–36n757–66).

502   *crowd . . . with mony gudly spring*. The Welsh "crwth" (*OED crowd* (n.1), sense a) is a bowed lyre. As a dance, the *spring* is attested in *HF*, where it is learnt by "Pipers of the Duche tonge" (lines 1234–35).

503   *Schalmis, clarionis, portativis hard I ring*. The shawm is a loud double-reeded woodwind instrument in various sizes; the clarion, a small soprano trumpet; the portative is a high-pitched organ truly portable enough to be carried; one regularly traveled along with the King from one royal household to another (*ALHTS*, pp. ccxxxii–ccxxxiii). These are all instruments suitable for use outdoors.

504   *Monycord*. Probably not the Pythagorean single-stringed instrument used pedagogically, but the clavichord, "sometimes called *monochordia* by 15th- and 16th-century writers" (*Grove Music Online*, "Monochord"); "a pare of monicordis"

accompanied James IV as he traveled from Aberdeen to Stirling in April 1497 (*ALHTS*, p. 329).

505   *Sytholl, psaltery*. The citole, a kind of lute widely used in the fourteenth century, would have been somewhat old-fashioned by Douglas' time, having been superseded by the cittern with its wire strings and prominent frets. By the end of the fifteenth century, the psaltery (the "gay sautrie" in *CT* I[A] 296, 3213) with its plucked strings was being developed into an instrument capable of producing chromatic notes. The line may suggest a traditional or even archaic aspect to the music of this court.

506   *releschyngis*. As a term for musical ornamentation, "releschyngis" may be related to the later use of "relish" in English (*OED relish* (n.3), earliest citation 1561, in Thomas Hoby's translation of Castiglione, *The Courtyer*).

507   *Fractyonis*. In late-medieval music, "fraction" can refer to time signatures and rhythmic proportion; by extension, Douglas' terms would pertain to rhythmic subdivision, silence, and convergence in performance.

508   *Pan of Archaid*. Pan is a pagan deity associated with woods and flocks. He played his syrinx in competition against Apollo and his lyre (*Met* 11.146–71, 2:130–33).

509–10   *Nor King David . . . . Kyng Saul confoundit*. David's playing of the harp initially exorcized King Saul's evil spirit, but not later; 1 Kings 16:23, 18:10–11, 19:9–10.

511–12   *Nor Amphion . . . . in his dayis*. Ovid refers to Jupiter's mortal son Amphion raising the walls of Thebes by playing his lyre (*Met* 6.178–79, 1:300–01; see *CT* IX[H] 116–18).

513   *Nor he that first the subtile craftis foundit*. Douglas, like Gower, names Jubal as the one who "fond" music (*CA* 4.2416–18, quoted at line 2418; Genesis 4:21).

517–18   *Na mare I understude . . . . or a swyne*. A comically overstated admission of ignorance that may recall a similar confession in Henryson's *Orpheus and Eurydice* (ed. Fox, lines 240–42).

521–25   *Na mair I . . . . na noyes compeir*. In "Did Chaucer know the ballad of *Glen Kindy*?" Richard Firth Green argues that by reducing Chaucer's list of four harpers (Orpheus, Arion, Chiron, and Glascurion; *HF*, lines 1203–08), Douglas is alluding to the special (and unhappy) associations with Venus shared by Orpheus and Glascurion. Green suggests that versions of what would become the ballad of *Glen Kindy* (Child, *English and Scottish Popular Ballads*, no. 67) may have been in circulation in the late middle ages, as were romances about Orpheus (ed. Purdie, *Shorter Scottish Medieval Romances*, pp. 23–33). For "Glaskeryane," see the note to line 525 below.

523   *And dulcer than the movyng of the speir*. The music of the spheres consists of the sounds generated by the harmonious revolutions of the planets and stars. According to the medieval encyclopedist Bartholomaeus, the outermost sphere, the "primum mobile" (see note to line 1840 below) "drawith aftir him the planetis, that metith therwith. And passith forth with armonye and acorde; for as Aristotel seith . . . of ordinate meovynge of the spere and of contrarye

metinge of planetes in the worlde cometh armonye and acorde" (Trev. *Prop.* 8.6, p. 458, lines 7–11).

525   *Glaskeryane.* As mentioned above (in the note to lines 521–25), "the Bret Glascurion" appears among the harpers at the House of Fame (*HF*, line 1208); Andrew Breeze posits that this figure may be traceable to "Gwydion son of Dôn, the famous otherworld magician, craftsman, story-teller, and bard of the Welsh: a Celtic Orpheus and more" ("The Bret Glascurion," p. 64). See further the note to lines 1722–27.

534   *Quhais lakkest weid was silkis, or brounvert.* The superlative idiom "the worst [*lakkest*] example was *x*" (where *x* is valuable) had been used by Richard Holland to emphasize the richness of cloth: "Cled our with clene clathis . . . The esiast was arras" (*BH*, line 673–75). The reading in L, "silkis or brounvert," makes sense, if not as straightforwardly as E's "ovirbroudart" ("embroidered over"); following L, the color is described using the heraldic terms "or" and "vert" (see the note to line 2 above); "broun" in combination with another color signifies "dark"; *DOST broun(e* (adj.), sense 1.3, as in line 433: the reference would thus be to gilt-and-green silk as the least valuable cloth.

535   *In vesturis quent of mony syndry gyse.* The various styles of garment worn at the court of Venus contrast against the "constant weid" in which Minerva's courtiers were dressed (line 203); and the dreamer-protagonist expressed satisfaction with the former.

537   *Purpur coulour, punyk and skarlot hewis.* In this sequence of colors, "punyk" refers to the color pomegranate, *punicum malum* (*MED punik* (n.)).

538–41 *Velvot robbis maid . . . . flouris and bewis.* The later 1490s witnessed a change of men's fashion, notably in the "enormously increased width of the sleeves" (*ALHTS*, p. clxxiv). The amply cut, richly piled silk gowns are "begaryit," decorated with variously colored strips of other materials: damask (silk cloth in which designs are woven), satin, "cramessy" (crimson) satin, and velvet appliqued onto them "in divers rewis." These strips may be embroidered with designs of flowers and foliage, or perhaps such designs cover the whole gown (*ALHTS*, p. clxix).

540   *Cramessy.* See *MED cremesin* (n.), sense a. This is the deep red dye from crushed kermes or the cloth so dyed. The old form *veluos* preserved in L (*DOST vellus*) recurs in the *ALHTS* in the late 1490s (pp. 13, 21, 24, 97, 164, 256, 273, 297, 392).

542–43 *Damesflure tere pyle . . . . every state renewis.* Adding details of special fineness of material and workmanship, these lines intensify the impression of sumptuousness. The "flure" (underlying) velvet is "three-pile"; the cloth has been woven with three threads, producing a luxurious nap. Appliqued with strips (compare *PH*, line 539), and embroidered with gold thread (*OED orphrey* (n.), sense 1) worked with pearls, this fabric is said to "renew" every "state" — perhaps, to enhance the eminence of every high rank. "[T]he term *terpoile* indicates that Spanish velvet was also being imported to Scotland" (*ALHTS*, p. 135).

544   *entire.* For this unusual spelling of "attire," see *DOST entyre.*

547   *pattrell.* See *MED peitrel* (n.1), sense a. This was the breastplate for a warhorse. By the late fifteenth century, it was more ornamental than practical: "Brydel & paytrel & al the gere / With fyn gold y-harneysed were" (*Sir Ferumbras*, line 3665); see also "bardyt" (line 551).

549–51 *palfray . . . . cursere.* The palfrey is a fine riding horse, fit for ladies; the larger courser has the power and speed for tournaments and battle: "Upon a courser stertlynge as the fyr . . . / Sit Eneas, lik Phebus to devyse" (*LGW*, line 1204). Elaborate gear for James IV's horses was being prepared in November 1495, including "velvous to covir twa sadillis and the harnessingis of the samyne," and a larger quantity of velvet for "the Kingis bardis"; this horse-armor was evidently overhung with trappings decorated with silk fringes and gold thread (*ALHTS*, pp. 261–62).

559–61 *Behaldand Venus . . . . ryde or gang.* On the adulterous love of Mars for Venus, see *Met* 4.171–89, 1:190–91, and Chaucer, *Mars.*

561   *Hir knycht hym clepis quare so he ryde or gang.* The line has the air of an English romance: even with the northern *-is* suffix, "clepe" is a borrowing, generally in Scots verse, from southern English (*DOST clep(e,* (v.), sense 1). Compare the English lyric "My lief is faren in londe" (*Secular Lyrics*, ed. Robbins, p. 152): "She hath my herte in holde / Wherever she ride or go".(lines 5–6).

562–64 *Thair wes Arsyte . . . . fals luf Enee.* The list of lovers begins in a Chaucerian register: Arcite, Palamon, and Emily, the love triangle of KnT; and a rather flatly characterized Troilus and Criseyde. Amidst this opening sequence, Dido and "fals" Aeneas seem to arise from Chaucer's depictions in *HF* (lines 329–82) and *LGW* (lines 924–1367), but the most important source is Ovid, *Heroides* 7.

562–97 *Thair wes Arsyte . . . . innumerabill.* The attendants at the court of Venus represent various aspects of fortune and conduct in love. The sequence deserves comparison with similar lists (for instance, *HF*, lines 388–432; *PF*, lines 286–92; *CLL*, lines 365–99), and Gower's parliament of exemplary lovers (*CA* 8.2440–744).

562–63 *Arsyte and Palemon . . . with fare Emylya.* Unlike Douglas, in *The Temple of Glas* Lydgate names Chaucer as the source for his reference to Palamon and Arcite (lines 102–10).

564   *hir fals luf Enee.* This emphasis on Aeneas' falseness is Chaucerian (Legend of Dido in *LGW*, e.g., lines 1236, 1265–76, 1285–86, 1325–31; *HF*, lines 253–92; see also *CA* 4.77–137, where faithless Aeneas is accused of "slowthe"). Compare Douglas' later skepticism on this account: Chaucer "set on Virgill and Eneas this wyte, / For he was evir (God wait) all womanis frend" (*Eneados* 1.prol.448–49, 2:16).

566   *The fair Paris and plesand Helena.* Though Paris and Helen appear in *TC*, Douglas may be thinking back toward Ovid's letters between Paris and Helen, as well as Oenone's letter to Paris (*Heroides* 16 and 17, 5).

567   *Constant Lucres and traist Penolype.* For Lucrece, see *LGW*, lines 1680–885, and
        Gower, *CA* 7.4754–5130 (and, given Douglas' interest in Livy, see also *History*,
        as in Bellenden's Scots translation, ed. Craigie, 1.58–60, 1:200–09); for
        Penelope, see *Heroides* 1 (see also *CA* 4.147–233).

568   *Kynd Pirramus and wobegone Thysbe.* For Pyramus and Thisbe, see *LGW*, lines
        706–923; also *Met* 4.55–166, 1:182–91.

569   *Dolorus Progne, triest Philomena.* Procne's husband raped and mutilated her sister
        Philomela: *Met* 6.438–674, 1:318–35; *CA* 5.5551–6074.

570   *King David's luif thare saw I, Barsabe.* Bathsheba is in the cavalcade, but not David
        "bestad" with love for her (2 Kings 11:2–5; quoted in *CA* 6.97).

571   *Ceix with the kynd Alcyon.* This refers to Ceyx and Alcyone (*Met* 11.410–748,
        2:148–73; *CA* 4.2927–3123); in Ovid, Alcyone learns in a dream that her
        husband, Ceyx, has drowned in a storm at sea, and the two of them are
        transformed into sea-birds.

572–73 *And Achilles wroth . . . . fra hym tane.* Briseis writes to Achilles to allay his anger at
        Agamemnon (*Heroides* 3).

574   *Wofull Phillys with hir luf Demophon.* "[T]raysed" and abandoned by her husband
        Demophon, Phyllis committed suicide (*HF*, line 390; see *LGW*, lines 2394–561
        and especially *Heroides* 2); see further, line 810 and the note to lines 809–16.

575   *Subtel Medea and hir knycht Jasone.* The tale of Medea and Jason elicits powerful,
        expansive narratives from Ovid (*Met* 7.1–403, 1:342–71) and Gower (*CA*
        5.3247–4222).

576   *Paris and Veane.* Pierre de la Cépède, *Histoire du chevalier Paris et de la belle Vienne*
        (1432); translated into English, *Thystorye of the Noble Ryght Valyaunt and Worthy
        Knyght Parys / And of the Fayr Vyenne the Daulphyns Doughter of Vyennoys* was
        printed by William Caxton in 1485 (*STC* 19206; also Antwerp: Gerard Leeu,
        1492; *STC* 19207).

577   *Phedra, Thesyus, and Adriane.* Phaedra, wife of Theseus, falls in love with her
        stepson Hippolytus (*Heroides* 4); Ariadne writes to Theseus about his abandoning
        her on Naxos (*Heroides* 10; *LGW*, lines 1886–2227).

578   *Ipomedon.* Hue de Rotelande's late twelfth-century Anglo-Norman romance
        Ipomedon gave rise to numerous versions, the fullest English translation being
        Ipomadon (ed. Purdie); the theme was perennially appealing of the ill-dressed
        knight who claims to prefer hunting to romantic pursuits but wins in disguise in
        the tournament and gains the hand of the princess.

579   *Asswere, Hester, irraprevabill Susane.* This line refers to indomitable Esther and the
        Persian king Ahasuerus, protagonists of the OT Book of Esther; and Susanna,
        ogled while bathing (as was Diana by Actaeon), and assertive of her innocence
        despite her male accusers' slander (Daniel 13).

580   *the fals unhappy Dalida.* Delilah outwits and betrays Samson: Judges 16:4–21.

581   *Cruel, wikkyt and curst Dyonera.* Deianira writes to her errant husband Hercules, whom she unwittingly kills with a robe soaked in the poison blood of the centaur Nessus (Ovid, *Heroides* 9; see further the note to line 586, below).

582   *Wareit Bibles and the fair Absolon.* Byblis is cursed with incestuous love for her brother (*Met* 9.454–665, 2:34–51); given the variation of classical and biblical figures in this sequence "fair Absolon" is likely the Absalom whose "gilte tresses clere" Chaucer praises (*LGW*, F prol.249; also *CA* 8.216–22), the handsome, usurping son of King David whom Chaucer comically refracts into the Absolon of MilT.

583   *Ysyphele, abhomynabil Sylla.* These refer to Hypsipyle, abandoned by Jason (*Heroides* 6; *LGW*, lines 1368–679; see further *PH*, line 1606); Scylla, betraying her father King Nisos for love of Minos (*Met* 8.1–151, 1:406–16; *LGW*, lines 1900–21) — or perhaps the Scylla aptly described as "abhomynabil" who was transformed into a sea monster by Circe (*Met* 13.730–37, 898–968, 2:280–81, 290–97; 14.1–74, 2:300–05).

584   *Trastram, Yside, Helcana and Anna.* A strikingly variegated yet apt pairing: Tristram and Iseult, Gower's example of love-drunkenness (*CA* 6.467–75); righteous Hannah, wife of Elkanah, accused of drunkenness while she prays under her breath for a son to devote to God (1 Kings 1:9–18).

585   *Cleopatra and worthy Mark Anthon.* Chaucer retells the tale of Cleopatra and Mark Antony (*LGW*, lines 580–705). See also Gower, *CA* 8.2571–77.

586   *Iole, Hercules, Alcest, Ixion.* Hercules abducts Iole and thereby earns the jealousy of his wife Deianira (*Met* 9.134–58, 2:12–15; see the note to line 581, above); while "Ixion" has been taken to refer to Hesione, rescued at Troy by Hercules (*Met* 11.211–15, 2:134–35), the name precisely echoes that of the would-be rapist of Juno, progenitor of the centaurs (*Met* 4.461, 1:210–11; 10.42, 2:66–67; 12.504, 2:216–17). Alcestis appears to be the odd one out in this line, dying for her husband; but Hercules is the linking factor, as he rescues her from Hades, a detail Chaucer includes (*LGW*, F prol.510–16) but Gower omits in his version of the tale (*CA* 7.1917–49).

587   *The onely pacient wyfe Gressillida.* Griselda, the protagonist of Chaucer's ClT.

588   *Nersissus that his hed brak on a ston.* In Gower's version of the tale of Narcissus, the hapless youth "agein a roche of ston / . . . smot himself til he was ded" (*CA* 1.2340, 2342; Bawcutt, "The 'Library,'" p. 120; compare *Met* 3.339–510, 1:148–61).

589–91 *Jacob with fair Rachel . . . firm hart immutabill.* Compare Genesis 29:16–30, where Jacob twice works seven years in order to wed Laban's daughter Rachel.

592–94 *Thair bene bot few . . . so stabyll.* Silk and fine linen betoken softness and whiteness (Whiting L22, S311, 313, 315), but also wealth and privilege. The relation between these fine materials and the decline of faithfulness, is a well-established moral topic, as in Chaucer's Parson's Tale: "Seint Jerome seith that 'wyves that been apparailled in silk and in precious purpre ne mowe nat clothen him in Jhesu Crist'" (*CT* X[I] 933).

601–02   *Sum leivys in . . . . his panys swage.* Conor Leahy notes the recurrence of the phrase "Sum levis in hoip" in *Eneados* 12.prol.206 (4:72), in a passage surveying men's diverse experiences, obsessions, and sensations in love ("Dreamscape into Landscape," pp. 163–64). In *KQ,* lines 605–09, a comparable survey of diverse lovers takes the form of a *repetitio* on "Sum."

606–38   *lay.* The dreamer's lyric is a "lay" in that it is "a poem for singing" (*DOST lay* (n.2)). However, it does not follow the pattern of such performances at court: the dreamer does not follow those poets "that the sciencis knewe, / Throwout the warld, of lufe in thair suete layes" (*KQ,* lines 593–94); nor is he one of those who "in the courte bene present, in thir dayis, / That ballattis brevis [*compose poems*] lustellie, and layis" (Lyndsay, *Testament of the Papyngo,* lines 37–38). The "lay" is more of a complaint, an expression of grief that is taken as a "formal statement of grievance to one in authority" (*DOST complaint* (n.)).

607–36   *Constrenyt hart . . . . and cursyt destané.* This complaint is formally distinguished by its virtuosic ten-line stanza (*aabaabbabb*). For discussion of this stanza form, see the Introduction to this edition, p. 36.

613   *O cative thrall, involupit in syte.* While Palamon is hiding in KnT, Arcite complains to Juno that he has been made "so caytyf and so thral" through her enmity (*CT* I[A] 1552).

615–16   *Divide in twane . . . . in miserabill endyte.* The pathetic image of the broken heart is merged into something more unsavory, with the issuing forth of bitter grievance in the form of "miserabill" writing.

625   *bysnyng.* In *BH,* the complaining owl likewise calls himself a "bysyn," a bad example, a portent (lines 107, 959). On the recurrence of this term, see the note to *PH,* line 834, below.

627–36   *Wo worth sik . . . . and cursyt destané.* The *repetitio* on "Wo worth" derives from *TC* 2.344–47.

639   *Venus on hir lyp did byte.* As in Skelton's *Bowge of Courte,* line 288, lip-biting betokens scorn (Burrow, *Gestures and Looks,* p. 45n115).

644   *disdenyeit.* See *OED disdain* (v.), sense 4b, for the impersonal construction "it disdains me."

648   *thayr hedis schuke.* John Burrow comments that such head-shaking often signifies anger or scorn in medieval literary narrative (*Gestures and Looks,* pp. 43, 62).

651   *Pluk at the craw.* "Pluk at the craw" is "a game in which the *craw* [crow] was an object of sport to other players, who tugged his clothes or hair" (Lyndsay, p. 232n230).

652   *with blek my face they bruke.* On the blackening of the fool's face in the Morris dance and the gloomy modern legacy of that practice, see Hornback, "'Extravagant and Wheeling Strangers,'" p. 201.

653–64   *Skrymmory fery gaif . . . . Mars, Cupyd, and Venus.* These assailants may be
          alarming, but their names have diminutive or playful associations. Their
          performance resembles that of the lapwing and cuckoo in *BH* (lines 820–45). A
          "fery skrimmar" is an agile fencer (*DOST skrimmar* (n.); *fery* (adj.)), but the verb
          to *skrym*, "to dart; to attack" (*DOST*) is attested as the action of birds (*BH*, line
          67; *Eneados* 12.5.68, 4:93); together with the verbal noun *skirming*, these forms
          are related to the modern *skirmish*. For "Chippynuty," *DOST* gives the definition
          "The name of a sprite or goblin" (*Chippynutie* (n.)) but also refers to an entry for
          3 December 1573 in the *Register of the Privy Council of Scotland*, recording the
          summoning of Sir Walter Scott of Branxholm with a group of men, several of
          whom have apparently unsavory nicknames: "Huttitill," "Blak Sande," and
          finally "David Graham chipenute" (ed. Fleming, 2:307). It is possible that the
          nuts cracked by such a character would include the heads of hapless victims.

654   *chaftis quuke.* Later, the dreamer's teeth chatter with fear (line 1330), and
          Catiline's "chaftis quuke" (the note to lines 1770–73 below).

658–63   *And so confoundit . . . . pane full sare.* The implication is that the dreamer is too
          upset to notice what the courtiers are wearing — but then one would expect he
          "micht nocht consydyr" it. Perhaps the point is that the dreamer is so upset that
          he finds himself taking indelible note of details of appearance.

664–702   *Entronit sat Mars . . . . now proponyt late.* The defense conforms to the practices of
          Scottish law (indictment, plea for mercy, declaration of innocence, objection to
          the competency of the court [*Habakkuk Bisset's Rolment of Courtis*, ed. Hamilton-
          Grierson, 1:174]).

665   *Varius.* Bawcutt (*SP*, p. 186n655) posits an allusion to Quintus Varius Hybrida,
          who famously passed a law to empower an irregular court, and who at last was
          sentenced and executed under his own law (Cicero called him a "barbarous
          creature" [*De Natura Deorum*, trans. Rackham, 3.81]); in the same note, Bawcutt
          also notes that the name may offer "a punning reference to the traditional
          fickleness and uncertainty" of Venus. The name "Varius" also has significant
          literary associations: Varius Rufus was a celebrated Latin poet whom the
          Emperor Augustus assigned to edit Virgil's *Aeneid* (Brill, "Varius"). It is possible
          that each of these associations is playing into Douglas' selection of this name.

666   *Me tyl accusyng.* The preposition "tyl" is the common form of the word "to" in
          late fifteenth-century Scots usage and appears frequently in L but not in E; in
          "accusyng," the *-ing* suffix indicates the infinitive, a prominent southernism in
          Scottish courtly style (see also line 729; also the Introduction, p. 31n102).

674   *cald as a key.* The simile is proverbial; see Whiting K16.

683   *mysmaid.* All the citations in *DOST* for the past participle *mismaid* are taken from
          PH; see the Glossary to the present edition for line references. As used here and
          elsewhere in *PH*, the word may be an innovative derivation from both *mismay*
          ("[t]o be discouraged, disheartened or dismayed"; *DOST mismay* (v.)) and *mismak*
          ("[t]o make (clothes etc.) badly, to misshape"; *DOST mismak* (v.), sense a).

691   *pietuus face*. Assuming a pathetic facial expression heightens the emotional impact of an oration (Cicero, *De oratore*, trans. Rackham, 2.189–96, pp. 332–39); Lydgate considers it the proper look for a poet about to recite (*ST*, line 175). Of course, one would predictably have a "pietuus face" in a mess like this.

697   *thocht I be void of lare*. In this hasty, rather *pro forma* allusion to his lack of learning, the dreamer is making the merest of gestures toward the sort of obsequiousness expected of court poets — even though before falling asleep, he had proclaimed that he serves ("deservis"; line 93) Venus and May. Later, he will abase himself much more lavishly in expressing gratitude to Calliope (lines 1061–67).

712   *Fyrst quhen thow come, with hart and hail entent*. This reference to the poet's first arrival at Venus' court may seem biographical; probably it refers, however, to the poet's entry into the pleasant place at the start of the poem.

716–17   *Ye clerkis bene . . . . as ony snalys*. The Wife of Bath is similarly unimpressed by clerks' criticisms of women (*CT* III[D] 703–10). There is a cluster of proverbs ironically referring to the speed and "sharpness" of snails (Whiting S416, S421, S425).

725   *Syne ye forswere baith body, treuth and handis*. To swear by one's body, faith ("truth"), or hand is conventional for oaths (*DOST hand* (n.), sense A.1.e); see also line 1001.

731   *The feverus hew in till my face dyd myith*. This is the third reference in *PH* to facial color (see lines 119–20 and the note to line 652 above); the dreamer, having had his face daubed with blacking, now turns pale with fear and anxiety.

732–35   *swa the horribill dreid . . . . thocht I had neid*. "Creid" refers to an established text setting forth the basic articles of Christian belief. Of the two principal Creeds so called, the term by itself usually refers to the Apostles' Creed; learning this text was fundamental to Catholic liturgy and religious instruction in the Middle Ages and beyond (*Catholic Encyclopedia*, "Apostles' Creed"). The dreamer's anticipation of imminent harm makes him unable to recite this canonical text and thereby claim immunity by right of being a cleric.

736   *I set not half a fle*. "Not to give (or set) half a fly" is proverbial (Whiting F262, where the term is glossed is as "flea") and related to several idiomatically dismissive expressions involving flies (and fleas) current in fifteenth-century Scots writings (Whiting F260, F261, F263).

740   *In till sum bysnyng best transfigurat me*. The tone of this passage may not be entirely serious. In *The Dreme*, Sir David Lyndsay recalls playing various roles, "And sumtyme lyke ane feind transfegurate," to entertain the young James V (line 15; Lyndsay, p. 1).

746   *Quhow that Diane transformyt Acteone*. The memory of Diana's transformation of Acteon should be fresh for the reader; see lines 316–27 and note.

747–51   *And Juno eik . . . . that danger depe*. Jupiter transformed his paramour Io into a heifer; Juno perceived the ruse and kept the heifer under the guard of hundred-eyed Argus until Mercury rescued it (*Met* 1.583–746, 1:42–55).

749   *yymyt.* This is from ʒym, to care for, guard, protect (*DOST* ʒem(e (v.), sense 1).

753   *The wyfe of Loth ichangit sore did wepe.* A telling instance of Douglas' syncretism:
            Lot's wife looks back at the destruction of Sodom and Gomorrah (see also line
            1503) and is turned into a pillar of salt (Genesis 19:26); it is Niobe who is turned
            to marble and weeps (*Met* 6.267–312, 1:306–09). In *CLL*, the poet invokes Niobe
            to infuse her tears into his pen (lines 178–79).

754–55   *Jove and ald Saturn. . . . did Lycaon turn.* Referring to Saturnian paternity but not
            Saturn's actual presence (*Met* 1.163, 1:12–13), Ovid has Jupiter alone punishing
            Lycaon for serving human flesh.

756–58   *Nabugodonosore . . . . wepe and murn.* Nebuchadnezzar, king of Babylon and
            dreamer of visionary dreams, is condemned to sojourn like a beast in the
            wilderness (Daniel 4; *CA* 1.2785–3042). Crawling through the wilderness (lines
            160, 647), the dreamer has a little in common with him.

760–62   *For by exemplys . . . . ane otheris lore.* These "oft heard" sayings (Whiting F116,
            M585) are related to a widely attested proverb, *Felix, quem faciunt aliena pericula
            cautum* ("Happy are those who take warning from the perils of others" [Walther,
            Proverbia Sententiaeque, no. 8952, 2:47; and Whiting M585]).

775–79   *He quhilk that . . . . for me.* A periphrasis for God, who has prepared a rescue
            because a blessed soul has interceded on the dreamer's behalf.

776   *in personis thre.* Douglas is alluding to the fundamental Christian doctrine of the
            Trinity, three "persons" ("modes of being," *OED trinity* (n.), sense 2a) of one
            God. A liturgically prominent statement of the this doctrine may be found in the
            Athanasian Creed (Schaff, *Creeds of Christendom*, § 10).

790   *With lawrere crownyt in robbis syd all new.* "The long or 'syde' gown was a loose
            garment which reached to the feet, open in front, and sometimes confined by
            a girdle. It was made both with sleeves and without them, sleeves being then
            frequently made as separate articles of dress" (*ALHTS*, p. clxviii).

799   *And sum of thaym ad lyram playit and sang.* Asserting that knowledge of poetry is
            necessary for the orator, Quintilian links the making of poetry to knowledge of
            music; this, he observes, is certainly true for those who compose songs for the
            lyre ("carmina ad lyram," quoted in Quint. *Inst.* 1.10.29, 1:226–27). The lyre is
            Apollo's instrument; Horace's Ode 1.32 addresses it (*Odes*, trans. Rudd, pp.
            82–83). It is also what David plays when he entertains Saul; see the note to lines
            509–10 above.

801   *Metyr Saphik and also elygee.* Horace wrote twenty-five of his Odes in Sapphics:
            four-line stanzas, the first three lines of eleven syllables and the last, of five. Ovid
            used elegiac couplets (alternating hexameter and pentameter lines) in various
            works, including *Heroides* and *Ars Amatoria*. Martial famously employed elegiacs
            in his epigrams.

802–04   *Thair instrumentis all . . . . a fair psaltree.* These refer to monochords and psalteries
            as in lines 504–05; the almost identical phrase "nevyr a wreist yeid wrang"
            appears in line 1080.

805–06   *On lutis sum thair accentis subtellé / Devydyt weil.* "Tonus is the scharpnesse of voice, and is difference and quantite of armony, and stondeth in accent and tenor of vois" (Trev. *Prop.* 19.131, p. 1387, lines 10–12).

808   *The ladyis sang in vocis dulcorate.* By having the women singing the *Heroides*, Douglas may be taking literally the allusions to sung performance in Ovid's writing, notably in *Ars Amatoria* 3.345, where an *epistola* (taken as a reference to some one of the *Heroides*) appears to be directed to be sung (*cantetur*; Cunningham, "The Novelty of Ovid's *Heroides*," pp. 101–02).

809–16   *Facund epistillis quhilkis . . . . myssyvis mony one.* Douglas alludes to the *Heroides* (written by Ovid in elegiac couplets, a form referenced in line 801): Phyllis and Demophon had already appeared among the courtiers of Venus (line 574 and note), as had Penelope (line 567 and note); now the poems themselves are performed. At the end of this stanza, Douglas also refers to another of the *Heroides*, number 20, the letter of Acontius to Cydippe.

813   *tone.* The past participle of the verb *tak* ("to take") would regularly be spelled "tane"; for the sake of the rhyme, an alternate spelling, "tone," is synthesized, on the analogy of the '*o* for *a*' variation that marks the appearance of southern forms in various genres of Scots poetry (Aitken and Macafee, "History of Scots to 1700," §9.3.1). A subsequent Scottish instance is cited in *OED* (*take* (v.), under the idiom "to take out of —"; Stewart, *Buik of the Croniclis of Scotland* [1858] 2:660, lines 40, 544).

819–21   *Of castis quent . . . . fyrme cadens regulere.* "*Castis quent* means fine touches of poetry" (Scott, p. 145). Subtle use of the colors of rhetoric and maintenance of clear, consistent meter are singled out as a poet's prime skills.

829   *My curage grew.* The expression "my curage grew" reappears in line 971, and "curage" itself reappears eleven more times throughout the poem; see the Glossary for line citations.

833   *our mate.* This is perhaps referring to Varius in his role as prosecutor, arguing for the prisoner to be condemned and sentenced (*DOST justify* (v.), sense 2d).

834   *bisning.* Venus' courtiers call the offensive poet a "bisning," a monster. The word recurs throughout this episode, having been used by the poet himself in his denunciatory song (line 625) but also in the narration proper, when the dreamer fears being transformed (line 740); further, Venus refers scornfully to him as a "bysnyng schrew" (line 943). From these varying perspectives, monstrousness seems more a consequence of one's own hateful discourse than mythic retaliation against it.

846   *joyus disciplyne.* This is not so much the "Horatian synthesis of the *dulce* and the *utile*" (Bawcutt, p. 57, citing Horace, *Art of Poetry*, line 343) as a continuation of the pattern of the previous two lines. Possibly the phrase recalls the Provençal *gai saber*, referring to the art of making poetry; at Toulouse, the *Consistòri del Gai Saber* was still holding its annual festival in Douglas' lifetime (ed. France, *New Oxford Companion*, "Jeux Floraux de Toulouse," p. 414).

852   *Thespis.* Calling the mother of the Muses Thespis rather than Mnemosyne
           (Memory) may arise from Ovid's reference to the Muses as "Thespiades" (*Met*
           5.310, 1:261–62) after Thespiae, a city at the foot of Mount Helicon in Boeotia
           (*Brill,* "Thespiades" and "Thespia").

853–79   *And nixt hir . . . . scho is maistres.* Douglas translates *De Musis,* a well-known short
           poem associated with the *Dicta Catonis* (*Minor Latin Poets,* trans. Duff and Duff,
           2:634–35), with particular expansion of the line on Calliope, into a whole stanza.

863   *psaltreis.* Terpsichore's interest in psalteries intensifies an earlier interest in this
           instrument (lines 505, 804), perhaps as an indication of the ancient affiliations
           of the Muses' court, as of the court of Venus. On the relevance of Terpsichore
           to the history of musical instruments in the fifteenth century, see Salmen, "The
           Muse Terpsichore."

866–67   *Polimnya . . . . rethorik cullouris mylde.* The corresponding line (7) in *De Musis* is
           "signat cuncta manu loquiturque Polymnia gestu," translated by Duff as
           "Polymnia's hand marks all — she speaks in act" (*Minor Latin Poets,* 2:634–35).
           Downplaying this emphasis on eloquent gesture, Douglas associates Polyhymnia
           with the command of the colors of rhetoric.

878   *heroicus.* To translate *heroicus* as *epic* may be misleading; Douglas is referring to
           a high courtly style, as when Chaucer's Host urges the Clerk to set aside "Youre
           termes, youre colours, and youre figures / . . . til so be ye endite / Heigh style, as
           whan that men to kynges write" (*CT* IV[E] 16–18); directing his poem to James
           IV, Douglas uses just such a "kyngly style." (*Eneados* 9.prol.34–35, 3:170; Blyth,
           "*The Knychtlyke Stile,*" pp. 164–67).

882–84   *Phanee . . . . Napee.* Fanae, nymphs ("from whom shrines [*fana*] are named") are
           included by Martianus Capella in a list of mythical beings (*De Nuptiis Philologiae
           et Mercurii* 2.167); the Pierides are the Thracian maids who challenged the
           Muses (*Met* 5.294–331, 671, 1:258–61, pp. 284–85; *Brill,* "Pierides"); the Nereids
           are sea-nymphs, the fifty daughters of Nereus and Doris (*Met* 13.742–43,
           2:280–81, and see further *PH,* lines 1849–54); Aones are associated with the
           Aonian mountains of Boeotia and hence Helicon (*Met* 1.313–47, 1:24–27;
           3.339–58, 1:148–49; 5.333, 1:260–61), and Ovid calls the Muses *Aonides* (*Met* 6.2,
           1:288–89); Napaeae are woodland nymphs (Statius 4.255, 1:224–25; 9.386,
           2:86–87).

888, 890   *afore . . . . tofore.* Note the close occurrence of the alternate forms "afore" and
           "tofore"; in E, *befoir* is used in both places.

897   *Maist eloquently, in quham all wyt aboundyt.* The wording recalls that of lines 204
           and 275; see also lines 1037, 1415, 1970, and 2069. Seen in this context,
           Homer's abounding wit correlates with plenitude in nature and human affairs.
           On Homer's reputation in fifteenth-century Scotland, see Wyntoun, 1.1, lines
           16–18: "The pohete Omere and Virgile / Fairly formyt there tretyss / And
           curiously dytit there storyis."

900   *Ditis, Daris, and eik the trew Lucane.* Dictys Cretensis (*Ephemeris Belli Troiani*) and
           Darius Phrygius (*De excidio Troiae*), the supposed eyewitness chroniclers of the

Trojan War, the former from the Greek perspective, the latter from the Trojan (cited, for instance, in *HF*, line 1467, and *Bruce* 1.521–26, 2:20; for circulation in late fifteenth-century Scotland, see Macfarlane, "William Elphinstone's Library Revisited," p. 68). Lucan is one of Chaucer's foundational poet-historians in *HF* (line 1499); in his unfinished commentary to his *Eneados*, Douglas extols Lucan's *Pharsalia* as a "gret volum" (1.5.102n, 2:39). These three may be linked by a shared reputation for veracity.

901   *Thare wes Plautus, Pogius, Parsius.* A trio connected through alliteration: Plautus the author of Roman comedies, Poggio Bracciolini the fifteenth-century humanist, hunter of classical manuscripts (and rediscoverer of Quintilian), and polemicist (see further line 1232 and note); and the satirist Persius; it may not be a strain to see a further connection via comedy, invective and satire.

902   *Thare wes Terens, Donat and Servius.* After Plautus, Terence is the second great Roman author of comedies; linking him with the late Roman grammarians Donatus and Servius, Douglas may be alluding to the curricular importance of Terence's plays, used as school texts for learning Latin grammar (Barsby, "Terence in Translation," pp. 446–48).

903   *Francys Petrark, Flakcus Valeriane.* Pairing Petrarch with Valerius Flaccus may allude to these poets' ambition to follow in Virgil's footsteps, Petrarch with *Africa*, and, much earlier, Flaccus with his *Argonautica*, the latter rediscovered by Poggio Bracciolini. Douglas may thus be contrasting mythological and historical epic narratives.

904   *Thare wes Ysop, Caton, and Alane.* Aesop and Cato (the *Distichs*) were primary authors in the medieval curriculum (Wheatley, *Mastering Aesop*, pp. 10, 17, 37, 62–63, 88–89). Somewhat more advanced would be Alan of Lille (Alanus de Insulis), whose *De planctu naturae* Chaucer mentions (*PF*, line 316).

905   *Galterus and Boetius.* Possibly Walter of Châtillon (Gualterus de Castellione), twelfth-century author of the epic *Alexandreis*, which continued to be copied into the fifteenth century. Anicius Manlius Severinus Boethius was a Roman consul who was subsequently imprisoned and executed (CE 524). Though he also wrote treatises on music and mathematics, the work of his that had extraordinary importance through the Middle Ages was *The Consolation of Philosophy*, a Platonic dialogue on the power of philosophical study to raise the mind out of the vicissitudes of earthly life.

906   *the gret Quintilliane.* Quintilian's eminence as a rhetorical authority rose in 1416, when Poggio Bracciolini discovered a manuscript of his *Instituto Oratoria* (Zürich, Zentralbibliothek MS C74a); that work was first printed in 1470.

907   *Juvinale.* Juvenal is the most celebrated Roman satirist, and his *Satires* (often accompanied by those of Persius) were frequently reprinted in the late fifteenth century. In their commentaries on Juvenal the humanists "proudly boasted of their own work, and often vilified that of their rivals with a flood of abuse far exceeding the bounds of scholarly dignity, and leading to counter-recriminations

and sometimes to long-continued controversy" (Sanford, "Renaissance Commentaries on Juvenal," p. 95).

908 *mixt*. Referring to the Roman poet Martial's versatility of mood and meter, as revealed in his *Epigrams*.

909 *Of Thebes bruyt thare wes the poete Stace*. Alluding to Statius as author of the *Thebaid*, Douglas here follows Chaucer's reference to "Stace, / That bar of Thebes up the fame" (*HF*, line 1461). See also lines 1583–84 and note.

910 *Faustus*. Fausto Andrelini (c. 1462–1518) was crowned with laurel in 1483 by his teacher Pomponio Leto (see note to line 911); in Paris by 1488, he was assailed in an invective by Gerolamo Balbi, the reigning Italian humanist in the French capital; Balbi's ally Cornellio Vitelli accused Andrelini of plagiarism, who responded by accusing Vitelli of "corrupting the Latin language" (Carlson, "Politicizing Tudor Court Literature," p. 289).

 Laurence of the Vale. John Mair depicted Douglas as especially fond of citing the authority of the humanist Lorenzo Valla (in Latin, Laurentius Valla; Broadie, "John Mair's Dialogues," pp. 421, 424, 428–29; see also *PH*, line 1233 and note to lines 1232–33, below). Giving this acerbic scholar's name in the vernacular, Douglas perhaps jocularly imports him into the domestic scene.

911–12 *Pomponeus*. (Pomponio Leto, 1428–1498), "the first humanist commentator on Virgil" (Grafton, *Defenders of the Text*, p. 49), led the Accademia Romana. That his fame has been "blawin wyd" (for this wording see also line 961) may allude to Fame's various fanfares in *HF*, lines 1545–867.

913 *wyse poete Orace*. Horace, Roman poet whose Odes (with his *Satires*, *Epodes*, *Epistles*, and *Art of Poetry*) found particular favor in the fifteenth century, when he was among the most highly regarded curricular authors (Friis-Jensen, "Commentaries on Horace's 'Art of Poetry,'" p. 229); extolling Horace as "moral" and "wise," Douglas pays tribute to his ethical authority. In his Prologue to Book 1 of *Eneados* (line 400, 2:14), Douglas admiringly cites "Horatius in hys Art of Poetry."

915 *Brunell*. David Irving speculated in 1861 (*History of Scotish Poetry*, p. 271n4) that this is "Daun Burnel the Asse" (*CT* VII[B^2] 4502), mock-hero of Nigel Wireker's *Speculum Stultorum* (late twelfth century) — an ascription rejected by Bawcutt because "Douglas could hardly have known the work well if he took the name of the ass for the name of its author" (*SP*, p. 191n915). Bawcutt proposes instead the celebrated fifteenth-century Italian humanist Leonardo Bruni. Either way, the line presents a very diverse set of personages. Also appearing here are Claudian (Roman author of political verse and an incomplete mythological epic on the abduction of Proserpina) and the important early humanist Giovanni Boccaccio (best known in Britain for his Latin writings). Boccaccio's *De Mulieribus Claris* (*Concerning Outstanding Women*) includes sections on controversial figures such as Semiramis, Medea, and Medusa, as well as several other women whom Douglas names in *PH*.

918–24   *Yit thare I . . . . on his hede.* Chaucer is called the best in "his" vernacular (*DOST vulgar(e* (adj. n), sense B.1), and of the English nation; in *Purse*, Chaucer calls Henry IV "conquerour of Brutes Albyon" (line 22), the nation as originating in Brutus' conquest. Douglas distinguishes between English poets and those of "this natioun." By 1513, he had a wider sense of nation and audience: he hoped that his *Eneados* "may be red and song / Our Albyon ile," in his "wlgar leid" (13.prol.104–05, 4:143).

          morell John Gowere. The epithet derives from *TC* 5.1856.

919   *A per se.* "The letter A 'by itself' [indicates] a unique or incomparable person or thing" (*OED A per se* (n.)). Beginning his first Prologue to *Eneados*, Douglas praises Virgil as "Lantarn, laid stern, myrrour, and A per se" (1.prol.8, 2:3).

921   *Lydgat the monk raid musand him allone.* Depicting a solitary, melancholy Lydgate, Douglas may be alluding to Lydgate's self-portrait in the Prologue to *ST*, where "after siknesse" he encounters Chaucer's Canterbury pilgrims (lines 72, 89, 103–04, 126, 175). Lydgate is not the only poet referred to as "him allone" in *PH*: compare Juvenal (line 1229) and, at the outset of his dream, the dreamer himself (see line 61 and note).

922–24   *Of this natioun . . . . on his hede.* The balance of a triad of Scots poets against the traditional grouping of the three English ones may broadly betoken comparability of worth (Bawcutt, p. 42). However, the Scots group are all more narrowly associated with *The Flyting of Dunbar and Kennedy*, perhaps fresh in memory when *PH* was being composed (Bawcutt, "The 'Library,'" p. 121). Alluding to this particular triad of poets — "[o]f this natioun" — Douglas assigns a defining importance to the *Flyting*, but (in his reference to Kennedy and Dunbar as still alive, "yit undede") perhaps also contributes to a running joke — how could they have survived the violence of one another's insults?

          Quyntyne with ane huttok on his hede. This line has occasioned debate whether he is the Quintin Schaw recorded at court, to whom a poem in the Maitland Folio is ascribed (opposed, *Poems*, ed. Bawcutt, 2:430–31n2; in favor, McDiarmid, "Early William Dunbar," p. 127); two Quintins are recorded as servitors at court, Schaw and Focart (*ALHTS*, 1:367; 2:60, 2:90, 2:106, 2:141, 2:151, etc.), but more frequently the latter. The word "huttok" may be related to "hattock," "little hat," later appearing in the incantatory expression "horse and hattock" (*OED hattock* (n.), sense 1; *DOST hattock* (n.), with supplement).

960   *Quhow may a fule your hie renoun chakmate.* Calliope's blunt comment that the dreamer is a mere "fule" deserves comparison with Alceste's defence of Chaucer (another offender against Venus) as well-meaning and diligent, "Al be hit that he kan nat wel endite" (*LGW*, F prol.414). The declaration of "chakmate" against persons derives from Chaucer (*TC* 2.754).

961   *Your fame so wyd is blaw.* It is neatly ironic that Calliope alludes to Venus' being subject to the arbitrary dispensations of Fame; the allusion can be seen as a stimulus to Venus' following expostulation against tyrannical women (e.g., lines 988–90).

964 *modefy*. This means "alter in the direction of mildness or moderation" (*OED modify* (v.), sense 1), with the earliest citation from KnT (*CT* I[A] 2542). For the precise signification "to lessen the severity of a law," *MED* (*modifien* (v.), sense b) provides various illustrations from Lydgate.

973 *but prayer, pryce, or cost*. This phrase may derive from Latin (*prece et pretio*, "by pleading and bribery"); see *DOST prayer* (n.), sense 4.3.

984–85 *No woman is . . . . devill of hell*. Comparing spiteful women to snakes and dragons, Venus is alluding to an important source of medieval antifeminism, Ecclesiasticus, chapters 25–26 (specifically here, verses 25:22–23; Kordecki, "Making Animals Mean," pp. 89–90).

1005 *perlour*. Scant evidence for this form has been found beyond its occurrence here (*DOST perlour* (n.1); "discussion, conference"; derived from Old French *parloir*, "speeches, collectively"). Compare *MED parlour* (n.), sense 3 (with a single citation, dated c. 1475). *OED* provides various spellings with the *perl-* root, but cites only a variant of the word in *TC* 2.82 (where the word denotes "a smaller room separate from the main hall"; *parlour* (n.), sense A.I.2).

1013 *Doun on a stok I set me suddanlye*. The speaker is sitting on a tree stump to compose a poem: see line 2114 and note.

1015–44 *Unwemmyt wit . . . . delyverit of dangare*. A prominent rhetorical figure in this florid lyric (in ten-line stanzas, aabaabbcbC, first and final lines identical) is periphrasis, the multiplication of synonyms: e.g., "glaid, fresche, lusty, grene" (line 1021). It is worth noting that this lyric is addressed to the poet's own powers of invention, now "unwemmyt" (unblemished, untarnished), and praise of Venus is provided only as a penultimate gesture (lines 1039–41).

1025–30 *Quha is in welth . . . . fortune doith avance*. The impression of abundance is further enhanced by the sequence of rhetorical questions with the anaphora (word prominently repeated through successive clauses) on "Quha."

1043 *dangare*. "Danger," a lady's resistance to a lover, is an important concept in traditions of courtly love. See *MED daunger* (n.), sense 4: "Resistance offered to a lover by his ladylove; disdain, aloofness, reluctance, reserve." The full range of senses in Older Scots repays attention: 1. "Power to command or control another"; 2. "Power to hurt or injure; range of doing harm"; 3. "Risk of harm or injury; peril"; 4. "Difficulty, reluctance, grudging"; 5. "Disdain; displeasure, enmity" (*DOST danger(e), dawngere* (n.)).

1047 *I stand content thow art obedient*. Some sixteenth-century Scottish evidence indicates that the phrase "stand content" may have been idiomatic; *DOST content* (adj.1), sense 1. As if to instantiate the poet's power to influence the thinking of his superiors, the phrase combines terms closely associated in the lyric (lines 1028–29).

1051 *And with that word all sodanly sche went*. As befits the sequence of events in a dream, suddenness is a recurrent quality of the narrative; see, e.g., lines 1307, 1314, 1979. The suddenness of sleep can be dangerous, as in lines 1334–38.

Suddenness can also be associated with books, as in lines 1749, 1772. See also the occurrence of semantically related adverbs such as "atonys" (e.g., line 1923), "sone" (e.g., line 189), and "swyth" (e.g., line 1934). For further discussion, see also notes to lines 121–24, 136–53 above.

1053   *on the bent*. "On the bent" is a phrase associated with heroic narrative; *DOST bent* (n.), sense 2; *MED bent* (n.1), sense 2c. See also line 1445.

1058   *I sall beseik the Godly Majesté*. An example of the poet's mingling of Christian doctrine and classical mythology: the dreamer will pray to God to bless the Muse Calliope.

1063   *Glore, honour, laude, and reverence*. Commenting on the use of the same phrase in William Dunbar's ballade honoring Bernard Stewart on his arrival in Edinburgh, Bawcutt identifies the source in the hymn "Gloria, laus et honor" sung following the procession on Palm Sunday (*Poems*, "The Ballade of . . . Barnard Stewart," line 8, 1:177, 2:408; *Catholic Encyclopedia*, "Gloria, Laus et Honor").

1071   *a swete Nymphe*. That the dreamer's guide would be a nymph, a semi-divine denizen of the world of classical gods and goddesses, seems appropriate. This nymph serves Calliope by teaching the dreamer about the visionary world and conveying him to his destination. As well, her command of Christian knowledge and moral principles makes her almost angelic; on the other hand, her broad sense of humor and zestful readiness to puncture masculine pretensions sometimes bring her close to the depictions of women in, for instance, Dunbar's *Tretis of the Tua Mariit Wemen and the Wedo*. Like the dreamer, the nymph is never named in the poem. Entrusted into her care, he calls her "my keeper," and indeed she has to guide and even carry him past dangerous obstacles (lines 1309–11, 1339–41, 1926–29). She is also his "governour" (line 1169), an instructor from whom he learns the significations of objects he sees on his journey; if much less grandiloquently, she functions as did the Eagle in *HF*. She is no meek, willowy little being: she can lift up the dreamer (by the hair, if necessary; line 1340), and does not hesitate to scold and insult him when he lags or fails (lines 1308, 1866–68, 1936–38).

1073   *Was harnyst all with wodbynd levis grene*. Evidence of traditional practices postdating *PH* in Scotland suggest that woodbine or honeysuckle, *Lonicera periclymenum*, "was considered to ward off evil especially around May Day" (*National Records of Scotland*, "Honeysuckle"; Wimberly 355). To celebrate the coming of May, Arcite gathers a "gerland" of "wodebynde or hawethorn leves" (*CT* I[A] 1507–08).

1077   *swyft as thocht*. This is proverbial; Whiting T231–34. Chaucer depicts Dido's hunting party "upon coursers swift as any thought" (*LGW*, line 1195).

1081   *Throw cuntreis seir, holtis, and rochys hie*. The phrase "cuntreis seir" recurs at line 1632, about Aeneas, who voyaged through distant lands as does the dreamer now. A similar formula for movement through varied landscapes occurs at line 1246. The aerial perspective is comparable with Geoffrey's in *HF* (lines 896–903).

1081–83 *Throw cuntreis seir . . . . mony strate montane*. Fittingly, the nymph guides the dreamer through a landscape marked by places associated already (lines 882–84) with local deities like herself.

1085–87 *Our horssis flaw . . . . up in Almane*. A zigzag itinerary (Hasler, *Court Poetry*, p. 104) is taken on "apparently Pegasean horses" (Spearing, *Medieval Dream-Poetry*, p. 207).

1087, 1090 *Almane . . . . Garmanie*. *DOST* lists *Almanie* (n.) as the usual name for Germany, but here it specifies northern Switzerland and Alpine Germany (Lyndsay, p. 221n708, n710).

1092–1134 *Ovir Ryne . . . . Musis Caballyne fontane*. Ovid lists mountains and rivers scorched in the disastrous flight of Phaethon (*Met* 2.216–71, 1:74–79; see note to lines 1100–30, below); as Sandra Cairns shows, Douglas handles this source by means of the much-reprinted commentary by the late fifteenth-century Raffaello Regio.

1093 *Ovir Alpheus, by Pyes the ryche citie*. Virgil alludes to the River Alpheus, flowing under the sea and re-emerging on Sicily (*Aeneid* 3.694–96, 1:418–19). Ovid lists the river (*Met* 2.250, 1:76–77) and later relates the story of Alpheus' pursuit of Arethusa, who is transformed into a stream. On the river's banks in the western Peloponnese was a Greek city named Pisa (*Met* 5.409, 494, 1:266–67, 272–73; Virgil, *Georgics* 3.180, pp. 188–89).

1095 *Ovir Ron, ovir Sane, ovir France and eik ovir Lare*. The sequence of French rivers seems disturbed by the reference to France itself, as if the name of the country were parallel to the names of the rivers. The occurrence may possibly be due to a misreading of a less familiar river name (e.g., Rance in Brittany).

1096 *And ovir Tagus the goldin sandyt ryvare*. The Tagus River of the Iberian Peninsula was famed in antiquity for its gold-bearing sands (e.g., *Met* 2.251, 1:76–77).

1097–98 *In Thessaly . . . . sepulture fand there*. Ovid describes the funeral pyre of Hercules on Mount Oeta but does not mention any sepulchre there (*Met* 9.211–72, 2:18–23); the reference may have been derived from Regio (Cairns, p. 20).

1100 *In Secil eik we passyt the mont Tmolus*. At the comparable point (*Met* 2.217, 1:74–75), Ovid refers to Cilicia rather than Sicily in relation to Taurus rather than Tmolus (in Lydia); Douglas appears to have applied the *Cilix* to both mountains. Douglas also follows Ovid in alluding to Tmolus' vineyards (*Met* 11.85–90, 2:126–27).

1105–07 *Ovir Carmelus . . . . Carmelitis come syne*. Mount Carmel, on the northern coast of Israel, was associated with the prophets Elijah and Elisha; though evidence exists of much earlier monastic settlements in the region, monks occupied the "cave of Elijah" on Mount Carmel by the 1160s (Jotischky, *Carmelites and Antiquity*, pp. 8–9). The Carmelite Order of mendicant friars was founded in the thirteenth century. In the fifteenth century, the Carmelites had convents in various Scottish burghs (for example, Historic Environment Scotland, "Edinburgh, Greenside Row, Carmelite Friary"; "Linlithgow, Carmelite Friary").

1109   *the flude Termodyon.* Cairns observes (p. 21) that Douglas transfers the quality of rapidity from the river Thermodon ("Thermodonque citus"; *Met* 2.249, 1:76–77) to the journey and hence his catalogue; speed of travel thus becomes a device of brevity in the catalogue.

1111   *Bachus Citheron.* Douglas recalls that Cithaeron is the site of the rites of the Bacchantes, the ecstatic female celebrants of the rites of the god Bacchus or Dionysus (*Met* 2.223, 1:74–75, 3.702, 1:172–73).

1114–15   *In that countré . . . . scheip blak anon.* Considering whether Douglas might have derived the detail of the water blackening the sheep from Boccaccio's *De Fluminibus,* Cairns (p. 22) argues instead for Regio as the source, and proposes that Douglas has read *Mygdoniae* there (in Ovid, "Mygdoniusque Melas"; *Met* 2.247, 1:76–77) as a reference to Macedonia, "that countré" specified a line before.

1118   *Achicorontes.* This has been recognized as an error for Orontes; Cairns identifies the occurrence of *arsitorontes* at this point in the marginal annotations "in a hand of the late fifteenth-early sixteenth century," in the Edinburgh University Library copy of *Metamorphoses* printed in 1493 with Regio's commentary (pp. 22–23).

1120   *Armany hillis and flude Eufrates.* Noah's Ark landed in the hills of Armenia (Genesis 8:4); the Euphrates is one of the two great rivers of Mesopotamia and the fourth river of Eden (Genesis 2:14). See also the note to line 1126 below.

1121   *the pretius flude Ganges.* The Ganges is "pretius"; Regio calls it *notissimus,* most famous (note to *Met* 2.249, 1:76–77). Andrew of Wyntoun follows the tradition that the Ganges was the same as the river Phison that flowed from Paradise (Wyntoun, 1.4.125–34). A gloss for "pretius" would be "holy," given the river's exalted source. See *MED preciouse* (adj.), sense 2.

1123   *the mont of Frygy Dindama.* On Mount Dindyma, in Phrygia, stood a shrine to the goddess Cybele (*Met* 2.223, 1:74–75).

1126   *fludis of Tygris and Phison.* Tigris is one of the two great rivers of Mesopotamia, and (named *Hiddekel* in Hebrew) is the third river flowing out of Eden (Genesis 2:14); Pison runs into the Black Sea, and is the first river of Eden (Genesis 2:11). See also the note to line 1120 above.

1128   *Modyn.* Modin is a hill fortification of the Maccabees (1 Maccabees 2:23, 13:30, 16:4; 2 Maccabees 13:14).

1130–31   *The mont Erix . . . . Venus en certane.* For the connection between Eryx and Venus, see *Met* 5.363, 1:262–63 and *Aeneid* 5.759–61, 1:522–23. The connection between Venus and Acheron, a river of the underworld, is more problematic. Possibly an Ovidian reference provides a clue: beginning Calliope's narrative of the rape of Proserpina, Ovid situates Venus at Mount Eryx, where she sees Dis, the god of the underworld (Cairns, p. 28). In declaring that Acheron is "didicat to Venus," however, Douglas appears to be going out of his way to stress the connection between Venus and the underworld, "en certane."

1132   *Lybane*. Though the form of the word suggests Lebanon, the allusion appears to be to Ovid's reference to Libya (*Met* 2.237, 1:76–77), glossed by Regio as *aridissima*.

1134   *Caballyne fontane*. Unless the Muses have doubled back towards Mount Helicon (line 1129), Douglas appears to distinguish between the Hippocrene and Caballine fountains, which are usually taken as the same place. The Caballine arose from Pegasus' hoofprint on Helicon (*Met* 5.256–59, 1:256–57).

1143   *That of the watir I micht never tast a drew*. Lack of cleansing refreshment at the Hippocrene spring (*fonte . . . caballino*) is what distinguishes the Roman satirist Persius (*Satires*, ed. Braund, prol.1, pp. 44–45) from the pack of conventionally eloquent poets. For a coarser version of the topic of failure to drink from the fount of eloquence, see *Flyting of Dunbar and Kennedie*, lines 337–44 (*Poems*, ed. Bawcutt, 1:211).

1150   *The byrriall stremys rynnand ovyr sterny greis*. Descriptions of the pleasant place may feature descriptions of clear water flowing over a sparkling stream-bed (for example, *CLL*, line 78). Describing the stream as crystal flowing over glittering steps ("sterny greis") anticipates the bejeweled stages in the presence-chamber of Venus (line 1473) and also in the heavens (line 1841). See *DOST* for this metaphorical extension of the adjective *sterny* (sense 2; see also *sternit* (ppl. adj.), sense 2).

1160   *Thair womanlynes writhyt the elementis*. The women's beauty is so dazzling that even Nature is thrown off kilter.

1162–66   *The warld may . . . . febill proces dryve*. On combinations of pagan and Christian in protestations of humility, see Curtius, pp. 407–13.

1179, 1234 *Dilligate meatis . . . . meatis diligate*. Delicacies at the court of James IV included dried fruits, candies, and condiments. Spices were much prized, including cloves, mace, nutmeg, cinnamon, and of course sugar (*ALHTS*, p. ccviii).

1181   *interludyis*. These refer to short, easily staged plays performed between courses of a banquet; such entertainments may include debate and farce, as the following performances indicate.

1182   *Gave problemys sere and mony fare demandis*. In the Scots *Buik of Alexander the Grit* (1438) a game of "demandis and fare answeris . . . Of amouris and his worshep all" (lines 2175, 2177, 2:159). Such literary references to posing questions such as "Who were the greatest lovers (or warriors)" may reflect actual pastimes during feasts. The *demande d'amour* ("question about love") is a frequent aspect of discourse about love in medieval literature, as, for example, with the question "what do women most desire" in the Wife of Bath's Tale (*CT* III[D] 904–05).

1186–87   *Than Caliope Ovid . . . . of regestere*. Bawcutt ("The 'Library,'" p. 113) contrasts Chaucer's reference to Ovid as "Venus clerk" (*HF*, line 1487) with Calliope's designation of Ovid as her "Clerk of Register" in *PH*.

1191–94   *the fetis of Hercules . . . . mychty giantis dang*. In Ovid's list of the labors of Hercules (*Met* 9.182–99, 2:16–17), Hercules drags the three-headed dog Cerberus out of

Hades, kills the Nemean Lion, destroys the snaky-headed Hydra, and defeats the giants Antaeus and Busiris. The "monstreis" referred to in line 1193 may include the sea-monster from which Hercules rescued Hesione (*Met* 11.211–14, 2:134–35).

1191   *schew*. "Showing" appears to be an uncomplicated synonym for "telling"; the term may foreshadow the showings the dreamer later views in the mirror of Venus (lines 1495 ff.).

1195–97   *Of Thesyus eik . . . . Mynotaure in Crete*. On Theseus at war against the Amazons, see Statius 12.163–64, 2:260–61, 523 ff., 2:286 ff.; see also *CT* I[A] 866–70.

1198–1200 *Of Persyus . . . . monsturis mony one*. Using the head of Medusa, Perseus defeats Atlas and the sea serpent (*Met* 4.604–752, 1:220–31).

1201–03   *Of Dianis bore . . . . the systeris mone*. Ovid (*Met* 8.260 ff., 1:424 ff.) recounts the tale of the Calydonian boar, wounded by the huntress Atalanta and killed by Meleager the prince of Calydon. When Meleager's uncles begrudge his gift to Atalanta of the boar's hide, Meleager kills them. Mourning her brothers' deaths, Meleager's mother burns the fated branch that measures the length of her son's life. The spelling "bore" (line 1201) may be authorial: where "bair" would be the usual form, the southern spelling of the word would intensify connections with Chaucer's handling of Cassandra's tale of Diana, Meleager, and the "mayde" (*TC* 5.1464–84).

1204–06   *Kyng Priamus sonne . . . . transformyt wes anon*. Trying to drown himself in remorse after Hesperie, the nymph he has been pursuing, dies by accident, Aesacus is transformed by Tethys into a merganser (*mergus*; *Met* 11.749–95, 2:172–77), here a "skarth" or cormorant; late in *Eneados*, Douglas alludes again to Aesacus who "completis hys pennance / In ryveris, fludis, and on euery laik" (12.prol.286–87, 4:74). Here as elsewhere in the poem, birds and humans mirror each other.

1208–15   *Quhow fers Achylles . . . . all his fere*. Realizing that Cycnus is impervious to wounding by weapons, Achilles strangles him (*Met* 12.64–145, 2:184–91).

1216–21   *He schew . . . . lustis suld be flemyt*. Referring to Ovid's *Metamorphoses*, *Heroides*, *Ars Amatoria*, and *Remedia Amoris*, respectively.

1224   *He wes expart in all thyng*. Douglas is not alone in regarding Ovid as a fount of knowledge; in the preface to his commentary on *Metamorphoses*, Raffaelo Regio establishes a key humanist perspective on Ovid as the conveyor of the breadth of curricular learning and on *Metamorphoses* as "the basis for geography, astrology, music, rhetoric, and philosophy, both moral and natural" (Knox, "Commenting on Ovid," p. 337).

1225–26   *Up rais . . . . Daphnis and Coridon*. Virgil may be "gret," but here he is confined to the comparatively light amusements of Eclogue 7, in which Corydon wins a singing match against Thyrsis, with Daphnis and Meliboeus as the judging audience.

1228   *Of Permeno, Thrason and wyse Gnaton.* The characters named are from the *Eunuchus* of the Roman dramatist Terence (see the note to line 902, above), whose comedies held their place in primary curriculum in the fifteenth century.

1229–30   *Juvynale lik a mower . . . . thay yeid by.* Juvenal is "hym allone" like Lydgate or like the dreamer. See notes to lines 61 and 921 above. More to the point, Juvenal's behavior is what is expected of a satirist at court; it is the stance William Dunbar adopts in his satires addressed to James IV (e.g., "Off benefice, Sir, at everie feist," line 7; "Schir, yit remember as befoir," lines 7–10 [*Poems*, ed. Bawcutt, 1:140, 225]). Such an attitude might explain why Juvenal is alone.

1231   *Marcyall was cuyk till rost, seith, fars or fry.* Martial continued into the fifteenth century to be known by his medieval nickname *Coquus* ("the Cook"; Sandys, *Classical Scholarship*, p. 643). Douglas fleshes out the connection by alluding·to Chaucer's portrait of the Cook: "He koude rooste, and sethe, and broille, and frye" (*CT* I[A] 383); Bawcutt adds that "we may compare modern colloquial senses of 'roast' or 'grill'" ("The 'Library,'" p. 112).

1232–33   *And Pogyus stude . . . . and cryand fy.* Poggio and Lorenzo famously exchanged invectives about their conflicting theories of textual analysis and Latin style (Camporeale, "Poggio Bracciolini versus Lorenzo Valla," pp. 29–37). Their exchanges were sometimes regarded as "a highly entertaining game of mockery" (Rizzi, "Violent Language in Early Fifteenth-Century Italy," p. 150). Douglas himself "spittit for dispyte" at Caxton's mishandling of the *Aeneid* (*Eneados* 1.prol.150, 2:7). On spitting as a sign of scorn, see Burrow, p. 44.

1237   *Retret wes blawyn lowd.* "Retreat" seems an obtrusively military term in this context, and its being announced by a fanfare ("blawyn lowd") strengthens the association.

1239   *Schynand for swete as thay had bene anoynt.* The horses shining with sweat recall Chaucer's sweat-anointed Monk (*CT* I[A] 198–99).

1244–45   *The Vail of Ebron . . . . the lusty vail.* Three biblical places of destiny: Hebron (site of Abraham's burial plot, Genesis 23:17–19, 50:13; and place of David's anointing, 2 Kings 2:1); the Damascene field (traditional site of Adam's creation, via readings of Genesis 2:7); and the Valley of Jehosaphat (Joel 3:2, 12, 14), the apocalyptic destination for prophesied doom.

1254   *fere trymlys my pen.* On the trembling pen, see Hammond, *English Verse Between Chaucer and Surrey*, pp. 437n4, 448n46. The topic is used by Chaucer (*TC* 4.13–14) and by Lydgate (repeatedly, including a passage Douglas would likely have encountered, *CLL*, line 181).

1255–58   *The hart . . . . joy to ken.* Part Two ends on a serious note, with a formal peroration. The topic of the inexpressibility of heavenly bliss is grounded on 1 Corinthians 2:9.

1259–62   *Quhilk now I saw . . . . to schaw.* The passage is tinged by recollection of the many tongues of pagan Fame (*HF*, line 1390; *Aeneid* 4.183, 1:434–35); see also *Aeneid* 6.625–27, 1:576–77, where the Sibyl claims inability to catalogue the torments of the damned in the fortress of Dis.

1261   *Thocht al my membris tongis were on raw.* The syntax is complicated here. The line might be loosely translated, "Even if all the parts of my body were tongues set out in a row."

1264–66   *For quhiddir . . . . gret God wait.* Douglas has returned to St. Paul (2 Corinthians 12:2); compare Chaucer's "wher in body or in gost / I not, ywys, but God, thou wost!" (*HF*, lines 981–82).

1269   *dremes quhilkis ar not worth a myte.* The assertion that dreams are "not worth a mite" is proverbial. See Whiting D387, M611.

1290   *Teche me your facund castis eloquent.* "*Teiche me zour castis eloquent,* your curious nice touches of eloquence, poetry is here meant" (Scott, p. 147); at the outset of his *Eneados,* Douglas refers to Virgil's "quent and curyus castis poeticall" (1.prol.255, 2:10); earlier in *PH,* the Muses' Ovidian songs are similarly said to exhibit "castis quent" (line 819).

1294   *Till make the heraris bousum and attent.* Quintilian upholds "Goodwill, Attentiveness, and Readiness to learn" as the aims of the *prooemium* or *exordium,* the introduction of an oration (Quint. *Inst* 4.1.5, 2:180–81).

1300–01   *Hewyn in the roch . . . . glas it schone.* The mountain on which Chaucer's House of Fame stands is like "alum de glas" (line 1124).

1322–23   *Till Xantus . . . . hest contrar Achill.* If Douglas is following Homer, he does so at some remove from this ultimate source, according to which, Hera (Juno) gets Hephæstus (Vulcan) to use fire against the river Xanthus in Achilles' fight against it (*Iliad* 21.328–82, 2:428–33). Douglas may have derived from Regio's commentary the unusual allusion to Xanthus burning at Venus' behest to oppose Achilles (Cairns, p. 37n27).

1340–41   *Caryit me . . . . brocht in Babilone.* The Old Testament prophet Habakkuk, who in an apocryphal chapter of the book of Daniel is dwelling in Judah and preparing a meal for the harvesters when an angel commands him to take the meal to Daniel, imprisoned by king Cyrus of Babylon. The angel "took him by the top of his head and carried him by the hair of his head, and set him in Babylon over the den in the force of his spirit" (Daniel 14:36). In his own scriptural Book, Habakkuk laments the prevalence of oppression and injustice, and receives a vision of the coming of God's rule (2:2–3).

1348–77   *This brukkill erth . . . . thay clam.* The Boethian image of "fortune's seas" with their "rushing waves" (*Consolation of Philosophy,* trans. Tester, p. 161, 1.m5.45–46; Curtius, pp. 128–30) had been picked up memorably in *KQ,* where the narrator voyages "Amang the wawis of this warld" (line 111). As if to give full sail to his eloquence (and perhaps to equal James I's inventive treatment; *KQ,* lines 101–33n), Douglas amplifies this theme substantially.

1348–50   *This brukkill erth . . . . na maner swage.* The combination of fire and stormy seas (compare the lake of fire in Apocalypse 19:20, 20:14–15) recalls the combination of "vyle wattyr" and "brynt," "[c]ombust" landscape in the nightmarish beginning to the First Part of *PH* (lines 139, 144 and note, 150).

1354   *palyce*. The irony instills a dire implication into the range of meanings of this key term throughout *PH*.

1360   *carvel*. This is a small two-masted ship with triangular (lateen) sails. Given the identification of this ship as the "Carvell of the State of Grace" (line 1386), its smallness and frailty are meaningful.

1380   *pepill drint*. On shipwreck as an emblem for the destruction of the faithless, see 1 Timothy 1:19.

1387   *sonnys of ire*. Douglas alludes to Ephesians 2:3; Chaucer's Parson also preaches: "be we alle born sones of wratthe and of dampnacioun perdurable" (*CT* X[I] 334).

1393–94 *Except bye fayth . . . . vorkyng gud vorkys*. The spelling "bye" occurs uniquely in these two lines; elsewhere "be" is consistently used thus. Douglas is expounding an orthodox doctrine of salvation through faith and good works; in the prologue to *Eneados* 11, he similarly argues that a sinner must act well in order to merit grace (lines 151–68, 4:5).

1408–09 *Impossibill wer . . . . abone my micht*. Douglas reverts to formulae of inexpressibility (compare lines 1255–62).

1410   *with ynk may do bot paper blek*. Re-using the word "blek" (now as a verb), the poet anticipates doing to the paper what Venus' impish courtiers did to him when they daubed his face with boot-blacking (line 652 and note); both actions seem degrading but also assert the dreamer/poet's presence in hostile surroundings. This scribal blackening may indicate some progress from the emptiness the poet previously ascribed to his pen (lines 1254, 1283).

1411   *I man draw furth; the yok lyis in my nek*. Where Chaucer's Knight compares ploughing to narration (*CT* I[A] 886–87), Douglas refers to himself as the ox.

1413–22 *Plenyst with plesance . . . . the littil volatill*. "Paradice js a richt nobile place of plesaunce, with sueit and temporit aire, quhare na trubile nore commocioune is of wynd, rayne, snaw or vthir trubile, that may put jmpediment to the plesaunce and dilectacioune of man" (*Meroure* 2:4, 1:77).

1421–22 *Till noy . . . . the littil volatill*. The visionary world of animals (and birds) at peace derives from Isaiah 11:6–7, where such peace comes when the kingdom is ruled by a true descendant of the royal line. The allusion combines the topic of the *locus amoenus*, the pleasant place (Curtius, pp. 193, 195–200), with that of ideal kingship. Appropriately enough, Douglas is about to commence his description of Honour's palace.

1423–24 *Still in the season . . . . but other noy or sare*. Douglas draws evocatively on Isaiah 6:9 with this reference to the perpetual seasonableness of all things, untouched by harm or suffering.

1429–37 *A palyce stude . . . . and plesand spryngis*. The "enumeration of technical details" is a rhetorical convention in the description of impressive buildings (Norton-Smith, pp. 242–43; *HF*, lines 1186–94; *Court of Sapience*, ed. Harvey, 2.1485–89, p. 51).

1434   *corbell*. The construction at Linlithgow Palace included "image corbels carved with an angelic orchestra"; later at Edinburgh Castle, the building of James IV's great hall included "precocious" stone corbels "supporting the roof wall posts, which are carved as sophisticatedly classical consoles" (Fawcett, *Scottish Architecture*, pp. 308, 312).

1437   *spryngis*. In architectural terminology, the modern equivalent to this word is "springer," referring to the section on the top of a pillar on which an arch rests and from which it begins to curve (or "spring"; *OED spring* (n.1), sense 9a; *springer* (n.1), sense 2).

1452   *beriall stone*. Chaucer's palace of Fame is built entirely of "ston of beryle" (*HF*, line 1184).

1453–54   *Bosiliall nor Oliab . . . . ryche and dere*. A list of inspired builders and their excellent works begins with Bezaleel, Aholiab, and their building of the Tabernacle, containing the ark of the Covenant (Exodus 31:1–6, 36:1–38).

1455   *Salomon*. Solomon is identified as the builder of the Temple (3 Kings 6:1–36).

1456   *he that beild the riall Ylyon*. Laomedon is aided by Apollo and Neptune in building the walls of the first Troy but denies them payment (*Met* 11.194–220, 2:132–35; Horace, *Odes* 3.3.21).

1457   *he that forgete Darius sepulture*. On Apelles and the making of the tomb of Darius, Walter of Châtillon wrote an influential ekphrasis, a passage with "sufficient cultural currency that Chaucer's Wife of Bath alludes to it in passing" (at *CT* III[D] 497–99; *Alexandreis*, ed. Townsend, 7.420–77, p. 156).

1460   *Thus in a stare quhy standis thou stupefak*. The Nymph begins to revel in her authority. Writing to Ferdinand and Isabella in 1497, Pedro de Ayala, Spanish ambassador, commented that Scotswomen "are really honest, though very bold" (*Calendar of Negotiations between England and Spain*, ed. Bergenroth, 1:174).

1461   *Govand*. "Govand, govan, gazing with wonder" (Scott, p. 148).

1464   *Quhat thow seyst, luke eftirwartis thow write*. Behind this command lies the divine order to John to "[w]rite therefore the things which thou hast seen, and which are, and which must be done hereafter" (Apocalypse 1:19); less exalted and more apposite may be the God of Love's command to the poet in Chaucer's *LGW*, F prol. 548–58.

1483–85   *With vertuus stanis . . . . wox hale*. Various jewels have the power to staunch the flow of blood: cornelian ("corneolus"), hematite ("emachite"), heliotrope ("eliotropia"), jasper, sapphire, smaragdus, and topaz (Trev. *Prop*. 16.33, 39, 40, 52, 86, 87, 95; pp. 843, 846, 853, 869, 871, 877).

1495–96   *In that myrrour . . . . every erdly wycht*. Precedents include the mirror Virgil devises in which Rome's enemies may be foreseen (*CA* 5.2031–2272; see Peck's note to line 2031) and the mirror sent to Canacee by the king of Arabia and India, in which adversity and treason may be foreseen (SqT, *CT* V[F] 132–45). Like those mirrors, this one will offer a glimpse into the future as well as a survey of the past; it shows the coming of the Antichrist (line 1701).

1500   *in the erth ysent*. This refers to Adam and Eve's banishment from Paradise (Genesis 3:23–24).

1503   *subversyoun*. Bawcutt (*SP*, p. 201n1503) points out that this echoes the term "subversione" in Genesis (19:29) for the fall of Sodom.

1505   *Hornyt Moyses with his ald Ebrew law*. The tradition that Moses' face was horned when he descended from Sinai derives from Scripture (Exodus 34:29–30). Douglas mentions Moses' horns and "ald Ebrew law" in anticipation of the Plagues and the crossing of the Red Sea.

1507–08   *In the Reid See . . . . wald nevir knaw*. When the Israelites depart from Egypt, Pharaoh pursues them as far as the Red Sea, which they are crossing miraculously, the waters having receded. When the Egyptians follow, the waters engulf them (Exodus 14:15–31). God destroys Pharaoh for breaking his word to let the Israelites leave Egypt; the drowning of Pharaoh and his "court" in the Red Sea is framed as an emblem of the limits on royal power.

1512   *Of Josuy I saw the worthy weris*. These wars, notably against Jericho, are the subject of Joshua, chapters 6–12.

1515   *Of Ameleth the cruel homosyd*. Son of the righteous judge Gideon, Abimelech of Shechem murdered his seventy brothers, all save the youngest (Judges 9:1–5).

1516–18   *The wonderful werkis . . . . in his pryde*. With a donkey's jawbone, Samson kills a thousand Philistines (Judges 15:15–17) and carries off the gates to the city of Gaza (Judges 16:3); captured, blinded, and fettered, he pulls down the temple of Dagon and destroys its occupants, including himself (16:29–30).

1520–21   *duke Sangor there . . . . a plewchis sok*. Shamgar, predecessor of Samson, routs six hundred Philistines with no other weapon than an ox-goad (not a "plewchis sok"; Judges 3:31).

1522–26   *The praphet Samuell . . . . thre hundreth uncis was*. Samuel anoints Saul as king of Israel; Saul's son Jonathan, unaided, defeats the Philistines; David fells the giant Goliath (1 Kings 10:1; 14:11–14; 17:40–54). The weight of Goliath's spearhead is given in 1 Kings 17:7 as six hundred shekels.

1527–32   *Jesbedonab the giant . . . . bryng to grond*. Late in life, David kills the Philistine giant, Jesbibenob, who has six fingers on each hand (2 Kings 21:16, 20–21). As a boy, he killed lions and bears that took his sheep (1 Kings 17:32–37). The victory over eight hundred at an onset seems ambiguously ascribed to David (*sedens in cathedra sapientissimus princeps*) rather than his foremost champion, Jesbaham (2 Kings 23:8).

1533–39   *Bananyas the strang . . . . did harm eneuch*. David's champion Benaiah kills two "lyonys" of Moab and, in the time of snow (*in diebus nivis*) climbs into a storage-well (*in media cisterna*) to kill a lion. He takes the spear from an enemy Egyptian (not an "Ethiop") "worthy to be a sight" and "slew him with his own spear" (2 Kings 23:20–21).

1542–45   *His sonne Roboam . . . . fra hym devyd.* This line refers to Rehoboam's oppression and the consequent division of the kingdom (3 Kings 12; 2 Chronicles 10; *CA* 7.4027–4146).

1546–48   *the angell sla . . . . with gret bost.* The angel's destruction of Sennacherib's army is narrated in 4 Kings 19:35; 2 Chronicles 32:21; Isaiah 37:36. For the "gret bost," see 4 Kings 19:10–13.

1549–50   *the lyfe . . . . Prolongit fifteen yere.* Hezekiah, repentant, merits recovery from illness (4 Kings 20:1–11; Isaiah 38:1–8); through Isaiah, God promises to add fifteen years to the king's life (2 Chronicles 32:24–26).

1550–51   *the prophet Hely . . . . to Paradyce went.* In triumphant counterbalance to the fall of Phaethon, Elijah ascends to heaven in a fiery chariot, witnessed by his successor Elisha (4 Kings 2:11–12).

1552   *The stories of Esdras and of Neamy.* These refer to 1 Ezra 7:1–10:17; 2 Ezra 1:1–7:5, 13.

1553–54   *And Danyell . . . . brak and schent.* Not Daniel's first, better-known stint in a lion's den (Daniel 6:17–25), this is his second, as punishment for wrecking an artificial dragon worshipped as the god Bel (Daniel 14:23, 27, 31); this time, Daniel is aided by Habakkuk (on whom see the note to lines 1340–41).

1555   *The chyldir thre amyd the fornace sent.* Three young men (Hananiah/Shadrach, Mishael/Meschach, and Azariah/Abed-nego) were thrown in the fiery furnace for refusing to worship the golden statue set up by Nebuchadnezzar (Daniel 1:6; 3:26, 27).

1556   *transmygracion.* The key term in 1 Ezra (6:16, 8:35) for the deportation of the Jews into Babylon (4 Kings 24:14, 25:11) is "transmigration."

1558–62   *the haly archangell . . . . as tha tel.* Tobias, son of Tobit, is to become the eighth husband of Sarah (daughter of Tobit's kinsman Raguel), but unless he manages to ward off Asmodeus, the evil demon jealously guarding her, he will suffer the same fate as the seven previous husbands; the angel Raphael advises him to drive the demon away with the stench from burning a "little piece" from a giant fish's heart (Tobias 3:8, 6:2, 6:8–10, 8:2).

1563–64   *And quhow Judyth . . . . town fra wrake.* Venturing into the encampment of the Assyrian army to be entertained by their general Holofernes, Judith beheaded him (Judith 13:8–10, 15:1–7).

1565–66   *Jonas . . . . at Ninive.* In Jonah 2:1–2, 2:11–3:2, the whale's vomiting happens a day's journey away from the inland city of Nineveh. Bawcutt notes (*SP*, p. 202n1566) that Douglas may be indebted to Chaucer for the detail that Jonah was "schot furth" at Nineveh (*CT* II[B^1] 486–87).

1568–71   *Of Alexander . . . . Jowrye he opprest.* The summary of Alexander's twelve years of conquest is scriptural, as is the reference to the oppression of the Jews by Antiochus Epiphanes (1 Maccabees 1:1–8; 1:20–26 ff.).

1572–74   *Of Macabeus . . . . throw his prowes.* The exploits of Judas Maccabeus are the subject of 1 Maccabees 3:1–9:18 and 2 Maccabees 8–15.

1575–76   *his brethir Symon . . . . thair dayis rang.* Jonathas is the subject of 1 Maccabees 9:28–13:23; Simon, of 13:1–16:22.

1577–82   *Of Tebes eik . . . . all his slychtis.* In part, Douglas is working through Chaucerian and Lydgatian precedents: on Tydeus at Thebes, see *TC* 5.1485–1501, *ST*, lines 2120–2235; on King Creon, his defeat by Theseus, and Theseus' conquest of Thebes, see *CT* I[A] 938–47, 960–64, 985–90.

1583–84   *as Stacius dois tell . . . . sank to Hel.* Douglas cites Statius (7.771–823, 1:454–59). A Chaucerian approach to the classics continues to be evident: naming Amphiaraus as "Amphiorax the bischop," Douglas may also be drawing on *TC* 2.104–05 (or *ST*, lines 4022–4103). This is one of several allusions in *PH* to sudden descents into infernal regions; see, for instance, Empedocles (note to line 257 above), the "sewch" (note to line 1316 above), Jonah (note to lines 1565–66 above), and Curtius (note to lines 1676–80 below).

1585–86   *The faithfull ladyis . . . . barfute pas togyddir.* The episode is familiar from *CT* I[A] 896–964; as Bawcutt notes, however (*SP*, p. 203n1585–93), Lydgate provides a more exact source for the phrases "alle in clothes blake" and "all in blak and barfoot" (*ST*, lines 4417, 4469).

1588–93   *Behald . . . . ar til avance.* The ironic praise of women is a hallmark of Lydgate's style (*ST*, lines 4448–52; Pearsall, *John Lydgate*, pp. 118–19, 134–36).

1594–96   *Of duke Pyrrotheus . . . . huge till se.* Achilles having defeated Cycnus (compare *PH*, lines 1207–15), Nestor tells in lingering and grisly detail the tale of the battle of the Lapiths and Centaurs at the wedding of Pirithoüs and Hippodame (*Met* 12.210–535, 2:194–219; *CA* 6.485–536).

1597–1602 *And Hercules . . . . the rial town.* For Hercules' rescue of Hesione (compare note to line 586) and his revenge against her ungrateful father Laomedon, see *Met* 11.211–15, 2:134–35 and *CA* 5.7195–7224 and 8.2515–24.

1603–05   *To wyn the fleys . . . . all Medeas slychtis.* Medea, sorceress and princess of Colchis, helped Jason steal the Golden Fleece (*Met* 7.1–158, 1:342–53; *CA* 5.3247–4222).

1606   *Quhow for Jason Ysiphile wes shent.* Hypsipyle, princess of Lemnos, was bedded by Jason and then abandoned en route to the Golden Fleece (*ST*, lines 3188–92); see *PH*, line 583 and note, above.

1607–11   *And quhow to Troy . . . . the town agane.* Having referred already (lines 1597–1602) to Ovid on the Greek overthrow of the Trojan king Laomedon, Douglas alludes afresh to Gower's version (*CA* 5.7195–7224).

1612–14   *The jugement of Parys . . . . goddes maist gudlye.* Judgment is significant at various points in the poem as the determiner of destiny. Its decisive operation is what distinguishes and exalts the god Honour (lines 2051–57 and note). Here it is applied ill-advisedly: disputing over the golden apple of Discord (to be awarded to the most beautiful), Juno, Minerva, and Venus appealed to the judgment of the Trojan prince Paris, who gave the apple to Venus and earned the enmity of the other two (*Heroides* 16.51–88, pp. 200–03; *CA* 5.7400–7585).

1619–20   *quhow be Ulixes . . . . brocht to Troy.* The sea-nymph Thetis disguised her not-quite-invulnerable son Achilles as a girl so that he would not be called to Troy; Ulysses tricked him into revealing his identity (*Met* 13.162–71, 2:238–41; Statius 1.198–960, 2:326–85; *CA* 5.2961–3201).

1624   *Grekis Troianys amang.* In verse, the preposition "amang" may appear after the noun or pronoun which it locates (*DOST amang* (prep. adv.), sense A.4; also *MED among(es* (prep.), occasionally in the quotations for senses 1 and 2)

1627   *baith hym and Troylus.* Yoking Troilus as an afterthought to Hector, Douglas adopts the style of Pandarus, but applies it, as finally does Chaucer, to the heroes' deaths rather than their victories (*TC* 2.170–98; 5.1800–06).

1630–56   *out of Troy. . . . kyng of Rutuleis.* In his summary of the wanderings and campaigns of Aeneas, Douglas draws on the *Aeneid* but also perhaps the *Metamorphoses* (13.623–14.582, 2:272–341). Where Chaucer had given most attention in his *Aeneid* summary to Book IV's tragic romance between Aeneas and Dido, Douglas — logically, given the theme and plot of his own poem — concentrates (lines 1637–46) on Book VI's prophetic journey of Aeneas into the Underworld.

1641   *The fludis four of Hell.* Five (sometimes, as in the *Odyssey*, four) rivers are generally associated with Hades: Lethe, Styx, Acheron, Cocytus, and Phlegethon; Gower refers to Jupiter's oath "Be Lethen and be Flegeton, / Be Cochitum and Acheron," which are "the chief flodes of the helle," along with two "depe pettes," Styx and "Segne" (*CA* 5.1109–15).

1643   *The weltrand stone wirk Sisipho mych cair.* The tale is widely alluded to in classical sources that Sisyphus was condemned by Jupiter to push a stone to the top of a hill, only to have it roll back each time (e.g., *Met* 4.460, 1:210–11; 13.27, 2:230–31).

           mych. This is the first occurrence in L of a Midlands form of "much" (as in the *Poems in the* Pearl *Manuscript*, eds. Andrew and Waldron, p. 334), while "mekill" is the usual form in *PH*. (See the Glossary for line references.) This southern form recurs in line 2122.

1644   *Camp Elysee.* The Elysian Fields, where the blessed souls dwell (*Aeneid* 6.640–59, vol. 1, pp. 576–79); Douglas echoes this line in *Eneados* 6.prol.100, 3:3.

1645–46   *Quhare ald Anchyses . . . . all his successyon.* Anchises revealed the future greatness of Rome (*Aeneid* 6.756–886, 1:586–597).

1652   *All his navy gret hunger did suppryse.* See *Aeneid* 7.107–34, 2:10–11. Earlier (*Aeneid* 3.255–57, 1:388–89), the Harpy Celaeno had foretold that the Trojans would not establish their destined city until hunger compelled them to eat their tables.

1653–54   *he in Italie . . . . strandis of Lavyne.* The couplet echoes *HF*, lines 147–48, "In Itayle with ful moche pyne, / Unto the strondes of Lavyne."

1656   *Tarnus slew, the kyng of Rutuleis*. Turnus was Aeneas' fiercest adversary in the battle for Latium; the *Aeneid* concludes with his death; Livy also refers to the defeat of Turnus as Aeneas' last exploit (*History* 1.2, 1:10–14).

1657   *Rome saw I beildit fyrst be Romulus*. Douglas identifies Romulus the builder but not Romulus the fratricide of Livy's *History* 1.6–7, 1:22–31.

1660–65   *wickit proud Terquinius . . . . wes cruelly opprest*. Livy brings the first book of his *History* to a close (1.58–60, 1:200–09) with Sextus Tarquinius' rape of Lucretia and the consequent expulsion of the Tarquins from Rome by Lucius Junius Brutus, to initiate the Roman republic. See also Gower's version of the tale as part of his discussion of good and bad kingship (*CA* 7.4593–5130; see line 4593n).

1666–84   *The Punik batalis . . . . Scipio clepyt Affrycane*. These stanzas focus on men's self-sacrificing acts for the good of their nation (Aeneas; Marcus Regulus; Marcus Curtius).

1671–74   *worthy Marcus Regulus . . . . for till de*. Marcus Atilius Regulus, Roman consul in 267 and 256 BCE, was captured by the Carthaginians, who deputed him to negotiate with Rome on their behalf; advising the Romans instead to keep fighting, he returned to a gruesome death in Carthage (Horace, *Odes* 3.5). A main source is Cicero, *De officiis* (especially 3.99–115, pp. 374–97, also 1.39, pp. 42–43); "common profyt" is a key theme of that work (1.20–24, pp. 20–23), as of *CA*, Book 7 (for example, lines 2957, 3006–11; also *PF*, line 47 and note).

1675   *Tullus Servilius dowchty in his daw*. This probably refers to Servius Tullius, the honored sixth king of Rome, whose doughty deeds Livy recounts (*History* 1.39–48, 1:138–71).

1676–80   *And Curtyus eik . . . . thairin lap*. The most fully developed but problematic instance in *PH* of plunging into a chasm (see notes to lines 257, 1583–84 above): Livy alludes to the sacrifice of Marcus Curtius who leapt (not unarmed but fully armed) into a chasm in the Forum (*History* 7.6, 3:372–77) but does not mention the fieriness of the chasm. See Textual Note for line 1676 for the emendation *Curtyus*.

1681–87   *And Hannyball . . . . Realme of Spane*. Calling the elder Scipio "Affrycane," Douglas follows *PF*, lines 41 ff.; Scipio, hero of the Second Punic War, took Spain and defeated Hannibal; he adopted the epithet Africanus.

1688–89   *Quhow Kyng Jugurtha . . . . were the fyne*. The references to Sallust's *Jugurthine War* here and in lines 1775–76 may indicate the esteem Douglas felt toward this book and its author. They may also point to his interest in the topic of aristocratic rebellion.

1690–91   *the batellis intestyne . . . . of Lentulus*. Linked with the previous reference to Jugurtha, the allusion to Sallust's *Conspiracy of Catiline* further exemplifies Douglas' interest in this Roman historian. The Catiline conspiracy, which involved Catalina and co-conspirator Lentulus, brought to light by Cicero, is described in Sallust's *Bellum Catalinae* and amply by Cicero (e.g., *Catilinarian Orations*).

1692   *atwine Pompey and Cesar Julyus*. This civil war is the subject of Lucan's epic *De bello civili*, commonly known as *Pharsalia*.

1693–94   *And breifly . . . . or cornackyll reid*. The dreamer sees heroic deeds in the mirror; compare his interpretation to the Nymph's more amatory understanding, lines 1760–64 and note.

1701   *the cumming of the Antecrist*. A vernacular depiction of the coming of the Antichrist that was widely available in the fifteenth century is in *The Prik of Conscience*, part 5.

1703–07   *al maner disportys . . . . handlyt hate*. Hunting waterfowl with falcons was considered a fine noble recreation. Of all such quarry, herons and bitterns, rare in Scotland, were regarded the finest; as they were more common, geese and ducks were used to 'enter' falcons, or train them to hunt: "the falconers rode on horseback, for the sake of following the rapid movements of the hawks"; dogs and "laddis" raised the quarry (*ALHTS*, pp. cclii–ccliii, 288, 305, 360). This scene of avian carnage contrasts strikingly with the depiction of the paradisal landscape outside Honour's palace, where "ravanus fowlis" do not harm "littil volatill" (line 1422). Douglas later associates the image of "fowlis plungit in laik or puyll" with the profusion of semantically complex terms in Latin (*Eneados*, Prologue to Book 1, line 376, 2:14]).

1705   *in periculo mortis*. That is, "in danger of death": a jocular allusion to the annotation accompanying the short forms of the sacrament of baptism in emergencies, in Canon Law (e.g., Canons 865.2, 867.2, 868.2).

1711–19   *Raf Coilyear . . . . in Madin land*. As preserved in E but not L, this stanza provides a register of entertaining narratives deemed traditional, some of which are identified by region, several of which are preserved in texts much later than *PH*, and some are no longer extant. This register evidently has a place among courtly entertainments; tellers of such *geistis* to the king and his inner household were duly rewarded (*ALHTS*, p. 176; compare *The Dreme*, lines 31–46, Lyndsay, p. 2). The adjective "auld" appears twice in this stanza, where the usual form in *PH* is "ald."

1711   *Raf Coilyear*. This is a fifteenth-century Scottish romance in alliterative stanzas about the Emperor Charlemagne's encounters incognito with a coal-peddler, involving much burlesque of courtly conventions (*Three Middle English Charlemagne Romances*, ed. Lupack, pp. 161–204).

1712   *Craibit Johne the Reif and auld Cowkewyis sow*. *John the Reeve* and *Rauf Coilyear* employ the theme of "a king incognito meeting the humblest of his subjects" (*Ten Bourdes*, ed. Furrow, p. 141). In three parts (like *HF* and *PH*), *Colkelbie's Sow* (in the Bannatyne Manuscript) is a wild burlesque of higher literary forms.

1713   *how the wran come out of Ailssay*. No tale has been found about a wren from Ailsa Craig, a volcanic outcrop in the Firth of Clyde. "Hunting the wren" is attested regionally, notably on the Isle of Man, with a traditional origin in the seductive depredations of "a fairy of uncommon beauty" who assumes the form of a wren each New Year's Day (Bullock, *History of the Isle of Man*, p. 370; Wentersdorf, "Folkloristic Significance of the Wren," pp. 193–94).

1714   *Peirs Plewman*. *Piers Plowman* B-text, Passus VI seems out of place in this list of burlesque and popular tales; its inclusion here as a *bourde* in which Piers invites Hunger to discipline some refractory workers suggests that at least part of Langland's work was valued as comedy.

1715–16   *Gret Gowmakmorne . . . . as thay say*. "It is with pleasure we find here, two of Ossian's celebrated heroes, *viz*. Gow or Gaul the son of Morni and Fyn Macoul or Fyngal — The last verse alludes to their heroic, or god-like exploits in Ireland" (Scott, p. 149). Goll mac Morna and Finn mac Cumhaill are heroes and sometime antagonists of the Fenian cycle of Irish epic tales, the circulation of which in late-medieval Scotland is attested in the Book of the Dean of Lismore (Meek, "Scots-Gaelic Scribes," pp. 264–66; Gillies, "The Book of the Dean of Lismore," pp. 183, 190, 201–03, 210).

1717   *Maitland upon auld Beird Gray*. Sir Richard Maitland, late thirteenth-century ancestor of the noble family of that name, "the hero of the well-known ballad of *Auld Maitland*, which deals largely with the brave defence of his 'darksome house' of Thirlestane in his old age against a large English force" (*Scots Peerage*, ed. Paul, 5:279); Maitland's old grey horse features prominently in this ballad (Lang, *Walter Scott and the Border Minstrelsy*, pp. 18–39); with allusions to it in the Maitland Quarto ("Ane Consolatore Ballad to Sir Richart Maitland of Lethingtoun knicht," ed. Martin, poem 46.105, and "Virgil his village Mantua," poem 68.145).

1718   *Robene Hude and Gilbert with the quhite hand*. In *A Gest of Robyn Hode*, "good Gylberte / With the Whyte Hande" rivals Robin Hood at archery (lines 1167–68, 1603–04; *Robin Hood and Other Outlaw Tales*, ed. Knight and Ohlgren).

1719   *How Hay of Nauchtoun flew in Madin land*. Though this tale has not been traced, the Hays of Naughton (near Balmerino in Fifeshire) are mentioned in fifteenth-century records (e.g., Royal Commission on Historical Manuscripts, *Manuscripts of the Duke of Athole and the Earl of Home*, p. 158); "Madin land" may refer to Mainland, the largest of the Shetland Islands (*DOST madin-land* (n.); *main-, mayn[e], mane-land* (n.), sense 1b), rather than the magical kingdom of maidens (*Sir Perceval of Galles*, ed. Braswell, lines 956, 1128, 1645; *Ywain and Gawain*, ed. Braswell, line 3010).

1721   *Bonitas*. Guido Bonatti, thirteenth-century astrologer, was mentioned by Dante in *Inferno* (20.108); Bonatti's *Introduction to Astrology* was printed in Augsburg in 1491 and is also included in Henry VII's astrological manuscript, now British Library, MS Arundel 66 (Carey, "Henry VII's Book of Astrology").

        Bongo. While the name appears to refer to Bacon's contemporary the Franciscan Thomas Bungay, it may have been conflated with that of "another Friar Bungay in the fifteenth century with a definite reputation as a magician" (Molland, "Roger Bacon," p. 449n23, citing *New Chronicles*, ed. Ellis, p. 661).

        Bacon. Roger Bacon, thirteenth-century Aristotelian scholar at Oxford and Paris, embraced mathematical and experimental sciences (especially optics) and "went some way towards meriting his later reputation as a magician (Molland, "Roger

Bacon," p. 460). It may be of interest that all three names in this line are connected with scientists of the thirteenth century.

1722–27   *With mony subtell poynt . . . . made ane ape.* These entertaining illusions of transformation (mostly involving foodstuffs) recall the much briefer trick with the windmill and the walnut shell in *HF* (lines 1280–81) and the "castis" and "cawtelis" performed by the Jay, "a iuglour" in *BH*, lines 770–80 (see p. 136n772–80). In *The Mabinogion*, the bard Gwydion displays similar transformative skills, "making horses and hounds out of toadstools, shoes out of seaweed, a woman out of flowers, and a sea filled with hostile vessels out of nothing" (Breeze, "Bret Glascurion," p. 64).

1724   *sychyng bone.* Bawcutt (*SP*, pp. 325–26n1724) points to another occurrence of this obscure term, in the Bannatyne Manuscript, in the first of a series of "Schort Epegrammis Aganis Women": "Will god I sall not weir the siching b[a]ne" (line 5); in this context, the "sighing bone" seems to be an emblem of having been jilted. Given the frequency of association between the heart and sighing (e.g., *KQ,* line 1216), a breastbone may be implied. In *The Romance and Prophecies of Thomas of Erceldoune* (ed. Murray, Thornton text, line 49), a saddle is made of "roelle bone" (ivory; "rewel boon" is parodied in the Tale of Sir Thopas, *CT* VIII[B^2] 2068).

1726   *penny py.* This is a simple, economical pastry usually filled with mutton, spice, and seasoning (Riddell, *Aberdeen and Its Folk,* pp. 121–22): at lunchtime, the rustic merrymakers of William Tennant's *Anster Fair* (1812) long for "wherewithal to sate / Their hunger, bread and beer, or penny pie" (4.47.373–74, p. 19).

1735   *Ye bene welcum.* Graciously acknowledging the dreamer with this greeting, Venus employs the polite second person plural pronoun, in contrast to her usual practice in addressing the dreamer in particular. The gracious gesture is made only once; by the next line, 1736, Venus has reverted to "thou" in addressing the dreamer.

1737   *I not more than a schepe.* The silliness and cowardice of sheep are proverbial. See Whiting S213, S204–05.

1749   *Than suddandly in hand a buke scho hynt.* "The poet's interview with someone who commands him to write was a popular theme, and often linked with the dream. It perhaps originated partly as a humorous development of the humility topos: the poet writes not out of 'vane presumptioun' but at the request of another" (Burrow, p. 189). This assignment recalls the task Alceste sets for Chaucer (*LGW,* F prol.479–91) with a difference: where Alceste tells Chaucer what to write, Venus shows Douglas the book he will write (Morse, "Gavin Douglas: 'Off Eloquence,'" pp. 111–12).

1752   *put in ryme that proces, than quyt tynt.* The sense may be that the authentic *Aeneid* has been supplanted in vernacular discourse by incorrect, inaccurate retellings (possibly including Chaucer's in *HF*). It is worth remembering that Douglas does not specify the *Aeneid* here — even though the accompanying marginal note in

L is categorical on this point (see Textual Note to line 1756; see also Introduction to this edition, pp. 7–8).

1757 *Sumtyme efter quhen I have mare lasere*. Thus the poet may be dropping a gentle hint that greater leisure would enable him to be more productive.

1760–64 *yone myrrour clere . . . . behald all gracis*. The images in the mirror of Venus give rise to conflicting interpretations. While previously the dreamer saw the reflected deeds as heroic (lines 1693–94), the Nymph calls them beautiful. Complicating the issue further, a marginal gloss is printed in L that the Nymph's interpretation is "The Auctors conclution of Venus merour" (see Textual Notes to this edition, line 1761). The difference has stirred critical debate: it is either a flaw or thematically significant (Norton-Smith, p. 240; *SP*, p. xlv; Kratzmann, *Anglo-Scottish Literary Relations*, p. 114; Morse, "Gavin Douglas: 'Off Eloquence,'" pp. 111–12; Hasler, *Court Poetry in Late-Medieval England and Scotland*, p. 105; Johnston and Rouse, "Facing the Mirror," pp. 171–73). Throughout the poem, combat and intimacy have been problematically, productively intertwined. (For further discussion, see the Introduction to this edition, pp. 23–24, 54.)

1770–73 *Lucyus Catalyn . . . . his chaftis quuke*. The allusion is to Cicero's invective orations against Catiline; paired with his allusions to Sallust, here and above (lines 1688–91, and note), this emphasis may reflect the "marked preference for the invective" that Kristeller detects in fifteenth-century humanist taste ("Humanism," p. 125) and that Bawcutt considers to be prominent in Douglas' literary taste, practice, and public life (Bawcutt, p. 2). It is a nice touch that Cicero strikes down Catiline with a "buke," the vehicle of his invective rhetoric.

1775 *tressonabill Tryphon*. Assuming the name of Tryphon, Diodotus claimed the throne after the Prince Antiochus VI's suspicious death; he had been the Prince's tutor and regent. Tryphon deceitfully captured and murdered Jonathan Maccabeus, but Antiochus VII defeated him (1 Maccabees 11:39; 12:39–52; 13:12–23, 31–32; 15:25).

1787–88 *Rycht vertuus young . . . . thair mindis sete*. "Young saint, old devil" is proverbial. See Whiting S19.

1792–1827 *The mychty prynce . . . . yone kyngis obbeysance*. This is a "short allegorical passage based on the hierarchies of a royal household . . . which has some generic similarities to *King Hart*" (Martin, *Kingship*, p. 132; see also *Court of Sapience*, lines 1471–652). Hepburn argues that Douglas represents the household as "a force for obedience and order in a sometimes unruly courtly world" ("Household of James IV," p. 37). In the Scottish royal household, some offices were held by young noblemen: "carvers, sewars, cupbearers, waiters at the board-end, henchmen, and pages" (*ALHTS*, pp. cxc–cxci).

1798, 1801 *Thesaurar, Comptrowere*. In the Scottish royal administration under James IV, while the Comptroller received regular income from rents, the Treasurer received irregular income from duties, fines, and taxes. The Treasurer's expenses included construction and repair of royal castles and houses; maintenance of the Chapel

Royal; alms, offerings, largess, rewards and gifts; officers' pensions and fees; the lodging and entertainment of ambassadors and guests (*ALHTS*, pp. xiv, xxv).

1800   *clerkis of closet and cubeculeris.* The clerk of closet and the cubicular were attendants to the king in his bedchamber, the first his private confessor, the second his groom or personal servant. In *The Dreme*, Lyndsay recalls carrying out various of these household tasks for the young James V: "seware," "coppare," "carvoure," "ischare," and "of thy chalmer cheiffe cubiculare" (lines 21–24, Lyndsay, p. 1).

1807   *Humylyté karvar, that na wycht lyst to greve.* Humility is the quality displayed by Chaucer's Squire in carving at table for his father; it is also displayed by the young James Douglas performing the same task for the Bishop of St. Andrews (*CT* I[A] 99–100; *Bruce*, 1.333–77, 2:14–15).

1810–11   *His Chanceller . . . . pronounce fals sentence.* The Chancellor of the Scottish court "presided over the king's parliaments and councils and kept the king's great seal" (Nicholson, *Scotland: The Later Middle Ages*, p. 22). The poet's father held this office in the 1490s (see Introduction, pp. 4–5).

1816   *As auditouris thay ovirseis quhat is spent.* The audit of the royal accounts was an annual affair performed by the Lords Auditors of the Exchequer, officers specially appointed for this duty (Murray, "Procedure of the Scottish Exchequer," pp. 91–93; Hepburn, "Household of James IV," pp. 168–69).

1818   *out stewartis.* Hepburn suggests these are equivalent to the *ballivi ad extra* of Scottish royal administration, "the financial administrators of the king's property" outside the burghs ("Household of James IV," p. 36n107).

1821   *almoseir.* In fifteenth-century Scotland, the almoner was "charged with distributing to the poor from a great household" (Houston, "What Did the Royal Almoner Do," pp. 306–07).

1824–25   *The kyngis mynyeon . . . . heicht Verité.* Naming Verity the king's intimate servant overturns the usually pejorative associations of *minion*; *DOST Min3(e)o(u)n, minio(u)n* (n.), sense 3, "A prince's or great man's favourite. Chiefly opprobriously: One who owes everything to his patron's favour, a 'hanger-on', a 'creature'."

1834–36   *yet of byrnyst gold . . . . in erd consave.* Golden doors decorated with scenes (but of military triumph not natural phenomena) open upon the shrine of Caesar in Virgil's *Georgics* (3.26–39, pp. 178–79); a closer parallel exists in Ovid's description of the silver doors of the palace of the Sun (*Met* 2.1–18, 1:60–61).

1837   *Thare wes the erth enveronyt wyth the see.* Ovid also begins his description of the doorway to the palace of the Sun with an account of the earth surrounded by the seas (*Met* 2.5–6, 1:60–61). Douglas alludes to *HF*, line 903, where the airborne Geoffrey glimpses "shippes seyllynge in the see"; a secondary allusion may exist in Troilus' view of the little earth, in the epilogue to *TC*.

1840   *The Speris Sevyn and primum mobile.* The seven spheres are the courses of the seven planets (outer to inner: Saturn, Jupiter, Mars, Venus, Mercury, the sun, the moon) revolving around the earth according to the Ptolemaic system; the "primum mobile," the source of planetary motion is the outermost sphere moving on an axis, at either end of which are the Pole Stars (lines 1843–44 and note).

1841–42   *The sygnis twelf . . . . as bukis represents.* A source is Ovid's reference to six signs of the zodiac on the right-hand doors of the palace of the Sun and six on the left (*Met* 2.18, 1:60–61).

1843–44   *The Poil Antertik . . . . the Poil Artik.* The Pole Stars are *arcticus*, the one which "alway schineth to us and never gooth doun to oure sight, for alwey he is above us," and *antarcticus*, "'the southeren sterre,'" which is "alwey unseyn to us" (Trev. *Prop.* 8.22, p. 501, lines 27–28, 30, 32); these two stars mark the uppermost and downmost points of the "spere of heven" on which, in Ptolemaic astronomy, the stars are fixed (8.6, p. 456, line 27).

1844–45   *the Ursis twane . . . . the Charle wane.* These refer to Ursa Major and Ursa Minor; as the "Charle wane" is another name for Ursa Major, some uncertainty may exist about terminology (*DOST Charle wain(e* (n.)). Situating Phaethon in the heavens with the Pleiades and the two Bears may suggest some vagueness about basic astronomy; it may, however, be an allusion to the wandering stars whose courses Ovid compares to falling Phaethon (*Met* 2.320–23, 1:82–83), and perhaps to the "impressioun" at the outset of the poem (lines 105–06). In the prologue to *Eneados* 8.prol.151 (3:121), a reference to the "son, the Sevyn Starnys, and the Charl Wayn" is part of the rough lore reeled off by a character in a dream. See also *Dialog* line 165 (Lyndsay, pp. 189, 319n165).

1846–48   *quhow that Ganamedis . . . . his cheif butlare.* Orpheus sings the tale of Jupiter's taking the form of an eagle to abduct the Trojan boy Ganymede, who then mixes and serves Jupiter's nectar (*Met* 10.155–61, 2:74–75). Here the tale of divine lust and aerial travel contrasts with the earlier emphasis on the moral worth of the officers at the court of Honour; Norton-Smith argues that Ganymede, the only human depicted on the doorway, is a figure for the poet (p. 249; compare *HF*, lines 588–92).

1849–54   *The douchters . . . . al sisteris beyng.* Douglas is translating Ovid's description of the engraving on the doors of the Sun's palace of the sea-nymph Doris and her daughters (*Met* 2.11–14, 1:60–61), with two changes: Ovid's nymphs have green hair, and some of them are riding on fishes.

1855   *Of the planetis all the conjunctionys.* In medieval astronomy, a conjunction (an "apparent proximity of two planets or other heavenly bodies . . . as viewed from the earth") was regarded as an especially significant influence on terrestrial affairs (*OED conjunction*, sense 3; Grant, *Planets, Stars, and Orbs*, p. 387).

1856   *Thare episciclis and oppositionis.* In Ptolemaic astronomy, each of the seven planets was supposed to revolve on its own orbit (or "epicycle"), but also to move spirally along a greater circle (the "deferent"). "Opposition" occurs when two planets are exactly opposite to one another from the perspective of the earth, or when a planet is opposite to the sun: "it is signe of parfite emnyte and bodeth worst happis, and namliche yif Mars hath soche aspecte to Saturnus othir to the sonne"; Trev. *Prop.* 8.9, p. 465, lines 23–24).

1857   *quhow thair coursis swagis.* Bartholomaeus identifies three kinds of planetary motion: direct, stationary, and retrograde: "Also in these cerclys thre maner meouynge of planetis is ful wiseliche ifounde of astronomers, that ben iclepide *motus directus, stacionarius,* and *retrogradus*" (Trev. *Prop.* 8.11, p. 477, lines 24–26).

1859   *aspectis, and degressyonys.* This is the position of a planet on the zodiac relative to another planet from the vantage point of the earth; "digression" is the apparent deviation in the courses of the lower planets, Venus and Mercury.

1862–63 *The werkmanschip excedyng . . . . wes fynest gold.* These lines translate *materiam superabat opus* at the outset of Ovid's description of the doors of the palace of the Sun (*Met* 2.5, 1:60–61); Cairns (p. 33) perceives a significant inversion of sequence, with Douglas placing this phrase at the end of his ekphrasis.

1865   *My Nymphe in grif schot me in at the yet.* This gesture recalls the impatient shove Africanus gives the erring dreamer in *PF* (lines 153–54).

1866–68 *Quhat Devyl . . . . on sic dotyng.* "What devil" is a common expletive phrase (*MED devel* (n.), sense 6c; *DOST devil* (n.), sense 1d). For all its raciness of style, the Nymph's scolding may recall the Sibyl Deiphobe's rebuke of Aeneas for staring overlong at the depictions on the doors to Daedalus' temple of Apollo (*Aeneid* 6.14–39, 1:532–35; Norton-Smith, p. 249).

1868   *tho for fere I swet.* Krantzmann observes that "Douglas's 'I', like Chaucer's, 'sweats' in fear" (*Anglo-Scottish Literary Relations,* p. 122; *HF,* line 1042).

1878   *It semyt lyk the hevyn imperiall.* The empyrean is the highest heaven, above the moving spheres; it is the home of the angels and the "contrey and wonynge of blisful men" (Trev. *Prop.* 8.4, p. 454, lines 28–29); Honour lives in a place "like" heaven (compare *The Dreme,* lines 514–18, Lyndsay, p. 19).

1879–80 *as the cedir . . . . in perfyt hycht.* The cedar is a traditional emblem for the high style (Curtius, p. 201); Douglas exaggerates the lowness of the low style by typifying it by a mere shrub (Norton-Smith, "Ekphrasis as a Stylistic Element," p. 247).

1891   *breddyt.* The doors and windows are shuttered, not completely sealed; his view thus obstructed, the dreamer "must view the interior of the palace in a single, circumscribed peep" (Norton-Smith, p. 253).

1893   *With byrnyst evyr baith palyce and touris.* Ovid's Palace of the Sun is similarly roofed with ivory (*Met* 2.3, 1:60–61).

1898   *Curius knottis, and many sle devyse.* By "knots," Douglas refers to ornamental patterns of interlace, worked in gold and enamel upon the ivory; a "devise" is an emblematic design inscribed with an explanatory motto.

1902   *thopas.* Topaz "schyneth most whan he is ysmyte with the sonne beeme, and passeth in clerenesse alle othere precious stones, and comforteth men and bestes to byholde and loke theronne . . . . And in tresorie of kynges nothing is more cleere ne more precious than this precious stone" (Trev. *Prop.* 16.95, p. 877, lines 33–36; p. 878, lines 1–2).

1903   *boir.* This may be a small space in the shutters on the door; see note to line 1891 above.

1904   *represent.* In Middle English, the word has associations with the mental impression resulting from perception (*MED represent* (n.)). Fradenburg considers this an especially significant, decisive choice of term (*City, Marriage, Tournament,* p. 186); in this moment, the dreamer registers his awareness of the impact of his vision upon his senses and mind, so that he is already smitten before he falls unconscious. Johnston and Rouse argue that the "represent" "mesmerizes the viewer — he feels both desire and fear while gazing on the alluring image of totalizing power, and he becomes a wretched captive" ("Facing the Mirror," p. 177).

1907   *amatist.* Amethyst traditionally has associations with sobriety (Trev. *Prop.* 16.9, p. 834). The twelfth foundation of the heavenly Jerusalem is amethyst (Apocalypse 21:20).

1913   *saphyrs.* The sapphire "hath vertue to reule and acorde hem that bene in stryf and helpeth moche to make pees and acorde"; it was reputedly "singulerliche yhalowed to Appolyn" (Trev. *Prop.* 16.86, p. 869, lines 32–33; p. 870, lines 28–29).

1916   *smaragdane.* The smaragd is "pris [most prized] of alle grene stones" (Trev. *Prop.* 16.87, p. 871, line 16). The name is etymologically related to "emerald," appropriately so since the two words refer to the same gemstone (*OED smaragd* (n.)).

1921   *Intronyt sat a god armypotent.* In Dunbar's *Goldyn Targe,* it is Mars who is "armypotent"; in *Eneados,* Douglas refers thus to both Pallas Athena and Deiphobus (2.7.113, 2:87; 6.8.37, 3:33). See further the Textual Note for this line.

1922–24   *On quhais . . . . all my bonys.* "And the schynand and fyry suerd that stoppis oure gait to paradice, js the just sentens of the diuinite agane the man, that wauld have turnit agane to paradice terrestir eftir the sentens of the trinite" (Ireland, *Meroure* 2:4, 1:79). Referring to lines 105–11, Johnston and Rouse see this collapse as "the second time that the poet-speaker is struck down by a blinding force" ("Facing the Mirror," p. 178). For Douglas Gray, the moment "is reminiscent in some ways of an intense spiritual experience, of a mystic vision perhaps, or of the way Lancelot is smitten down in the *Queste del Saint Graal*" ("Gavin Douglas," p. 155).

1942   *Carlyng.* This is the feminine equivalent to "carl" or "churl," an abusive colloquialism (*DOST carling* (n.), sense 1).

1944   *For kyrkmen wer ay jentill to ther wyvys.* Small records the tradition that Douglas had a relationship that produced a daughter and perhaps other children, and observes that "[a]ccording to the sentiments of the age, transgressions of this kind were treated with indulgence" (*Poetical Works*, 1:cxxv–cxxvi; Fraser, *Douglas Book*, 2:139n1; Paul, *Scots Peerage* 1:185). Less controversially, *ther* may also be a variant of *thir*, "these" (*DOST thir* (adj.), sense A.1).

1953   *malt.* Later the dreamer regrets having a "megyr hart," (line 2029); here, it appears his heart is soft, easily overcome (derived from *MED melten* (v.), senses 1b and 2b; *DOST melt* (v.1), sense 2). The form might be related to "molten" as past participle, (see *DOST melt* (v.1), for the form "moltine").

1957   *My lydyis court in thair gudly array.* This refers to the court of the Muses.

1978–94   *For erdly glore . . . . of thair estatis.* A summary of various traditional expressions about the transience of earthly glory, including proverbial images such as the dream, the sunbeam, and the weltering sea; the passage ends with a catalogue of the mighty, all under the term of Death (Whiting L241, S107, 113; Woolf, *English Religious Lyric*, pp. 325, 343–47).

1981–89   *Behald . . . . the wally see.* Life is a dream, and its good things pass away in an instant; the Nymph's moralizing recalls aspects of ephemerality elsewhere in the poem. See note to line 1051 above.

1987   *sonne beme.* The sunbeam as an emblem of ephemeral brilliance conveys a deeply-rooted sentiment (Whiting S906); the simile may recall the flash of the "impressioun" at the outset (lines 105–06).

1995   *And not ellis bot vertuus werkis richt.* Behind this allusion to the doctrine of good works may lie an exemplary tale such as the ubiquitous parable of Barlaam and Josaphat, appearing, for example, in *The Golden Legend*.

2019   *Nobillis Nyne.* The tradition of the Nine Worthies — three pagan heroes (Hector, Alexander the Great, Julius Caesar), three Jews (Joshua, David, Judas Maccabeus), and three Christians (Arthur, Charlemagne, and Godfrey of Boulogne) — "became increasingly popular across medieval European art, drama, and literature" and gave rise in mid-fifteenth-century Scotland to *The Balletis of the Nine Nobles*, with Robert the Bruce added as a worthy tenth (Wingfield, *Trojan Legend in Medieval Scottish Literature*, pp. 64–73, quoted at pp. 64–65).

2020   *Pompeyus the ald.* This is Gnaeus Pompeius Magnus (Pompey the Great), Roman conqueror of Asian kingdoms, including Pontus, Syria, and Judea; he was defeated by Caesar at the Battle of Pharsalus. Gower alludes to him as the epitome of the mighty conqueror (*CA* 5.5533–34).

2024   *Semiramis, Thamar, Ypolytha.* Semiramis, an Assyrian queen whom Gower calls a whore (*CA* 5.1432–33) and Chaucer a "virago" (*CT* II[B¹] 359), is also famed for building a wall around Babylon (*LGW*, line 707; Utley, pp. 224–25); Tamar is one of two wronged women in the Old Testament: the daughter-in-law of Judah (Genesis 38:6, 8, 12–30) or the daughter of David, raped by her brother Amnon (2 Kings 13:1–32; 1 Chronicles 3:9); Hippolyta, Amazon queen, defeated and married by Theseus (as in lines 1195–96).

2025   *Pantyssalé, Medus, Cenobia.* For Penthesilea, see note to line 341 above. Ovid depicts Medusa, once the most beautiful and desirable of women, as raped by

Neptune. Jealous or angered, Minerva punished Medusa by changing her hair to snakes; Perseus beheaded her after showing her reflection; and her blood produced the flying horse Pegasus (*Met* 4.790–803, 1:234–35; *CA* 1.389–435). Zenobia is the militant queen of Chaucer's MkT (*CT* VII[B²] 3437–564).

2027   *The kyngis Gregor, Kened and Kyng Robert.* These are three victorious kings of Scots: "Gregor," Giric I, identified in *Scotichronicon* (4.17, ed. Watt, 2:320–21) as commencing his reign in 875 and conquering Ireland and most of (*ac pene totam*) England (ed. Watt, 2:318–21); "Kened," Kenneth I mac Alpin, conqueror of the Picts, whose reign commenced in 834 (*Scotichronicon* 4.273; ed. Watt, 2:273–74); "Kyng Robert," Robert the Bruce (1274–1329), who re-established Scottish kingship and defeated Edward II at Bannockburn in 1314.

2034   *A huge pepyl punyst for thair trespas.* Expecting to see a "huge people" rightfully punished might be comparable to avidly anticipating the discourse of a "man of gret auctorite" at the end of *HF* (line 2158). What may strengthen the connection to *HF* is that the man of great authority arrives shortly after Geoffrey has described men of evil fame — liars and such — who deserve punishment (lines 2121–30). The moment in *PH* may also involve an appeal to the King to live up to his reputation for judicial rigor; according to the Spanish ambassador Pedro de Ayala, James IV was "a severe judge, especially in the case of murderers" (*Calendar of Negotiations between England and Spain*, ed. Bergenroth, 1:169).

2035–49   *Quhilkis be wilfull . . . . honour away is.* The displacement of sons of noble birth by upstarts and the corruption of morals among the nobility are topics of Dunbar's court satires (e.g., "Schir, ʒit remember as befoir," lines 11–25; "Complane I wald, wist I quhome till," lines 15–38; "Quhom to sall I compleine my wo," lines 21–30 [*Poems*, ed. Bawcutt, 1:225–26, 67–68, 171–72]). The justice meted out by Honour might be compared with Fame's treatment of the "shrewes" who request and receive lasting notoriety for their evil deeds (*HF*, lines 1823–68).

2044–47   *And nobillis cumyn . . . . corruppit, covatus invy.* The poet's father, Archibald Douglas, fifth earl of Angus, was deprived of the chancellorship in 1497 (see the Introduction to this edition, pp. 4–5).

2051–57   *And thair gret . . . . na mare prescryve.* The Spanish ambassador Pedro de Ayala reported approvingly on the young James IV's characteristically decisive execution of justice: "He lends a willing ear to his counselors, and decides nothing without asking them; but in great matters he acts according to his own judgment." Civil strife, Pedro reported, had been suppressed among the Scots: "since the present King succeeded to the throne they do not dare to quarrel so much with one another as formerly, especially since he came of age. They have learnt by experience that he executes the law without respect to rich or poor" (*Calendar of Negotiations between England and Spain*, ed. Bergenroth, 1:171).

2059   *My spreit desyris to se thair torment fane.* See note to lines 2107–12 below. The dreamer's longing to witness "thair torment" may recall Apocalypse 21:8–9, where the torture of the unrighteous proceeds "in the presence of the holy angels and the Lamb."

2062–76   *Bot first . . . . thair nebbis grew.* In writing about *PH*, the Edinburgh advocate and historian Patrick Fraser Tytler took special note of this passage: "the Poet, under the protection of her who has so faithfully conducted him, proposes to visit a delightful garden, where the Muses are employed in gathering the choicest flowers of poesy, which spring beneath trees bearing precious stones instead of fruit. In the description of this retreat there is a strange admixture of the beautiful and the ridiculous. The scenery is sweetly painted; but what shall we say of the trees on which geese or chickens are seen growing; to the transplanting of the extraordinary fables of Boece into the gardens of the Palace of Honour?" (*Lives of Scottish Worthies*, 3:168).

2065   *bissy as the beis.* On the Muses as busy bees, see note to line 45 above.

2066   *colouris of rethoreis.* Compare "Youre termes, youre colours, and youre figures," which Chaucer's Host associates with the high style, "as whan that men to kynges write" (*CT* IV[E] 16, 18). Chaucer's Franklin professes ignorance of such devices: "Colours ne knowe I none . . . / But swiche colours as growen in the mede" (*CT* V[F] 723–24). The lyric concluding *PH* (lines 2143–69) would thus exemplify the poet's own skill at gathering, selecting, and applying such colors for such purposes, but also display his reluctance to claim such skill — a display that is itself a "color."

2075–76   *out of growand treis . . . . thair nebbis grew.* The birth of barnacle geese out of trees growing over the water may be presented as an insular marvel, a myth of nature that originates back home in the British Isles, as it is in *Mandeville's Travels*, about the *bernakes*, born like fruit from trees (*Buke of John Maundevill*, ed. Warner, pp. 130, 213; eds. Kohanski and Benson, lines 2346–48, and "introduced to bestiary lore in 1187 by Geraldus Cambrensis"; 2342–47n). In his *Chronicles of Scotland* (1527), Hector Boece asserted that "we can not beleif that thir clakis [barnacle geese] ar producit be ony nature of treis or rutis thairof, bot allanerly be the nature of the occeane see, quhilk is the caus and production of mony wonderful thingis" ("Cosmographe and Discription of Albion," trans. Bellenden, chapter xiv; *History and Chronicles*, ed. Maitland, p. xlix).

2078   *Wes laid a tre ovir quhilk behovyt we pas.* Not for the first time or the last, a tree trunk occupies a significant place in the narrative; see, e.g., lines 199, 230, 313, 316, 345, 1474, and notes to lines 1013 and 2114.

2086–88   *Quhyl I fell . . . . in point to droun.* Cairns (p. 34) detects an Ovidian link to Phaethon's final fall into a river, this link is strengthened via Regio's gloss *in caput cadit* ("[he] falls headlong").

2098   *The byrdis sang.* Chaucer (*PF*, lines 491–93) influentially exaggerates the effects of this sound; here it both counters and recalls the birdsong at the outset of the poem but also the apocalyptic cries the fish make, at the start of the dream proper (*PH*, lines 22–25, 146–47).

2106   *fund.* Middle English *finden* has a wealth of meanings from "discover," "find," "ascertain," and "judge," to "compose," "invent," "counterfeit," or "tell" (*MED* provides twenty-three separate entries, each with various shades of meaning).

The dreamer longs to remain in the country of poetic invention that he "fund" in his dream.

2107–12   *And maist of . . . . slane or schent.* The dreamer in Dunbar's *Ballat of the Abbot of Tungland*, lines 125–28 (*Poems*, ed. Bawcutt, 1:59) is angry about waking, Bawcutt suggests, because he too has thus been prevented from seeing justice executed (*Dunbar the Makar*, p. 279).

2114   *sittand under a tre.* This is not the first time the narrator-protagonist places himself near a tree to compose a poem; see line 1013 and note, and, implicitly, the recitation of the song against Venus, lines 607 ff.

2116–69   *O hie Honour . . . . I end tha.* These two lyrics merit comparison with the lyrics inset earlier (lines 163–92, 607–36, 1015–44). Where those earlier effusions each begin with a strong focus on the speaker himself (addressing the dreamer's fate, his heart, and his wit), these closing stanzas are addressed to other, exalted entities: Honor, King James IV. It is worthwhile to trace the relation between the objective values presented here (Honour, kingship) and the representation of the poet's own need for protection and patronage, however unworthy his book may be (lines 2142–43, 2150–51, 2154 ff.).

2116–42   *O hie Honour . . . . to thy devyse.* These stanzas attain new stylistic heights. Internal rhyme is a memorable device of closure in other late fifteenth-century Scottish poems: Henryson, *Prayer for the Pest* (*Poems of Robert Henryson*, ed. Fox, lines 65–88), Dunbar and Kennedie, *Flyting*, lines 233–48, 545–52 (*Poems*, ed. Bawcutt, 1:208, 218); for further discussion of internal rhyme in *PH*, see the Introduction to this edition, pp. 31, 36). Bawcutt notes that "the imagery has religious associations, several of the figures being traditionally applied to Christ or the Virgin; and Douglas frequently addresses Honour as if he were addressing God" (*SP*, p. 213n2116–42). In the first stanza, the dominant images are the flower and the gem; in the second, it is first the shining "face" of the sun and then (line 2130) a harbor. The first three lines of the third stanza present a sequence of images: rose, gem, dew. Several of these images are regularly associated with Christ.

2116–18   *swete hevynly flour . . . . guerdoun condyng.* Honour is a flower in that it is the "best or finest," or "the perfection" of virtue (*DOST flour* (n.), senses 2b and c). Similarly, it a gem in that it is the most powerful ("vertuus"), precious, and beautiful ("gudlyest") of qualities. This concept of Honour might be compared with the virtue of magnificence, "that is to seyn, whan a man dooth and parfourneth the werkes of goodnesse; and that is the ende why that men sholde do goode werkes, for in the accomplissynge of grete goode werkes lith the grete gerdoun" (ParsT, *CT* X[I] 736).

2122   *poverale.* In earlier Scottish poems, the word has an association with military rank-and-file — or often, camp-followers (e.g., *Bruce*, 8.275, 368, 2:199, p. 203; *DOST poveraill* (n.), sense a); more generally, it is associated with the common people who ideally support and are protected by the nobility (*MED poverail(e* (n.), sense a).

myche. See note to line 1643 above and "mekill" in the Glossary.

2124 *That efter this in thy hie blys we ryng*. The request is to "reign with" Honour; that is, to persist or flourish "in thy hie blys." The language recalls prayers for eternal life (*DOST ring* (v.3), sense 7).

2125–27 *thy face . . . . Thy glore*. The image is of royal power drawing all subjects to bow to it, the way sunshine attracts all living things. The phrase "baith heid and feit" indicates the completeness of Honour's power over his subjects, but also suggests that he rules both high and low in the kingdom; the idea that even the poor are under his care has been stated in line 2122.

2134–35 *Hail rois . . . . trone of lycht*. The language of flowers and jewels that has recurred in various situations throughout the poem is now given its concluding synthesis. Jewels (ruby, jasper, emerald) are associated with the throne in heaven and the one seated upon it (Apocalypse 4:2–3).

2136 *dew*. As an image of blessings and favored destiny, "dew" is scriptural (e.g., Genesis 27:28; Judges 6:36–37). The image also appears in medieval descriptions of the visionary pleasant place (e.g., *LGW*, line 775; see *PH*, line 13). The term is one of several used literally at the beginning of the poem and that reappear in fully allegorical guise in its closing lines.

2139 *Thow stant ordant as sant of grant maist wyse*. Compared to a saint, the god Honour is dedicated to awarding favor with discernment.

2140 *Til be supplé and the hie gre of pryce*. Naming the supreme virtue as itself a "gre," a platform, gives final utterance to the language of steps and levels that has taken prominence at key points throughout *PH* (e.g., lines 21–22, 1150–51, 1472–74, 1900–02).

2157 *variance*. The use of "variance" here may be compared with its structurally significant previous appearances. At the outset of the Prologue, the word refers to variation of visual effects as an aspect of beauty (line 9, "wariance"). At the end of the Second Part (line 1286), Douglas prays for a style purged of "variance" — of inconsistency, imperfection. Now he begs the King's pardon for the sins of his "variance" in a style that recalls the varying ornamentation with which *PH* began.

2159 *Remyttand my pretendit negligence*. Similarly, the god of Love dismisses Chaucer's balade-making as "necligence" but assigns him to compose *LGW* (F prol.537; G prol.525).

2161–63 *Breif, burall quair . . . . not pretend tha*. This is an intensification of Chaucer's envoy to *TC* (5.1786–92; see also *KQ*, lines 1352–65).

2163 *Til cum in plane se thow not pretend tha*. The realization that the poem ought not to come into the open recalls the dreamer's impulse to seek cover at the outset of the dream.

2164–69 *Thy barrant termis . . . . I end tha*. Antony Hasler describes this conclusion as "an unusually explosive dismissal" in which "The poet suddenly turns into a 'flyter' against his own text, rehearsing, with a barrage of internal rhyme, charges with which we are by now familiar. His poem is purloined, sterile, worthless — waste matter, in effect" (*Court Poetry*, p. 106).

2164   *barrant termis*. Barrenness is a recurrent concept, having been applied to the poet's mind (line 127), the trees in the nightmare wasteland and the wasteland itself (lines 150, 661), and the erstwhile pleasant Maytime garden (line 2100). It is also evidently a relative concept.

2166   *quytcleme*. Douglas is pressing a legal term into a more general meaning, to "repudiate, disavow, deny" (*DOST quite-clame* (v.), sense 1b); more formally and precisely, the verb refers to giving up "a possession, claim, right, title, etc." (sense 1); it can also denote a declaration of being released from a claim once a debt has been paid or an obligation performed (sense 2). The assertion thus involves both a submission to the King's authority and an assertion of the poet's own prerogative in declaring his work over and done with.

2167   *stouth . . . but lyte*. Calling the poem "theft," "stolen property," or "something done by stealth" (*DOST stouth* (n.), senses 1, 1b, 2), the poet is dismissing his allusive, ornate style as mere plagiarism. On a more serious level, Douglas may be bringing his conclusion into line with Richard Holland's final stanzas to *BH*, where the owl presents himself as a "merour" of poverty and mortality, become "lathast [most hateful]" once the other birds have reclaimed the feathers in which he had been decked (lines 969–70; see pp. 146–48n969–76). The line ends sententiously (Whiting E184, T75).

2168–69   *Not worth a myte . . . . I end tha*. Rather as dreams had been earlier (line 1269), the poem is depicted as trash, before it is roughly dismissed as if it were an unwelcome vagrant. The book heads off on its wanderings, in need of a charitable reception from each person it encounters.

TEXTUAL NOTES

ABBREVIATIONS: **D**: The fragments of a print likely by the Edinburgh printer Thomas Davidson (Edinburgh University Library De.6.123); **DOST**: *The Dictionary of the Older Scottish Tongue*; **E**: The Edinburgh print of *PH* (as in National Library of Scotland, H.29.b.12); **E1**: The handwritten emendations in E; **L**: The London print of *PH* (as in John Rylands Library, 2039.2; base text); **ME**: Middle English; **MED**: *The Middle English Dictionary*; **OE**: Old English; **OF**: Old French; **SP**: *The Palice of Honour*, ed. Bawcutt (in *The Shorter Poems of Gavin Douglas*).

All printed rubrics and notes are recorded. Some alternations recurrent through the text of L (with, for instance, *a/ai, en/in, er/ir, i/y* with *i* regularly used for *j, u/v,* suffix *-y/ie, c/k, c/t,* double/single *l, o/ou/u,* thorn/*th,* final *-e*) are generally not recorded. Suspensions and abbreviations are expanded silently. D is present only for fragments of lines 10–29, 39–58, 68–87, 97–115, 125–26, 136–55, and 165–184. E1, comprising the handwritten emendations in the NLS copy of E, is present only intermittently in the witness. Hyphens, inconsistently provided in the marginal notes, are normalized editorially.

Heading	*Prologue*. L: omitted.
3	*be*. So L. E: *the*. The reading in E stems from a misreading of *circumstance* as "surroundings" (*DOST, circumstance*, sense 4).
8	*sole*. So L. E: *Sol*. E1: *Soil*. E1 apparently attempts to resolve an ambiguity in E between soil and Sol, the sun; see also note to line 57 below.
	amyable. So L. E1: *dilectabil[l]*. E1 thus avoids the repetition of the rhyme-word from line 5.
21	*Above*. So L. D: . . . *ue* [initial letters lost]. E: *Abone*.
25	*eccon*. So L. E: *Echo*. The spelling in L is unique but may be authorial.
29	*Replennessed*. So L. E: *Replenischit*. The spelling in L reflects a form etymologically consistent with the OF source *replenisser*, well-distributed in ME and attested in fifteenth-century Scots texts (see *DOST, replenis(c)hit, -ist*; *MED, replenishen*).
35	*restored*. So L. E: *restorit*.
36	*Reconfort*. So L. E: *Recomfort*.
39	*preserve*. So L. E: *reserve*. E's reading may maintain the sense of protection that is foremost in L's (*DOST, reserve* (v.), sense 6).
48	*vigitant*. So L. E: *vegetant*. The spelling in L is unusual; see note to line 25 above.
57	*soyl*. So L. E: *Sol*. E1: *Soil*. See note to line 8 above.

88   *auchtys*. L: *auchtyst*. E: *auchtis*. The reading in L may involve a mistaken use of the second person suffix in the impersonal construction (*DOST*, *aucht* (v.), sense 1, possibly confused with sense 2b).

97   *Confort*. So L. E: *Comfort*.

99   *puncys*. So L. E: *pulsis*. L preserves a form well-attested in fifteenth-century Scottish texts (*DOST*, *punse*, *punce*, (n.2)).

101   *dasyt*. So L. E: *desie*. L's reading indicates that the immediate situation has dazed the protagonist (*DOST*, *dasit*, *daisit* (ppl. a.)), while E's may imply that giddiness is the narrator's normal condition (*DOST*, *desy*, *desie* (adj.)); see also note to line 109 below.

    vary. L: *veray*. L's reading can at best be described as an idiosyncratic spelling (*DOST*, *varie*, *vary* (v.); alternate spellings are *var(y)e*, *war(i)e*, *-y(e*, *verré*).

109   *so dasyt*. So L. D: *so da . . .* [final letters lost]. E: *sa desyit*.

111   *hetis*. So L. E: *heiring*. In referring to body temperature, L's reading can be taken as somewhat more learned, as well as being more apposite in the context of signs of conscious life.

114   *Corruppis*. So L. D: *Corruppys*. E: *Corruptis*. As confirmed by D, the reading in L reflects an authentic form (*DOST*, *corrupt*, *corrup* (v.)).

118   *quhou*. So L. E: *how*. L provides a form current in Scots writing from the late fifteenth century to the mid-sixteenth century but rare thereafter (*DOST*, *quhow* (adv.)).

126   *avision*. So L. E: *Visioun*. Douglas is among the latest Scots writers to employ the older form *avision* (*DOST*, *avisioun*, *avisione*); compare the occurrence in L of the alternate *vision*, line 60.

Final rubric   *Finis*. So L. Below this rubric appears a woodcut of the royal arms of the Tudors. D: *. . . ambyl. And now nixt efter | the Palyce of HONOUR | n. & c.* (Below is a fragment of a woodcut with a vertical type ornament.) E: *Finis Prologi*.

Heading   *The First Part*. L: *The Palys of Honour*. E: *The Palice of | Honour, Compylit be M. | GAWINE DOWGLAS | Bischop of Dunkeld. | ¶The First Part.*

132   *ranys*. So L. E: *rymis*. *DOST* identifies *rane* (n.) as possibly Gaelic in origin (*rann*, meaning a verse; stanza), but used typically pejoratively by the predecessors and contemporaries of Douglas; E would thus be offering a simplified counterpart.

134   *thir*. L: *their*. Copland has apparently mistaken a standard demonstrative adjective in Douglas' usage.

139   *trubbyll*. So L. E: *trubil*. E1: *tribil*. Though the reading in E1 is attractive, *trubbyll* is attested elsewhere with this meaning (*DOST*, *trubil(l*, *troubil(l*, *trib(b)ill*).

144   *skauppis*. So L. D: *sk . . . uppis* [letter lost]. E: *swappis*. E1: *skappis*. The apparently meaningless reading in E is opposed by all the other witnesses.

148   *monsturis*. L: *monstruis*. E: *monstures*. The form in L likelier results from a mistake in the typesetting than from an idiosyncratic spelling.

157   *royk*. So L. E: *Rock*. L's spelling is etymologically significant (*DOST*, *rok(e*, *roik*, *rouk* (n.2)).

165	L: printed in the left hand margin, *A discrip-	tion of the	inconstance	of fortune*.
186	*Suythly*. So L. E: *Surelie*.
189	*this*. So E. L: *thus*. The reading in L may have resulted from the occurrence of *thus* directly above, in the previous line.
197	*quhow afferyt wes*. So L. E: *how affrayit was*. *Afferyt* derives from OE *afæran*; the semantically similar *affrayit* derives from OF *afrayer*.
201	L: printed in the right hand margin, *The quen	of sapyence	wyth hyr	court*.
213	*four*. So L. So E1. E: *all*.
221	*Twelve*. L: *Xii*. E: *Twelf*.
230	L: printed in the left hand margin, *Craftye	Synone	and false	Architefel*.
233	*tothir*. So L. E: *vther*. The form attested in L is frequent in fifteenth-century and early sixteenth-century usage (*DOST, tothir* (adj., pron.)).
242	*twelve*. L: *xii*. E: *Twelf*.
246	*Prophetis*. So L, E. E1: *Prophetes*. With this emendation, E1 clarifies that the noun is singular and has a feminine suffix.
251	L: printed in the right hand margin, *Wyse and	lerned men*.
276	L: printed in the left hand margin, *Architefel	confessis	hys owne	craftenes	deceyt and	abused	wit*. In contrast to the generally positive associations of Douglas' own usage, the commentator uses "craft" pejoratively.
284	*overwhort*. So L. E: *ouirthort*. The spelling in L preserves a rarer form (*DOST, overwhort, -hort, -whart* (adv., prep.)).
285	L: printed in the left hand margin, *Sinons	craftines*.
289	*bene*. So L. So E1. E: *haue bene*. Metrical regularity is preserved if "schrewis" is pronounced with two syllables.
290	*optene*. So L. E: *obtene*. The spelling in L is attested in fifteenth-century and early sixteenth-century Scots sources (*DOST, optene* (v.)). See also note to line 974 below.
302	*Imagynand feil syse*. L: *Imagynand feil lyse*. E: *Imagining feill syse*. L's reading *lyse* can be explained as resulting from mistaking a long *s* for an *l*.
308	L: printed in the left hand margin, *Feare*.
315	*and of hir*. So L. E: *or hir*. E regularizes a departure from metrical regularity in L.
319	*tofore*. So L. E: *befoir*. Here as elsewhere (e.g., lines 120, 385, 661, 760, 828, 890, 1440, 1985), L preserves a form attested in fifteenth-century Scots usage (*DOST, to-for(e, to-forn(e)*.
342	*Effygyn*. So L. E: *Effyoin*. E1: *Effygin*. A descender is added by E1 to the printed *o* of E. Bawcutt comments that "E's reading is not necessarily corrupt" (*SP*, p. 179n342).
360–61	*Proportion soundis dulcest . . . . did tak kepe*. Lines inverted from L, E. Bawcutt proposes the logical emendation (*SP*, p. 179n360).
360	*soundis*. So L. E: *sounding*. E provides a simplification of the syntax and significance of the line, in which "proportion" is likeliest to have a precise musical signification (*DOST, proportio(u)n(e* (n.), sense 3).
363	*caryit*. So E. L: *carit*.
372	*Inoth*. So L. E: *Inwith*. The form in L derives from *inouth*, a fifteenth-century variant of *inwith* (*DOST, in(n)outh, innowth*).
379	*inoth*. So L. E: *Inwith*. See note to line 372 above.

385   *tofore*. So L. E: *befoir*. See note to line 319 above.

388   *Lang ere*. L: *Langere*. E: *Langer*. Compare the variants in the note to line 1946.

394   L: printed in the left hand margin, *A sorow- | ful harte | can not be | mery.*

404   L: printed in the left hand margin, *Heuinlye | harmonye.*

413   *dymmyt*. So L. E: *dynnit*. While the reading in L appears to involve a thematically significant synaesthesia, by which an over-excelling representation may overwhelm human senses, E appears to refer more straightforwardly to a superabundance of sound.

419   L: printed in the left hand margin, *Goodly | apparell.*

435   *plate*. So L, E1. E: *claith*. E repeats the phrasing "claith of gold" from line 433.

444   *ordours*. So E. L: *ordour.*

446   L: printed in the left hand margin, *Venus & | hyr court.*

472   *wondryt*. So L. E: *wonder*. E1 emends with *wondert.*

477   L: printed in the right hand margin, *Blynd | Cupid.*

486   *yit*. L: *yf.*

491   L: printed in the right hand margin, *Musyke.*

495   *Sesque*. So L. E: *Seque.*

497   *songin*. So L. E: *soung.*

510   *quhilk Kyng Saul*. So L. E: *quhilk Saul*. E appears to resolve a hypermetrical line; if the first word in the line, "Conjurit," is pronounced as two syllables, then the metrical difficulty in L is somewhat alleviated.

514   *igroundit*. So E. L: *groundit*. The prefix is metrically valuable and grammatically correct with the past participle.

518   *gekgo*. So L. E: *greik*. E1: . . . *eko* [initial letters lost]. Here is a telling instance of lexical misunderstanding in E. The form in L is an unusual spelling of the imitative *gukgo* (*DOST*, *gukgo* (n.); *gekgo*).

534   *or brounvert*. So L. E: *ovirbrouderit*. E1: *ovirbroudart*. Despite its lexical difficulties, the reading in L might be preferable as possible evidence of an otherwise rare idiom. See the corresponding Explanatory Note for further discussion of this line.

540   *velvos*. So L. E: *velvot*. The term in L is attested in fifteenth-century and early sixteenth-century Scots usage (*DOST*, *vell(o)us*, *well(o)us*, *velu(o)us* (n.)).

547   *pattrell*. So L, E1. E: *yattrell*. The idiosyncratic reading in E is most readily explained as a misprint.

549   *lusum*. So L. E: *luifsum*. L preserves the reduced variant current in earlier usage (*DOST*, *lusum* (adj.), sense a).

550   L: printed in the right hand margin, *Mars.*

563   L: printed in the left hand margin, *Louers.*

574   *Demophon*. L: *Demoophan*. E: *Demophoon*. The chosen spelling matches L, line 810. L appears at this point to have confused the rhyme, with the a-rhymes on -*on* and the b-rhymes on -*an.*

576   *France*. So E. L: *Fare*. The reading in E has the advantage of straightforwardness but may possibly involve a misunderstanding of *fare* as denoting "good fortune" (*MED*, *fare* (n.1), sense 7).

591   *Fourteen*. L: *Xiiii*. E: *Fourtene.*

607   L: printed in the right hand margin, *A ballet of | inconstant | loue.*

613   *involupit in syte*. So E. L: *involvit in dispyte*. The rhyme word in L is repeated from the previous line. In E, the Chaucerian word "involupit" reflects the

poet's use elsewhere (*DOST, envolup* (v.); *involup* (v.); compare *CT* VI [C] 942). As well, "syte" is a distinctive northernism (*MED, sit(e* (n.1)). The reading in L may conceivably have arisen from a sixteenth-century southern English speaker's modification of unfamiliar terms.

617 *fait.* So L, E1. E: *fact.* Bawcutt comments that "the self-pitying mood of the passage supports L's *fait*" (*SP*, p. 185n617).

630 L: printed in the left hand margin, *He curseth* | *the worlds* | *felycite. for-* | *tune and all* | *his plea-* | *sure.* See the Introduction to this edition, p. 14.

644 *in greif.* So L. E: *and greit.* E's reading is stylistically more straightforward, but L is retained in case it reflects an early adjectival use of "disdenyeit," as "scornful" (*OED, disdained* (adj.), sense 2; the only citation is Shakespeare's *Henry IV, Part 1* 1.3.181).

660 L: printed in the left hand margin: *He curseth* | *the worlds felycite for-* | *tune and al* | *his plea-* | *sure.*

665 L: printed in the right hand margin, *The Auc-* | *tor accused.*

666 *accusyng as of.* So L. E: *accusen of.* In L, the final syllable of "accusyng" can be read in elision with the following "as."

684 L: printed in the left hand margin, *Answer.*

693 L: printed in the left hand margin, *Appelati-* | *onem.*

698 *am and aucht.* L: *am aucht.*

706 L: printed in the right hand margin, *A thret-* | *nyng.*

716 *Ye.* So L, E1. E: *Yit.*

737 *de.* L: *be.* E: *die.*

740 *transfigurit.* So L. E: *transfigurat.* E1: *transf . . . rmit.* This is an instance in which E1's unique reading may indicate either editorial intervention or access to an independent witness.

Heading *The Seconde Parte.* So L. E: *THE SECVND PART.*

772 *Lo.* So L. E: *To.*

776 L: printed in the right hand margin, *Consolation.*

786 *lusty.* So L. E: *luik.* E1: *lus . . . .* Bawcutt suggests that E may reflect an early use of *lucky*, otherwise not attested in Scots writing before the early sixteenth-century (*DOST, lukkie* (adj., n.); *SP*, p. 188n786).

792 L: printed in the left hand margin, *Poetis.*

805 *On lutis sum thair accentis subtellé.* So L. E: omitted. E1: *. . . tes sum . . . ccents . . . e.*

806 *held the.* So E. L: *held.*

818 *na way.* So L. E: *na.*

827 *the gate.* So L. E: *thair gait.*

831 *knawlage.* L: *knawlagis.* E: *knawledge.*

833 *rout wyll stop our mate.* So L. E: *court will stop or meit.* E1: *our . . .*

836 *polit termys sang.* So L. E: *Poet termis singand.* E1: *sang;* E1 provides only the single word in support of L's reading.

837 *historyis.* So L. E: *storeis.* With elision, L's reading is metrically regular.

855 L: printed in the left hand margin, *The nyue* | *muses.*

859 *cronikillis doith.* So L. E: *Chronikill dois.*

860 *endityth.* So L. E: *endytis.* Here and in line 859, the southern suffix may be editorial.

862   *humyll*. So L. E: *humbill*. The spelling in L is typical of fifteenth-century Scots
        (*DOST*, *humil(l* (adj.)).

865   *syng, play, dans, and leip*. So L. E: *sing, daunce, and leip*. The version in E
        produces a hypometrical line.

869   *and sistir schene*. So L. E: *sister with Croun*. The reading in E makes the rhyme
        (with "bedene") imperfect.

870   *all bedene*. So L. E1: . . . *ai ar*.

875   *nobillis*. So L. E: *Nobill*.

882   *Phanee*. So L. E: *fair*. L preserves the specialized term that is glossed in the
        remainder of the line.

886   *dempt*. So L. E: *demit*. The form in L is "commonest in legal use" (*DOST*,
        deme, deym(e (v.1)).

888   *afore*. So L. E: *befoir*.

889   *suddand*. So L. E: *suddane*. With its excrescent final *-d*, the form in L reflects
        a widespread tendency in fifteenth-century Scots writing (*DOST*, *suddan(e,
        suddand* (adj.)).

890   *tofore*. So L. E: *befoir*.

891   *brest*. So L. E: *spreit*.

892   *Behaldand*. So L. E: *Behalding*. The form in L maintains the preferred form
        of the present participle in fifteenth-century Scots writing.

896   *Grew*. So L. E: *Greik*. The form in L is current until the mid-sixteenth-
        century in Scots.
        L: printed in the right hand margin, *Homer*.

898   L: printed in the right hand margin, *Virgil & | other latin | poetis*.

910   *of the Vale*. So E. L: *of Vale*. E is preferred for metrical regularity.

914   *other clerkis*. So L. E: *uther Clerk*.

917   *hunder part thare namys is*. So L. E: *hundreth part thair names ar*. The reading
        in L is grammatically correct; the reduced form of the numeral is
        prevalent in fifteenth-century Scots, but a rarer option in northern ME
        (*DOST*, *hundir, hunder* (num.)).

918   *thare I saw*. E: *saw I thair*.

919   L: printed in the left hand margin, *Chauser & | other eng- | lyshe and |
        Scottishe | Poetis*.

921   *musand*. So L. E: *musing*. The *-and* suffix is typical of the present participle
        in fifteenth-century Scots.

926   *bonteis*. So L. E: *bounteis*. The spelling witnessed in L is etymologically
        consistent (ME *bonté*; OF *bonté*; *DOST*, *bonté, bontie* (n.)); see note to line
        1488 below.

928   *Twychand*. So L. E: *Tuiching*.

933   *the*. So L. E: *my*.

934   *sammyn thir*. So L. E: *thir samin*.

939   *as here make na lang*. L: *as here make na langer*. E: *not heir mak na lang*. The
        idiom *as here* is authentic (e.g., *CT* VI [C] 103).

942   *the cause thair of hir*. So L. E: *cause of hir thair*. E1: *thair hir*. E1 emends only
        the last two words.

943   *schrew*. So L, E1. E: *schew*.

944   L: printed in the right hand margin, *Venus | complaint*.

948   *dispitefull subtellé.* So L. E: *dispitefull and subtell.* E1: *subtellie.* E1 emends only the last word.

949   *on hie.* So L. E: *and hie.*

950   *wallaway.* So L. E: *velanie.* E1: *vela[nie, . . .].* The remainder of the emendation in E1 has been lost.

951   *my court.* So L. E: *our court.*

954   *rebell renygate.* So L. E: *Rebald Rennigait.* The reading in E can be taken as a spelling variant of that in L (*DOST, rebel(l, rabel(l* (adj.)); alternately, it can be read as a form of *ribald,* referring to a "low, base or contemptible fellow" (*DOST, rebald, ribald* (n., adj.), sense 2). Venus is denouncing her captor for his rebellion against her.

956   *leis.* So L. E: *lois.* The form in L is current in fifteenth-century Scots (*DOST, lese, leis* (v.1)).

959   *All out than wes his sclander or sich plede.* So L. E: *To sic as he to mak conter pleid.* E1: *all out t . . . mischief or . . . .* [The whole printed line has been scored out.] It is possible to read E here as a clarification of a difficult idiom in L, with "or" meaning "before" (*DOST, or* (conj.1)) and the form "sich" instead of the more common "sik" (*DOST, sic, sik*).

960   *renoun.* So L. E: *honour.*

961   *Your fame so wyd.* So L. E: *sa wide your fame.* The sequence in L maintains balance with the syntax of the next line.

966   *eft.* L: *oft.* E: *efter.*

968   *this.* So L. E: *his.*

971   *afore.* So L. E: *befoir.*

974   *Opteynit.* So L. E: *Obtenit.* See note to line 290 above.

978   *be not.* So L. E: *not be.*

981   L: printed in the left hand margin, *Mercy be- | cumys all | men & speci- | ly gentyl- | wemen.*

984   *No woman is, rather.* So L. E: *Ane vennome is rather and.* E1: *vennomous ather.* Remnants of other E1 emendations can be traced in the cropped margin; *vennemous* also appears in line 985 in E.

986   *inequyté.* So L. E: *Iniquitie.* In the context of false judgment, the reading in L is semantically apposite.

988   *ane.* So L. E: *one.*

990   *serve.* So L. E: *have.* Douglas uses the idiom "[de]serve reproof" elsewhere (*Eneados* 1.prol.78, 2:5).

1000   *go.* So L. E: *gang.*

1004   *releschit.* So L. E: *relevit.* The form in L is "rare after c. 1520" (*DOST, relesch(e* (v.1)); see also line 1017 and note.

1005   *perlour.* So L. E: *Parlour.* E1: *Parrel. DOST* accepts the spelling in L, but cites no other occurrences than this line (*parl-, perlour* (n.1)). The reading in E1 suggests editorial intervention, and may be a gloss rather than a variant.

1015   L: printed in the right hand margin, *a ballat for | venus ple- | sour.*

1016   *preservit.* So L. E: *deliverit.* E1: *prese . . .*

1017   *Releschit.* So L. E: *Relevit.*

1022   *lait and air.* So L. E: *but dispair.*

1024   *Quhair thou in joy and plesour may repair.* So L. E: *In lestand blis to remane and repair.* Possibly E substitutes a Christianizing allusion to heaven in place of the Epicurean pleasures of L; see the note below to line 1921.

1026   *peace, dissoverit.* So L. E: *pietie disseverit.* Again, the possibility exists that E's reading stems from a Christianizing emendation.

1029   *and lat.* So L. E: *or lait.*

1030   *doith.* So L. E: *dois.*

1031   *replenyst with.* So L. E: *replenischit of.*

1034   *now be.* So L. E: *thow be.*

1037   *purifyit.* So L. E: *perfite.*

1040   *gard.* So L. E: *guerdoun.* The reading in E produces a hypermetrical line.

1043   *Be glaid and lycht now in thy lusty flouris.* So L. E: omitted. E1: *. . . now in . . . hes lustie.*

1044   *dangare.* So L. E: *all dangeir.* E1: *dangair.*

1048   *campion.* So L. E: *companioun.*

1052   *In ane.* So E. L: *In.*

1053   *thir Musis.* So E. L: *hir musis.*

1065   L: printed in the right hand margin, *Thankes | gyuyng.*

1066   *Submyttand.* So L. E: *Submitting.*

1069   *passe.* So L. E: *wend.*

1074   *On.* So L. E: *Of.*

1083   L: printed in the left hand margin, *The auc- | tours | vyage.*

1088   *in Ytalie.* So L. E: *into Italie.*

1090   *montayns we passit of all.* So L. E: *hie Montanes we passit of.*

1115   *makith.* So L. E: *makis.*

1135   *strand.* So L. E: *well.* See *DOST, strand* (n.2), sense 1: "A stream, brook; a flow of water from a well or spring."

1144   *hors.* So L. E: *horsis.* The reading in L offers the older plural form, which becomes less prevalent by the late sixteenth century (*DOST, hors* (n.), sense 2).

1150   *sterny.* So L. E: *stanerie.* E provides a more prosaic alternative ("pebbly") for L's metaphorical term ("starry, glittering").

1173   L: printed in the right hand margin, *The gates.*

1176   *Musis.* So L. E: *Ladyis.* The choice in E might be explained as an attempt to resolve the arithmetical difficulty of seating the nine Muses two by two.

1177   *deace.* So L. E: *deissis.*

1189   L: printed in the right hand margin, *Valiant | Knightis.*

1194   *to the.* So E. L: *to.*

1195   *tald.* So L. E: *schew.*

1201   *bore.* So L. E: *bair.* L provides the southern form of *boar*, an option in Scots (*DOST, bore, boir* (n.2); the prevalent form is *bare, bair*).

1205   *dede.* So L. E: *deith.* L provides the northern ME and Scots variant of *deth(e* (*DOST, dede, deid* (n.2)).

1218   *hondris.* So L. E: *hundreths.*

1225   L: printed in the right hand margin, *Poetis.*

1239   *anoynt.* So L. E: *anoyit.* In L, *anoynt* represents an older form of the past participle (*OED, anoint* (ppl. adj.), sense a; *MED, enointen* [for ppl. *enoint(ed)*]). See also note to line 1523 below.

1253	*that*. So L. E: *this*.
	rydyng. So L. E: *ryden*.
1265	*doth*. L: *duth*. E: *dois*.
1280	*rememorance*. So L. E: *remembrance*. L attests to the occurrence in Scots of a late ME form (*DOST, rememora(u)nce*; *MED, rememoraunce*; OF *rememorance*).
Heading	*The Thyrd Parte*. So L. E: *THE THRID PART*.
1288	L: printed in the right hand margin, *Inuoca-* | *cion*.
1302	*Ascens*. So L. E: *The ascence*.
1309	*mismaid*. So L. E: *dismaid*.
1313	*clam we*. So L. E: *clam I*. Logic prevails in E, with the presumption that only the dreamer is experiencing difficulty and not causing any to his guide.
1317	*hol*. So L. E: *how*. Meaning "deep, sunken," L's *hol* is current in fifteenth-century Scots (*DOST, holl* (adj.), sense 1).
	heill. So L. E: *hell*. The spelling *heill* is unusual for *Hell*, regularly in the forms *hell, hel*.
1318	*bulnyng*. So L. E: *bulling*. The spelling is rare but not necessarily erroneous (compare *bulnyng* in Calle-Martín, "*Practica Urinarum*," p. 42).
1327	*nene*. So L. E: *na*. The spelling in L recurs occasionally in sixteenth-century Scots writing (*DOST, nan(e* (pron., adj.1, adv.)).
1330	*Trymland*. So L. E: *Trimbland*. The reading in L attests to a persistent spelling variant (*DOST, trimbil(l, trim(m)ill* (v.)).
1331	*Lat be*. So E. L: *lat se*.
1336	L: printed in the right hand margin, *Idyll peo-* | *ple puny-* | *shed*.
1338	*drynt*. So L. E: *drownit*. The spelling in L is one Douglas uses elsewhere (e.g., *Eneados* 4.prol.82, 2:149; *DOST, drint, drynt*). See also notes to lines 1376 and 1508 below.
1354	*palyce, folk to*. So L. E: *place folk for to*. E1: *~~for to~~ to*. The reading in L is thematically significant as well as metrically regular.
1363	*boldyn*. So L. E: *bairdin*. E1: *bo* . . . . L's reading is consistent with Douglas' idiom in his other descriptions of storms at sea (*DOST, boldin, bowdin* (v.), sense 1). Bawcutt notes that the reading in E is not readily explainable (*SP*, p. 199n1363).
1364	*bustuus*. So L. E: *busteous*. E1: *busteus*.
1365	*schip*. So L, E1. E: *schipis*.
1368	*tobryst*. So L. E: *did brist*. The intensive prefix *to-* reflects fifteenth-century usage (*DOST, to-brist, to-brest* (v.)).
1373	*firre*. So L. E: *Fir tre*. E1: *fir*.
1374	*apon takill*. So L. E: *upon a Takill*.
1376	*drynt, and*. So L. E: *drownit*.
1379	*tha*. So L, E1. E: *that*.
1380	*drint*. So L, E1. E: *drownit*.
1381	L: printed in the left hand margin, *Faythles* | *peopill*.
1388	*baptyme*. So L. E: *Baptisme*. Etymologically reflecting the OF source *bapteme*, the spelling in L is prevalent in fifteenth-century Scots (*DOST, baptime, bapteme* (n.)).
1399	*endytyng*. So L. E: *endyten*.
1423	*thyng*. So L. E: *things*.
1424	*sare*. L: *fare*. E: *sair*.

1427   L: printed in the left hand margin, *The dis-* | *cription of* | *the palace.*

1428   *of.* So L. E: *with.* The idiom in E is prevalent, but "replete of" is witnessed elsewhere in Scots (*DOST, replet(e* (adj.), sense 2[2]).

1431   *fanys.* So L. E: *Thanis.* The spelling in E is a legitimate variant of *fane* (*DOST, than(e* (n.2)).

1443   *at that.* So L. E: *at the.*

1456   *beild.* So L. E: *beildit.* The form of the past tense in L is rare (*DOST, beild, beld* (v.)).

1464   *eftirwartis.* So L. E: *efterwart.*

1473   *Twelf amarant stagis stude, twelf grene precius greis.* So L. E: *Stude emeraut stagis, twelf grene precious greis.* The line is hypermetrical in L and contains a repetition of the word "twelf." Deletion of the second of these would produce a metrically regular line, but the syntactic parallel between the two phrases would be somewhat challenging. One hypothesis for the form of the line in E would then be that this stylistic complication has been simplified by editorial revision.

1475   *Sustenttand.* So L. E: *Upstandand.* L preserves a rare variant (compare to Latin *sustentandum*) of the more common *sustenand* (*DOST, sustent* (v.)).

        aforne. So L. E: *beforne.*

        L: printed in the right hand margin, *Venus mer-* | *rour.*

1487   *purifyed, precius.* So L. E: *purifyit and precious.*

1488   *bontyis.* So L. E: *bounteis.* See note to line 926 above.

1498   *creacion.* So L. E: *creatiounis.*

1503   *Sodomus.* So L. E: *Sodomes.*

1504   *Abram.* So L. E: *Abraham.*

1506   *Twelf.* So L. E: *Ten.* The number of plagues was in fact ten; the error may be authorial.

1508   *drynt.* So L. E: *drownit.*

1509   L: printed in the right hand margin, *A lang ca-* | *tathaloge* | *of nobyll* | *men and* | *wemen* | *both of* | *scriptur &* | *gentyll* | *stories.*

1513   *In.* So L. E: *Of.*

1523   *Anoynt.* So L. E: *Anoyntit.* See the discussion of this variant at the note to line 1239 above.

1528   *douchty.* So L. E: *michtie.*

1537   *champion.* So L. E: *Campioun.*

1540   L: printed in the left hand margin, *Salomon.*

1547   *Four.* So L, E. E1: . . . *e.*

1571   *tyrrand lyk all Jowrye he.* So L. E: *tyranlie he Jowrie all.*

1572   *mony.* So L. E: *mony ane.*

1581   *Wes distroyit.* So L. E: *Destroyit was.* The metrical inversions in L are not sufficiently unusual to call for emendation.

1586   L: printed in the right hand margin, *Faythfull* | *& constent* | *women.*

1615   *revest.* So L. E: *revischit.*

1616   *navyne.* So L. E: *Navie.* E1: *Navine.* The form in L is prevalent in fifteenth-century Scots writing (*DOST, navyn(e* (n.); compare *navy* (n.)).

1653   *huge.* So L. E: *greit.*

1661   L: printed in the left hand margin, *Chast Lu-* | *cretia.*

1667   *Atwene.* So L. E: *Betwene.*

1670	*Atwene thair*. So L. E: *Betwene thir*. E1: *their*.
1671	L: printed in the left hand margin, *The con-* | *stancye of* | *Marcus* | *regulus*.
1676	*Curtyus*. L: *Quincyus*. E: *Marcus Curtius*. The error in L might be due to a misreading of handwritten *C*, a mis-distribution of minims, and a misrecognition of a *t* as an exceptionally angular *c* (as typical of Scottish secretary hands).
1677	*in the*. L: *in*.
1687	*to Rome conquerit all*. So L. E: *sine to Rome conquerit*.
1692	*atwine*. So L. E: *betwene*.
1705	*Newand*. So E. L, E1: *Mewand*. As Bawcutt notes, E's reading "is an aphetic form of ME *enew* (OF *enewer*), a hawking term" (*SP*, p. 205n1705). L substitutes a more familiar term pertaining to falconry.
1709	*syrchand*. So L. E: *seirching*.
1711–19	*I saw Raf . . . . in Madin land*. So E. L: omitted.
1720	*saw I*. L: *saw*.
1721	L: printed in the left hand margin, *Nigraman-* | *sye*.
1726	*a small penny*. So L. E: *ane penny*. E1 *. . . all penny*.
1740	*I*. So L, E1. E: *scho*.
1746	*ay*. So L. E: *all*.
1756	L: printed in the right hand margin, *By thys* | *boke he me-* | *nis Virgil*.
1758	*tho*. So L. E: *scho*.
1761	*afore*. So L. E: *befoir*.
	L: printed in the right hand margin, *The Auc-* | *tors con-* | *clution of* | *Venus me-* | *rour*.
1767	L: printed in the right hand margin, *The Pa-* | *lice of ho-* | *nour is pa-* | *tent for ho* | *nest vertu-* | *us men an* | *not for vi-* | *cius fals &* | *craftye pe-* | *pyll*.
1779	L: printed in the left hand margin, *Falsehed* | *the moder* | *of al vice*.
1783	*The garatour, my Nymphe tho to*. So L. E: *That Garitour tho my Nimphe unto*.
1784	*the*. So L. E: *that*.
1788	*mindis*. So L. E: *minde is*.
1791	L: printed in the left hand margin, *Patience*.
1792	L: printed in the left hand margin, *The discri-* | *ptio of the* | *Prince of* | *hie honore* | *wyth hys* | *Palys &* | *Court*. | *Charity* | *Constance*. | *Liberalite* | *Innocens* | *deuocyon*.
1794	*disservys*. So L. E: *dois serve*.
1795	*the*. So E. L: *is the*.
1801	L: printed in the left hand margin, *discrecion* | *Humanite* | *Trew re-* | *lation* | *peace tem-* | *perance*.
1803	*morow and eve*. So L. E: *morne and evin*.
1807	*lyst to*. L: *lyst*. E: *list to*.
1808	L: printed in the right hand margin, *Humilite*. | *discypline* | *mercye*.
1811	*pronounce*. L: *pronounce a*.
	L: printed in the right hand margin, *Conscience* | *iustyce pru-* | *dence dili-* | *gens clene* | *lyuyng*.
1814	*lyst committing*. So L. E: *listin commit*.
1816	*ovirseis*. So L. E: *overse*. The form in L displays the third person plural *-is* suffix as is is normal in Scots verb inflection.
1821	L: printed in the right hand margin, *Hope*. | *Piety*. | *Fortitud*, | *Veryte*.

1835	*was*. So E. L: *of*.
1841	L: printed in the left hand margin, *Astronami*.
1856	*episciclis and oppositionis*. L: *episciclis and opposionis*. E: *Epistillis and oppositiounis*. E1: . . . *ne coursis*.
1857	*porturyt*. So L. E: *portrait*. The form of the past participle attested in L occurs in fifteenth-century and early sixteenth-century Scots writing, along with its counterpart *portrait* (*DOST*, *porture*, -*our* (v.); see also *portra*(*y* (v.)).
1860	*I mony*. So L. E: *I and mony*.
1879	*surmontyth*. So L. E: *surmountis*.
1884	*Swa*. So E. L: *Fra*.
1886	*soithlie as me*. L: *soithla as my*. E: *surelie as me*.
1890	*paithit*. So L. E: *pachit*.
1898	*sle*. So L. E: *hie*.
1903	*Schit*. So L. E: *Schute*. The form attested in L is an infrequent variant in Scots writing of the past participle of *shut* (*DOST*, *s*(*c*)*hut*, *s*(*c*)*hute* (v.)).
1908	*ne*. So L. E: *not*.
1921	*a god armypotent*. So L. E: *ane God Omnipotent*. This variation, thematically the most significant between the witnesses, epitomizes the contrast between pagan and Christian understandings of *Honour*; E resolves the contrast by providing an explicitly Christian term. See Introduction, pp. 23–24. In this regard, the line deserves comparison with the similarly varied readings in lines 1024, 1026, and 1966 (as noted).
1925	*blaucht*. So L. E: *blancht*. The form in L is the past participle of *bleche* ("bleach"; *MED*, *blechen* (v.1); *DOST*, *bleche*, *bleitch*; see *DOST*, *blacht*, *blaucht*).
1930	*Held up*. So L. E: *Upheld*.
1933	*of my*. So L. E: *of that*.
1938	*is so*. So L. E: *was sa*. In E, the protagonist was "mysmaid" when he fell unconscious; in L, the Nymph is deriding him for continuing to be so. The joke, and the insult, seem stronger in L.
1942	*at*. So L. E: *that*. In fifteenth-century Scots, as earlier in northern ME (deriving from Old Norse), the form attested in L is the relative pronoun corresponding to *that* (*DOST*, *at* (rel. pron., conj.)).
1944	*to ther*. So L. E: *to thair*. E1: *Unto*. E1 softens the Nymph's gibe.
1946	*Lang ere*. L: *Langere*. E: *Lang eir*.
1953	*malt*. So L. E: *mad*. See the corresponding Explanatory Note for a discussion of these variants.
1954	*quod scho, na mare*. So L. E: *na mair quod scho*.
1961	*passage*. So E. L: *passagis*.
1962	*within the*. So L. E: *within that*.
1966	*Victoriusly*. So L. E: *Verteouslie*. The reading in E may be related to the variation in line 1921, as noted above.
1968	*mane*. So E. L: *name*. The reading in L is semantically weak and loses the alliteration of the phrase. It may have arisen from a faulty distribution of the *m* and *n* in typesetting.
1972	*ryng*. So L. E: *King*.
1973	*honoring*. So L. E: *governing*. E1: . . . *ouring*.
1981	*warldly glore*. So L. E: *warldis glorie*. E1: *gloir*.

1982	*transitore.* So L. E: *transitorie.* E1: . . . *toir.*
	L: printed in the right hand margin, *Al warldly	glorye is	bot a drea-	me.*
1985	*to fore.* So L. E: *befoir.*
2000	L: printed in the right hand margin, *A comenda-	cion of ver-	tue quhilk	is the vay	to honour	and not ri-	ches or hie	blud.*
2001	*ma.* So L. E: *can.*
2009	*honour lestand.* So L. E: *lestand honour.*
2011	*glory vanys.* So L. E: *glore vanische.* The form in L is prevalent in fifteenth-century Scots writing.
2019	L: printed in the left hand margin, *Exemplis	of vertuus	men & wo-	men.*
2021	*afore.* So L. E: *befoir.*
2028	*otheris.* So L. E: *uther.*
2031	L: printed in the left hand margin, *Vicious	people	punyshed.	Inuye	Pryde.*
2037	L: printed in the right hand margin, *Ignorante	Disseyt.*
2038	*thair selvyn.* So L. E: *thair selfis.*
2044	L: printed in the right hand margin, *Dissate &	craftynes	ar haldyn	wisdome	now a day-	es verite &	iustice is	callyt sim-	plycitye &	folyshnes.*
2066	*colouris.* So L. E: *flouris.*
2068	*For.* So L, E1. E: *And.*
2069	*doyth.* So L. E: *dois.*
2077	*the.* L: *thay.*
2080	*folow.* L: *felow.* E: *follow.*
2085	*trymlyt.* So L. E: *trimblit.*
2090	L: printed in the left hand margin, *The auc-	thour retur-	nes frome	his dreame	to him self	agane.*
2094	*herbere.* So L. E: *herbrie.* E1: *herber.*
2095	*herd.* So L. E: *hard.*
2097	*swounyt.* So L. E: *swemit.* E1: *swenit.*
2105	*In purpose.* So L. E: *I purpoisit.*
2116	L: printed in the right hand margin, *A ballade	in the com-	mendatioun	of honour	& verteu.*
2118	*renoun.* So L. E: *Honour.* E1: . . . *noune.*
2122	*myche.* So L. E: *mekill.*
Heading	*The auctor direkit . . . . Kyng of Scottis.* So L. E: *The Author directis his buik	to the richt Nobill and Illuster Prince Iames	the Feird King of Scottis.*
2155	*humely.* So L. E: *humbillie.*
2161	*burall.* So L, E1. E: *buriall.*
2163	*tha.* So L. E: *the.*
2166	*tha.* So L. E: *the.*
2166–67	With no deletion indicated, E1 provides the following additional note: *pas hy . . . way as . . . best can . . .*
Finis	So E. L: *Imprinted at London in Fletestrete at the sygne of the Rose garland, by Wyllyam Coplande.*

❧ GLOSSARY

PRINCIPLES

This list is designed to enhance understanding of Douglas' general usage insofar as it is embodied in the forms and spellings of the London text of *The Palis of Honoure* (L). Here is a selection from the lexis of the poem in which attention is paid to "false friends" — words that resemble ones in present-day English but that have different uses and/or meanings. Specialized terms and unique occurrences generally do not appear below but are glossed marginally in the text; some problematic and especially interesting usages are discussed further in the Explanatory Notes. Where citations of a form or meaning are abundant, only the first twelve occurrences are provided. When used as a vowel, the letter *y* is placed alphabetically with *i*. With common irregular verbs such as *be*, emphasis is placed on obsolete forms and meanings.

ABBREVIATIONS: **2nd p.**: second person; **3rd p.**: third person; **adj.**: adjective; **adv.**: adverb; **conj.**: conjunction; **inf.**: infinitive; **n.**: noun; **p. ppl.**: past participle; **p. t.**: verb, past tense; **pl.**: plural; **poss.**: possessive noun; **prep.**: preposition; **pres. ppl.**: present participle; **pron.**: pronoun; **sing.**: singular; **subj.**: subjunctive; **v.**: verb; **vbl. n.**: verbal noun.

abaid, abayd (p. t.) *remained, stayed* 228, 1053, 1306, 1830

abone (adv., prep.) *above* 432, 1164, 1409, 1659, 1833

abound, habond (v.) *abound* 372, 2069; (p.t.) **abondyt, aboundit, aboundyt** 204, 275, 897, 1415, 1970

about (adv., prep.) *around* 3, 40, 232, 242, 1298, 1888, 2092

addresse (v.) *prepare, dedicate [oneself]* 626; (pres. ppl.) **addressand** 87

ado (adv.) *afoot, underway* 1866

adoun (adv.) *down, below* 66, 402, 432, 1161, 1347, 2087

afferyt (p. ppl.) *frightened* 197

affray (n.) *alarm, upset* 94, 658, 2089; see **effray**

afore, aforne (adv.) *before, in front of* 888, 971, 975, 1472, 1475, 1761, 2021, 2127

agane, aganne, agayne (adv.) *in return, back, again* 235, 271, 299, 560, 936, 1151, 1393, 1591, 1611, 1744, 2058, 2097

agane, aganys (prep.) *against* 688, 1196, 1301, 1864

agast (adj.) *afraid* 154, 2081

aggreabill, agreabyl (adj.) *pleasing* 76, 488

aggrevance (n.) *distress* 616

ay (adv.) *always, forever* 276, 464, 635, 951, 1122, 1425, 1746, 1932, 1944, 1997, 2004, 2009, etc.

aill, ale (v.) *affect, suffer* 115, 1332; (2nd p.) **alys** 178, 715; (p. t.) **alyt** 1948

ayr, ayre (n.) *air* 25, 56, 105, 352, 366, 373, 374, 379, 1839, 1930, 2061

air, ayr, ayrly (adv.) *early* 87, 1022, 1029, 1708

ald, auld (adj.) *old, aged, ancient* 50, 151, 206, 548, 754, 855, 882, 1505, 1645, 1712, 1717, 1787

ald (adj.) *elder* 2020

alychtit, alychtyt (p. t.) *dismounted* 1137, 1304

alkyn, alkynde (adj.) *every sort of* 1140, 1417; see **kyn, kynd** (n.)

all hail, alhalely, all halely (adv.) *entirely* 781, 1138, 1580

allace, allake, allas (interjection) *alas* 165, 168, 185, 188, 325, 1369, 2096

allane, allone, alone (adv.) *alone* 228, 230, 921, 1578; see **myn alone, hym allane**

als, also, alswa (adv.) *also, as* 248, 415, 479, 562, 717, 752, 801, 906, 922, 1014, 1077, 1179, etc.

als (conj.) *but* 832

als swyth, alswyith (adv.) *immediately* 727, 1014

amang; amangis (prep.) *among* 26, 44, 81, 1141, 1624, 1819

amyabyll, amyable (adj.) *kindly, loving* 5, 8, 102

amid, amyd, amyddys (prep.) *within, upon, among* 61, 107, 123, 199, 211, 330, 445, 619, 657, 772, 891, 1022, etc.

anamallyt, anamalyt (p. ppl.) *enameled* 435, 1896

ane (indefinite article) *a, an* 105, 201, 211, 227, 232, 233, 239, 299, 330, 367, 400, 418, etc.

ane (adj.) *one* 526; (pron.) *one* 221, 232, 644, 762, 988

anon, anone (adv.) *straightaway, readily* 200, 337, 745, 785, 814, 922, 1115, 1206, 1225, 1340, 1513, 1720, etc.

apon, apone (prep.) *at, into, upon, onto* 233, 1211, 1374, 1485, 1852, 1939, 2084, 2135

appeir, appere (v.) *appear* 49, 550, 1186, 1353, 1912; (p. t.) **opperyt** 358

approchit (p. t.) *came* 137, 1315; **approchyng** (inf.) 194, 824

ar, are see **be** (v.)

arrasyt (p. ppl.) *overcome, abducted* 98, 164

array (n.) *clothing* 457, 529, 659, 1957

arrayit (p. ppl.) *dressed, arrayed, ordered* 202, 792, 1440; see **rayed**

art, arte (n.) *art, skill, technique* 532, 818

art (n.) *district, place* 1397, 2030, 2105

art (v. 2nd p. sing.) *are ("thou art")* 1047, 1333, 1462, 1738, 1945, 1956, 2118, 2123, 2167

assay (v.) *test* 1954; (p. t.) **assait** 205

at rychtis *in every respect* 1440

atwene, atwine (prep.) *between* 1667, 1670, 1692

aucht (v.) *ought, should* 698; (2nd p.) **auchtyst** 88

aucht (n.) *eighth* 869

aucht (adj.) *eight* 1532

auld see **ald**

availe, avayle (n.) *benefit, wellbeing* 914, 2122

avaylys (v. 3rd p.) *benefits* 173

avale (v.) *descend* 114

avance (v.) *advance, benefit, commend* 449, 1030, 1593, 2038, 2121, 2160

aw (n.) *dread* 965, 1268, 1679

away (adv.) *away, banished* 98, 298, 955, 1595, 1782, 2011, 2049, 2083, 2093

awyn (adj.) *own* 1536

bad (adj.) *malevolent, deplorable* 51, 129

bad (p. t.) *ordered, wanted* 1003, 1831

bair, bare, bore (n.) *boar* 741, 1201, 1710

baith, bayth (adj.) *both* 35, 99, 289,
    344, 414, 422, 516, 635, 725, 865,
    868, 874, etc.

bald (adj.) *bold, fierce* 551, 987, 1786,
    2018

ballat (n.) *ballade, song* 995; (pl.)
    ballattis 498

balmy (adj.) *soothing, mild* 13, 58

band (n.) *fetter, shackle, strap* 1004; pl.
    bandis 1214

bare (p. t.) *carried, wore* 478, 553, 604,
    1928

bare (adj.) *naked* 142, 347, 661, 771

bare see **bair**

barrant (adj.) *barren* 127, 150, 661,
    2100, 2164

battel, battell (n.) *battle, war, combat*
    1447, 1596, 1968; (pl.) **batalis,
    batellis, battellys** 1513, 1621,
    1666, 1690

be (v.) (See *DOST, be* [v.], with the
    comment that the "normal forms
    are confused and augmented in
    various ways," including the
    extension of indicative *beis* and
    war(e to the subjective, as well as
    the use of southern English forms,
    such as *bene* for *are* and *werren* for
    were. Following are some
    illustrations of such augmented
    and extended forms.) (pl.) **ben,
    bene, beyng** 236, 240, 274, 289,
    294, 527, 592, 718ff., etc.; (subj.)
    beis 708, 2028; (p. t. pl.) **werren**
    528 (See also the separate
    disambiguating entry for **art**.)

be, bye, by (prep.) *by, with* 3, 42, 54,
    95, 194, 280, 284, 288, 296, 304,
    352, 363, etc.

bedene (adv.) *fully, together, at once*
    383, 870, 1076, 1187, 1243

behald, beholde (v.) *see* 55, 461, 544,
    743, 943, 1021, 1352, 1397, 1404,
    1406, 1465, 1588, etc.; (p. t.)
    beheld 464, 1331, 1904; (pres.
    ppl.) **behaldand** 559, 892

beheist, behest (n.) *vow, order* 724,
    1002

beild (p. t.) *built* 1456; (p. ppl.)
    beildit, beildyt 1362, 1502, 1657

beir, bere (n.) *bear* 741, 1530

beis (n. pl.) *bees* 45, 1152, 2065

beis (subj.) see **be** (v.)

belive, belyve (adv.) *at once, promptly*
    685, 929, 1004, 1163, 2053

ben, bene (v. pl.) see **be** (v.)

bene, beyn, beyng, byn (p. ppl.) see
    be (v.)

bent (n.) *open ground, field, grass* 1053,
    1445; (pl.) **bentis** 1154

beriall, byrriall (n., adj.) *crystal, beryl,
    sparkling* 53, 1150, 1452, 1478,
    1888

beseik (v.) *beseech, beg* 700, 1058;
    (pres. ppl.) **besekand** 938, 2156

best (n.) *beast, animal* 170, 740; (pl.)
    bestis 74, 196, 201, 303, 1417,
    1421

best (adj.) *best* 1138, 1183, 1664, 2123

betrais (v.) *betray* 672; (p. t.) **betrasyt**
    166; (pres. ppl.) **betraisand** 2041

bewrays (v. pres. pl.) *disclose* 718

bewté, bewtie, bewty, bewtye (n.)
    beauty 405, 449, 452, 460, 464,
    794, 873, 1157, 1763

bye see **be** (prep.)

byn see **be** (v.)

byrriall see **beriall**

bisning, bysnyng (n.) *monster* 625,
    740, 834, 943

blast (n.) *gust, wind, sound* 158; (pl.)
    blastis 144, 857

blaw (v.) *blow* 1364; (p. ppl.) **blaw,
    blawyn** *sounded, trumpeted* 912,
    961, 1237

blenk (n.) *look, glance* 785; (pl.)
    blenkis 470, 599

blenk (v.) *look, gaze* 1885; (p. t.) **blent**
    326, 1347, 1485, 1903, 1922,
    2092

bonty (n.) *goodness, virtue, power* 788;
    (pl.) **bonteis, bontyis** 885, 926,
    1488

bot (conj., adv.) *but, except, unless* 144, 149, 162, 170, 197, 304, 307, 336, 368, 376, 378, 393, etc.

bot gif, **bot gyf** (conj.) *unless* 291, 378, 471

braid, **breid** (adj.) *broad* 557, 1325, 1329, 1569, 2072

brethir (pl.) *brothers* 1575, 1688; (pl. poss.) **bretheris** 1203

but (adv.) *only* 1974

but (prep.) *without* 163, 241, 254, 380, 381, 643, 676, 693, 857, 973, 1041, 1424, etc.

but (conj.) *but* 387, 434, 738, 967, 1166, 1325, 1787

but weir, **but were** (adv.) *certainly, doubtless* 878, 1453, 1529, 1910

cace (n.) *occurrence, situation; legal case* 121, 694

cair, **care** (n.) *sorrow* 399, 1019, 1338, 1643, 1927

cais (n.) *frame* 1482

campion (n.) *champion, advocate* 1048 (pl.) **campyonys** 1579

caryit (p. t.) *conveyed, carried* 363, 369, 1084, 1340

castis (n. pl.) *devices* 819, 1290

cast (v.) *direct* 1934; (pres. ppl.) **castand** 452

cative, **catyve** (n.) *wretch* 357, 668, 728, 946, 1905; (pl.) **cativis**, **catyvis** 231, 269, 393, 1320

cative, **catyve** (adj.) *wretched, miserable* 613

celestiall (adj.) *heavenly* 417, 493, 838

chaftis (n.) *jaws* 654, 1773

chaire, **chare** (n.) *chariot* 32, 211, 445, 475, 550, 657, 1551

charge (v.) *load, press, impose* 998; (p. ppl.) **chargyt** 2070; (pres. ppl.) **chargeand** 2080

charge (n.) *weight, load, command* 1359; (pl.) **chargis** *orders* 679

circumstance (n.) *elaborateness, detail* 3, 1279

clam see **clym**

clepis (v. 3rd p.) *calls* 561; (2nd p. pl.) **clepys** 723; (p. ppl.) **clepit**, **clepyt**, **clyped** 665, 698, 878, 1119, 1684, 1784, 1791, 1801, 1810

clerk (n.) *scholar, cleric, secretary, lawyer* 665, 710, 1187; (pl.) **clerkis** 249, 378, 716, 914, 987, 1800

clym (v.) *climb* 1769, 1777, 1786; (p. t.) **clam** 1304, 1313, 1377; (pres. ppl.) **clymmand** 1774

clois (v.) *enclose* 2134; (p. ppl.) **closyd** 216

clois, **close** (n.) *courtyard* 1875, 1890, 1929

clos (adv.) *close together* 507

colour, **colowr**, **coulour**, **cullour** (n.) *color* 34, 57, 1925; (pl.) **colouris**, **coullouris**, **cullouris** 819, 867, 1896, 2066, 2106

comfort (n.) *delight, consolation* 1032, 2130

comfort, **confort** (v.) *console, soothe* 1823; (p. ppl.) 59; (3rd p.) **comfortes** 841; (pres. ppl.) **confortand** 156

compare (n.) *comparison* 986, 2095

comparit (p. t.) *likened* 1321

compeir, **compere** (n.) *peer, equivalent, comparison* 525, 818, 871, 986

condyng (adj.) *worthy* 1063, 2118

confortand see **comfort**, **confort**

confoundit, **confoundyt** (p. t.) *defeated, overcame* 510, 658, 894

consave (v.) *survey, plan* 1302, 1343, 1836

considdir (v.) *contemplate, perceive* 1274, 1344, 1585, 1779, 1882, 1953, 2062; (p. t.) **considerit** 1327

constance (n.) *loyalty, steadfastness* 1592, 1797, 2039, 2158

constand, **constant** (adj.) *matching, dependable*, 203, 467, 567, 837, 845, 1042

constrenis (v. 3rd p. pl.) *compels* 68;
(p. t.) **constrenyt** 399; (p. ppl.)
constrenit 86, 607

contrar, contrare (adj.) *unfavorable*
51, 396; (adv.) *against* 768, 1323,
1682; see **in contrar**

contrarius (adj.) *hostile, in opposition*
172, 182, 192

contrariusly (adv.) 1364

convoy (v.) *convey* 1466; (p. t.)
convoyit, convoyt 1078, 1765

corage, curage (n.) *vital spirits,
liveliness, spirit, desire, mood* 70, 82,
103, 488, 599, 605, 683, 829, 971,
1021, 1947, 2107

coulour see **colour**

craft (n.) *skill, art, discipline* 128, 1220;
(pl.) **craftis** 513

craftely (adv.) *skilfully* 10, 488, 854,
1458, 1894

craftines (n.) *skilfulness* 67

crap see **creip**

creature (n.) *being, human* 72, 473,
707; (pl.) **creaturis** 96

creip (v.) *creep* 1336; **crap** (p. t.) 160,
300, 647

crewel, crewell, cruel, cruell (adj.)
cruel, fierce 166, 303, 581, 617,
981, 1200, 1515, 1561, 1621

cristall, crystall (n., adj.) *crystal,
shining* 469, 1135, 1420, 1451,
1478, 1796, 1829, 1884

cruelly (adv.) 1665

cry (v.) *call, resound, cry, yell* 171,
1269; (3rd p.) **cryis** 25; (p. t.)
cryit 651; (pres. ppl.) **cryand**
1233

cry (n.) *clamor* 196, 1370

cullour see **colour**

cum (v.) *come, arrive* 792, 1958, 2163;
(3rd p.) **cummis** 296; (p. ppl.)
cumyn 2044; (vbl. n.) **cumming,
cummyng** 319, 1701

cunning, cunnyng (n.) *knowledge, skill*
73, 135, 596, 2151

cunnyng (adj.) *adept, skilful* 497

curage see **corage**

cure (n.) *care, attention, project* 70,
134, 361, 455, 700, 1458, 1754

curius (adj.) *difficult, involved, intricate*
249, 1474, 1898

curiusly (adv.) *intricately* 1835

cursand (pres. ppl.) *cursing* 2102

cursit, curst (adj.) *accursed* 288, 581,
636, 707

dangare, dangear, danger, dangere
(n.) *mishap, harm, danger, peril*
115, 188, 751, 1015, 1044, 1634,
1742

dant (v.) *tame, intimidate, overcome*
188; (3rd p.) **dantis** 74, 469, 2006

dasyt (p. ppl.) *dazed, stupefied* 101,
109, 355

de, die (v.) *die* 633, 737, 956, 1057,
1674; (p. t.) **deyt** 2013

debate, debbat (n.) *discussion, strife,
quarrel* 1026, 1622; (pl.) **debatis**
407

debaitmentis (n. pl.) *entertainments*
1702

declare (v.) *put in words* 383, 925,
1188, 1426, 1729, 1760, 2079; (p.
t.) **declarit** 319

declyne (v.) *reject* 707; *turn* 930

decore (adj.) *comely* 1071

dede, deid (adj.) *dead* 34, 168, 952,
1319

dede, deid, deth, deith (n.) *death* 193,
304, 633, 967, 1205, 2006, 2131;
(poss.) **dedis** 1535

dedes, dedis see **deid**

defence (n.) *refutation, protection, legal
representative* 254, 302, 1048

degest (adj.) *composed, dignified, calm*
204, 793, 1135, 1190, 1567, 2116

degraid (v.) *debase* 706, 947; (vbl. n.)
degradyng *debasement* 958

deid (adj.) *dead*; (n.) *death*; see **dede**
(adj. and n.)

deid (n.) *act, deed* 717, 1572, 1693;
(pl.) **dedes, dedis** 1198, 1449,
1496, 1626

deill, dele (n.) *detail, part* 515, 1481

deir, dere (v.) *harm, disturb* 1213,
  1825; (3rd p.) **deris** 373

deith, deth (n.) *death* 642, 736, 952,
  1194, 1203, 1992, 2006; see **dede**
  (n.)

deliverit (p. t.) *decided* 704

deliverit, delyverit (p. t.) *rescued* 751,
  1015, 1044, 1743

delyte (n.) *delight* 219, 842, 1831

delyte (v.) *please* 2141

dellicius, delycious (adj.) *pleasant*
  1489, 2000

demand (n.) *question* 1174; (pl.)
  demandis; 1182

demandit (p. t.) *asked* 682

deme (n.) *mother* 1986

demyng (inf.) 729; (p. t.) **demit,
  dempt, demyt** *judged, criticized,
  expressed opinions* 832, 886, 1222

den (n.) *ravine* 153, 1321

deny (v.) *disagree, disallow, withhold*
  788; (2nd p.) **denyis** 179; (p. ppl.)
  denyit 678, 1600

dere (adj.) *precious, beloved* 1209,
  1454

dere (v.) see **deir, dere**

descryve, discrive, discryve (v.)
  describe 125, 545, 596, 1162, 1407;
  (3rd p.) **discrivis, discrivys** 1631,
  1963

desert (adj.) *deserted* 122

desert, deserte (n.) *deserted place,
  wasteland* 136, 164, 169, 346,
  1132, 1511

destané, destany (n.) *fate* 287, 620,
  636

deth see **deith**

devaill (v.) *lower, sink* 1251; (3rd p.)
  devailys 174

device, devys, devyse (n.) *plan, device*
  31, 1898, 2142

devyd (v.) *separate* 1545; (p. ppl.)
  devydyt 806, 1509; (pres. ppl.)
  devydand 1091

devise, devyis, devyse (v.) *imagine,
  describe, consider* 536, 766, 1281,
  1649

dew, dewe (n.) *dew* 13, 2136

dew (adj.) *due* 429, 2155

dewly, dewlye (adv.) *suitably,
  appropriately* 926, 1292

deyt see **de**

diffine, diffyne (v.) *describe, recount*
  521, 1480, 1613, 2022

diligate, dilligat, dilligate (adj.)
  luxurious 1032, 1179, 1234

dyn (n.) *noise* 194, 370, 373

dynnyt (p. t.) *resounded* 1151

diseis (n.) *hardship, distress* 630; pl.
  diseyses 1018

dispite, dispyte (n.) *hatred, offence*
  612, 642

disportis, disportys (n. pl.) *pastimes,
  entertainments* 498, 1703

disserve (v.) *merit, serve* 966; (3rd p.)
  deservis, diservis, disservys 93,
  642, 1794; (p. t.) **deservit** 952

do (v.) *do, perform, send, make, show,
  cause* 6, 626, 947, 978, 1003,
  1020, 1410; (3rd p.) **dois** 283,
  357, 372, 518, 633, 840, 854, 856,
  877, 1583, 1989; (p. ppl.) **doyn**
  727

doun, doune (adv., prep.) *down* 108,
  865, 1006, 1013, 1074, 1137,
  1304, 1343, 1518, 1638, 1773,
  1804, etc.

dout (n.) *doubt* 241, 376

doutyt (p. t.) *dreaded* 148

draw (v.) *pull, proceed* 1411; (3rd p.)
  drawis 31; (p. ppl.) **draw, drawin**
  213, 284, 418

dred (p. t.) *feared* 738

dredis (n. pl.) *terrors, doubts* 1201,
  1850

drynt (p. ppl.) *drowned* 1338, 1376,
  1508

droppes, droppis (n. pl.) *droplets* 16,
  27, 58

dulce (adj.) *sweet* 15, 391, 506, 523,
  857

dulcest (adj.) *sweetest* 360

dume, dome (n.) *judgment, opinion*
  296, 1491

e (n.) *eye* 462, 1084, 1256; (pl.) **eyn, eyne** 469, 480, 749, 1247, 1934

effere (n.) *ceremony,* 208, 1739

effere (n.) *fear* 737

effray (v.) *terrify* 1955; (p. ppl.) **effrayit** 90, 1309; see **affray**

eik (adv.) *also* 244, 322, 378, 747, 856, 900, 951, 1049, 1095, 1100, 1116, 1195, etc.

enbroude (p. ppl.) *embroidered* 57, 540

encres, incres (v.) *grow* 68, 877, 1035; (3rd p.) **incressys** 331

endyt, endyte (n.) *writing, composition, style* 616, 798, 2164

endyte, indyte (v.) *compose, write* 925, 1267, 1292; (inf.) **endytyng** 1399; (3rd p.) **endityth** 860, 1292

enforcis (v. 3rd p.) *intensifies, exerts* 83, 2038

entalyeit (p. ppl.) *built* 477, 555

entre (v.) *enter* 368, 1790; (3rd p.) **entres** 1094

entres (n.) *access* 290, 1771

erd (n.) *earth* 516, 1836, 1983, 2148

erd quake (n.) *earthquake* 272

erdly (adj.) *earthly* 485, 1408, 1496, 1881, 1974, 2007, 2013, 2043, 2100

escheve (v.) *achieve* 1278; (p. ppl.) **eschevyt, eschewyt** *escaped, emerged* 466, 787, 2108

estait, estat, estate (n.) *rank, mode of existence, conditions, nobility* 221, 225, 405, 706, 812, 830, 958, 1028, 1235, 1343, 1540, 1975, etc.

expell (v.) *expell* 1018; **expellis** 75

expremit, expremyt (p. ppl.) *described* 828, 1218

expres (v.) *bring forth* 71, 847

expres (adj.) *actual* 487

expres (adv.) *actually* 1695, 1770

extasy (n.) *trance* 106, 193, 1923

facund (adj.) *ample, eloquent* 261, 838, 940, 1129, 1290

fair, fare (adj.) *fine, attractive* 202, 224, 407, 473, 498, 560, 563, 566, 582, 589, 593, 660, etc.

fair (v.) *go* 1639

fait (n.) *fate* 617; (pl.) **faitis** 191

fall (n.) *downfall* 1499

fall (v.) 142, 1391, 1948; (p. ppl.) **fallen** 1778; (p. t.) **fell** 108, 1337, 1769, 2086, 2091

fantasy (n.) *mind's eye, illusion, understanding* 358, 413, 1867; (pl.) **fantasyis** 127, 384, 763

fanton (n.) *delusion* 60, 97

fare (v.) *happen, befall, travel* 397, 2169

fare (adv.) *far, at a great distance* 2072

fare (adj.) see **fair, fare** (adj.)

fary (n.) *daze* 107, 1872

fatal, fatale, fatall (adj.) *fated, fateful* 100, 167, 245, 614, 2149

fate (n.) *action* 1543

faucht (p. t.) *fought* 1212, 1655

febil, febill, febyl (adj.) *feeble* 100, 103, 305, 770, 970, 1166, 1427, 1910, 2032

feblyt (p. ppl.) *enfeebled* 108

fede, feid (n.) *hostility* 955, 989, 2133

feil, fele (adj.) *many, great* 237, 297, 302, 650, 720, 1194, 1284, 1430, 1503

feil (n.) *sense, inkling* 1477

fell (adj.) *terrible, frightful* 658, 984, 1193

fell (p. t.) see **fall** (v.)

fere (n.) *strength* 1215

fere (n.) *comrade* 2015

fere, feir (n.) *fear* 99, 734, 1254, 1308, 1356, 1868

fere (v.) *fear* 1263

fere see **in fere**

ferly, ferlye (n.) *marvel, spectacle* 113, 1732

ferly (adj.) *marvelous* 121

flaw, flew (p. t.) *flew* 1085, 1719

flewour (n.) *scent* 15, 2064

florist (adj.) *flowery* 2066

flour, floure (n.) *flower* 1416, 1580, 1795, 2116; (pl.) **flouris, flowris**

5, 19, 35, 343, 541, 603, 1043,
1140, 1148, 1425, 1897, 2098

flud, flude, fluid (n.) *river, flood* 123,
137, 145, 1109, 1114, 1116, 1118,
1120, 1121, 1128, 1322, 1418,
etc.; (pl.) **fludis** 1083, 1092, 1126,
1641

fors (n.) *force, matter, strength* 1215,
1738, 1946

forsuith, forsuyth (adv.) *indeed* 378,
480, 735, 953, 1753

forsy (adj.) *powerful* 2018

forvay (v.) *err* 92; (p. t.) **forvayt** 206

foryet (p. t.) *forgot* 780, 781; (p. ppl.)
994

fowlis, fowlys (n. pl.) *birds* 35, 1422,
1705

fra (prep.) *from, once, after* 1485,
1545, 1564, 1587, 1669, 1709,
1787, 1993, 2083, 2113, 2151

fresch, fresche (adj.) *fresh, young* 14,
85, 405, 491, 599, 721, 794, 881,
1021, 1157, 1291

freuch (adj.) *fragile* 185, 629

fulfill (v.) 1746; (p. t.) **fulfyllyt**
satisfied, 276; (p. ppl.) **fulfyllet,
fulfyllyt** *replete, abounding* 251,
445

furious, furyus (adj.) *raging, insane*
190, 394, 668

gam, game (n.) *fun, pastime,
entertainment* 181, 410, 708; (pl.)
gemmys 1730

gang, go (v.) *walk, go* 561, 1000, 1537

gar (v.) *make, cause* 2137; (3rd p.)
garrys 114; (p. t.) **gart** 101, 279,
759, 1573

garding, gardyng (n.) *garden* 7, 2063

garth (n.) *enclosed garden* 62, 93,
1466, 2071, 2101

gate (n.) *path, direction, route* 227, 708,
827, 1704

gent (adj.) *noble* 338, 861

gentyll, jentill (adj.) *noble, courteous*
849, 1944

geve, gyf (v.) *give* 326, 701, 964; (p.
t.) **gave** 239, 650, 1182, 1535,
1613; (p. ppl.) **gyvyn** 1975

gyf (conj.) *if* 529, 729, 730, 744, 788,
1267; see **bot gyf**

glance (n.) *look, reflection, sparkle* 452,
1880; (pl.) **glancis** 54

glore (v.) *glorify* 88

glore (n.) *glory* 1063, 1978, 1981,
2043, 2127

godly, godlyk (adj.) *divine* 73, 416,
431, 1058

gone (v.) *go* 1297, 1673

gone (p. ppl.) *gone* 248, 611, 1497,
2013

grace (n.) *mercy, highness, favor* 72,
125, 625, 678, 692, 933, 978,
1010, 1028, 1386, 2125, 2157

gracius (adj.) *favorable, merciful* 701,
2145

gram (n.) *trouble* 181, 990

gre (n.) *degree* 1841; (pl.) **greis** *levels,
tiers, steps* 22, 1150, 1473

greif (n.) *grief, injury* 619, 644, 993

grein, grene (adj., n.) *green* 54, 58,
419, 479, 599, 1073, 1145, 1184,
1246, 1416, 1473, 2067

greve (v.) *grieve, annoy* 1807; (p. ppl.)
grevyt 1947

gryis, gryse (v.) *horrify* 764, 1287

grym (adj., adv.) *grim* 148, 554, 649,
1949

grysly (adj.) *frightening, ugly* 124,
384, 1192, 1314, 1352, 1525

gros (adj.) *huge, coarse, rude* 353, 843

groundit (p. ppl.) *established, schooled,
rooted* 247, 608; see **igroundit**

gud, gude (adj.) *good, virtuous,
beautiful* 178, 208, 456, 519, 778,
798, 1242, 1330, 1394, 1415,
1463, 1817, etc.

gudliest, gudlyest (adj.) *most
beautiful, finest* 1168, 1664, 2117

gudly (adj.) *beautiful, virtuous, noble*
202, 409, 502, 530, 598, 827,
1157, 1243, 1303, 1360, 1614,
1860, etc.

guerdoun, gwardoun (n.) *reward* 1062, 2118

habond see **abound**

hail, hale (adv.) *together, wholly, exactly* 781, 1580, 1788, 1842

hailsum, halsom (adj.) *healthy* 46, 1930

hald, halde (n.) *dwelling, fortress* 1170, 1784, 2017

hald (v.) *hold, keep* 1776; (p. ppl.) **halden** *kept* 1238

hale (adj.) *healthy, firm* 177, 712, 1485

halely see **all hail, alhalely, all halely**

hant (n.) *dwelling, residence* 189, 2068

hant (v.) *reside, accompany* 52, 336

harm (n.) *injury* 1539; (pl.) **harmys** 288

hart (n.) *heart* 115, 311, 531, 591, 607, 619, 674, 712, 786, 1156, 1255, 1937, etc.; (pl.) **hartis** 332, 849, 1287, 1543, 1780

hart (n.) *male deer* 316, 324, 1710

havinges, havyngis (n. pl.) *manners* 456, 1158

hecht, heicht, heycht (v. 3rd p.) *is called* 1110, 1386, 1798, 1825

heich (adv.) *high* 330, 1087, 1113; see **hie** (adv.)

heid (n.) *head, top* 30, 101, 465, 1175, 1315, 1563, 2126

heir, here (adv.) *here* 174, 267, 368, 670, 672, 688, 917, 939, 1218, 1381, 1738, 1956, etc.

heir, here (v.) *hear* 53, 361, 364, 380, 447, 519, 606, 798, 1256, 1370, 1756

heit, hete (n.) *heat, warmth* 43, 56, 119, 891, 1147; (pl.) **hetis** 111

herbis, herbys (n. pl.) *plants, edible plants* 68, 143, 1148, 1416, 1425

hes (v. 3rd p.) *has* 166, 167, 186, 187, 237, 297, 324, 875, 946, 949, 952, 969, etc.

hew (n.) *color, complexion* 1137, 2077

hewyn (p. ppl.) *hewn, cut* 1300

hewyt (p. ppl.) *colored* 463

hycht, height (n.) *summit, height, exaltation* 1299, 1405, 1735, 1880, 1992

hie (adj.) *high* 70, 207, 225, 449, 460, 706, 949, 960, 963, 1009, 1064, 1081, etc.

hie (adv.) *aloft* 174, 1366, 1405

hiest (adj.) *highest* 451

hym allane, hym allone (adv.) *by himself* 1229, 1524

hyng (v.) *hang* 621; (3rd p.) **hyngis** 426; (p. t.) **hangit** 281; (p. ppl.) **hang** 436, 1074, 1374; (pres. ppl.) **hyngand** 2076

hynt (p. t.) *took* 1339, 1749, 1758

hors (n.) *horse* 31, 233, 285, 1072, 1242, 1628, 1680; (pl.) **hors, horssis, horsys** 266, 640, 1085, 1136, 1144, 1238

igroundit, ygroundyt (p. ppl.) *taught, trained* 514, 895

ilk (adj.) *each, very, same* 215, 221, 296, 1647, 2137, 2168

implore (v.) *beg, request* 675, 1065, 2127

imprent (v.) *print, stamp, affix* 859, 1293; (3rd p.) **imprentis** 1156

in contrar, in contrare (adv.) *against, in opposition* 303, 995

in fere (adv.) *together* 600, 1356, 1759, 1959

in til, in till, in tyl, in tyll (prep.) *in, within, into* 107, 274, 337, 694, 731, 740, 755, 789, 832, 1088, 1206, 1805, etc.

inclyne (v.) *turn, adapt, bow* 849, 2126; (pres. ppl.) **inclynand** 1000

inconstant (adj.) *disloyal, changeable, undependable* 333, 620, 1982

incres see **encres**

indyt see **endyt** (v.)

infynyt, infynyte (adj.) *unending* 609, 1059, 1296, 2144

ingraf, ingrave (p. ppl.) *engraved, cut* 619, 1299, 1835, 1846

ingres (n.) *entry* 292, 1767
inoth (prep.) *within* 372, 379
is see **be** (v.)

jape (n.) *trick* 738, 1728
jentill see **gentyll**
justefy (v.) *pass sentence [on]* 834, 954

keip, kepe (v.) *keep, protect* 747, 1333;
   (p. ppl.) **kepit** 1419; (vbl. n.)
   kepyng 1070
ken (v.) *know, understand, realize* 1258;
   (p. t.) **kend** 1905, 2166; (p. ppl.)
   kend 1270, 2119
kepar, keper (n.) *protector, guard*
   1307, 1784
kepe (n.) *attention* 361, 747
kyith, kyth (v.) *show* 728, 1011
kyn, kynd (n.) *variety, sort* 598, 1148;
   see also **alkyn, alkynde**
kynd (adj.) *loving, gentle* 568, 571
kyndly (adj.) *own, natural* 23; (adv.)
   naturally 13
kyndnes (n.) *generosity, good will* 1589
knaw (v.) *know, recognize* 1265, 1508;
   (p. t.) **knew** 922, 1734; (p. ppl.)
   knaw 962

lady (n.) *lady* 65, 242, 315, 338, 446,
   483, 573, 670, 854, 872, 983,
   1056, etc.; (pl.) **ladyis** 202, 224,
   328, 332, 407, 491, 532, 549, 593,
   695, 794, 808, etc.; (poss.) **ladyis,
   lydyis** 1202, 1449, 1763, 1957
lay (n.) *song* 606, 638, 1014, 1045;
   (pl.) **layis** 511, 817
lay (v.) *place, set, impute*; (p. t.) **laid,
   layd** 686, 1445, 1929, 2078
lay (p. t.) *lay* 34, 38, 1298, 1319,
   1324, 1925, 2090
layf, lave (n.) *remainder* 623, 1141
lait, lat (adj., adv.) *late* 1022, 1029
laithly, laythly (adj.) *repulsive* 145,
   1334
lake (n.) *lack* 101
lake (n.) *linen* 593

lamentabill, lamentable (adj.)
   sorrowful 1, 1371
lang, long (adj, adv.) *long, tall* 92,
   558, 594, 748, 802, 806, 939,
   1174, 1195, 1577, 1622, 1658,
   etc.; (comparative) **langer** 104,
   267, 676
lang (v.) *belong*; (3rd p.) **langyth** 1061

lang (v.) *yearn, wish*; (p. t.) **langyt**
   2097
lap see **leip**
lare (n.) *learning, knowledge* 697, 849
lat, late (v.) *let* 728, 980, 1331, 1993
late (adv.) *recently* 702, 911
latis (n. pl.) *habit, behavior* 1589
lauchys (v. 3rd p.) *laughs* 176; (p. t.)
   leuch 1952; (vbl. n.) **lauchyng**
   1252
laud, laude (n.) *praise* 996, 1059,
   1063, 2115, 2143; (pl.) **laudis** 95
laurere, lawrere (n.) *laurel* 1189,
   2144; (pl.) **laurers** 27
law (adj., adv.) *low* 175, 225, 647,
   691, 1074, 1175, 1251, 1366,
   1598, 1985; (adv.) **lawly** 1006,
   1755
law (n.) *law* 964, 1505
lawté (n.) *loyalty* 1970, 2039, 2049
lede (n.) *language* 843
left, levyt (p. ppl.) *left, abandoned* 151,
   345
leid (n.) *lead* 478, 1318
leip (v.) *leap* 865; (p. t.) **lap** 1680
leiris (v. pl.) *learn* 380; (p. t.) **lerit**
   1104
leis (v.) *lose* 956; (p. ppl.) **losyt** 813
leis (v. 3rd p.) *tell lies* 378
leivys, levys (v. 3rd p.) *lives, exists*
   601, 1027
lele (adj.) *loyal* 723
lest (adj.) *least, of lowest status* 1138
lest (v.) *last, endure* 2120; (pres. ppl.)
   lestand 2009
let, lete (n.) *interruption* 857, 1472,
   1864, 2051
levand (v. pres. ppl.) *living* 112

leve (n.) *exit, departure* 1755

leve (v.) *live, exist* 2004

leves, levis, levys (n. pl.) *leaves* 20, 38, 76, 1073

leyl (adj.) *loyal* 1825

lycht (n.) *light* 106, 113, 359, 381, 403, 2135, 2137, 2167

lycht (v.) *alight, dismount* 938

lycht (adj.) *joyful, frivolous* 1043, 1589

lychtly (adv.) *readily* 415

lyfe (n.) *life* 964, 1549, 1931; (poss.) **lyvys** 698; (pl.) **lyvys** 1634, 1964; see **on lyve**

liggis (n. pl.) *leagues* 265

ligis (n. pl. poss.) *lieges'* 1543

lyis (v. 3rd p.) *lies, extends* 27, 128, 263, 387, 542, 1411

lik, lyk, lyke (adj.) *like* 138, 142, 299, 820, 864, 879, 1571, 1878, 2094; (adv.) *about* 329, 354, 430, 451, 855, 1229, 1301, 1413, 1433, 1497, 1876, 1984, etc.

lymmes, lymmys (n. pl.) *limbs* 476, 555

list, lyst (v.) *please, choose, wish* 533, 1807, 1814, 1822; (p. t.) 49, 104

lytell, lityll, littil, littyl (n., adj.) *little* 119, 307, 1348, 1422

lois (n.) *loss* 1882

lore (n.) *learning, lesson, teaching* 73, 762, 1295

lovys (v. 3rd p.) *praises* 181; (vbl. n. pl.) **lovyngis** 1039

lovys (v. 3rd p.) *loves* 2167

luf, luif (n.) *love* 84, 485, 498, 559, 564, 570, 574, 595, 1037, 1590; (poss.) **luffis** 86

lufsum, lusum (adj.) *lovely* 407, 549

luk, luke (n.) *look, expression* 554

lukand (pres. ppl.) 200

luke (v.) *look, glance, take care* 1312, 1464

lusty (adj.) *vigorous, youthful, fine, attractive, pleasing* 85, 201, 223, 328, 338, 408, 448, 490, 599, 721, 786, 816, etc.

ma, mo (adj.) *more* 262, 1218, 2028

magnify (v.) *praise* 88; (3rd p.) **magnifyis** *gains importance* 175

mair, mare (adj., adv.) *more* 131, 309, 320, 462, 517, 520, 521, 522, 532, 556, 684, 693, etc.

maist, mast (adv., adj.) *most* 48, 74, 80, 212, 217, 299, 303, 329, 353, 396, 400, 401, etc.

maister (n.) *master* 1796, 1808

maistres (n.) *mistress* 65, 879

mak, make (v.) *make* 399, 529, 939, 1271, 1294, 1648, 2114; (3rd p.) **makis, makith** 863, 1115, 2002, 2003; (p. t., p. ppl.) **maid, makyt** 77, 139, 271, 284, 301, 410, 525, 538, 758, 779, 935, 1151, etc.; (pres. ppl.) **makand** 23

make (n.) *spouse* 589

man (n.) *man* 394, 697, 868, 1159, 1230, 1635, 1825, 1935, 1984, 2168; (poss.) **manis, mannys** 341, 442, 1255; (pl.) **men** 53, 153, 202, 235, 285, 380, 509, 536, 718, 719, 720, 723, etc.

man (v.) *must* 1411

mandate (n.) *command* 677, 1067

mane (n.) *strength* 1527, 1968

manere (n.) *manner, way, kind* 795, 820, 1350, 1418, 1649, 1703

mate (n.) *companion* 833, 1241

mater (n.) *topic, substance* 1863; (pl.) **materis** 1222

me think (v.) *seems to me* 519, 714; (p. t.) **me thocht** 417, 660, 673, 737, 1349, 1452, 1886, 1907, 1946, 2088, 2094, 2100

med, meid (n.) *meadow* 1140, 1146, 1167, 1428

megyr (adj.) *small, puny* 436, 2029

megyrnes (n.) *inadequacy* 312

meid (n.) *mead* 1178

meid (n.) *bribe* 1811

meyne, mene (v.) *mean* 31, 382, 1079

mekill (adj., adv.) *great, much* 1313, 1345, 1527, 1871; see **mych, myche**

membris (n. pl.) *body parts* 116, 1261

menys (n. pl.) *means* 237

menstral, **menstrall** (n.) *minstrel, musical performer* 497, 1820

menstraly (n.) *minstrelsy, performance* 409, 487

my self, **my sell**, **my selvyn** (pron.) *myself* 154, 187, 281, 306

mych, **myche** (adj.) *much* 1643, 2122

micht, **mycht** (n.) *power* 109, 1409, 1499, 1734, 1946, 1975, 1996, 2006, 2132, 2134, 2160

micht, **mycht**, **myght** (p. t.) *could* 53, 159, 392, 459, 461, 473, 536, 659, 663, 733, 818, 1143, etc.

mychtis (n. pl.) *forces* 1581, 1609

myn alone (adv.) *by myself* 61

mirrour, **myrrour** (n.) *acme, paragon, mirror* 64, 1476, 1485, 1493, 1495, 1623, 1666, 1676, 1695, 1731, 1760

myrth (n.) *joy, pleasure* 78, 486, 605, 1958; (pl.) **myrthys** 1234, 1875

mismaid, **mysmaid** (p. ppl.) *upset, overcome, downcast* 683, 941, 1309, 1938

mocht (p. t.) *might* 637, 683, 1885

modolation (n.) *music, melody* 499, 863

monsture (n.) *monster* 1599; (pl.) **monsturis**, **monstreis** 148, 1193, 1200

mot (v.) *may* 635, 2146

motion, **motione** (n.) *motion, course* 111, 374; (pl.) **motionis** 1858

mow (n.) *jest* 1728, 1820

mower (n.) *jester* 1229

na (adj., adv.) *no* 113, 143, 295, 304, 333, 450, 466, 517, 520, 521, 525, 527, etc.

na (conj.) *but* 468

na thing, **nothing**, **nothyng** (n.) *nothing* 156, 207, 380, 381, 443, 1762, 1994

nicht (n.) *night* 38; (poss.) **nychtis** 1546, 1564

nocht, **not** (n.) *nothing* 149, 162, 459, 710, 829, 967, 1866, 1978, 2009, 2128

nocht, **not** (adv.) *not* 49, 102, 116, 163, 177, 206, 272, 292, 307, 311, 340, 368, etc.

noy (n.) *trouble* 1424

noy (v.) *hurt* 1421

noyes, **noys** (n.) *sound* 372, 525

not (v.) *do not know, cannot* 60, 118, 336, 382, 1488, 1737

nother, **nothir**, **nothyr** (adj.) *neither* 110, 1353, 1946, 1996

obeysance (n.) *bidding, obedience* 446, 624

observance, **observans** (n.) *duty, service* 6, 87

ocht (n.) *anything* 1263, 1272

on lyve (adj.) *alive* 2056

on rowme (adv.) *apart* 294

on till, **on tyl**, **on to** (prep.) *to, into* 115, 1253, 1459, 1489, 1848, 1941, 2071; see **untill**

onabisitly, **onabysytly** (adv.) *boldly* 1537, 1679

one (adj.) 1812; see **ane** (adj.)

one (prep.) *on* 1320, 1788

one (pron.) 229, 749, 816, 1200, 1298, 1432, 1777; see **ane** (pron.)

onely (adv.) *only* 587, 711

opprest (p. t.) *overcome, crowded, oppressed,* 453, 628, 1142, 1571, 1665

or (conj.) *before* 266, 959, 1400, 1750, 1753

or (conj.) *or* 60, 106, 291, 314, 394, 395, 434, 463, 507, 518, 556, 561, etc.

or (n.) *gold* 534

ordour, **ordur** (n.) *sacred order, sequence* 209, 1107, 1649; (pl.) **ordours** 444

other, **othir**, **uther**, **uthir**, **uthyr** (adj., pron.) *other, another, opposite* 165, 169, 262, 343, 434, 708, 738, 816, 871, 914, 1222, 1273, etc.; (pl.) **otheris**, **utheris** 533, 762, 2028

over fret, ovirfret, ovyrfret (p. ppl.)
adorned 10, 212, 429, 1468

overspred, ovirspred (p. ppl.) *covered*
20, 660, 1895

ovirset, ovyrset (p. t.) *overcame,*
overwhelmed 733, 1950; (p. ppl.)
overset 127, 1359

palace, palyce (n.) *enclosure, refuge*
52, 1354

palice, palyce (n.) *palace* 264, 293,
1403, 1429, 1443, 1451, 1790,
1793, 1829, 1873, 1893, 1901

pastance (n.) *entertainment* 409, 1446,
1730, 1739

peirles (adj.) *peerless* 454, 474, 544,
962

pere (n.) *equal, peer* 919, 1450, 1998,
2123

perfyt, perfyte (adj.) *complete,*
absolute, perfect 1258, 1266, 1289,
1465, 1467, 1832, 1880, 1899,
2002, 2008

perfytly (adv.) *completely* 320, 1280,
1841, 1883

peryst (p. t.) *shipwrecked* 1357; (p.
ppl.) 1371, 1384

picht, pycht (p. ppl.) *set, pitched* 1167,
1483

pieté, pyeté (n.) *pity* 979, 1009

pieteous, pietuus (adj.) *merciful,*
pitiful, pious 531, 631, 691, 1334,
1369, 1668

pyne (n.) *suffering, difficulty* 825, 933,
1653

plane (adj.) *plain, open, smooth* 1917,
1969, 2163

plane (n.) *open area, field* 1144, 1243,
1249, 1414, 1442, 1685

plene (v.) *lament, complain* 171; (p. t.)
plenyeit 641

plenist, plenyst (p. ppl.) *filled* 1101,
1413, 2068

plesance, plesans (n.) *pleasure,*
pleasant place 7, 62, 173, 396, 404,
445, 618, 1020, 1031, 1282, 1338,
1413, etc.

plesand (adj.) *pleasing, beautiful* 401,
431, 566, 662, 794, 807, 844,
1144, 1249, 1437, 1446, 1487, etc.

polist, pollist, pollyst, polyst (adj.)
polished 1419, 1452, 1487, 1917

polit, polyte (adj.) *polished, refined*
217, 836

pompe (n.) *reputation, display* 1974,
1996, 2013

port (n.) *gate* 290, 1443, 2130

portrait, porturyt (p. ppl.) *portrayed*
41, 1857

precius, precyus, prectius, pretius
(adj.) *costly, prized* 428, 1121,
1435, 1473, 1487, 1723, 1863,
1909, 1920, 1999, 2069, 2117

preclare (adj.) *clear, shining* 63, 212

preis, pres (n.) *crowd* 916, 1142, 1180

pres (v.) *push, throng* 1767, 1771;
(pres. ppl.) **preissand, presand,**
pressand 1769, 1777, 1786

pretend (v.) *assert, profess* 1277, 2163;
(p. ppl.) **pretendit** 1336, 2036,
2159

pryce, pryse (n.) *worth, value, payment*
32, 973, 2140

pryse (v.) *praise* 79

proces (n.) *proceedings, discourse* 689,
928, 1166, 1277, 1663, 1752, 1906

prolixt, prolyxt (adj.) *wordy, verbose*
927, 1462

proportion (n.) *melody, symmetry* 360,
429; (pl.) **proportionis** 493

pure (adj.) *clean* 457

pure, puyr (adj.) *poor* 1986, 2151

purgit (p. ppl.) *cleansed, rid of*
impurities 56

purifyed, purifyit (p. ppl.) *cleansed*
1037, 1420, 1487, 1886

purpos, purpose (n.) *goal* 724, 847,
1278, 1297, 2105

purpur (adj.) *purple, dark* 215, 433

quare so (adv.) *wherever* 561

quent (adj.) *elegant, cunning* 535, 716,
819, 1430, 1492, 1919

quha (pron.) *who, whoever* 86, 183, 184, 464, 1025, 1026, 1027, 1028, 1029, 1030, 1064, 1184, etc.

quhair, quhar, quhare (adv.) *where* 143, 153, 200, 208, 294, 349, 443, 476, 632, 641, 825, 931, etc.

quhair of (adv.) *of what* 458

quhair on, quhare on (adv.) *on which* 542, 1835, 1838

quhairfore (adv.) *for which reason* 154, 280, 1263, 1383, 1609, 1616

quhairfra, quharefra (adv.) *from which* 436, 840

quhairin (adv.) *in which, where* 151, 204

quhairin, quhare in (adv.) *in which* 1415, 1494, 1764

quhairof, quhare of (adv.) *of which* 1649, 1908, 2079

quhairthrow (adv.) *by which* 286

quhais, quhois, quhoys (pron.) *whose* 24, 70, 106, 446, 509, 534, 1115, 1276, 1488, 1519, 1526, 1597, etc.

quham, quhame, quhom, quhome (pron.) *that, which, whom* 101, 146, 156, 211, 317, 330, 347, 460, 788, 871, 873, 885, etc.

quhat (pron., adj.) *what* 173, 235, 238, 382, 385, 403, 404, 405, 406, 407, 408, 409, etc.

quhat so (adv.) *whatever* 1745

quhen (adv.) *when* 1, 116, 394, 712, 1370, 1742, 2013, 2061

quhy (adv.) *why* 166, 167, 782, 956

quhyddyr (adv.) *whence, whether* 189, 1264

quhyil (n.) *duration of time* 976

quhil, quhill, quhyll (adv.) *while, until, so that* 14, 28, 110, 285, 369, 605, 644, 724, 800, 1214, 1368, 1381, etc.

quhilk (adj., pron.) *which, who, that* 17, 21, 31, 33, 93, 120, 139, 157, 185, 195, 216, 280, etc.; (pl.) **quhilkis** 79, 135, 222, 247, 430,

437, 439, 533, 809, 818, 868, 1080, etc.

quhilum, quilum (adv.) *formerly, previously* 809, 1602, 1786, 1986

quhou, quhow (adv.) *how* 92, 118, 197, 756, 814, 960, 970, 1192, 1197, 1202, 1204, 1208, etc.

quhowbeit (adv.) *even though* 1279

quyte (v.) *acquit* 687

quod (p. t.) *said* 92, 238, 268, 287, 292, 691, 693, 727, 835, 955, 1000, 1012, etc.

rage (n.) *passion, fury* 86, 1349, 1632

raid see **ryde**

rais, rays, rasit, rasyt (p. t.) *arose, started, raised* 6, 89, 282, 356, 665, 784, 1225, 1405, 1670

rang (p. t.) *resounded* 800

rang (p. t.) *reigned, prevailed* 1576, 1659

ravyst (p. t.) *abducted* 136, 1610

raw (n.) *row, line* 1261, 1360, 1507; (pl.) **rewis** 540

raw (adj.) *untreated* 426

rayed (p. ppl.) *dressed, arrayed* 220; see **arrayit**

recomfort, reconfort (v. p. ppl., p. t.) *comforted* 36, 306, 890

recompence (n.) *atonement* 968, 1049

recompence (v.) *repay* 1062

red, reid (adj.) *red* 33, 140, 1316, 1507

rede, reid (n.) *recourse, guidance* 169, 2130

reid (v.) *read* 1591, 1694; (3rd p.) **redis** 1199, 1847; (p. t., p. ppl.) **red** 667, 1045; (pres. ppl.) **redand** 1295

rejois (v.) *rejoice* 1022; (p. ppl.) **rejoysit, rejosyt** *comforted, consoled* 59, 1029, 2060; (pres. ppl.) **rejosand** 888

relatioun (n.) *report, discourse* 1802; (pl.) **relationys** 1223

remane (v.) *remain, stay, reside* 267, 295, 953, 1147, 1389, 1395, 1590,

1746, 1965; (3rd p.) **remanis,
remanys** 1819, 1994; (p. t.)
remanit, remanyt *remained* 110,
1106, 1423, 2101; (pres. ppl.)
remanand 230, 313, 1636, 2033,
2053

remede, remeid (n.) *remedy* 304, 765,
2127

replenyst, replennessed (p. ppl.)
supplied 29, 1031

replete (adj.) *full* 62, 1428

represent (n.) *appearance* 1904; (pl.)
representis 1157

represent (v.) *uphold, expound* 710;
(3rd p. pl.) **representis** 1842

rethoreis, rethoryis (n. pl.)
rhetoricians 130, 2066

return (v.) *revert, reverse* 383; (p. ppl.)
returnyt 612

richt, rycht (adj., adv.) *right, straight,
very, just, rightly* 116, 154, 179,
199, 377, 680, 822, 1690, 1702,
1787, 1945, 1952, etc.

richt, rycht (n.) *truth* 1822, 1963,
2120; see **at rychtis**

ryde (v.) *ride* 561; (3rd p. pl.) **rydyng**
210, 227, 600, 1076, 1253; (p. t.)
raid *rode* 233, 298, 345, 892, 921,
934, 1085, 1111, 1114, 1116,
1117, 1242, etc.; (pres. ppl.)
rydand 231

ryme (n.) *poem, verse* 670, 948, 1752

ryng (n.) *realm* 1972

ryng (v.) *reign, prevail* 2124; (3rd p.)
ryngis 1997; (pres. ppl.) **ryngand**
776

ryngis (n. pl.) *rings* 424

roch (n.) *crag, cliff* 1249, 1253, 1300,
1304; (pl.) **rochis, rochys** 142,
800, 1081

rout, route (n.) *throng, herd* 201, 223,
229, 238, 447, 787, 833, 851, 930,
1240, 1305

routyt (p. t.) *roared* 145

rowme see **on rowme**

rowmed (p. t.) *roamed* 28; (pres. ppl.)
rowmyng 61

sa (adv.) *so* 185, 189, 281, 284, 467,
474, 526, 528, 560, 618, 726, 957,
etc.

sair, sare (adj.) *bitter, grievous* 663,
769, 861, 1018, 1041

sair, sare (n.) *suffering* 1041, 1424

sall (v.) *shall* 92, 168, 188, 415, 594,
709, 966, 969, 992, 1000, 1002,
1058, etc.

sammyn (adv.) *together* 934, 1076,
1242, 1759

sare, sore (adv.) *greatly* 90, 154, 472,
685, 738, 753, 759, 2097

sary, sory (adj.) *paltry, sad* 103, 932

saw (n.) *speech, saying* 968; (pl.) **sawis**
254

scharp, scharpe (adj.) *witty, keen* 717,
1223, 1286, 1291

schaw (n.) *grove, thicket* 1151

schaw (v.) *show* 128, 129, 130, 131,
132, 133, 134, 1260, 1262, 1284,
1400, 1663, etc.; (p. t.) **schew**
207, 385, 794, 977, 1191, 1204,
1207, 1216, 1623, 1646

schene (adj.) *beautiful, shining* 869,
1419, 2133

schynis, schynys (v. 3rd p.) *shines*
874, 1987, 2125; (p. t.) **schane,
schone** 63, 430, 452, 1133, 1301,
1433, 1877, 1884, 1910, 2135;
(pres. ppl.) **schynand** 359, 1239

se (v.) *see* 293, 417, 710, 998, 1079,
1248, 1256, 1289, 1489, 1495,
1834, 1870, etc.; (3rd p.) **seis** 381;
(3rd p. pl.) **seyng** 1853; (inf.)
sene 1180; (p. t.) **saw** 112, 325,
336, 337, 475, 536, 550, 570, 576,
639, 792, 895, etc.; (p. ppl.) **sene**
385, 1238, 1250, 1439, 1703,
2010, 2030, 2112; (pres. ppl.)
seand 770, 2109

sea, see (n.) *sea* 30, 157, 881, 1094,
1350, 1367, 1418, 1507, 1509,
1837, 1850, 1989; (poss.) **seis**
1632; (pl.) **seis** 379

seir, sere (adj.) *many, diverse, various* 365, 497, 546, 603, 796, 817, 1081, 1179, 1182, 1379, 1632, 1669, etc.

seis (n. pl.) *places* 19

self, selvyn see **my self**

semis, semys (v. 3rd p.) *seems, appears* 33, 1113; (p. t.) **semit, semyt** 222, 443, 831, 1224, 1861, 1878, 1890

sen (conj.) *since* 402, 611, 672, 1956, 2123

send (v.) 2138; (p. ppl.) *sent* 810, 1493

set (v.) *put, place, value, put in writing, sit* 854, 1159, 1867; (3rd p.) **settis** 1992, 2045, 2048; (p. t.) **set, sete** 736, 1013, 1788; (p. ppl.) **set** 122, 214, 218, 476, 657, 1469, 1625, 2052

set (adv.) *although* 686

sic, sich, sik (adj.) *such* 489, 627, 642, 959, 965, 990, 1275, 1502, 1592, 1868, 1955, 1975, etc.

sic (pron.) *such* 592, 982

sicht, sycht (n.) *sight* 110, 401, 461, 466, 786, 889, 1250, 1282, 1314, 1324, 1404, 1406, etc.

syne (adv.) *then, afterwards* 220, 328, 374, 725, 853, 1107, 1203, 1227, 1377, 1388, 1511, 1566, etc.

syng (n.) *sign* 320, 331; (pl.) **syngis** 1438

syng, synge (v.) *sing* 95, 499, 606, 865; (pres. ppl.) **syngand** 64, 795, 1154; (vbl. n.) **syngyng** 1252; (p. t.) **sang** 403, 491, 559, 604, 799, 808, 823, 836, 1077, 1080, 1152, 2089

syte (n.) *sorrow* 613, 928, 2141, 2169

slychtis, slychtys (n. pl.) *tricks* 1582, 1605, 2040

slyd, slyde (adj.) *slippery* 620, 1300, 1982

solace, soles (n.) *comfort, delight* 64, 404, 486, 612

sone (adv.) *soon, promptly* 168, 189, 704, 714, 1003, 1173, 1375, 1873, 2011, 2032, 2108, 2122

sore see **sare, sore**

sort (n.) *fate* 287

sort (n.) *group, kind* 826, 1819; (pl.) 496, 1706

soun, sound (n.) *sound* 102, 366, 389, 437, 440, 493, 524, 862, 1155; (pl.) **soundis** 360, 364, 412, 519, 527, 798, 807

space (n.) *time, duration* 118, 698

spak (p. t.) *spoke* 680, 1459

speir, spere (n.) *sphere* 50, 451, 523; **speris** (pl.) 1840

spere (n.) *spear* 1212, 1536, 1967

spreit, sprete (n.) *spirit, mood* 59, 98, 136, 510, 730, 841, 888, 1955, 2059, 2126; (poss.) **spretis** 778; (pl.) **spretis** 148, 163, 203, 628, 1950, 2081

stand (v.) *stand, remain, continue, experience* 159, 294, 1047, 1268, 1573, 1748, 1761, 1951; (3rd p.) **standis** 485, 722, 945, 965, 1028, 1460; (pres. ppl.) **standand** 932

stank (n.) *ditch, moat* 2077, 2087

stank (p. t.) *stank* 161, 348

stare (n.) *stair* 1928

stare (n.) *state of wonderment* 1460

stare (v.) *stare* 472

sted, stede, steid (n.) *place* 477, 953, 1171, 1887, 2070

stede (n.) *steed* 546

stere (n.) *control* 875

sternis, sternys, sterris (n. pl.) *stars* 430, 870, 1845

sterny (adj.) *starry, glittering* 1150

stok (n.) *tree trunk, base* 199, 300, 1013, 1482

strait, strate (adj.) *narrow, impassable, strict* 976, 1083, 1302, 1310, 1346

sua, swa (adv.) *so* 117, 732, 994, 1171, 1247, 1786, 1884, 1910, 1950, 2057, 2082, 2085

subtel, subtell, subtil, subtile, subtyle (adj.) *clever, skilfully made* 511, 513, 575, 705, 716, 820, 908, 944, 1492, 1722, 1728

subtellé (adv.) *skilfully, cunningly* 805, 948

suyth (n.) *truth* 662, 1951

suythly (adv.) *surely* 186, 1956

sum (adj., pron.) *some* 170, 186, 302, 314, 386, 437, 601, 602, 624, 649, 650, 738, etc.

sum tyme (adv.) *sometimes* 305, 1447

supplé (n.) *help, rescue* 684, 1055, 2140

sustene (v.) *endure, bear* 102, 2133; (p. ppl.) **sustenit** 1624; (pres. ppl.) **sustenttand** 1475

swa see **sua**

swage (v.) *diminish, alleviate* 602, 1020, 1350; (3rd p.) **swagis** 1857

swet (p. t.) *sweat* 1868

swete (adj., adv.) *sweet, sweetly* 58, 214, 391, 406, 470, 492, 505, 519, 521, 599, 795, 807, etc.

swete (n.) *sweat* 1239

swyth (adv.) *quickly* 1934, 1959; see **als swyth**

swoun (n.) *swoon* 106, 1159, 1925, 1933, 2090

swounyt (p. t.) *swooned* 2097

tak, take (v.) *take, pay* 361, 1463, 1930; (3rd p.) **takis** 2050; (p. t.) **tuke** 1311, 1755; (p. ppl.) **tane** 573, 2061

tald (p. t.) *noticed, noted, narrated* 547, 1195, 1198, 1219, 1783; (p. ppl.) 885, 2021

tender (adj.) *delicate, soft* 4, 58, 1023, 2067

terme (n.) *limit, end date* 1992; (pl.) **termes, termis, termys** *words* 126, 131, 836, 2164

thay, they (pron.) *they* 205, 210, 226, 227, 235, 264, 292, 298, 319, 345, 410, 443, etc.

thay (adv.) *those* 1774, 1785, 2023, 2109

thaim, thaym, them (pron.) *them* 223, 234, 310, 326, 327, 334, 377, 635, 799, 936, 938, 1136, etc.

thaim self (pron.) *themselves* 2042

thair, thayr, thare, their, thir (pron.) *their* 19, 23, 38, 45, 78, 147, 205, 207, 226, 263, 327, 408, etc.

thair, thare (adv.) *there* 110, 174, 248, 266, 368, 379, 381, 450, 456, 466, 542, 562, etc.

thair selvyn (pron.) *themselves* 2038

thairby (adv.) *by that* 1593

thairfore (adv.) *for that reason* 1296

thairin (adv.) *into that* 1680

thairof (adv.) *in that way* 714, 1738

thairon, thair on (adv.) *on that* 1165, 1489, 1754, 1885, 1910

thairto (adv.) *to that* 1185, *in that direction* 2050

thairwith, thair with (adv.) *with that* 392, 1395, 1466

thynk (v.) *think* 1255; (3rd p.) **thinkis** 1764; (p. t.) **thocht, thought** 122, 2096; see **me think**

thir (adj., pron.) *these, the* 134, 471, 517, 593, 686, 702, 759, 864, 867, 880, 882, 929, etc.

tho (adv.) *then* 92, 121, 639, 665, 745, 781, 991, 1006, 1076, 1176, 1308, 1378, etc.

tho (pron.) *those* 988

thocht (adv.) *though* 370, 411, 697, 735, 1260, 1261, 1273, 1863, 2043

thocht (n.) *thought* 1077, 2128; (pl.) **thochtis** 764

thocht (p. t.) *see* **thynk**

thou, thow (pron.) *thou* (informal or intimate form of *you*) 64, 127, 166, 167, 179, 673, 705, 712, 713, 714, 730, 1031, etc.

thrang (n.) *crowd, melée* 1078, 1580

thrang (p. t.) *forced* 1139, 1536

throu, throw (prep.) *through* 36, 106, 149, 160, 231, 263, 291, 370, 739, 787, 912, 1081, etc.

throw out (prep.) *directly through* 1140, 1901

til, till, tyl, tyll (prep.) *to* 5, 48, 51, 55, 66, 68, 71, 77, 88, 124, 138, 198, etc.; see **in til, on till**

tyne (v.) *lose* 520; (3rd p.) **tynis** 2128; (p. t., p. ppl.) **tynt** 1384, 1543, 1628, 1752

tyte (adv.) *at once, quickly* 615, 2141

tofore (adv., prep.) *before, previously, in front of* 319, 385, 661, 760, 828, 890, 1440

torment (n.) *corporal punishment, torture* 2059

torment (p. ppl.) *tormented, tortured* 655, 825, 2109

traist (adj.) *loyal, secure* 567, 1184, 1360, 1794

traist (v.) *trust, expect* 779, 1591; (p. t.) **traistit** 742

travail, travel (n.) *effort, travel* 678, 1248

tre, tree (n.) *tree, mast, timber* 228, 230, 313, 316, 345, 643, 1149, 1416, 2114; (pl.) **trees, treis, treys** 26, 40, 149, 161, 1146, 1474, 2063, 2069, 2075

treuth (n.) *loyalty, faithfulness* 725, 1590

trew (adj.) *genuine, loyal, faithful, truthful* 335, 565, 793, 900, 1038, 1802, 2136

twa (adj.) *two* 690, 1102, 1105, 1176, 1306, 1534, 2101

twychand (pres. ppl.) *concerning* 928, 1282, 1396, 1699, 1756

uneth (adv.) *hardly* 159, 789

untill, untyll (prep.) *to, into* 1108, 1686; see **on til**

uther see **other**

variabill (adj.) *changeable, fickle* 484

variance, wariance (n.) *variation, inconsistency* 9, 1286, 2157

variant (adj.) *varying, ephemeral* 54, 185, 334

vary (v.) *wander, rave* 101, 1871

varyit see **wary**

vertew, vertu (n.) *virtue, power* 1826, 1977, 1997, 1999, 2007, 2015, 2136; (pl.) **vertuys** 874

vertuus (adj.) *powerful, virtuous* 1483, 1787, 1808, 1911, 1964, 1980, 1995, 2045, 2117

vincus, wyncus *vanquish* 1524, 1685; (p. t.) **vincussyt** 1199

vysit, vissy, vysy (v.) *look about, survey, tour* 209, 1069, 1828; (p. ppl.) **vissyte** 1461

vissage (n.) *face* 89, 557, 649, 744, 784, 1406, 1472, 1922, 1949

voce (n.) *voice* 63, 110, 442, 491, 674, 704; (pl.) **vocis** 406, 505, 808

void, voyde (adj.) *empty* 120, 618, 697

voydit (p. ppl.) *empty* 1286

wail, wale (v.) *enjoy* 1249, 1875

wait, wate (v.) *wait, expect, know, serve* 169, 197, 223, 238, 334, 387, 408, 673, 705, 730, 815, 829, etc.; (3rd p.) **watys** 1993; (p. t.) **watyt** 321

wake (adj.) *weak* 596, 1372

wald (v.) *would* 545, 743, 978, 1079, 1159, 1753, 2111

wale (v.) *wail* 171

wall (n.) *wall* 1779; (pl.) **wallis, wallys** 1769, 1774, 1877, 1883, 1908

wallit (p. ppl.) *built* 512

wally (adj.) *wave-tossed* 1082, 1989

wallys (n. pl.) *waves* 1351, 1357, 1363

wan (adj.) *dark* 1246

wan (v. p. t.) *conquered* 1569, 1582

warld (n.) *world* 172, 182, 192, 402, 1162, 1326, 1344, 1519, 1569, 1989, 2001; (poss.) **warldis** 610, 1390

warldly (adj.) *worldly, secular* 1699, 1973, 1981, 2046

wary (v.) *curse* 100; (p. ppl.) **varyit, wareit, waryit** *cursed* 582, 635, 2029; (pres. ppl.) **wariand** 2103

wast (adj.) *waste* 152, 155

water, watir, watyr, watter, wattir, wattyr (n.) *water; fresh water* 139,

348, 364, 367, 372, 374, 375, 376,
881, 1115, 1143, 1420, etc.; (pl.)
waters 379, 1246

weid (n.) *clothing* 203, 534, 2162

weil, weill, wele (adv.) *well, very
much, surely* 88, 203, 277, 467,
477, 514, 526, 555, 792, 806, 815,
888, etc.

weilfare (n.) *well-being, happiness* 624,
1032, 1042, 1833, 2113

weir, were (n.) *war* 1670, 1689

weir, were (n.) *doubt*; see **but weir**

weir (v.) *wage war* 1548

welth (n.) *well-being, happiness* 1025,
1402

werd (n.) *fate, destiny* 100, 2149; (pl.)
weirdes 245

wes (p. t.) *was* 59, 60, 109, 156, 197,
213, 223, 229, 275, 280, 282, 286,
etc.

wit, wyt (n.) *sense, mental faculty,
intelligence* 98, 100, 114, 127, 204,
275, 411, 414, 545, 771, 897,
1015, etc.

wicht, wycht (n.) *person* 112, 186,
392, 400, 440, 466, 469, 489, 624,
631, 767, 941, etc.; (pl.) **wychtis**
1439

wod, wode (n.) *wood* 160, 208, 231,
787; (pl.) **woddis** 1082, 1246

wod (adj.) *insane* 668

wone (n.) *abode, dwelling* 431, 1887

worth (v.) *befall* 627, 629, 630, 631,
633, 634, 635, 636, 2032

worth (adj.) *of [the] value of* 1269, 2168

wrang (adj.) *wrong* 803, 1080

wrang (n.) *wrong* 1662; (pl.) **wrangis**
2051

writ, write, wryt, wryte (v.) *write* 134,
728, 876, 926, 1254, 1263, 1283,
1464, 1488; (3rd p.) **wrytis** 869,
1658; (p. t.) **wrait, wrate** 809, 815,
1014, 2115; (p. ppl.) **wryttyn** 769

wryt (n.) *writing, composition* 859, 879,
1295, 1591, 2111

wrocht (v. p. t.; p. ppl.) *constructed* 45,
1436, 1452, 1455, 1883

wycht (adj.) *strong* 1945

ya (adv.) *yes* 187, 239, 1951

ye (pron.) *you* 91, 96, 238, 268, 289,
290, 559, 606, 694, 716, 718, 719,
etc.

yeid (p. t.) *went* 1080, 1230

yeir, yere (n.) *year, years* 46, 591,
1550, 1667; (pl.) **yeris** 1184,
1335, 1511, 1569, 1624

yet, yete (n.) *gate* 1440, 1789, 1834,
1865; (pl.) **yettis** 1518

yet (p. ppl.) *poured* 17, 47, 1888

yon, yone (adj., pron.) *that* 238, 241,
248, 290, 641, 833, 835, 838, 839,
844, 845, 846, etc.

yow (pron.) *you* 93, 95, 700, 703, 723,
1060, 1064, 1296, 1943

INDEX

Following is a list of all names appearing in *PH*, accompanied with their usual modern forms and line references in *PH*. **OT**: Old Testament.

Abacuk. OT Habakkuk. 1341

Abram. OT Abraham. 1504

Absolon. OT Absalom. 582

Achalles, Achil, Achill, Achilles, Achylles. Achilles. 572, 1208, 1212, 1214, 1323, 1620, 1627, 2019

Acheron. The River Acheron. 1130

Achicorontes. The River Orontes. 1118

Achitefel, Achitefell, Achittefell. OT Ahithophel. 236, 271, 1768

Acontus. Acontius. 814

Action, Acteone. Actaeon. 321, 746

Adam. 402, 1500

Adriane. Ariadne. 577

Affricane, Affrycane. See **Scipio**

Ailssay. Ailsa Craig. 1713

Alane. Alan of Lille. 904

Albion. See **Brutus Albion**

Alcest. Alcestis. 586

Alcyon. Alcyone. 571

Alexander the Great. 1568

Almane. Southwest Germany. 1087

Alpheus. The River Alpheus. 1093

Ameleth. OT Abimelech. 1515

Amphion. 511

Amphiorax. Amphiaraus, Greek king. 1584

Amyson. The land of the Amazons. 1108

Anchyses. Anchises, father of Aeneas. 1645

Anna. OT Hannah. 584

Antecrist. Antichrist. 1701

Antertik. See **Poil Antertik**

Anthiacus. Antiochus. 1570

Anthon, Mark. Mark Antony. 585

Aones. Dwellers on Mount Helicon. 884

Appenynus. Apennine Mountains. 1091

Appollo. Apollo. 1133

Araby. Arabia. 438

Archaid. Arcadia. 508

Arestotyl. Aristotle. 251

Argos. Argus. 749

Armany. Armenia. 1120

Arsyte. Arcite. 562

Artik. See **Poil Artik**

Aurora. 1

Averroes. 258

Babillon, Babilon, Babilone. Babylon. 1341, 1502, 1556

Bachus. Bacchus. 1111

Bacon. Roger Bacon. 1721

Bananyas. OT Benaiah. 1533

Barsabe. Bathsheba. 570

Beird Gray. Graybeard, Maitland's horse. 1717

Bibles. Byblis. 582

Bocace. Giovanni Boccaccio. 915

Boetius. Boethius. 905

Bongo. Thomas Bungay. 1721

Bonitas, Bonytas. Guido Bonatti. 1721, 1727

Bosiliall. Bezaleel, OT builder. 1453

Brunell. Possibly Brunellus. 915
Brutus Albion. Britain. 918
Brutus Junius. Lucius Brutus Junius 1661
Bryssida. Briseis. 573
Bybyl. The Bible. 277

Caballyne. The Hippocrene spring. 1134
Cacasus. Mount Caucasus. 1125
Caliope. The Muse Calliope. 872, 940, 955, 991, 1000, 1007, 1048, 1054, 1186
Callydon. Calydon, ancient Greek city. 1201
Camp Elysee. Elysian Fields. 1644
Campe Damascene. The Damascene field. 1244
Canyce. Canacee of Chaucer's Squire's Tale. 1493
Carmelitis. The Carmelite Order. 1107
Carmelus. Mount Carmel. 1105
Carone. Charon. 1640
Cartage. Carthage. 1636, 1667, 1686
Cassandra. 244
Catalyn, Lucyus, Catulyna. Catiline. 1691, 1770
Caton. Cato. 904
Cedippa. Cydippe. 814
Ceix. Ceyx. 571
Cenobia. Zenobia, warrior queen. 2025
Centauris. Centaurs. 1595
Cesar Julyus. Julius Caesar. 1692
Charité. Charity, third Theological Virtue. 1795
Charle Wain. Ursa Major. 1845
Chaucere, Goffryd. Geoffrey Chaucer. 919
Chyppynuty. 654
Chryst. Jesus Christ. 1394
Cicero. 261, 1772
Cignus. Cycnus. 1209
Cinthus. Mount Cynthus. 1133
Circis. Circe. 244
Citheron. Mount Cithaeron. 1111

Claudyus. Claudian, Latin poet. 915
Cleo. The Muse Clio. 854
Cleopatra. 585
Cochyte. The River Cocytus. 138
Coilyear. See **Raf Coilyear**
Colchos. Colchis. 1607
Coridon. Corydon, shepherd in Virgil's *Eclogues*. 1226
Cowkewyis sow. *Colkelbie's Sow*. 1712
Creon. King of Thebes. 1582
Cressida. Criseyde. 565
Crete. 1197
Cupid, Cupyd. Son of Venus, god of love. 482, 634, 664, 931, 1470
Curtyus. Marcus Curtius. 1676

Dalida. Delilah. 580
Damascene. See **Campe Damascene**
Danyell. OT Daniel. 1553
Daphnis. Shepherd in Virgil's *Eclogues*. 1226
Daris. Darius Phrygius, Trojan chronicler. 900
Darius. Persian king. 1457
David, Davyd, Davidis. OT king. 509, 570, 1525, 1528, 1530
Delbora. OT prophet and judge. 244
Demophon. Demophoon. 574, 810
Dian, Diane. Diana. 297, 317, 321, 332, 336, 746, 1201
Dido. Queen of Carthage. 564, 1636, 1669
Dindama. Mount Dindyma. 1123
Diogenes. Cynic philosopher. 259
Dyonera. Deianeira. 581
Ditis. Dictys Cretensis, Trojan chronicler. 900
Donat. Donatus, Roman grammarian. 902
Dorida. The sea-nymph Doris. 1850
Dryades. Dryads, the tree-nymphs. 883
Dunbar. William Dunbar. 923

Ebrewes. Jews. 1505, 1510
Ebron. Hebron. 1244
Effygyn. Iphigenia. 342

Ptholomeus. Claudius Ptolemy the ancient scientist. 256

Quintilliane. Quintilian. 906
Quyntyne. Scottish poet. 924

Rachel. OT 589
Raf Coilyear. 1711
Raguell. OT 1559
Raphell. Raphael. 1558
Regulus, Marcus. Marcus Atilius Regulus. 1671
Reid See. The Red Sea. 1507
Ryne. The Rhine River. 1092
Robene Hude. Robin Hood. 1718
Robert. Robert Bruce. 2027
Roboam. OT Rehoboam. 1542
Romanis, Romanys. The Romans. 1667, 1682
Rome. 1492, 1657, 1659, 1687
Romulus. 1657
Ron. The Rhone River. 1095
Rutuleis. The Rutulians. 1656

Salomon. OT Solomon. 250, 1455, 1540
Salust. Sallust. 252
Sampson, Sampsone. OT Samson. 1516, 2017
Samuell. OT Samuel. 1522
Sancta Sanctorum. OT Ark of the Covenant. 1454
Sane. The Seine River. 1095
Sangor. OT Shamgar. 1520
Saphik. Sapphic. 801
Sara. OT Sarah, bride of Tobias. 1559
Saturee. Satyrs. 883
Saturn, Saturne. 50, 754
Saul, Saule. OT king. 510, 1523
Scipio Affricane. Scipio Africanus, Roman general. 1683, 1684, 2020
Secyle. Sicily. 1122
Secundus. Julius Secundus, Roman orator. 255
Semiramis. 2024
Senek. Seneca. 252
Servius. Latin grammarian. 902.

Sextus. See **Sextus Terquine**
Sibillais. Sibyls. 243
Sidrag. Sidrak. 255
Sylla. Scylla, female sea-monster. 583
Symon. Simon Maccabeus. 1575
Synachoryb. Sennacherib, Assyrian king. 1547
Synon, Synone. Sinon. 236, 239, 282, 1768
Sisipho. Sisiphus. 1643
Sythia. Scythia. 1125
Skrymmory. 653
Socrates. 256
Sodomus. OT Sodom. 1503
Solenyus. Solinus, Roman geographer. 255
Spane. Spain. 1089, 1687
Sparthiades. The River Spercheios. 1117
Stace, Stacius. Statius. 909, 1583
Stix. The River Styx. 1639
Strymon. The River Strymon. 1127
Surry. Syria. 1118
Susane. OT Susanna. 579

Tagus. The Tagus River. 1096
Tarnus. Turnus. 1656
Tarpsychore. The Muse Terpsichore. 862
Tebes, Thebes. Greek city. 512, 1577, 1587
Terens, Therens. Terence the Roman dramatist. 902, 1227
Termodyon. The River Thermodon. 1109
Terquine, Sextus. Sextus Tarquinius. 1665
Terquinius. Tarquin the Proud. 1660
Thalia. The Muse. 858.
Thamar. OT Tamar. 2024
Thanas. The Don River. 1116
Thedeus. Tydeus. 1578
Thesyus. Theseus. 577, 1195, 1581
Thespis. The Boeotian goddess. 852
Thessaly. 1097
Thysbe. Thisbe. 568
Thobyas. OT Tobias. 1560

BIBLIOGRAPHY

Acta Facultatis Artium Universitatis Sanctiandree 1413–1588. Ed. Annie I. Dunlop. 2 vols. Scottish History Society. Edinburgh: Oliver & Boyd, 1964.

Acts of the Lords of Council in Civil Causes. Ed. George Neilson and Henry M. A. Paton. Vol. II. Edinburgh: H.M. Stationery Office, 1918.

[*ALHTS.*] *Accounts of the Lord High Treasurer of Scotland*. *Vol. I. A.D. 1473–1498*. Ed. Thomas Dickson. Edinburgh: H. M. General Register House, 1877.

Andrew of Wyntoun. *The Original Chronicle of Andrew of Wyntoun*. Ed. F. J. Amours. 6 vols. STS 1st series 50, 53, 54, 56, 57, 63. Edinburgh: Blackwood, 1903–14.

Amsler, Mark E. "The Quest for the Present Tense: The Poet and the Dreamer in Douglas' *The Palice of Honour*." *Studies in Scottish Literature* 17.1 (1982), 186–208.

Aristotle. *Metaphysics*. Trans. Hugh Tredennick. Cambridge, MA: Harvard University Press, 1933.

———. *The Physics*. Ed. Philip H. Wicksteed and Francis M. Cornford. 2 vols. Cambridge, MA: Harvard University Press, 1934.

———. *Parts of Animals*. Trans. A. L. Peck. Cambridge, MA: Harvard University Press, 1937.

———. *On the Soul. Parva Naturalia. On Breath*. Trans. W. S. Hett. Cambridge, MA: Harvard University Press, 1957.

Armstrong, Adrian, and Sarah Kay. *Knowing Poetry: Verse in Medieval France from the "Rose" to the "Rhétoriqueurs."* Ithaca and London: Cornell University Press, 2011.

Arthour and Merlin. Ed. O. D. Macrae-Gibson. 2 vols. EETS o.s. 268, 279. London: Oxford University Press, 1973–79.

The Awntyrs off Arthure at the Terne Wathelyn. Ed. Ralph Hanna III. Manchester: Manchester University Press, 1974.

The Bannatyne Manuscript. Ed. W. Tod Ritchie. 4 vols. STS 3rd series 5, 22, 23, 26. Edinburgh: William Blackwood and Sons, 1928–34.

Barberis, Philippus de. *Opuscula*. [Rome: Georg Herolt and Sixtus Riessinger, c.1482.]

Barbour, John. *Barbour's Bruce*. Ed. Matthew P. McDiarmid and James A. C. Stevenson. 3 vols. STS 4th series 12, 13, 15. Edinburgh: William Blackwood and Sons, 1980–85.

Barsby, John. "Terence in Translation." In *A Companion to Terence*. Ed. Anthony Augoustakis and Ariana Traill. Oxford: Blackwell, 2013. Pp. 446–65.

Bawcutt, Priscilla. *Gavin Douglas: A Critical Study*. Edinburgh: Edinburgh University Press, 1976.

———. "The 'Library' of Gavin Douglas." In *Bards and Makars*. Ed. Adam J. Aitken, Matthew P. McDiarmid and Derick S. Thomson. Glasgow: University of Glasgow Press, 1977. Pp. 107–26.

———. *Dunbar the Makar*. Oxford: Clarendon Press, 1992.

———. "New Light on Gavin Douglas." In *The Renaissance in Scotland: Studies in Literature, Religion, History and Culture Offered to John Durkan*. Ed. A. Alasdair MacDonald, Michael Lynch and Ian B. Cowan. Leiden: Brill, 1994. Pp. 95–106.

———. "Crossing the Border: Scottish Poetry and English Readers in the Sixteenth Century." In *The Rose and the Thistle*. Pp. 59–76.

Beattie, William. "Fragments of 'The Palyce of Honour.'" *Edinburgh Bibliographical Society Transactions* 3.1 (1951), 33–46.

Bellenden, John. "The Proheme of the Cosmographe." In *The History and Chronicles of Scotland Written in Latin by Hector Boece, Canon of Aberdeen and Translated by John Bellenden*. Ed. Thomas Maitland. 2 vols. Edinburgh: W. And C. Tait, 1821. 1:v–xvi.

———, trans. *Livy's History of Rome*. Ed. William A. Craigie. 2 vols. STS 1st series 47, 51. Edinburgh: William Blackwood and Sons, 1901–03.

———, trans. *The Chronicles of Scotland Compiled by Hector Boece*. Ed. Walter Seton, R. W. Chambers, and Edith C. Batho. 2 vols. STS 3rd series 10, 15. Edinburgh: William Blackwood and Sons, 1938–41.

Bergstein, Mary. "Donatello's *Gattamelata* and Its Humanist Audience." *Renaissance Quarterly* 55.3 (2002), 833–68.

Bisset, Habakkuk. *Habakkuk Bisset's Rolment of Courtis*. Ed. Philip J. Hamilton-Grierson. 3 vols. STS 2nd series 10, 13, 18. Edinburgh: William Blackwood and Sons, 1920–26.

Blyth, Charles R. *"The Knychtlyke Stile": A Study of Gavin Douglas's Aeneid*. New York: Garland, 1987.

Boethius. *The Consolation of Philosophy*. In *Boethius: Theological Tractates; The Consolation of Philosophy*. Trans. H. F. Stewart, E. K. Rand, and S. J. Tester. Second edition. Cambridge, MA: Harvard University Press, 1973. Pp. 130–435. Originally published 1918.

Boffey, Julia, and A. S. G. Edwards. "Literary Texts." In *The Cambridge History of the Book in Britain. Volume 3: 1400–1557*. Ed. Lotte Hellinga and J. B. Trapp. Cambridge: Cambridge University Press, 1999. Pp. 555–75.

Le Bone Florence of Rome. Ed. Carol Falvo Heffernan. Manchester: Manchester University Press, 1976.

The Book of Pluscarden. Ed. and trans. Felix J. H. Skene. 2 vols. Edinburgh: Paterson, 1877.

Boutcher, Warren. "Vernacular Humanism in the Sixteenth Century." In *The Cambridge Companion to Renaissance Humanism*. Ed. Jill Kraye. Cambridge: Cambridge University Press, 1996. Pp. 189–202.

Bower, Walter. *Scotichronicon: In Latin and English*. Ed. D. E. R. Watt. 9 vols. Aberdeen: Aberdeen University Press, 1987–98.

Braund, Susanna Morton, ed. *Juvenal and Persius*. Cambridge, MA: Harvard University Press, 2004.

Breeze, Andrew. "The Bret Glascurion and Chaucer's House of Fame." *The Review of English Studies* 45.177 (1994), 63–69.

Brill's New Pauly: Encyclopedia of the Ancient World. Ed. Hubert Canok, et al. Leiden: Brill, 2002–10. Online at http://referenceworks.brillonline.com.

Broadie, Alexander. "John Mair's *Dialogus de materia theologo tractanda*: Introduction, Text and Translation." In *Christian Humanism: Essays in Honour of Arjo Vanderjagt*. Ed. Alasdair A. MacDonald, Zweder R. W. M. von Martels, and Jan R. Veenstra. Leiden: Brill, 2009. Pp. 419–30.

Broun, Dauvit. *The Irish Identity of the Kingdom of the Scots in the Twelfth and Thirteenth Centuries*. Woodbridge: Boydell, 1999.

Buchanan, George. *The History of Scotland Translated from the Latin of George Buchanan*. Trans. James Aikman. 4 vols. Glasgow: Blackie, Fullarton & Co., 1827.

Bühler, Curt F. "'Kynge Melyzyus' and *The Pastime of Pleasure*." *The Review of English Studies* 10.40 (1934), 438–41.

The Buik of Alexander. Ed. R. L. Graeme Ritchie. 4 vols. STS 2nd series 17, 12, 21, 25. Edinburgh: William Blackwood and Sons, 1921–25.

Bullock, Hannah A. *History of the Isle of Man*. London: Longman, Hurst, Rees, Orme, and Brown, 1816.

Burel, John. *The Passage of the Pilgremer, Devidit into Twa Pairts*. Ed. Harriet Harvey Wood. In *James Watson's Choice Collection of Comic and Serious Scots Poems*. 2 vols. STS 4th series 10, 20. Edinburgh: William Blackwood and Sons, 1977–91. 1.2:16–53; 2:123–28.

Burrow, John A. *Gestures and Looks in Medieval Narrative*. Cambridge: Cambridge University Press, 2002.

Cairns, Sandra. *"The Palice of Honour* of Gavin Douglas, Ovid and Raffaello Regio's Commentary on Ovid's *Metamorphoses*." *Res Publica Litterarum* 7 (1984), 17–38.

Calendar of Letters, Despatches and State Papers Relating to the Negotiations between England and Spain. Henry VII. 1485–1509. Ed. G. A. Bergenroth. Vol. 1. London: Longman, Green, Longman & Roberts, 1862.

Calin, William. *The Lily and the Thistle: The French Tradition and the Older Literature of Scotland – Essays in Criticism.* Toronto: University of Toronto Press, 2014.

Calle-Martín, Javier. "The Late Middle English Version of *Practica Urinarum* in London, Wellcome Library, MS 537 (ff. 15r–40v)." In *From Clerks to Corpora: Essays in the English Language Yesterday and Today.* Ed. Philip Shaw, Britt Erman, Gunnel Melchers, and Peter Sundkvist. Stockholm: Stockholm University Press, 2015. Pp. 35–52.

Camporeale, Salvatore I. "Poggio Bracciolini versus Lorenzo Valla: The *Orationes* in *Laurentium Vallam.*" In *Perspectives on Early Modern and Modern Intellectual History: Essays in Honor of Nancy S. Struever.* Ed. Joseph Marino and Melinda W. Schlitt. Rochester, NY: University of Rochester Press, 2001. Pp. 27–48.

Capella, Martianus. *De nuptiis Philologiae et Mercurii.* Vol. 2. Hildesheim: Weidmann, 2011. Accessed August 2017. Online at http://clt.brepolis.net/llta/pages/Toc.aspx?ctx=980024.

Carey, Hilary M. "Henry VII's Book of Astrology and the Tudor Renaissance." *Renaissance Quarterly* 65.3 (2012), 661–710.

Carlson, David. "Politicizing Tudor Court Literature: Gaguin's Embassy and Henry VIII's Humanists' Response." *Studies in Philology* 85.3 (Summer 1988), 279–304.

Carter, Henry Holland. *A Dictionary of Middle English Musical Terms.* Ed. George B. Gerhard. Bloomington: Indiana University Press, 1961; Rpt. New York: Kraus, 1968.

The Catholic Encyclopedia. Gen. Ed. Kevin Knight, 1995–2017. Accessed 29 August 2017. Online at http://www.newadvent.org/cathen/.

Chaucer, Geoffrey. *The Riverside Chaucer.* Ed. Larry D. Benson. Third edition. Boston: Houghton Mifflin, 1987.

———. *The House of Fame.* Ed. Nick Havely. Second edition. Toronto: Pontifical Institute of Mediaeval Studies, 2013.

———. *Troilus and Criseyde.* Ed. Barry Windeatt. London: Penguin, 2013.

Chaucerian Dream Visions and Complaints. Ed. Dana M. Symons. Kalamazoo, MI: Medieval Institute Publications, 2004.

Chism, Christine. *Alliterative Revivals.* Philadelphia: University of Pennsylvania Press, 2002.

Cicero. *De Officiis.* Ed. Walter Miller. Cambridge, MA: Harvard University Press, 1913.

———. *De Oratore.* Ed. E. W. Sutton and H. Rackham. Cambridge, MA: Harvard University Press, 1942.

———. *De Natura Deorum; Academica.* Trans. H. W. Rackham. Second edition. Cambridge, MA: Harvard University Press, 1951. Originally published 1933.

Code of Canon Law. Washington, DC: Canon Law Society of America, 1998. Accessed August 2017. Online at vatican.va/archive/ENG1104/_INDEX.HTM.

Contemporaries of Erasmus: A Biographical Register of the Renaissance and Reformation. Ed. Peter G. Bietenholz and Thomas B. Deutscher. 3 vols. Toronto: University of Toronto Press, 1985–87.

Cooper, Scott. "Ornamental Structures in the Medieval Gardens of Scotland." *Proceedings of the Society of Antiquaries of Scotland* 129 (1999), 817–39.

The Court of Sapience. Ed. Ruth E. Harvey. Toronto: University of Toronto Press, 1984.

Cunningham, Maurice P. "The Novelty of Ovid's *Heroides.*" *Classical Philology* 44:2 (1949): 100–06.

Curtius, Ernst Robert. *European Literature and the Latin Middle Ages.* Trans. Willard R. Trask. New York: Pantheon Books, 1953; Rpt. Princeton: Princeton University Press, 1990.

Davidson, Clifford, Martin W. Walsh, and Ton J. Broos, ed. *Everyman and Its Dutch Original, Elckerlijc.* Kalamazoo, MI: Medieval Institute Publications, 2007.

Dickson, Robert, and John Philip Edmond. *Annals of Scottish Printing from the Introduction of the Art in 1507 to the Beginning of the Seventeenth Century.* 2 vols. Cambridge: Macmillan and Bowes, 1890.

DIMEV: An Open-Access, Digital Version of the Index of Middle English Verse. Ed. Linne R. Mooney, et al. Accessed 21 July 2016. Online at www.dimev.net.

Donaldson, Gordon, and Henry M. Paton, ed. *Protocol Book of James Young 1485–1515*. Edinburgh: J. Skinner, 1941–52.

[DOST]. Dictionary of the Scots Language. Ed. William A. Craigie, et al. Accessed August 2017. Online at www.dsl.ac.uk.

Douglas, Gavin. *Select Works of Gawin Douglass, Bishop of Dunkeld*. [Ed. James Scott.] Vol. 2. Perth: Robert Morison, 1787.

———. *The Palice of Honour, Compylit be Mr. Gawine Douglas, Bishop of Dunkeld*. In *Scotish Poems: Reprinted from Scarce Editions*. Ed. John Pinkerton. Pp. xvi–xv, 51–142.

———. *The Palice of Honour by Gawyn Douglas, Bishop of Dunkeld*. Ed. John G. Kinnear. Bannatyne Club. Edinburgh: James Ballantyne, 1827.

———. *The Poetical Works of Gavin Douglas, Bishop of Dunkeld*. Ed. John Small. 4 vols. Edinburgh: William Paterson, 1874.

———. *Virgil's Aeneid Translated into Scottish Verse by Gavin Douglas, Bishop of Dunkeld*. Ed. David F. C. Coldwell. 4 vols. STS 3rd series 30, 25, 27, and 28. Edinburgh: Blackwood, 1956–60.

———. *The Palis of Honoure*. Ed. David Parkinson. Kalamazoo, MI: Medieval Institute Publications, 1992.

———. *The Shorter Poems of Gavin Douglas*. Ed. Priscilla Bawcutt. Second edition. STS 5th series 2. Edinburgh: Scottish Text Society, 2003.

Dunbar, John G. *Scottish Royal Palaces: The Architecture of the Royal Residences during the Late Medieval and Early Renaissance Periods*. East Linton: Tuckwell Press, 1999.

Dunbar, William. *The Poems of William Dunbar*. Ed. Priscilla Bawcutt. 2 vols. Glasgow: Association for Scottish Literary Studies, 1998.

Durkan, John. "The Observant Franciscan Province in Scotland." *The Innes Review* 35.2 (1984), 51–57.

Ebin, Lois A. *Illuminator Makar Vates: Visions of Poetry in the Fifteenth Century*. Lincoln: University of Nebraska Press, 1988.

Edwards, A. S. G. "Lydgate in Scotland." *Nottingham Medieval Studies* 54 (2010), 185–94.

Eneados. See Douglas, Gavin. *Virgil's Aeneid*.

The English and Scottish Popular Ballads. Ed. Francis James Child. 5 vols. Boston and New York: Houghton Mifflin, 1882–98.

English Mediaeval Lapidaries. Ed. Joan Evans and Mary S. Serjeantson. EETS o.s. 190. London: Oxford University Press, 1933.

Ewan, Elizabeth. "Disorderly Damsels? Women and Interpersonal Violence in Pre-Reformation Scotland." *Scottish Historical Review* 89.2 (2010), 153–71.

Fabyan, Robert. *The New Chronicles of England and France, in Two Parts*. Ed. Henry Ellis. London: Rivington [etc.], 1811.

Fawcett, Richard. *Scottish Architecture from the Accession of the Stewarts to the Reformation 1371–1560*. Edinburgh: Edinburgh University Press, 1994.

Flynn, Caitlin. "The Grotesque in Late Medieval Scottish and English Literature." PhD dissertation, University of St Andrews, 2016.

Fox, Denton. "The Scottish Chaucerians." In *Chaucer and Chaucerians: Critical Studies in Middle English Literature*. Ed. D. S. Brewer. London: Nelson, 1966. Pp. 164–200.

Fradenburg, Louise O. *City, Marriage, Tournament: Arts of Rule in Late Medieval Scotland*. Madison: University of Wisconsin Press, 1991.

Fraser, William. *The Douglas Book*. 4 vols. Edinburgh: Edinburgh University Press, 1885.

Friis-Jensen, Karsten. "Commentaries on Horace's 'Art of Poetry' in the Incunable Period." *Renaissance Studies* 9.2 (1995), 228–39.

Galloway, Andrew. "John Lydgate and the Origins of Vernacular Humanism." *The Journal of English and Germanic Philology* 107.4 (2008), 445–71.

Geddie, William. *A Bibliography of Middle Scots Poets, with an Introduction on the History of their Reputations*. STS 1st series 61. Edinburgh: William Blackwood and Sons, 1912.

Gillies, William. "The Book of the Dean of Lismore: The Literary Perspective." In *Fresche Fontanis: Studies in the Culture of Medieval and Early Modern Scotland*. Ed. Janet Hadley Williams and J. Derrick McClure. Newcastle: Cambridge Scholars Publishing, 2013. Pp. 179–216.

Gower, John. *Confessio Amantis*. Ed. Russell A. Peck. 3 vols. Second edition. Kalamazoo, MI: Medieval Institute Publications, 2004–13.

Grafton, Anthony. *Defenders of the Text: The Traditions of Scholarship in an Age of Science, 1450–1800*. Cambridge, MA: Harvard University Press, 1991.

Grant, Edward. *Planets, Stars and Orbs: the Medieval Cosmos, 1200–1687*. Cambridge, New York: Cambridge University Press, 1994.

Gray, Douglas. "Gavin Douglas." In *A Companion to Medieval Scottish Poetry*. Ed. Priscilla Bawcutt and Janet Hadley Williams. Cambridge: D. S. Brewer, 2006. Pp. 149–64.

Green, Richard Firth. "Did Chaucer Know the Ballad of Glen Kindy?" *Neophilologus* 92.2 (April 2008), 351–58.

Grove Music Online. Oxford University Press, 2007–18. Accessed February 2017. Online at www.oxfordmusiconline.com.

Guido delle Colonne. *Historia Destructionis Troiae*. Trans. Mary Elizabeth Meek. Bloomington: Indiana University Press, 1974.

Hall, Alaric. "The Etymology and Meanings of *Eldritch*." *Scottish Language* 26 (2007), 16–22.

Hammond, Eleanor Prescott. *English Verse Between Chaucer and Surrey*. Rpt. New York: Octagon Books, 1969. Originally published 1927.

Harrison, Frank Lloyd. *Music in Medieval Britain*. London: Routledge and Kegan Paul, 1958.

Hansen, Elaine Tuttle. "Irony and the Antifeminist Narrator in Chaucer's 'Legend of Good Women.'" *Journal of English and Germanic Philology* 82.1 (January 1983): 11–31.

Hasler, Antony J. *Court Poetry in Late Medieval England and Scotland: Allegories of Authority*. Cambridge: Cambridge University Press, 2011.

Hay, Gilbert. *The Buik of King Alexander the Conquerour by Sir Gilbert Hay*. Ed. John Cartwright. 2 vols. STS 4th series 16, 18. Edinburgh: The Scottish Text Society, 1986–90.

———. *The Prose Works of Sir Gilbert Hay*. Ed. Jonathan A. Glenn. 2 vols. STS 5th series 21, 3. Edinburgh: Scottish Text Society, 1993–2005.

Heijnsbergen, Theo van. "Advice to a Princess: The Literary Articulation of a Religious, Political and Cultural Programme for Mary Queen of Scots, 1562." In *Sixteenth-Century Scotland: Essays in Honour of Michael Lynch*. Ed. Julian Goodare and Alasdair A. MacDonald. Leiden: Brill, 2008. Pp. 99–122.

Heist, William W. *The Fifteen Signs Before Doomsday*. East Lansing: Michigan State College Press, 1952.

Henryson, Robert. *The Poems of Robert Henryson*. Ed. Denton Fox. Oxford: Clarendon Press, 1981.

Hepburn, William Rendall. "The Household of James IV, 1488–1513." PhD dissertation, University of Glasgow, 2013.

Heroic Women from the Old Testament. Ed. Russell A. Peck. Kalamazoo, MI: Medieval Institute Publications, 1991.

Historic Environment Scotland. "Edinburgh, Greenside Row, Carmelite Friary." *Canmore: National Record of the Historic Environment*. Accessed 21 August 2017. Online at http://canmore.org.uk/site /52403.

———. "Linlithgow, Carmelite Friary." *Canmore: National Record of the Historic Environment*. Accessed 21 August 2017. Online at http://canmore.org.uk/site/49244.

———. "Tantallon Castle." *Canmore: National Record of the Historic Environment*. Accessed 15 July 2017. Online at http://canmore.org.uk/site/56630.

Historical Manuscripts Commission. *The Manuscripts of the Duke of Athole, K. T., and the Earl of Home*. 12th Report, Appendix, part 8. London: Eyre & Spottiswoode, 1891.

Die Historie vanden stercken Hercules. Antwerp: Jan van Doesborch, 1521.

The Holy Bible: Douay-Rheims Version. Ed. Bishop Richard Challoner. Rockford, IL: Tan Books and Publishers, 1989. Originally published Baltimore: John Murphy, 1899.

Holland, Richard. *The Buke of the Howlat*. Ed. Ralph Hanna. STS 5th series 12. Rochester, NY: Boydell, 2014.

Hollander, John. *The Untuning of the Sky: Ideas of Music in English Poetry, 1500–1700*. Princeton: Princeton University Press, 1961.

Homer. *The Odyssey*. Trans. A. T. Murray. 2 vols. Cambridge, MA: Harvard University Press, 1995.

———. *Iliad*. Ed. A. T. Murray and William F. Wyatt. Second edition. 2 vols. Cambridge, MA: Harvard University Press, 1999.

Honeyman, Chelsea. "*The Palice of Honour*: Gavin Douglas' Renovation of Chaucer's House of Fame." In *Standing in the Shadow of the Master? Chaucerian Influences and Interpretations*. Ed Kathleen A. Bishop. Newcastle: Cambridge Scholars Press, 2010. Pp. 65–81.

Horace. *Ars Poetica*. In *Satires, Epistles, The Art of Poetry*. Trans. H. Rushton Fairclough. Cambridge, MA: Harvard University Press, 1926. Pp. 442–88.

———. *Odes and Epodes*. Ed. and trans. Niall Rudd. Cambridge, MA: Harvard University Press, 2004.

Hornback, Robert. "'Extravagant and Wheeling Strangers': Early Blackface Dancing Fools, Racial Impersonation, and the Limits of Identification." *Exemplaria* 20.2 (2008), 197–223.

Houston, R. A. "What Did the Royal Almoner Do in Britain and Ireland, c.1450–1700?" *The English Historical Review* 125.513 (2010), 279–313.

Hume, David [of Godscroft]. *The History of the House of Angus*. Ed. David Reid. 2 vols. STS 5th series 4, 5. Edinburgh: Scottish Text Society, 2005.

Ipomadon. Ed. Rhiannon Purdie. EETS o.s. 316. Oxford: Oxford University Press, 2001.

Ireland, John. *The Meroure of Wysdome by Johannes de Irlandia*. Ed. Charles MacPherson, F. Quinn, and Craig McDonald. 3 vols. STS 2nd series 19; 4th series 2, 19. Edinburgh: Scottish Text Society, 1926–90.

Irving, David. *The History of Scotish Poetry*. Ed. John Aitken Carlyle. Edinburgh: Edmonston and Douglas, 1861.

Isabella Breviary. British Library, Additional MS 18851. Accessed August 2017. Online at http://www.bl.uk/manuscripts/FullDisplay.aspx?ref=Add_MS_18851.

Jack, R. D. S. *The Italian Influence on Scottish Literature*. Edinburgh: Edinburgh University Press, 1972.

James I of Scotland. *The Kingis Quair*. Ed. John Norton-Smith. Second edition. Leiden: Brill, 1981. Originally published 1971.

———. *The Kingis Quair and Other Prison Poems*. Ed. Linne R. Mooney and Mary-Jo Arn. Kalamazoo, MI: Medieval Institute Publications, 2005.

James IV. *The Letters of James the Fourth, 1505–1513*. Ed. Robert Kerr Hannay and Robert L. Mackie. Scottish History Society. Edinburgh: T & A. Constable, 1953.

James, Heather. "Ovid and the Question of Politics in Early Modern England." *ELH* 70.2 (2003), 343–73.

Johnston, Andrew James, and Margitta Rouse. "Facing the Mirror: Ekphrasis, Vision, and Knowledge in Gavin Douglas's *Palice of Honour*." In *The Art of Vision: Ekphrasis in Medieval Literature and Culture*. Ed. Andrew James Johnston, Ethan Knapp, and Margitta Rouse. Columbus: Ohio State University Press, 2015. Pp. 166–83.

Jotischky, Andrew. *The Carmelites and Antiquity: Mendicants and their Pasts in the Middle Ages*. Oxford: Oxford University Press, 2002.

Juvenal. See Braund, Susanna Morton.

Kallendorf, Craig W. "Renaissance." In *A Companion to the Classical Tradition*. Ed. Craig W. Kallendorf. Oxford: Blackwell, 2007. Pp. 30–43.

Kilgour, Maggie. *Milton and the Metamorphosis of Ovid*. Oxford: Clarendon Press, 2012.

Kinneavy, Gerald B. "The Poet in *The Palice of Honour*." *Chaucer Review* 3.4 (1969), 280–303.

The Knightly Tale of Golagros and Gawane. Ed. Ralph Hanna. STS 5th series 7. Rochester, NY: Boydell, 2008.

Knox, Peter E. "Commenting on Ovid." In *A Companion to Ovid*. Ed. Peter E. Knox. Chichester: Wiley-Blackwell, 2013. Pp. 327–40.

Kordecki, Lesley. "Making Animals Mean: Speciest Hermeneutics in the *Physiologus* of Theobaldus." In *Animals in the Middle Ages: A Book of Essays*. Ed. Nora C. Flores. London: Garland, 2016. Pp. 85–101.

Kratzmann, Gregory. *Anglo-Scottish Literary Relations, 1430–1550*. Cambridge: Cambridge University Press, 1980.

Kristeller, Paul Oskar. "Humanism." *The Cambridge History of Renaissance Philosophy*. Ed. Charles B. Schmitt, et al. Cambridge: Cambridge University Press, 1988. Pp. 111–38.

Lactantius. *Divine Institutes. Ante-Nicene Fathers*. Trans. William Fletcher. Vol. 7. Ed. Alexander Roberts, James Donaldson, and A. Cleveland Coxe. Buffalo, NY: Christian Literature Publishing, 1886. Pp. 3–223. Accessed 29 August 2017. Online at http://newadvent.org/fathers/0701.htm.

Laing, David, Walter Scott, and Thomas Thomson, eds. "The Wills of Thomas Bassandyne, and Other Printers, &c. in Edinburgh, 1577–1687." In *The Bannatyne Miscellany: Containing Original Papers and Tracts, Chiefly Relating to the History and Literature of Scotland*. Vol. 2. Edinburgh: Bannatyne Club, 1836. Pp. 185–296.

Lang, Andrew. *Sir Walter Scott and the Border Minstrelsy*. London: Longmans, Green, & Co., 1910.

Lange, P. "Chaucer's Einfluss auf die Original-dichtungen des Schotten Douglas." *Anglia* 6 (1883), 46–95.

Langland, William. *Piers Plowman: A Parallel-Text Edition of the A, B, C, and Z Versions*. Ed. A. V. C. Schmidt. Second edition. 2 vols. Kalamazoo, MI: Medieval Institute Publications, 2011.

Lawton, David. "Dullness and the Fifteenth Century." *ELH* 54 (1987), 761–99.

Leahy, Conor. "Dreamscape into Landscape in Gavin Douglas." *Essays in Criticism* 66.2 (2016), 149–67.

Leonard, Frances McNeely. *Laughter in the Courts of Love: Comedy in Allegory from Chaucer to Spenser*. Norman, OK: Pilgrim Books, 1981.

Lesley, John. *The History of Scotland, from the Death of King James I in the Year 1436, to the Year 1561 by John Lesley, Bishop of Ross*. Ed. Thomas Thomson. Edinburgh: Bannatyne Club, 1830.

Lewis, C. S. *The Allegory of Love: A Study in Medieval Tradition*. London: Oxford University Press, 1936.

———. *English Literature in the Sixteenth Century*. Oxford: Clarendon Press, 1954.

Lindesay, Robert. *The Historie and Cronicles of Scotland: from the Slauchter of King James the First to the Ane Thousande Fyve Hundreith Thrie Scoir Fyftein Zeir*. Ed. Æ. J. G. Mackay. 3 vols. STS 1st series 42, 43, 60. Edinburgh: William Blackwood and Sons, 1899–1911.

Livy. *History of Rome*. Trans. B. O. Foster, et al. 14 vols. Cambridge, MA: Harvard University Press, 1919–59.

Lyall, R. J. "The Stylistic Relationship between Dunbar and Douglas." In *William Dunbar, 'The Nobill Poyet': Essays in Honour of Priscilla Bawcutt*. Ed. Sally Mapstone. East Linton: Tuckwell Press, 2001. Pp. 69–84.

Lydgate, John. *Poems*. Ed. John Norton-Smith. Oxford: Clarendon Press, 1966.

———. *The Siege of Thebes*. Ed. Robert R. Edwards. Kalamazoo, MI: Medieval Institute Publications, 2001.

———. *The Temple of Glas*. Ed. J. Allan Mitchell. Kalamazoo, MI: Medieval Institute Publications, 2007.

Lyndsay, David. *The Works of Sir David Lindsay*. Ed. Douglas Hamer. 4 vols. STS 3rd series 1, 2, 6, 8. Edinburgh: William Blackwood and Sons, 1931–36.

———. *Sir David Lyndsay: Selected Poems*. Ed. Janet Hadley Williams. Glasgow: Association for Scottish Literary Studies, 2000.

Macafee, Caroline M., and A. J. Aitken, "A History of Scots to 1700." *Dictionary of the Scottish Language*. Accessed February 2017. Online at www.dsl.ac.uk/about-scots/history-of-scots.

MacDonald, Alasdair A. "Anglo-Scottish Literary Relations: Problems and Possibilities." *Studies in Scottish Literature* 26.1 (1991), 172–84.

———. "Princely Culture in Scotland under James III and James IV." In *Princes and Princely Culture, 1450–1650*. Ed. Martin Gosman, Alasdair MacDonald, and Arjo Vanderjagt. 2 vols. Leiden: Brill, 2003. 1:147–72.

Macdougall, Norman. *James IV*. Edinburgh: John Donald, 1989.

Macfarlane, Leslie J. "William Elphinstone's Library Revisited." In *The Renaissance in Scotland: Studies in Literature, Religion, History and Culture Offered to John Durkhan*. Ed. A. A. MacDonald, Michael Lynch and Ian Borthwick Cowan. Leiden and New York: Brill, 1994. Pp. 66–81.

Macrobius. *Commentary on the Dream of Scipio*. Trans. William Harris Stahl. New York and London: Columbia University Press, 1952.

Mair, John. *A History of Greater Britain as well England as Scotland by John Major*. Ed. and trans. Archibald Constable. Edinburgh: Edinburgh University Press, 1892.

The Maitland Quarto: A New Edition of Cambridge, Magdalene College, Pepys Library MS 1408. Ed. Joanna M. Martin. STS 5th series 13. Edinburgh: Scottish Text Society, 2015.

Mandeville, John. *The Buke of John Maundevill*. Ed. George F. Warner. Westminster: Nichols and Sons, 1889. Accessed 10 November 2017. Online at http://www.medievaltravel.amdigital.co.uk /collections/doc-detail.aspx?documentid=3137.

———. *The Book of John Mandeville*. Ed. Tamarah Kohanski and C. David Benson. Kalamazoo, MI: Medieval Institute Publications, 2007.

Mann, Alastair. *The Scottish Book Trade, 1500 to 1720: Print Commerce and Print Control in Early Modern Scotland: An Historiographical Survey of the Early Modern Book in Scotland*. East Linton: Tuckwell Press, 2000.

Mapstone, Sally. "Was There a Court Literature in Fifteenth-Century Scotland?" *Studies in Scottish Literature* 26.1 (1991). Accessed 15 February 2017. Online at http://scholarcommons.sc. edu/ssl/vol26/ iss1/35/.

———. "Editing Older Scots Texts." In *Probable Truth: Editing Medieval Texts from Britain in the Twenty-First Century*. Ed. Vincent Gillespie and Anne Hudson. Turnhout: Brepols, 2013. Pp. 311–25.

Markus, Manfred. "The Isle of Ladies (1475) as Satire." *Studies in Philology* 93.3 (1998), 221–36.

Martin, Joanna M. *Kingship and Love in Scottish Poetry, 1424–1540*. Aldershot: Ashgate, 2008.

———. "Responses to the Frame Narrative of John Gower's *Confessio Amantis* in Fifteenth- and Sixteenth-Century Scottish Literature," *Review of English Studies* 60.246 (2009), 561–77.

McDiarmid, Matthew P. "The Early William Dunbar and His Poems." *Scottish Historical Review* 59.168 (1980) 126–39.

McKerrow, Ronald B. *Printers' and Publishers' Devices in England and Scotland 1485–1640*. London: Chiswick Press, 1913.

[*MED*] *Middle English Dictionary*. Ann Arbor: University of Michigan Press, 2001–. Online at http://quod.lib.umich.edu/m/med/.

Meek, Donald E. "The Scots-Gaelic Scribes of Late Medieval Perthshire: An Overview of the Orthography and Contents of the Book of the Dean of Lismore." In *Stewart Style 1513–1542: Essays on the Court of James V*. Ed. Janet Hadley Williams. East Lothian: Tuckwell Press, 1996. Pp. 254–72.

Melville, Elizabeth. *Ane Godlie Dreame, Compylit in Scottish Meter be M. M. Gentelwoman in Culros, at the Requeist of her Freindes*. Edinburgh: Robert Charteris, 1603.

Meyer-Lee, Robert J. *Poets and Power from Chaucer to Wyatt*. Cambridge: Cambridge University Press, 2007.

Minor Latin Poets. Trans. John Wight Duff and Arnold Mackay Duff. 2 vols. Cambridge, MA: Harvard University Press, 1934.

Miskimin, Alice. "The Design of Douglas's *Palice of Honour*." In *Actes du 2e Colloque de langue et de littérature écossaises (Moyen Age et Renaissance)*. Ed. Claude Graf and Jean-Jacques Blanchot. Strasbourg: University of Strasbourg Press, 1979. Pp. 396–421.

Mitchell, W. J. T. *Picture Theory: Essays on Verbal and Visual Representation*. Chicago: University of Chicago Press, 1994.

Molland, A. G. "Roger Bacon as Magician." *Traditio* 30 (1974), 445–60.

Morse, Ruth. "Gavin Douglas: 'Off Eloquence the Flowand Balmy Strand.'" In *Chaucer Traditions: Studies in Honour of Derek Brewer*. Ed. Ruth Morse and Barry Windeatt. Cambridge: Cambridge University Press, 1990. Pp. 107–21.

Moss, Ann. *Latin Commentaries on Ovid from the Renaissance*. Signal Mountain, TN: Summertown Press, 1998.

———. *Renaissance Truth and the Latin Language Turn*. Oxford and New York: Oxford University Press, 2003.

Murphy, James J. *Rhetoric in the Middle Ages: A History of the Rhetorical Theory from Saint Augustine to the Renaissance*. Berkeley: University of California Press, 1974; Rpt. Tempe: Arizona Center for Medieval and Renaissance Studies, 2001.

Murray, Athol. "The Procedure of the Scottish Exchequer in the Early Sixteenth Century." *Scottish Historical Review* 40.130 (1961), 89–117.

Murray, James A. H., ed. *The Romance and Prophecies of Thomas of Erceldoune*. EETS o.s. 61. London: N. Trübner & Co., 1875.

National Records of Scotland. *Archivists' Garden*. Accessed 16 June 2016. Online at https://www.nrscotland.gov.uk/research/archivists-garden.

Nauta, Lodi. "Lorenzo Valla." In *The Stanford Encyclopedia of Philosophy*. Ed. Edward N. Zalta. Metaphysics Research Lab in the Center for the Study of Language and Information, 2009. Accessed 29 July 2016. Online at http://plato.stanford.edu/index. html.

The New Jerusalem Bible. Ed. Henry Wansbrough, et al. New York: Doubleday, 1998.

The New Oxford Companion to Literature in French. Ed. Peter France. Oxford: Clarendon Press, 1995.

Nicholson, Ranald. *Scotland: The Later Middle Ages*. Edinburgh: Oliver & Boyd, 1974.

[NLS] National Library of Scotland. *Scottish Books 1505–1700*. Accessed 16 June 2016. Online at https://www.nls.uk.

The Northern Homily Cycle. Ed. Anne B. Thompson. Kalamazoo, MI: Medieval Institute Publications, 2008.

Norton-Smith, John. "Ekphrasis as a Stylistic Element in Douglas's *Palis of Honoure*." *Medium Ævum* 48.2 (1979), 240–53.

[OCD] *The Oxford Classical Dictionary*. Ed. Simon Hornblower, Antony Spawforth, and Esther Eidinow. Fourth Edition. Oxford: Oxford University Press, 2012. Online at http://classics.oxfordre.com/.

Octovien de Saint-Gelais. *Le Séjour d'Honneur*. Ed. Frédéric Duval. Geneva: Droz, 2002.

[ODNB] *The Oxford Dictionary of National Biography*. Ed. H. C. G. Matthew, et al. Accessed 21 July 2016. Online at www.oxforddnb.com.

[OED] *The Oxford English Dictionary*. Ed. J. A. Simpson and E. S. C. Weiner. Second edition. Accessed September 2017. Online at http://www.oed.com/.

Ovid. *Heroides and Amores*. Ed. and trans. Grant Showerman. Second edition. Rev. G. P. Goold. Cambridge, MA: Harvard University Press, 1977.

———. *The Art of Love and Other Poems*. Trans. J. H. Mozley. Rev. G. P. Goold. Cambridge, MA: Harvard University Press, 1979.

———. *Metamorphoses*. Trans. Frank Justus Miller. Rev. G. P. Goold. 6 vols. 1916; Rpt. Cambridge, MA: Harvard University Press, 2014.

The Oxford Book of Late Medieval Verse and Prose. Ed. Douglas Gray. Oxford: Clarendon Press, 1985.

Panofsky, Erwin. *Studies in Iconology: Humanistic Themes In the Art of the Renaissance*. New York: Harper & Row, 1972.

Parkinson, David J. "Henryson's Fox and Hary's Potter." *Notes and Queries* 57.4 (2010), 476–80.

Patch, Howard Rollin. *The Goddess Fortuna in Mediaeval Literature*. Cambridge, MA: Harvard University Press, 1927.

Paul, James Balfour. *The Scots Peerage: Founded on Wood's Edition of Sir Robert Douglas's Peerage of Scotland; Containing an Historical and Genealogical Account of the Nobility of that Kingdom*. 9 vols. Edinburgh: David Douglas, 1904–14.

Pearl-poet. *The Poems of the Pearl Manuscript*. Ed. Malcolm Andrew and Ronald Waldron, Fifth edition. Exeter: University of Exeter Press, 2007.

Pearsall, Derek. *John Lydgate*. Charlottesville: University Press of Virginia, 1970.

Persius. See Braund, Susanna Morton.

Pliny. *Natural History*. Trans. H. Rackham and W. H. Jones. 10 vols. Cambridge, MA: Harvard University Press, 1938–63.

The Prik of Conscience. Ed. James H. Morey. Kalamazoo, MI: Medieval Institute Publications, 2012.

The Quare of Jelusy. Ed. John Norton-Smith and I. Pravda. Heidelberg: Carl Winter, 1976.

Quintilian. *The Orator's Education*. Ed. Donald A. Russell. 5 vols. Cambridge, MA: Harvard University Press, 2001.

———. *Quintiliani Institutionis oratoriae Libri XII*. Zurich: Zentralbibliothek. Accessed August 2017. Online at http://www.e-codices.unifr.ch/en/list/one/zbz/C0074a.

Ratis Raving and other Early Scots Poems on Morals. Ed. Ritchie Girvan. STS 3rd series 11. Edinburgh: William Blackwood and Sons, 1939.

Records of the Parliaments of Scotland to 1707. Ed. Keith M. Brown, et al. University of St. Andrews, 2007–16. Accessed August 2017. Online at www.rps.ac.uk.

The Register of the Privy Seal of Scotland. Ed. David Hay Fleming. Vol. 2. Edinburgh: H. M. General Register House, 1921.

Riddell, James. *Aberdeen and Its Folk: from the 20th to the 50th Year of the Present Century*. Montreal: J. Campbell & Son, 1868.

Rizzi, Andrea. "Violent Language in Early Fifteenth-Century Italy: The Emotions of Invectives." In *Violence and Emotions in Early Modern Europe*. Ed. Susan Broomhall and Sarah Finn. New York: Routledge, 2016. Pp. 145–58.

Ridley, Florence H. "Did Gawin Douglas Write King Hart?" *Speculum* 34.3 (1959), 402–12.

Robin Hood and Other Outlaw Tales. Ed. Stephen Knight and Thomas H. Ohlgren. Kalamazoo, MI: Medieval Institute Publications, 1997.

Rolland, John. *Ane Treatise Callit The Court of Venus, devidit into four Buikis, Newlie Compylit be Johne Rolland in Dalkeith, 1575*. Ed. Walter Gregor. STS 1st series 3. Edinburgh: William Blackwood and Sons, 1884.

The Rose and the Thistle: Essays on the Culture of Late Medieval and Renaissance Scotland. Ed. Sally Mapstone and Juliette Wood. East Linton: Tuckwell, 1998.

Rush, Sally. "French Fashion in Sixteenth-Century Scotland: The 1539 Inventory of James V's Wardrobe." *Furniture History* 42 (2006), 1–25.

Rutledge, Thomas. "Gavin Douglas and John Bellenden: Poetic Relations and Political Affiliations." In *Langage Cleir Illumynate: Scottish Poetry from Barbour to Drummond, 1375–1630*. Ed. Nicola Royan. Amsterdam: Rodopi, 2007. Pp. 93–116.

———. "The Development of Humanism in Late-Fifteenth-Century Scotland." In *Humanism in Fifteenth-Century Europe*. Ed. David Rundle. Oxford: Society for the Study of Medieval Languages and Literature, 2012. Pp. 237–63.

Sage, John. "The Life of Gawin Douglas Bishop of Dunkeld." In *Virgil's Aeneis, translated into Scottish verse, by the famous Gavin Douglas Bishop of Dunkeld. To the whole is prefix'd an exact account of the author's life and writings, from the best histories and records*. Ed. Thomas Ruddiman and John Sage. Edinburgh: Symson and Freebairn, 1710. Pp. 1–19.

Saintsbury, George. *A History of English Prosody from the Twelfth Century to the Present Day*. 3 vols. Second edition. London: Macmillan, 1923.

Salmen, Walter. "The Muse Terpsichore in Pictures and Texts from the 14th to 18th Centuries." *Music in Art: International Journal for Music Iconography* 23.1 (1998), 79–85.

Sandys, John Edwin. *A History of Classical Scholarship*. 3 vols. Third edition. Cambridge: Cambridge University Press, 1908–21.

Sanford, Eva Matthews. "Renaissance Commentaries on Juvenal." *Transactions and Proceedings of the American Philological Association* 79 (1948), 92–112.

Schaff, Philip. "The Athanasian Creed." In *The Creeds of Christendom, with a History and Critical Notes*. Vol. 1. Fourth edition. New York: Harper, 1877. Pp. 35–42. Online at https://www.ccel.org/ccel/schaff/creeds1.iv.v.html?highlight=athanasian#highlight.

Scotish Poems, Reprinted from Scarce Editions. Ed. John Pinkerton. 3 vols. London: John Nichols Publishing, 1792.

Secular Lyrics of the XIV and XV Centuries. Ed. Rossell Hope Robbins. Second edition. Oxford: Clarendon Press, 1955.

Shakespeare, William. *King Henry IV, Part 1*. Ed. David Scott Kastan. London: Sydney Bloomsbury, 2016.

Shorter Scottish Medieval Romances. Ed. Rhiannon Purdie. STS 5th series 11. Edinburgh: Boydell, 2013.

The Siege of Milan. Ed. Sidney J. Herrtage. EETS e.s. 35. London: Trübner, 1880.

Sir Perceval of Galles and Ywain and Gawain. Ed. Mary Flowers Braswell. Kalamazoo, MI: Medieval Institute Publications, 1995.

Simmons, Elizabeth Pope. "The Rejection of the Manege Tradition in Early Modern England: 'Equestrian Elegance at Odds with English Sporting Tradition.'" M. A. thesis. University of North Florida, 2001.

Simpson, Grant G. *Scottish Handwriting 1150–1650: An Introduction to the Reading of Documents.* Edinburgh: Bratton, 1973; Rpt. Edinburgh: John Donald, 2009.

Sinclair, George. *The Principles of Astronomy and Navigation.* Edinburgh: Heir of Andrew Anderson, 1688.

Sir Ferumbras: Edited from the Unique Manuscript Bodleian MS Ashmole 33. Ed. Sidney J. Herrtage. EETS e.s. 34. London: Oxford University Press, 1879.

Smith, Jeremy J. *Older Scots: A Linguistic Reader.* STS 5th series 9. Rochester, NY: Boydell, 2012.

Spearing, A. C. *Medieval Dream-Poetry.* Cambridge: Cambridge University Press, 1976.

———. *The Medieval Poet as Voyeur: Looking and Listening in Medieval Love-Narratives.* Cambridge: Cambridge University Press, 1993.

Statius. *Thebaid.* Ed. D. R. Shackleton Bailey. 2 vols. Cambridge, MA: Harvard University Press, 2003.

Stewart, John. *Poems of John Stewart of Baldynneis.* Ed. Thomas Crockett. STS 2nd series 5. Edinburgh: William Blackwood and Sons, 1913.

Stewart, William. *The Buik of the Croniclis of Scotland: Or, A Metrical Version of the History of Hector Boece.* Ed. William B. Turnbull. Vol. 2. London: Longman, 1858.

Suetonius. "The Life of Virgil." In *Suetonius.* Vol. 2. Ed. J. C. Rolfe and K. R. Bradley. Cambridge, MA: Harvard University Press, 1998. Pp. 448–65.

Ten Bourdes. Ed. Melissa M. Furrow. Kalamazoo, MI: Medieval Institute Publications, 2013.

Tennant, William. *Anster Fair and Other Poems.* Second edition. Edinburgh: Colburn, 1814. Accessed 10 November 2017. Online at http://gateway.proquest.com/openurl?ctx_ver=Z39.88-2003&xri: pqil:res_ver=0.2&res_id=xri:lion&rft_id=xri:lion:ft:po:Z000506514:0&rft.accountid=13567.

Three Middle English Charlemagne Romances. Ed. Alan Lupack. Kalamazoo, MI: Medieval Institute Publications, 1990.

Trevisa, John. *On the Properties of Things: John Trevisa's Translation of Bartholomaeus Anglicus De Proprietatibus Rerum.* Ed. M. C. Seymour, et al. 2 vols. Oxford: Clarendon Press, 1975.

Tytler, Patrick Fraser. *Lives of Scottish Worthies.* Vol. 3. London: John Murray, 1840.

Utley, Francis Lee. *The Crooked Rib: An Analytical Index to the Argument about Women in English and Scots Literature to the End of the Year 1568.* Columbus: Ohio State University, 1944; Rpt. New York: Octagon, 1970.

Vergil, Polydore. *Polydore Vergil's English History. Vol. I. Containing the First Eight Books Comprising The Period Prior To The Norman Conquest.* Ed. Henry Ellis. London: J. B. Nichols & Son, 1846.

Virgil. *Eclogues. Georgics. Aeneid.* Trans. H. Rushton Fairclough. Rev. G. P. Goold. 2 vols. Cambridge, MA: Harvard University Press, 1999.

Walker, John. *Your Sky.* Fourmilab, 2003. Accessed 24 August 2017. Online at http://www.fourmilab.ch/cgi-bin/Yoursky.

Wallace, Andrew. *Virgil's Schoolboys: The Poetics of Pedagogy in Renaissance England.* Oxford: Oxford University Press, 2010.

Walther, Hans. *Proverbia Sententiaeque Latinitatis Medii Aevi: Lateinische Sprichwörter und Sentenzen des Mittelalteus in alphabetischer Anerdnung.* 5 vols. Göttingen: Vandenhoeek & Ruprecht, 1963.

Walter of Châtillon. *The Alexandreis: A Twelfth-Century Epic: Walter of Châtillon.* Trans. David Townsend. Peterborough: Broadview Press, 2007.

Warton, Thomas. *The History of English Poetry, from the Close of the Eleventh to the Commencement of the Eighteenth Century.* 4 vols. London: Dodsley et al., 1774–81.

Wentersdorf, Karl P. "The Folkloristic Significance of the Wren." *The Journal of American Folklore* 90.356 (1977), 192–98.

Wheatley, Edward. *Mastering Aesop: Medieval Education, Chaucer, and His Followers.* Gainsville: University Press of Florida, 2000.

Whiting, Bartlett Jere, and Helen Prescott Whiting. *Proverbs, Sentences, and Proverbial Phrases from English Writings Mainly before 1500.* Cambridge, MA: Belknap, 1968.

William of Touris. *Contemplacyon of Synners.* London: Wynkyn de Worde, 1499.

Wilson, Florence (Florentius Volusenus). *De animi tranquillitate dialogus*. Ed. Dana F. Sutton. Irvine: University of California, 2008. *The Philological Museum*. Accessed June 2016. Online at http://www.philological.bham.ac.uk/wilson/.

Wilson-Lee, Edward. "Romance and Resistance: Narratives of Chivalry in Mid-Tudor England." *Renaissance Studies* 24 (2010), 482–95.

Wimberly, Lowry Charles. *Folklore in the English and Scottish Ballads*. New York: Frederick Ungar Publishing Co., 1928.

Wingfield, Emily. *The Trojan Legend in Medieval Scottish Literature*. Cambridge and Rochester, NY: D. S. Brewer, 2014.

Wood, Juliette. "Folkloric Patterns in Scottish Chronicles." In *The Rose and the Thistle*. Pp. 116–35.

Woolf, Rosemary. *The English Religious Lyric in the Middle Ages*. Oxford: Clarendon Press, 1968.

✒ MIDDLE ENGLISH TEXTS SERIES

The Floure and the Leafe, The Assembly of Ladies, The Isle of Ladies, edited by Derek Pearsall (1990)

Three Middle English Charlemagne Romances, edited by Alan Lupack (1990)

Six Ecclesiastical Satires, edited by James M. Dean (1991)

Heroic Women from the Old Testament in Middle English Verse, edited by Russell A. Peck (1991)

The Canterbury Tales: Fifteenth-Century Continuations and Additions, edited by John M. Bowers (1992)

Gavin Douglas, *The Palis of Honoure*, edited by David Parkinson (1992)

Wynnere and Wastoure and The Parlement of the Thre Ages, edited by Warren Ginsberg (1992)

The Shewings of Julian of Norwich, edited by Georgia Ronan Crampton (1994)

King Arthur's Death: The Middle English Stanzaic Morte Arthur and Alliterative Morte Arthure, edited by
  Larry D. Benson, revised by Edward E. Foster (1994)

Lancelot of the Laik and Sir Tristrem, edited by Alan Lupack (1994)

Sir Gawain: Eleven Romances and Tales, edited by Thomas Hahn (1995)

The Middle English Breton Lays, edited by Anne Laskaya and Eve Salisbury (1995)

Sir Perceval of Galles and Ywain and Gawain, edited by Mary Flowers Braswell (1995)

Four Middle English Romances: Sir Isumbras, Octavian, Sir Eglamour of Artois, Sir Tryamour, edited by
  Harriet Hudson (1996; second edition 2006)

The Poems of Laurence Minot, 1333–1352, edited by Richard H. Osberg (1996)

Medieval English Political Writings, edited by James M. Dean (1996)

The Book of Margery Kempe, edited by Lynn Staley (1996)

Amis and Amiloun, Robert of Cisyle, and Sir Amadace, edited by Edward E. Foster (1997; second edition 2007)

The Cloud of Unknowing, edited by Patrick J. Gallacher (1997)

Robin Hood and Other Outlaw Tales, edited by Stephen Knight and Thomas Ohlgren (1997; second
  edition 2000)

The Poems of Robert Henryson, edited by Robert L. Kindrick with the assistance of Kristie A. Bixby (1997)

Moral Love Songs and Laments, edited by Susanna Greer Fein (1998)

John Lydgate, *Troy Book Selections*, edited by Robert R. Edwards (1998)

Thomas Usk, *The Testament of Love*, edited by R. Allen Shoaf (1998)

Prose Merlin, edited by John Conlee (1998)

Middle English Marian Lyrics, edited by Karen Saupe (1998)

John Metham, *Amoryus and Cleopes*, edited by Stephen F. Page (1999)

Four Romances of England: King Horn, Havelok the Dane, Bevis of Hampton, Athelston, edited by Ronald B.
  Herzman, Graham Drake, and Eve Salisbury (1999)

*The Assembly of Gods: Le Assemble de Dyeus, or Banquet of Gods and Goddesses, with the Discourse of
Reason and Sensuality*, edited by Jane Chance (1999)

Thomas Hoccleve, *The Regiment of Princes*, edited by Charles R. Blyth (1999)

John Capgrave, *The Life of Saint Katherine*, edited by Karen A. Winstead (1999)

John Gower, *Confessio Amantis*, Vol. 1, edited by Russell A. Peck; with Latin translations by Andrew
  Galloway (2000; second edition 2006); Vol. 2 (2003); Vol. 3 (2004)

Richard the Redeless and Mum and the Sothsegger, edited by James M. Dean (2000)

Ancrene Wisse, edited by Robert Hasenfratz (2000)

Walter Hilton, *The Scale of Perfection*, edited by Thomas H. Bestul (2000)

John Lydgate, *The Siege of Thebes*, edited by Robert R. Edwards (2001)

Pearl, edited by Sarah Stanbury (2001)

The Trials and Joys of Marriage, edited by Eve Salisbury (2002)

Middle English Legends of Women Saints, edited by Sherry L. Reames, with the assistance of Martha G.
  Blalock and Wendy R. Larson (2003)

The Wallace: Selections, edited by Anne McKim (2003)

Richard Maidstone, *Concordia (The Reconciliation of Richard II with London)*, edited by David R. Carlson,
  with a verse translation by A. G. Rigg (2003)

Three Purgatory Poems: The Gast of Gy, Sir Owain, The Vision of Tundale, edited by Edward E. Foster (2004)

William Dunbar, *The Complete Works*, edited by John Conlee (2004)

Chaucerian Dream Visions and Complaints, edited by Dana M. Symons (2004)

Stanzaic Guy of Warwick, edited by Alison Wiggins (2004)

Saints' Lives in Middle English Collections, edited by E. Gordon Whatley, with Anne B. Thompson and
  Robert K. Upchurch (2004)

🖋 COMMENTARY SERIES

Rabbi Ezra Ben Solomon of Gerona, *Commentary on the Song of Songs and Other Kabbalistic Commentaries*, selected, translated, and annotated by Seth Brody (1999)

John Wyclif, *On the Truth of Holy Scripture*, translated with an introduction and notes by Ian Christopher Levy (2001)

Second Thessalonians: Two Early Medieval Apocalyptic Commentaries, introduced and translated by Steven R. Cartwright and Kevin L. Hughes (2001)

The "Glossa Ordinaria" on the Song of Songs, translated with an introduction and notes by Mary Dove (2004)

The Seven Seals of the Apocalypse: Medieval Texts in Translation, translated with an introduction and notes by Francis X. Gumerlock (2009)

The "Glossa Ordinaria" on Romans, translated with an introduction and notes by Michael Scott Woodward (2011)

Nicholas of Lyra, *Literal Commentary on Galatians*, translated with an introduction and notes by Edward Arthur Naumann (2015)

Early Latin Commentaries on the Apocalypse, edited by Francis X. Gumerlock (2016)

Rabbi Eliezer of Beaugency: Commentaries on Amos and Jonah (with selections from Isaiah and Ezekiel), by Robert A. Harris (2018)

🖋 SECULAR COMMENTARY SERIES

Accessus ad auctores: Medieval Introduction to the Authors, edited and translated by Stephen M. Wheeler (2015)

The Vulgate Commentary on Ovid's Metamorphoses, Book 1, edited and translated by Frank Coulson (2015)

Brunetto Latini, La rettorica, edited and translated by Stefania D'Agata D'Ottavi (2016)

🖋 DOCUMENTS OF PRACTICE SERIES

Love and Marriage in Late Medieval London, selected, translated, and introduced by Shannon McSheffrey (1995)

Sources for the History of Medicine in Late Medieval England, selected, introduced, and translated by Carole Rawcliffe (1995)

A Slice of Life: Selected Documents of Medieval English Peasant Experience, edited, translated, and with an introduction by Edwin Brezette DeWindt (1996)

Regular Life: Monastic, Canonical, and Mendicant "Rules," selected and introduced by Douglas J. McMillan and Kathryn Smith Fladenmuller (1997); second edition, selected and introduced by Daniel Marcel La Corte and Douglas J. McMillan (2004)

Women and Monasticism in Medieval Europe: Sisters and Patrons of the Cistercian Reform, selected, translated, and with an introduction by Constance H. Berman (2002)

Medieval Notaries and Their Acts: The 1327–1328 Register of Jean Holanie, introduced, edited, and translated by Kathryn L. Reyerson and Debra A. Salata (2004)

John Stone's Chronicle: Christ Church Priory, Canterbury, 1417–1472, selected, translated, and introduced by Meriel Connor (2010)

Medieval Latin Liturgy in English Translation, edited by by Matthew Cheung Salisbury (2017)

🖋 MEDIEVAL GERMAN TEXTS IN BILINGUAL EDITIONS SERIES

Sovereignty and Salvation in the Vernacular, 1050–1150, introduction, translations, and notes by James A. Schultz (2000)

Ava's New Testament Narratives: "When the Old Law Passed Away," introduction, translation, and notes by James A. Rushing, Jr. (2003)

History as Literature: German World Chronicles of the Thirteenth Century in Verse, introduction, translation, and notes by R. Graeme Dunphy (2003)

Thomasin von Zirclaria, *Der Welsche Gast (The Italian Guest)*, translated by Marion Gibbs and Winder McConnell (2009)

Ladies, Whores, and Holy Women: A Sourcebook in Courtly, Religious, and Urban Cultures of Late Medieval Germany, introductions, translations, and notes by Ann Marie Rasmussen and Sarah Westphal-Wihl (2010)

Neidhart: Selected Songs from the Riedegg Manuscript, introduction, translation, and commentary by Kathryn Starkey and Edith Wenzel (2016)

📖 VARIA

The Study of Chivalry: Resources and Approaches, edited by Howell Chickering and Thomas H. Seiler (1988)

Studies in the Harley Manuscript: The Scribes, Contents, and Social Contexts of British Library MS Harley 2253, edited by Susanna Fein (2000)

The Liturgy of the Medieval Church, edited by Thomas J. Heffernan and E. Ann Matter (2001; second edition 2005)

Johannes de Grocheio, *Ars musice*, edited and translated by Constant J. Mews, John N. Crossley, Catherine Jeffreys, Leigh McKinnon, and Carol J. Williams (2011)

Aribo, De musica *and* Sententiae, edited and translated by T.J.H. McCarthy (2015)

Guy of Saint-Denis, Tractatus de Tonis, edited and translated by Constant J. Mews, Carol J. Williams, John N. Crossley, and Catherine Jeffreys (2017)

Typeset in 10/13 New Baskerville
and Golden Cockerel Ornaments display

Medieval Institute Publications
College of Arts and Sciences
Western Michigan University
1903 W. Michigan Avenue
Kalamazoo, MI 49008-5432
http://www.wmich.edu/medievalpublications

 WESTERN MICHIGAN UNIVERSITY